The Collapse
of Rome

To Alex and Thomas; you are my inspiration and my life.

The Collapse of Rome

Marius, Sulla and the First Civil War (91–70 BC)

Gareth C Sampson

Pen & Sword
MILITARY

First published in Great Britain in 2013
and reprinted in this format in 2020 by
Pen & Sword Military
an imprint of
Pen & Sword Books Ltd
47 Church Street
Barnsley
South Yorkshire
S70 2AS

ISBN 978 1 52678 191 8

Typeset in Ehrhardt by Mac Style
Printed and bound in the in Great Britain by CPI Group (UK) Ltd,
Croydon, CR0 4YY

Pen & Sword Books Ltd incorporates the imprints of Pen & Sword
Archaeology, Atlas, Aviation, Battleground, Discovery, Family
History, History, Maritime, Military, Naval, Politics, Railways,
Select, Social History, Transport, True Crime, and Claymore Press,
Frontline Books, Leo Cooper, Praetorian Press, Remember When,
Seaforth Publishing and Wharncliffe.

For a complete list of Pen & Sword titles please contact
PEN & SWORD BOOKS LIMITED
47 Church Street, Barnsley, South Yorkshire, S70 2AS, England
E-mail: enquiries@pen-and-sword.co.uk
Website: www.pen-and-sword.co.uk

Contents

Acknowledgements

As always, the greatest acknowledgement goes to my wife Alex, without whose support this book would never have been written. Supporting a husband in writing a book, whilst writing one of your own and looking after a young baby is a truly Herculean effort.

A notable mention goes to our new son Thomas, whose arrival, though anticipated, had such an all-consuming impact on our lives that this book very nearly didn't get finished and is a year later than it should have been. But he's worth it.

My editor Phil Sidnell needs an especial vote of thanks for putting up with the huge delay caused by the arrival or our firstborn. And this time I won't tempt fate by adding that one day one of my books will be completed on time.

There are a number of individuals who through the years have inspired the love of Roman history in me and mentored me along the way: Michael Gracey at William Hulme, David Shotter at Lancaster and Tim Cornell at Manchester. My heartfelt thanks go out to them all.

As always, greetings go to all the guys and gals who form part of the Manchester Diaspora, Gary, Ian, James, Jason, Greg and Sam. Also, big hugs go out to Pete and Nicki back in the US, and a slap on the back to Carsten in Denmark. Special thanks must go to Jason, still holding out in academia, for the additional bibliographic assistance.

On a more practical note, thanks to the University of Exeter Library for having the best collection in the southwest and for being located in such a congenial setting. The Central Library at Plymouth also gets a vote of thanks for their truly excellent inter-library service, which would frankly put most university libraries to shame. Also, thanks go to the Alumni society at Manchester for organizing JSTOR access for alumni, which arrived just in the nick of time.

List of Plates

Maps and Diagrams

Strategic Maps

Tactical Diagrams

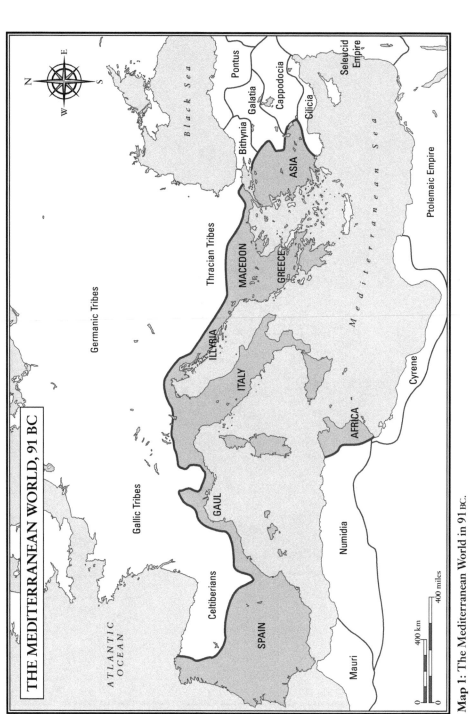

THE MEDITERRANEAN WORLD, 91 BC

N
E
W
S

ATLANTIC
OCEAN

Gallic Tribes

Germanic Tribes

Black Sea

Bithynia

Pontus

Galatia

Cappodocia

Seleucid
Empire

Cilicia

Thracian Tribes

MACEDON

GREECE

ASIA

Mediterranean Sea

ILLYRIA

ITALY

GAUL

Celtiberians

SPAIN

Mauri

Numidia

AFRICA

Cyrene

Ptolemaic Empire

400 km

400 miles

0

0

Map 1: The Mediterranean World in 91 BC.

Map 2: Campaigns in Italy, 90 BC.

Map 3: Campaigns in Italy, 89 BC.

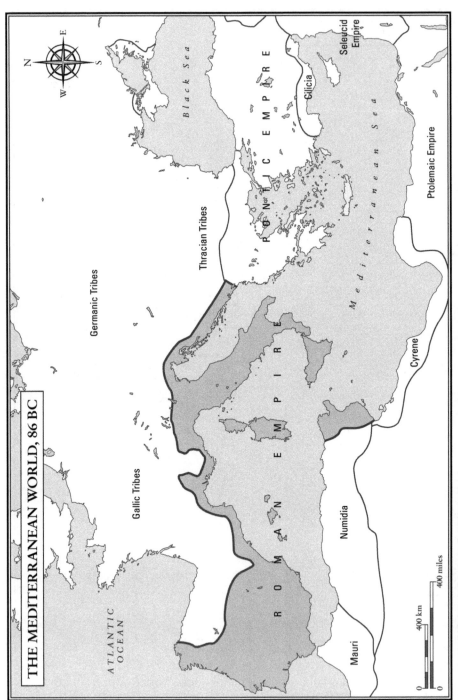

Map 4: The Mediterranean World in 86 BC.

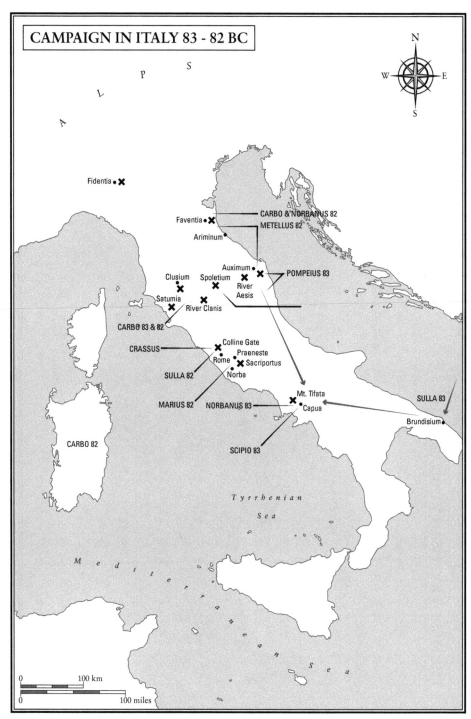

Map 5: Campaigns in Italy, 83–82 BC.

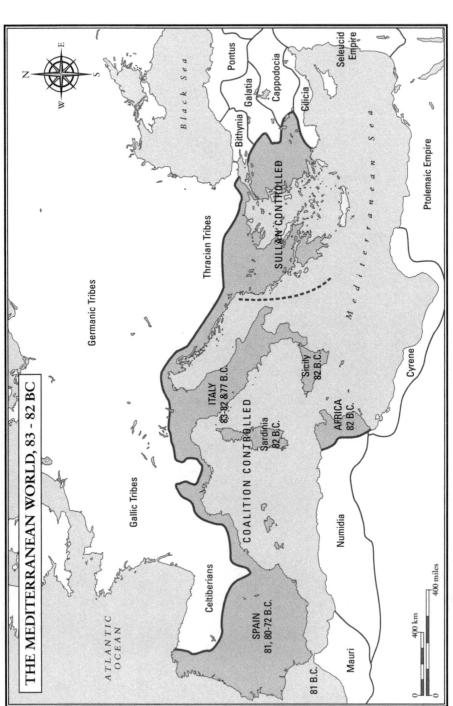

Map 6: The Mediterranean World in 83–82 BC.

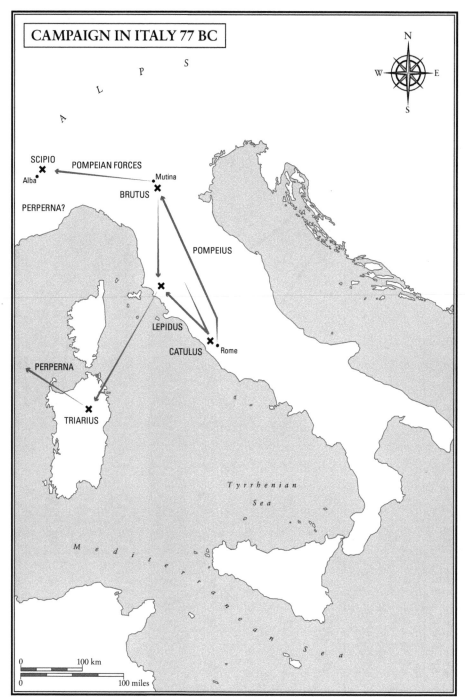

Map 7: Campaigns in Italy, 77 BC.

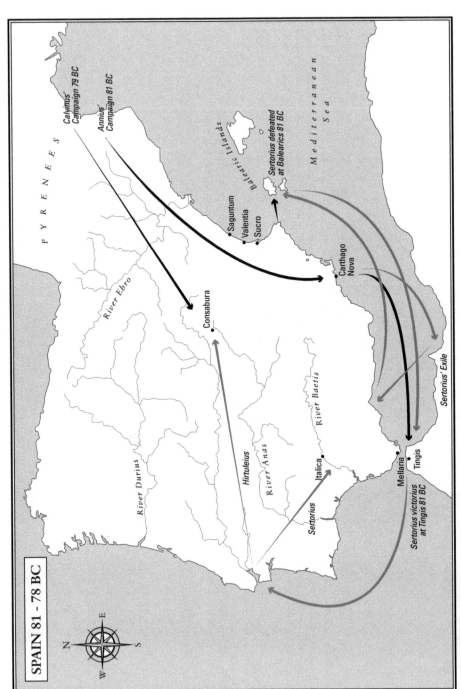

Map 8: Campaigns in Spain, 81–77 BC.

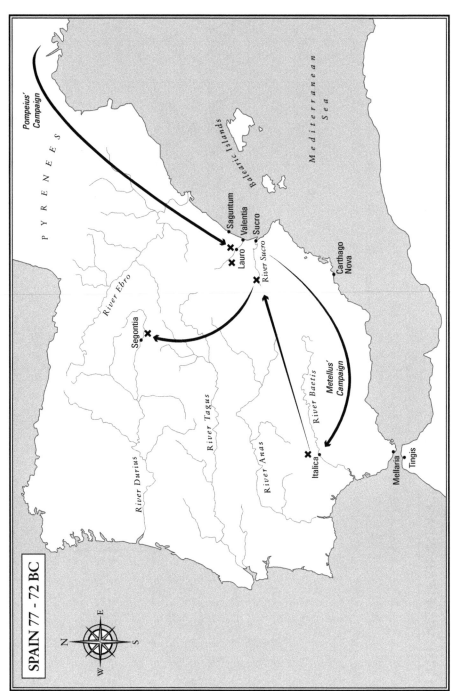

Map 9: Campaigns in Spain, 77–72 BC.

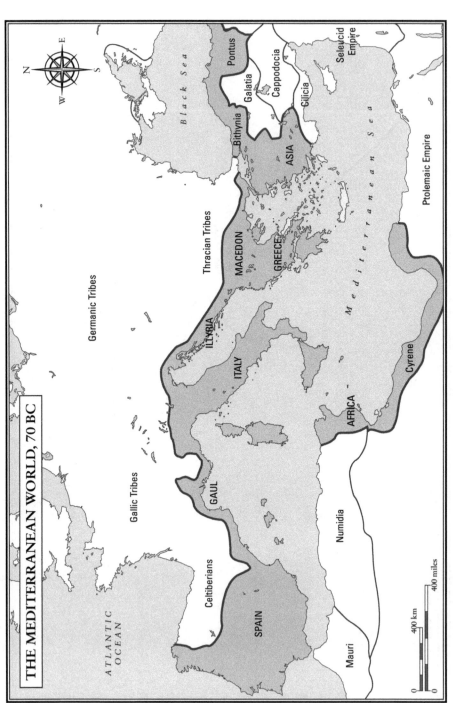

Map 10: The Mediterranean World in 70 BC.

Introduction – When is a Civil War
not a Civil War?

Although this may sound like the opening line to a particularly unfunny joke, it is an important question that faces anyone who examines the period 91–70 BC of the Roman Republic. It was during this period that the Republican system, which underpinned Rome's rise to Mediterranean pre-eminence, collapsed. There are two crucial differences between this event and the fall of the Roman Empire some 500 years later. Firstly, this collapse was not due to Rome being overrun by external enemies but internal ones, with sections of Italy and Rome's own aristocracy taking up arms against each other. Secondly, on this occasion the collapse of the Roman system, whilst severe, was not permanent, and a new Republic was able to emerge from the ashes of the old one.

This conflict was the greatest that Rome had seen, surpassing even the Second Punic War. Not only did the conflicts that made up the war span two decades, but fighting ranged across the whole Mediterranean world, from Spain in the west to Asia Minor in the east, encompassing Africa, Sicily and Sardinia, Gaul, Illyria, Greece and Macedon. Most importantly, however, was the fact that Italy itself and the city of Rome were turned into battlegrounds as the various factions fought for supremacy.

Conflicts raged across the peninsula between the years 91 and 87, again in 83 and 82, and finally in 77 BC. Furthermore, whilst neither Pyrrhus nor Hannibal had managed to attack Rome itself, which had lain untouched for 300 years at this point, the city was attacked on five occasions in just two decades; it was taken by force on no less than three of them, one of which resulted in what can only be described as a sacking. As well as the scope of the war was the significant number of fighting men involved and the casualties sustained, with well over 200,000 men under arms at the peak of the war and estimates of the casualties varying between 150,000 and 300,000 killed across the whole period.

This collapse and recovery spanned over two decades, and yet historiography on these events, both ancient and modern, has struggled to define them properly, with the various elements of this twenty-year period being compartmentalized and studied separately. It seems that for many, the answer to the initial question 'When is a civil war not a civil war?' is 'When it's an Italian or a Social War, a Lepidian Revolt or a Sertorian War.' The Romans themselves had no consistent historiographical approach for this period, with various commentators holding different opinions. Cicero himself, who was contemporaneous to these events, used a variety of conflicting terms for the conflicts throughout his works. In modern times, the First Roman Civil War is considered to be either between the years 88 and 82 BC or composed of two periods of 88–87 BC and 83–82 BC. I subscribe to neither argument.

To my mind this has always been a case of not seeing the wood for the trees. During these two decades the Republican system was taken considerably beyond the brink, and faced social, political, military and economic collapse. Rome was affected by a series of crises that were all interlinked and overlapping, forming into one whole, stretching from the Italian rebellion of 91 BC to the consulships of the younger Pompeius and Crassus, and spanning two generations. After more than a decade of studying this period, I am more convinced than ever that by studying these crises in separation, or drawing artificial boundaries between the various crises, one fails to appreciate the whole picture of the 'collapse and recovery' of the Republic.

Yet this work is a not a narrative of decline, but an analysis of the underlying strengths of the Republican system, by which it was able not only to survive these collective onslaughts, but to reconstitute a working Republican system, albeit one that was different to the Republic of 91 BC. The other issue that needs to be addressed is the over-emphasis given to the individual figure, rather than the wider issues, a tendency that is partially a result of the apparent compartmentalization of the various conflicts within the period. Although these conflicts involved a number of important and fascinating historical figures, both well known (Marius, Sulla, Sertorius and Pompeius Magnus) and not so well known (Pompeius Rufus, Pompeius Strabo, Cinna and Lepidus), this book is not simply a narrative of great men, but also an account of the forces that shaped them and the events in which they took part.

In a similar vein, we must move away from seeing this civil war in modern terms, based on the European model, with two clear-cut sides separated by an ideological argument, such as with the American or English Civil Wars. To this end, we must move beyond seeing the war as Marians vs. Sullans, terms used by many both in ancient and modern times. This was not a war of Optimates vs. Populares, but a civil war more marked by the collapse of central authority and the rise of warlords, as seen in the collapse of the Chinese Empire in the early twentieth century or many of the modern African civil wars. Throughout this period we do see the rise of alliances and factions, sometimes coalesced under either one leader, such as Sulla, or two leaders, most notably the duumvirate of Marius and Cinna. Yet these factions and alliances were at best temporary and were aimed solely at the gaining of power or the holding onto it.

The period in question covers a huge range of military activity, especially in the Italian and Spanish theatres of conflict. Yet regrettably, due to the limited number of surviving ancient sources, we have only the barest detail for the vast majority of the military engagements in this period. The lack of a surviving detailed narrative history, such as Livy, Sisenna, or even Lucceius, does leave us analysing scraps of information on what were key events at the time. In military terms, this robs us of the ability to analyse in-depth the first time that the Roman legionary system was used on both sides of a conflict, legion vs. legion, which would have been a truly fascinating analysis.

Whilst this does mean that these twenty years of conflict can be covered within one volume, it also means that for a number of what must have been crucial military engagements there is very little surviving detail for us to discuss and analyse. One of the most frustrating aspects of the poor state of our ancient sources is that there are certain key periods (90–89, 83–82 and 77–72 BC) during which we know there were a large number of battles being fought, yet for which we have only one or two lines of evidence. For most of the conflicts of this period, we know neither the size of the armies involved nor the tactics used, and thus we must construct whole campaign narratives from the slightest of evidence. Where possible the author has provided the few ancient sources that survive in order to allow the reader the opportunity to see for themselves how little detail actually remains.

This work is the culmination of over a decade of thought and sometimes obsession. It began life in the spring of 2001 as a master's thesis at the University of Manchester entitled *Crisis and Renewal; The Two Decades of the First Civil War 91–70 BC*, under the auspices of Professor Tim Cornell, who had the patience to supervise and guide my endeavours. Naturally, the end product represents my own views and not his. The work has been honed with several papers, notably *Still Waiting For Sulla* at the 2002 Classical Association Conference and *The Twenty Years War; the Collapse and Recovery of the Roman Republic 91–70 BC* in Manchester during 2004. On both occasions, vociferous debate ensued, and I am under no illusions that the views expressed in this work will find favour with everyone, but I present them nonetheless.

After more than a decade of working on the subject, I still find the topic a fascinating one and hope that others will do likewise.

Timeline

Key conflicts of the First Civil War, 91–70 BC

91–87	**Civil war in Italy**
91–88	Marsic campaign
91–87	Samnite campaign
88–87	**Civil war in Rome**
88	Sulpician-Marian coup and consular counter-coup
87	Civil war between the consuls
86–84	**Cinnan domination of Rome**
86–84	**Civil war in Rome's empire**
86–84	Civil war in Greece and Asia Minor
84	Civil war in northern Africa
83–82	**Civil war in Italy**
83–82	Civil war in Italy between the coalition and Sulla
82	Samnite campaign
82–79	**Sullan domination of Rome**
82	**Civil war in Rome's empire**
82	Civil war in Sicily
82	Civil war in northern Africa
82–81	Civil war in Spain
77	**Civil war in Italy**
81–71	**Civil war in Rome's empire**
81–71	Civil war in Spain
74–73	Civil war in Asia Minor
70	**Consulship of Pompeius and Crassus**

Notes on Roman Names

All Roman names in the following text will be given in their traditional form, including the abbreviated first name. Below is a list of the Roman first names referred to in the text and their abbreviations, along with the abbreviations for the terms tribune and consul.

A.	Aulus.
Ap.	Appius
C.	Caius
Cn.	Cnaeus
Cos.	consul
D.	Decimus
Faustus	(No abbreviated form exists.)
K.	Kaeso
L.	Lucius
M.	Marcus
Mam.	Mamercus
P.	Publius
Q.	Quintus
Ser.	Servius
Sex.	Sextus
Sp.	Spurius
T.	Titus
Ti.	Tiberius
Trib.	tribune

The Oncoming Storm

Chapter 1

The Road to Civil War

W ars, especially civil wars, do not occur spontaneously, even if that's how they may seem at the time. Historians, both ancient and modern, have spent millennia studying the causes of the catastrophe that struck Rome in this period. Sallust famously saw it in moral terms: the decline of the traditional Roman (aristocratic) spirit that followed Rome's final victory over Carthage in 146 BC.[1] Others saw it as a madness caused by individuals; for Appian it began with Ti. Sempronius Gracchus, while others chose either C. Marius or L. Cornelius Sulla, or both.[2] Yet the interlocking wars that formed this period had common causes and roots, many of which had been present in the Roman system for some time. To gain a better understanding of the various conflicts that made up Rome's First Civil War, one must be acquainted with the key issues that brought about these conflicts and that fuelled them for so long.

The Bloody Evolution of Republican Politics, 133–100 BC

Infamously, the previous four decades of Roman Republican politics had seen a number of unwanted innovations. On three occasions (in 133, 121 and 100 BC), Roman political arguments had ended in bloodshed and massacre. Technically, bloodshed in Roman politics was not a new feature. The Augustan poets took great pains to point out that Roman society had been founded on civil bloodshed, with Romulus slaying Remus, according to the most widely accepted tradition. Some variant traditions even had this act being the culmination of an earlier eighth century BC civil war between the brothers and their followers.[3] It is true that the early centuries of the Republic had seen three prominent politicians executed: Sp. Cassius, Sp. Maelius and M. Manlius.[4] Yet these second-century Republican murders and massacres had taken matters to a new level. Even within the span of thirty years, we can see the evolution of political murder. Ti. Sempronius Gracchus was lynched along with a handful of supporters. Yet commissions were established to try others who supported him.[5] In retaliation, P. Cornelius Scipio Aemilianus, the destroyer of Numantia and Carthage, was suspected of being assassinated by pro-Gracchan supporters.[6] C. Sempronius Gracchus was murdered with the state's full blessing under the *senatus consultum ultimum* along with a number of his supporters. By 100 BC, Marius had brought his veterans onto the streets of Rome to 'restore order'.

This bloodshed was centred upon particular holders of the office of tribunate of the plebs, which had always had a radical history, but it too was undergoing a rapid period of evolution in these years.[7] Ti. Sempronius Gracchus used it to depose another magistrate from office, overrule the Senate on foreign affairs and disrupt landholding patterns across Italy. C. Sempronius Gracchus used it to propose citizenship to the Italians (see below), undertake judicial reform and hand out subsidised grain to Roman citizens. An anonymous tribune of 107 used it to transfer a military command from one general to another against the Senate's wishes. By 100 BC, L. Appuleius Saturninus was using it to exile his political enemies from Rome. Whilst the tribunate was never the quiescent office that many commentators would have us believe in the two centuries preceding 133 BC, this period was evolution on a massive scale in the practical application of its powers.

Thus, within the space of a few decades, Roman politics had evolved rapidly and seemingly out of the Senate's control. Huge numbers of commentators, both ancient and modern, have attempted rational explanations for these changes, whether it be a Sallustian decline in morality or a symptom of the greater wealth that their empire had brought into the political system. Recently, Hölkeskamp has undertaken a fascinating analysis of the Roman senatorial culture and postulated that as the Republic grew more successful Roman politicians, who culturally were attuned to at least emulating if not outdoing the actions of their ancestors, had to take increasingly greater steps to match their illustrious forebears and this placed the self and family glory ahead of that of the state, to the exclusion of the common good.[8] The rise of the powerful individual was nothing new to Roman history; their annals are littered with them. P. Cornelius Scipio Africanus took personal glory and popularity to new levels, yet was laid low by the combined actions of his senatorial rivals.

A common theme linking all of the key individuals of this period (the Gracchi, Marius or Saturninus) is the sense that, despite a range of individual motives, they all placed their own success at a higher cost than the common good. The Gracchi in particular seemed to have had the innate belief that their reforms were the best remedy for the Republic and that their opponents were damaging the Republic and therefore needed to be overcome. Factions and rivalries had always existed in Roman politics, but there seemed to exist a number of factions, not all by any means, that believed that for the 'good of the state' any actions were justified, whether it be the Gracchi or their opponents. With C. Marius it can be argued that he had an outsider's perspective on the Roman system (he was an Italian nobleman with Roman citizenship) and could manipulate the system for his own ends, without worrying about the wider consequences. Saturninus and his political partner C. Servilius Glaucia were Roman noblemen through and through, yet appear to have understood that routes to personal power were available without having to wait until the age of 42 for a consulship and military command. Personal glory and power could be had through the domestic political route using a mixture of office and street violence.

Thus, by the end of 100 BC there were a range of factors in Roman politics that had not been present in previous generations, from the evolution of the powers of the tribunate as the chief domestic political office of state, consecutive consulships in times of military emergencies, through to murder as a legitimate means of ending political disputes. Other factors included the deposition of officials, the overriding of military commands, the use of armed supporters and military veterans on the streets of Rome, special commissions to root out enemies of the state and political exile of one's domestic opponents. All of these factors were present and developed within this crucial thirty-year period and were to become staples of the war that followed.

However, as always, it must be stressed that this did not make a civil war inevitable; it is merely that these factors were all present in the background, a powder keg in need of a spark to explode.

Rome and Italy: A Changing Balance of Power

Crucial to understanding the wars of this period is an understanding of the nature of Italy at the time. Until this civil war period, Italy was not a unified country or a unified culture. Rome was not the capital of Italy, but one of several different cities, governments, peoples and cultures; these ranged from the Celtic races of northern Italy, to the Latins, Etruscans and Samnites of central Italy, through to the Greek cities of the south. The only factor that bound these disparate races and peoples together was the fact that they were all dominated by Rome. From Rome's foundation in the eighth century the history of Italy was one of perpetual warfare between the various peoples of the region, only ending with the Roman conquest of the Gauls of northern Italy in the late third century BC. Rome's early empire was first and foremost an Italian one and one which bore all the hallmarks of the Roman imperial mentality: an absence of close (or invasive) governance and a focus on ensuring military and economic supremacy.

In the early stages of the Roman conquest of Italy (in the regions closest to Rome), enemies had been destroyed and their peoples incorporated into the Roman citizenship system. However, as Rome exerted her control throughout the peninsula such full integration was not possible or even desirable. Thus was born the Roman system of control, with a fundamental inequality binding all the peoples of Italy to Rome. Each defeated city or people was bound to Rome by treaty. They retained their own language, culture and domestic governance but had to follow a centralized foreign policy dictated by Rome and, most important, had to supply manpower to fight in Roman armies. Thus was born a system unique to the ancient world, in which the Romans were able to harness the manpower of the whole peninsula to fight their wars, whilst leaving the individual peoples with a large degree of internal autonomy. In the early stages of this process, these treaties were supported by a series of Roman military colonies throughout Italy, built on captured land, to ensure a passive military dominance of the peninsula.

Such a system provided Rome with a near limitless supply of soldiers, enabling her to withstand massive military losses, which would have exhausted any single state, yet at the same time without the need to enforce strict Roman rule on the conquered peoples. This is not to say that the peoples of Italy meekly accepted Roman dominance or saw it as anything other than such. This system of alliances was the result of the dissolution of the Latin League, which followed a 'revolt' or civil war between the Latin States and Rome over their dominance (340–338 BC). The other notable revolt within the Roman alliance system came in the Second Punic War, when the Carthaginian general Hannibal correctly identified that the key factor in defeating Rome was not to be found solely on the battlefield, or by siege, but in destroying Rome's system of alliances and thus limitless manpower. During the early stages of the war, a number of cities within the Roman system did defect to Hannibal, primarily the cities of southern Italy, most famously Capua. However, these rebels soon found themselves targeted by Rome, which sought to make an example of them and discourage the others.[9]

Key to this system was the extension of benefits and opportunities for the elites of the various peoples and regions of Italy, should they partake in the Roman system. Thus we see a steady stream of Italian noblemen gaining Roman citizenship, and within a generation or two moving to Rome and establishing themselves amongst the Roman nobility. The most notable examples of this were M. Porcius Cato (the elder), C. Marius and M. Tullius Cicero. The Roman oligarchic system gained fresh blood and the local elites kept their own communities quiescent in Rome's name. McDonald perhaps sums this system up the most succinctly:

> The Roman hegemony in Italy rested upon the alliance of the Roman senatorial nobility with the Latin and Italian aristocracy, in accordance with a set social structure and political organization in the Italian Confederation, and Roman and Italian nobility were of one mind in persevering the foundations of their power and authority.[10]

Two other key elements bound the peoples of Italy to Rome. One was shared experience in Rome's military, in which Latin was the official language. This brought together a vast number of young men from the various peoples of Italy, all of whom served in Rome's armies, a fact that created bonds between them and provided them with a rudimentary education in Latin. The other was the Roman citizenship system, which as the centuries passed became more and more disjointed. At its heart lay three categories of citizenship. At the highest level was Roman citizenship with full citizen status, the right to live and vote in Rome (if it could be afforded) and the full protection of Roman law, including the principal of protection from punishment without a trial. All citizens were enrolled into thirty-five tribes, for voting purposes. Whilst these tribes were originally geographically organized (including four tribes for those inhabitants of the city of Rome itself), by the first century BC the members of these tribes were scattered across Italy, with huge variations in each tribe in terms of both numbers and location. No new tribe had been created since 242 BC and any new citizens created were distributed across the existing thirty-five. Furthermore, the process of creating new citizens was haphazard and unplanned. Individuals could receive citizenship as a reward, as could whole communities. Even with a census every five years, determining who was, and who was not, a citizen became increasingly complex. The sources frequently report non-citizens moving to Rome and claiming some citizen rights.[11]

This problem was exacerbated by the fact that the other two categories of citizenship, Latin and Italian, were of far lower status, at least in Roman eyes. Neither brought electoral rights in Rome and neither had the full protection of Roman law. However, it has to be pointed out that, away from a Roman context, these citizens could take full part in their own communities and were only of second-class status when they found themselves dealing with a Roman. Thus, when it was designed, this system was a sound one. The Italian peoples maintained domestic autonomy and their own laws, religion and culture, despite being militarily defeated. The Romans had an endless supply of manpower and a graduated system of citizenship, which limited the number of citizens who could vote in Rome's elections, thus maintaining the oligarchy's grip on the Roman political system but allowing for progression, which in turn encouraged compliance to Roman demands. By the second century BC the number of Roman citizens was between 300,000 to 400,000, out of a total Italian population in its millions.

However, as with many Roman institutions, what worked in the fourth century BC did not automatically work in the second century. From the Roman side, the system still worked perfectly, with available manpower, a limited number of voters and eager and compliant local elites. However, it was the other side of this pact that appeared to be increasingly under strain. By the mid to late second century BC, in most cases, well over 100 years had passed since these Italian peoples had been defeated, with time dulling the memory. All that remained was a military burden and an unequal citizenship system. Furthermore, a Roman system that had been designed to supply Rome's armies with manpower to fight immediate threats in Italy now found itself being used to conquer and maintain a vast Mediterranean empire. Short summer campaigns within the peninsula now became decade-long wars in Spain, Africa, Greece or Asia Minor. To many, it must have seemed that the Italians supplied the manpower while the Romans (or at least the nobles) reaped the rewards. Furthermore, after 167 BC and the conquest of Macedonia, *tributum* (taxation) had been lifted from Roman citizens but not Latin or Italian ones.[12]

This inequality was not helped by an extension of Roman influence across the peninsula into domestic matters. Originally, the Romans had little interest in the internal laws or governance of an Italian state, aside from compliance to Rome's demands. From the start, wherever Roman and Italian interests interacted (such as trade), Roman law and Roman courts took precedence, which naturally put the Italians at a disadvantage. However, as the second century progressed there was an increasing number of laws, made in Rome by Romans that affected communities across the whole peninsula.[13] Perhaps one of the most famous examples of this was the laws suppressing the Bacchanal cults in Italy in 186 BC.

However, despite the fame of this example, its impact on the average Italian was limited. The case of agrarian legislation, however, was a different matter. Ironically, agrarian legislation, such as that proposed by the Gracchi (see above) was designed in Rome, by Romans, to solve a Roman problem: namely that the citizen soldiers were believed to be losing their land due to neglect while they were away fighting on long campaigns, thus making them ineligible for future service, and thus reducing Roman citizen manpower. However, the agrarian laws proposed and enacted, entangled Italian communities across the peninsula due to Roman repossessions of Roman public lands (*ager publicus*), on which many Italians had been living for generations. Exactly to what degree these laws affected the Italian communities has long been a matter of scholarly debate,[14] but Appian records Italian communities making representations to P. Cornelius Scipio Aemilianus in 129 BC about the chaos caused by the Gracchan land commission.[15] In fact, it is Scipio who first explicitly raises Italian concerns in Roman politics.[16]

This process reached a watershed in 125 BC when the consul M. Fulvius Flaccus, himself a member of the Gracchan land commission, proposed that Roman citizenship should be extended. We only have two references to this major proposal, so our details on its exact nature are unclear.[17] Mouritsen argues that the proposal was to extend Roman citizenship to those with Latin status only, as they were more integrated into the Roman system.[18] Nevertheless, the details count less than the precedent; a Roman politician, and a consul at that, had proposed a mass enfranchisement (to whatever degree) of the peoples within the Roman alliance system. For the Latins and Italians, this meant that such an outcome was possible, and at the passing of a law. For the Roman elite it meant that the question of mass enfranchisement of the Italians was now in the political arena.

Furthermore, another precedent was set in 125 BC, when the majority of the Senate rejected Flaccus' proposal. Not only did this send a clear message that citizenship was being denied to the Italians by the Senate of Rome, but the Latin town of Fregellae rose in revolt against Rome, possibly as part of a wider planned rebellion.[19] Naturally, one lone town was soon crushed militarily, but the precedent had been set. Furthermore, Flaccus' proposal has been linked to the passing of a law in 126 by M. Iunius Pennus, the tribune of that year, expelling non-citizens from Rome.[20] Nevertheless, within three years the issue of mass enfranchisement of the Italians was being proposed once more in Rome, this time by Flaccus' ally, the tribune C. Sempronius Gracchus. However, once again, this hope was crushed by the Senate, as were Gracchus and Flaccus themselves, who were murdered. Thus the two men to propose Italian enfranchisement had both been murdered on the orders of the Senate. Whilst the Senate had far more to worry about than what message they sent to the Italian people of the Roman alliance, a message had been sent nonetheless: peaceful reform of the system would not be tolerated.

The Calm Between Storms; Rome in the 90s BC

The decade between the death of Saturninus and Marius' sixth consulship (100 BC) and the tribunate of M. Livius Drusus is considered to be something of a quiet decade in Roman Republican history. There are two clear reasons for this. First is the lack of a detailed narrative source for this period (such as Livy) combined with very few snippets from other sources, leaving us in the dark about a great many events that must have taken place. The second reason is that these years were sandwiched between two of the most tumultuous periods in the Republic: the massive tribal invasions of Rome's empire, which resulted in the invasion of Italy itself and the threatened destruction of Roman power; and the outbreak of the First Civil War itself. [21]

Yet this apparent calm between storms may well be deceptive. The period saw the eclipse of both the Metellan clan, which had dominated Roman politics for the previous twenty years, and that of Marius himself, who had done likewise between 104 and 100. The Metellan dominance was based around a group of Metelli occupying the consulship and censorship within a few years of each other.[22] Yet by 98 BC they had exhausted that generation of Metelli and had been eclipsed by the (temporary) dominance of Marius and Saturninus. The fallout from the murder of Saturninus and his followers seems to have dominated the first few years of this period, with a number of supporters and opponents of Saturninus being put on trial.

Lurking throughout this decade is the figure of Marius himself. Regardless of the fallout from the murder of Saturninus, Marius' powerbase had been built on military success. The end of the Northern Wars had brought glory, power and wealth to Marius and established him as a major player in Roman politics, but it also robbed him of his monopoly of high office and the very reason for his success and his toleration by other factions in the Senate. With both the Metelli and Marius removed from their dominant positions, a large amount of manoeuvring between the individuals, families and factions appears to have taken place.

The surviving sources for these years are dominated by court cases, and one case in particular, that of P. Rutilius Rufus.[23] The Rutilius case seems to have been a notorious one, and it highlighted a growing additional rift in domestic politics at Rome between the Senate and the equestrian orders. By the late Republic the equestrian order was the business class. Traditionally, trade was seen as being beneath the senatorial class and law prevented any senator from indulging in it. However, given the vast opportunities and huge profits to be made from trade in Rome's growing empire, a number of rich Romans, many of them from aristocratic backgrounds, forsook a political career for a business one.

Until the tribunate of the younger Gracchus, this class of businessmen had remained in the shadows of Roman politics, not taking an active role; if they were involved at all, they limited themselves to financing allies and kinsmen. Gracchus, however, wanting to counterbalance the Senate's power, made the equestrians the majority of the jurors on each trial, thus giving them control of the courts. Whilst in most cases this was not an issue, it did give them control of trials involving charges of corruption and fraud, especially in cases from the provinces, and especially ones involving their colleagues.

During this period, Rutilius (Cos. 105) had served as legate to his friend Q. Mucius Scaevola (Cos. 95) who served as governor of Asia, Rome's richest province. Thanks to C. Gracchus, the collection of taxes in the Roman province of Asia was tendered to the highest bidder, with cartels of equestrian businessmen eager for the contract. The principle was a simple one: the winners had to deliver the winning amount to the Roman treasury and anything above that which they managed to collect in taxes they kept. Thus the equestrian tax collectors became universally loathed throughout the Roman province of Asia and used every method they could to extract taxes from the inhabitants. Both Scaevola and Rutilius set about clamping down on these practices, winning respect in the province and the enmity of certain equestrian cartels. In 92 BC, Rutilius himself was put on trial for extortion by equestrian jurors, despite his famous reputation as an honest and upright man.[24] Unsurprisingly, he was found guilty and chose exile from Rome, eventually settling in Smyrna, where he remained until his death after 78 BC. The case scandalized Rome at the time and showed the growing rift between the senatorial and equestrian orders, with the courts now a political weapon.

Another issue that seems to have dominated the domestic scene was that of Italians living in Rome and usurping citizen rights. This phenomenon appears to have been a part of the drift from Italian towns and countryside to live in Rome. This caused consternation in both the Italian and Roman elites, one losing clients, the other being swamped by them, with all the fears that such an influx of 'foreign' immigrants created in the minds of both the urban elites and the urban plebs, jealous of their privileges. In truth, this was not a new phenomenon, and various attempts had been made to return these non-citizens back to their place of origin.[25] In 95 BC, however, the consuls and Senate decided to act decisively and passed the *Lex Licinia Mucia*, which ordered the expulsion of all those who held Latin or Italian citizenship from Rome and the prosecution of any who determined to usurp citizens' rights. In an already tense situation, this could be seen as provocative or at least using a sledgehammer to crack a nut. Asconius, in fact, ascribes this as one of the key factors in the Italian rebellion and civil war that followed.[26] Once again, the Senate (or at least a majority of it) had seemingly failed to grasp the potential consequences of their actions.

Whilst Rome was occupied with political manoeuvrings, courtroom battles and the expulsion of immigrants, military matters were far from peaceful. Again, we suffer from a lack of solid narrative sources, but we must remember that the Roman army had taken heavy losses (over 100,000) in the various defeats inflicted on them by the invasions of Spain, Gaul and Italy by the Cimbri and Teutones, a few years earlier. Not only did Rome suffer numerical losses, but Gaul and Spain had been overrun and Italy invaded. Although ultimately successful, this must have created an impression that Rome's vaunted military superiority was at least shaken. Both provinces and northern Italy must also have been recovering from the devastation caused by these invasions. The same could have been said for Sicily, itself recovering from the Second Servile War (104–101 BC).

Throughout the 90s, we hear of military campaigns by Roman commanders in Spain.[27] The year 93 BC saw two separate triumphs celebrated for Spain, one for each province, by T. Didius (Cos. 98) and P. Licinius Crassus (Cos. 95). Both of these seem to have been lengthy campaigns, indicating the severity of the rebellions. Furthermore, it seems that these triumphs did not mark the end the rebellions, as Spain still remained a consular command. By 92 BC, we are told of C. Valerius Flaccus (Cos. 93) fighting a major campaign there.[28] Thus Spain seemed to have been a perpetual conflict zone throughout this period.

Macedonia also appears to have been a problem for Rome in this period. Diodorus reports an uprising led by a man claiming to be a descendant of the Kings of Macedon and attempting to restore Macedonian independence, although this soon petered out.[29] Military activity is recorded against the Thracians and Illyrian tribes in both 97 and 92 BC, the latter when the Macedonian governor C. Sentius was defeated in battle by Thracian incursions.[30] In northern Africa, Rome technically acquired fresh territory in 96 BC, when King Ptolemy Apion of Cyrene died and bequeathed his kingdom to Rome (see Map 1). At the time the Romans did not annex it, but left it to govern itself (see Appendix I).[31]

Asia Minor too appeared to be falling into instability. Although Rome only had the one province (Asia) their policy, such as it was, was for a series of weak client kings in the region (creating a buffer zone between Rome and the other rising power of the ancient world, the Parthian Empire[32]). Unfortunately for Rome's policy, there was one man in particular who did not share their view. This was the King of Pontus (on the south coast of the Black Sea, see Map1), Mithridates VI, who harboured ambitions of creating a Pontic Empire. He began quietly enough (from Rome's point of view) by invading and annexing the Crimea. However, by the 90s he soon turned his attention back to Asia Minor and his weak neighbours. On two occasions during the 90s (the exact chronology is confused) he contrived to annex the neighbouring kingdom of Cappodocia, first by allying with Nicomedes III of Bithynia (who subsequently double crossed him) and then with Tigranes of Armenia. On each occasion puppet kings were installed on the Cappodocian throne and on each occasion Rome intervened to restore a 'free' Cappodocia.[33]

Whilst Mithridates may have been a minor nuisance to Rome at the time, the potential for conflict did not seem to elude C. Marius, who in 98 BC left Rome and met with Mithridates during a tour of Asia. Plutarch records that Marius issued him with what could be construed as either a warning or a challenge, that he should either be stronger than Rome or do her bidding, in other words 'to put up or shut up'.[34] Whilst Plutarch is clearly using his knowledge of future events, the meeting between the two is an interesting encounter and may indicate that Marius had an Asian campaign in mind.[35] Coincidently, one of the Roman interventions over Cappodocia was led by L. Cornelius Sulla, Marius' deputy in the Jugurthine War.[36] As well as restoring client kings in Asia, Sulla received an envoy from the Parthian Empire the first formal meeting between representatives of the two growing empires of the ancient world.[37]

Thus, on both the domestic and foreign fronts, although we have no clear narrative for the events, it is clear that this period was both eventful and important. In Rome, the various factions were jostling for position and clashes were breaking out between senators and equestrians over the control of the courts. Furthermore, the Senate seemed to be fanning the flames of Italian discontent over citizenship, more by short-sightedness than design. Further afield, Rome was still recovering from the devastating Northern Wars and was suffering from rebellions and tribal uprisings, accompanied by heavy fighting in Spain and to a lesser degree Macedonia. Compared to these, events in Asia seemed to pale in comparison, yet Mithridates was intent on disrupting Rome's influence in the region and now Parthia appeared to be taking an interest in the region.[38] It was against this backdrop, with a mixture of volatile domestic and foreign issues, that M. Livius Drusus stood for a tribunate for 91 BC and unveiled a programme of political reforms.

The Powderkeg and the Spark: The Tribunate of Livius Drusus

However, despite all of these factors, there was nothing that made a collapse into civil war inevitable; they remained in the background and had done so for a number of years. It was the tribunate of M. Livius Drusus in 91 BC that turned these from being background factors into a crisis the likes of which the Republic had never seen, and which led to the collapse (albeit temporarily) of the Roman Republican system.

M. Livius Drusus was no radical maverick politician in the mould of L. Appuleius Saturninus. In fact, he had impeccable senatorial credentials. His father had been the tribune who had opposed C. Sempronius Gracchus in 122 BC and had earned a consulship (in 112 BC). Cicero, who was a young man during this period, informs us that Drusus was one of a group of young men who belonged to one of Rome's leading political factions, led by the eminent senators: Q. Mucius Scaevola (Cos. 95), M. Antonius (Cos. 99) and P. Licinius Crassus (Cos. 95). Cicero specifically states that these men had a programme of political reforms designed to strengthen the power and position of the Senate and sponsored Drusus as tribune for 91 BC to introduce them. They also had two friends of Drusus, C. Aurelius Cotta and P. Sulpicius, to stand as tribune for 90 and 89 BC, to ensure the smooth introduction of these measures.[39]

These proposals contained a number of measures.[40] There was a variety of lesser reforms, such as colonies for the urban plebs, corn laws, some coinage reform and measures to allow equestrians to be tried for bribery. At the heart of the programme, however, lay two major reforms: firstly, the addition of 300 equestrians to the Senate, with this enlarged body supplying jurors for the courts; and secondly, the extension of Roman citizenship to the Italians.[41]

Thus this grouping had proposed a series of reforms that offered, on the face of it, some benefits to all groups, and they hoped to solve the various issues that had been raised in recent years. However, they faced two key problems. Firstly, although the proposals offered a little something to everyone, they seemed to alienate more groups than they mollified. Appian provides an excellent summary of the main objections. Many in the Senate were apparently opposed to adding 300 equestrians to their number, while the equestrians disagreed on who the 300 should be and objected to the bribery laws, and even elements among the Italians objected to the new colonies proposed for Italy.[42] Furthermore, there would have been elements of the urban populace who would not want to leave Rome for colonies or share their citizenship privileges. Finally, there would have been those in the Senate who simply mistrusted the motives behind these reforms.

The second major problem was that this once again raised the hopes of the Italians, who wanted greater recognition for their efforts. In fact, it is recorded that prominent Italian noblemen came to Drusus' house and discussed the proposals with him. Notable amongst them was a Marsic nobleman, Q. Poppaedius Silo.[43] Diodorus even reports that a group of Italians swore an oath to Drusus personally to consider him their benefactor if he gained them citizenship, though, as always, such evidence must be questioned.[44]

Naturally enough, this legislation soon ran into difficulties in both the Senate and the assemblies. The principal opponent seems to have been L. Marcius Philippus (Cos. 91 BC). Philippus used his position as an augur to declare the auspices unfavourable whenever legislation was due to be voted on, making any measure passed technically null and void. In a familiar pattern, Drusus seems to have reacted badly to being opposed in such manner, and on one occasion attacked Philippus in the assembly, throttling him and giving him a bloody nose.[45] He also allegedly threatened to hurl another opponent (Q. Servilius Caepio) from the Tarpeian Rock.[46]

Interestingly, the sources record that Poppaedius took a young M. Porcius Cato to the roof and threatened to hurl him off it if he did not assist Drusus.[47] The *Periochae* of Livy reports that by using violence, and in defiance of the auspices, Drusus passed laws on currency reform and, more importantly, on rebalancing juries between senators and equestrians.[48]

However, Drusus' methods seem to have alienated the vast majority of the Senate and a number of the People, and his proposal on Italian enfranchisement was blocked. This stalemate seems to have been the final straw for a number of Italian nobles who engaged in a conspiracy to remove what they saw as the main obstacle, the consuls. Florus reports a plot being hatched to murder both Philippus and his colleague Sex. Iulius Caesar while sacrificing on the Alban Mount during the Latin Festival.[49] The *de viris illustribus* reports that it was Drusus who discovered this conspiracy and actually warned Philippus of the danger, and so it came to nought.[50] However, it seems that he became tainted by this conspiracy, being seen as a prime motivator, if not actually being a part of it, and was denounced in the Senate House.

Diodorus alone reports an extraordinary incident in which Poppaedius, the Marsic nobleman and friend of Drusus, assembled a force of 10,000 supporters, armed with concealed swords, and marched them on Rome. The intention was apparently to enter Rome and then surround the Senate (or assembly) and force them to pass legislation enfranchising the Italians. Upon their approach to Rome they encountered a senator named Domitius (possibly Cn. Domitius Ahenobarbus, Cos. 96) who was able to persuade Poppaedius that the Senate would never give way to force, but that they could gain what they desired through legitimate political means. Given the fragmentary nature of these books of Diodorus, we have no clear chronology for this incident within the year 91 BC. Whilst Poppaedius may have truly been marching against the Senate, he did apparently state that he was bidden to Rome at the invitation of the tribunes, and these 10,000 may have been intended to flood the assembly for the crucial votes and ensure that Drusus' proposals were passed.[51]

However, whilst bloodshed may have been averted on this occasion, shortly after his denouncement in the Senate, Drusus was assassinated at night by unknown assailants as he returned to his own house, thus adding to the list of murdered tribunes.[52] Following his death, the two laws that he had managed to pass were overturned by the consul Philippus, with a senatorial decree, as being passed against the auspices.[53] Appian reports that this murder was the final straw for a number of Italian communities who, convinced that Rome would never willingly grant them Roman citizenship, agreed that force was the only option. Thus a number of peoples and cities sent envoys to each other and formed an alliance with the purpose of opposing Rome by force.[54]

Given that they were aware of the failed Italian conspiracy to murder the consuls, the Senate was well aware that the feelings amongst certain Italian communities close to Drusus would be running high. Thus a number of Roman commanders were sent across Italy to communities that were considered to pose a potential risk. As it turned out, this action had the opposite effect. One of these emissaries was a praetor named Q. Servilius, who was dispatched to Asculum in Picenum (see Map 2). According to the few surviving sources, Servilius adopted a high-handed and contemptuous manner in his dealings with the Picentines.

Whether in a pre-planned move or an act of spontaneity, Servilius, his legate
Fonetius and the rest of his entourage were slaughtered by the inhabitants of
Asculum, whilst at a festival. This was followed by the slaughter of all Roman
citizens in the city.[55] This murder signalled the beginning of the rebellion of a
number of Italian peoples against Rome. Servilius had become the first casualty
of Rome's First Civil War, soon to be followed by hundreds of thousands more,
in a war which would last twenty years and cause the temporary collapse of the
Roman Republic.

Chapter 2

War in Italy (91–87 BC)

D espite the fact that this war encompassed military operations on a number of fronts ranging across Italy and was one of the most serious that Rome ever faced, in terms of our sources we must rely on short overview narrative accounts, mostly from Appian, supplemented by a series of more detailed fragments. The loss of detailed narrative histories – be they Livy's, those of Sisenna, or even Lucceius – force us to view such a major war in a condensed and fragmentary manner.[1] Furthermore, although the war took place in Italy, the surviving sources are all written from the winner's perspective, as is usually the case with Rome's wars, although we do possess some numismatic evidence from the Italian side (see images).

1. Italy Divided: Romans and Italians

The Italian Federation

The massacre at Asculum can be seen as the trigger point for the opening of hostilities between Rome and the peoples of Italy that rebelled from her control. However, as seen from Poppaedius' abortive march on Rome earlier in 91 BC, it seems that a number of the Italian peoples had already mobilized and thus were ready and waiting when the signal for revolt came. At the outset we must avoid all simplifications that make these wars simply a revolt by the oppressed peoples of Italy against their Roman overlords. Upward of twelve different Italian peoples took arms against Rome in the initial phase of the war, each with differing backgrounds and reasons for doing so. The *Periochae* of Livy, Diodorus and Appian all provide details on the peoples who rebelled, but each with a different perspective:

> The following Italian nations revolted: the Picentes, Vestinians, Marsians, Paelignians, Marrucinians, Samnites, and Lucanians.[2]
>
> Engaged in the war with the Romans were the Samnites, the people of Asculum, the Lucanians, the Picentines, the people of Nola and other cities and nations.[3]
>
> When the revolt broke out all the neighbouring peoples showed their preparedness at the same time, the Marsi, the Peligni, the Vestini, the Marrucini; and after them the Picentines, the Frentani, the Hirpini, the Pompeiians, the

Venusini, the Apulians, the Lucanians, and the Samnites, all of whom had been hostile to the Romans before.[4]

We can see that Livy and Diodorus provide far fewer names than Appian, who seems to combine the two. Appian provides us with far more than the names, however, as his account seems to indicate two waves of rebellion; with the Marsi, Peligni, Vestini and Marrucini in the first wave, who rebelled following the massacre at Asculum, and a second grouping who rose up later, in 91 BC. Interestingly, the first four peoples had been in alliance prior to their conquest by Rome and thus seem to have resurrected a pre-Roman alliance.

Salmon argues that this clearly indicates the presence of two separate, but allied, groupings amongst the rebels, one composed of peoples of central and eastern Italy who were predominantly Latin speakers, and another one composed of predominantly Oscan speakers to the south, making twelve key peoples in total. Livy and Diodorus are thus only preserving details of one of the two groupings in their accounts.[5] For Salmon, these two groupings can be supported by the variations in the coinage issued by the Italian rebels, with some in Latin and others in Oscan.

Each of these two groupings appears to have been centred around, or led by, a dominant people. In the central alliance this was the Marsi, and in the southern one it was the Samnites. Diodorus even refers to the two groupings agreeing a boundary between their spheres of influence, set at the Cercola.[6] This is generally considered to be a reference to a particular natural boundary between the Marsic and Samnite territories, but exactly what it refers to has been lost to us. These two groupings then seem to have created one overarching federation, with a federal capital Corfinum, which was renamed Italia. This capital was the location of a common treasury and store of supplies, as well having a federal council, giving this system all the trapping of a federation. Diodorus also provides details of a unified command structure, with two annual consuls and twelve praetors, one for each of the peoples. The first consuls were Q. Poppaedius Silo, for the Marsi, commander of the central alliance, and a Samnite named either as C. Aponius Motylus or C. Papius Mutilus.[7]

Thus Diodorus provides us with what is a particularly Greek view of the Italian rebels: a Greek federation, albeit with borrowed Roman magistracies and institutions. However, there are three key questions. The first one centres around how much Diodorus' view and the language he used reflected the reality of the situation, and the extent to which he saw it though a Greek filter? Again, we have no Italian records for how they organized themselves. Secondly, did the sources Diodorus used view the Italian Federation through Roman eyes, by giving it consuls and praetors and making it resemble a Roman system?[8] Thirdly, there is the question of whether these arrangements were meant to be permanent or were just for the duration of the war.

In terms of command structure, it does seem that the 'Italian Federation' did have a joint command structure, but only in so far as there were two major groupings within the rebellion, one centred on the Marsi and one on the Samnites. The Marsi were led by Q. Poppaedius Silo and the Samnites by C. Papius Mutilus. Thus the rebellion had two principal centres of command, each with its own leader. To Greek eyes, this may have looked like a traditional Greek federation. To Roman eyes, it may well have looked like the consular arrangement. However, this does not mean that the term 'consul' was used, nor that annual elections were held, nor that any other race could provide one of the two principal leaders. Thus Rome faced one Italian Federation, combined of two principal sub-groups or regional alliances. This meant that Rome faced a war on two fronts: central and southern Italy, or a Marsic and a Samnite campaign.

However, rather than fight two separate and unconnected wars, the two groupings of states created an overarching federation, with all the trappings necessary to co-ordinate their efforts and seemingly to provide governance for life after Rome. A Roman alliance in Italy would seemingly be replaced by an Italian federation, run for the benefit of all states rather than just one. In many ways, this harked back to the Greek model of federations created by the Greek city states, such as the Achaean and Aetolian leagues, to counterbalance the great Hellenistic kingdoms they faced. This overarching federation would also allow for the pooling of manpower, the benefits of which the Romans had ably demonstrated over the previous two centuries.

This brings us to the all-important question of what the Italian rebels' aims were?[9] Initially, it seems that the Marsic grouping sent ambassadors to Rome following the Asculum massacre to try to negotiate Roman citizenship for their citizens. Appian provides the following:

> They sent ambassadors to Rome to complain that although they had cooperated in all ways with the Romans in building up the empire, the latter had not been willing to admit their helpers to citizenship. The Senate answered sternly that if they repented of what they had done they could send ambassadors, otherwise not. The Italians, in despair of any other remedy, went on with their preparations for war. Besides the soldiers who were kept for guards at each town, they had forces in common amounting to about 100,000 foot and horse. The Romans sent an equal force against them, made up of their own citizens and of the Italian peoples who were still in alliance with them.[10]

A negotiated settlement was always an unlikely outcome, especially given the massacre at Asculum, which meant that armed struggle and the defeat of Rome was the only option. However, this still leaves us with the question of what were their longer terms aims? Some have argued that independence from Rome was the ultimate goal, others that this was the first stage of a desire for Italian unification; neither seems likely. Unification can be ruled out on account of the fact that the races which occupied the peninsula in this period were not of common ancestry, blood or culture, ranging from Gauls in the north through Etruscans, Latins and Oscans to the Greeks in the south, to name but a few. If nothing else, two centuries of Roman rule had shown the clear benefits, both at home and abroad, of abolishing the warfare that had racked the peninsula prior to the Roman conquest. Cooperation brought with it peace and prosperity at home and a large empire overseas.

With the creation of the Italian Federation, a demand for equality within the Roman system transformed itself into a desire to replace the Roman-dominated alliances with a more equitable system. Even if they were victorious on the battlefield and gained Roman citizenship, could the balance of power between Rome and the peoples of Italy remain the same? By its very nature, an Italian victory would end Roman supremacy within the peninsula and bring about a more balanced system of alliance, for the benefit of all, not just one city. Under such circumstances, the victors would not so much gain Roman citizenship for themselves as abolish Roman citizenship altogether, with everyone having equal citizenship in the Italian Federation. Thus Roman citizens would become Italian federal citizens, which would offer full rights and legal protection to all. Rome would thus then become another state within the federation, with no one hegemon.

As always, a note of caution must be sounded with any speculative reconstruction. The Italian Federation may have looked and even preached equality between its members, but it was dominated by two powers: the Marsi and the Samnites. Furthermore, many would have been looking no further than defeating Rome on the battlefield and ending their hegemony in the peninsula, rather than having a clear idea of what structures would be raised in their place. Finally, there must have been a myriad of different views within each of the rebel peoples, never mind between them.

Another interesting question arises regarding the Italian Federation and Rome's empire. Given the undoubted wealth and prosperity that the Romans had reaped and the key role that the Italians (through their manpower) had played in this process, would the Italians have done anything other than usurp Rome at the head of the empire? The question of whether this federation would have survived beyond the duration of the war must be linked to this issue of the empire. The Roman system had demonstrated the great rewards that unity brought with it, from peace and security at home to empire overseas. If the desire was to see an Italian federation with an Italian empire, the key question is whether such a thing would have been possible.

In terms of the empire, the armies would be the same; it would simply be the Senate of Corfinum issuing the orders, rather than that of Rome. The crucial difference is the fact that Rome's empire was for the benefit of the few and controlled by the few. At the centre lay an alliance of Roman noble families, who had solved their internal differences (notably the patrician-plebeian dissensions) before they gained their empire. If the Federal Italian Council was to replace that of Rome, how would it cope with so many conflicting peoples and voices, especially as the rebellion seemed to centre on the Marsi and the Samnites? Would such a federal system accommodate a number of competing peoples in the longer term, or would it have been doomed to dissension and further bloodshed?

This in turn leads to the question of Italian tactics. Although the rebellious peoples were geographically unified, Rome still maintained a number of colonies throughout rebel territory, most notably on the coast, along with a number of cities that remained loyal, all of which would have remained thorns in the rebels' sides until captured. Key to their longer term success, however, would be to persuade enough of the neutral Italian peoples to defect to the new Italian Federation to ensure that the manpower balance swung in their favour. Thus, in many ways, we have a repeat of Hannibal's initial tactics in the Second Punic War: score swift victories against Rome and strip her of her manpower resources, which in the long term would prove the decisive factor in any war. Although the rebels could field over 100,000 men, Rome still had control of large parts of northern and southern Italy, control of the seas and a large overseas empire (both formal and informal), from which they could call up further resources. If this war became a drawn-out affair then the rebels would surely suffer Hannibal's fate, worn down by the endless Roman military machine.

The Roman Alliance

Viewed from the Roman perspective, it must have been the scale of the rebellions that caught them by surprise. They had already received a warning through Poppaedius' march on Rome and had sent representatives out to monitor areas whose loyalty was suspect, which led the Praetor Servilius to Asculum in the first place. Furthermore, in 125 BC the city of Fregellae had revolted following the aborted citizenship proposals of M. Fulvius Flaccus, which may well have been part of a wider abortive revolt. As it was, the revolt of Fregellae on its own was isolated and easily crushed.[11] On this occasion, however, a number of Italian peoples across central and southern Italy had risen in arms. Furthermore, whilst one city could be isolated, these rebellions had united to form a rival alliance that offered all the benefits of the Roman one, such as peace and security in Italy and the prosperity of an overseas empire, with apparently none of the drawbacks, such as Roman interference in internal affairs or second-class status in Italy.

Although a number of the surviving sources, such as Florus, deploy calamitous rhetoric for the opening of the war, as the situation stood in 91 BC, Rome's position was far from hopeless.[12] The core of the early Roman state – Latium, Etruria and Campania – remained loyal, or at least had not openly rebelled, giving Rome a solid block of territory on Italy's western coast and a buffer around Rome itself. In the north, both Umbria and Cisalpine Gaul remained loyal, while in the south, the Greek cities remained loyal also (see Map 2).[13] Rome was also strategically in a far stronger position than in any previous war fought in Italy, given her vast resources in the Mediterranean from both her provinces and her allies. We have references to Gallic and African contingents fighting in Italy, as well as additional naval forces from Asia.[14] The key to Roman success again harked back to the Hannibalic invasion a century earlier: avoid the quick military defeats and ensure that her remaining allies, including those in the wider empire, did not desert to the opposition.

Fighting during the latter stages of 91 BC appears to have been limited, as both sides continued with their mobilizations. Appian refers to Rome ultimately fielding 100,000 men, to match the size of the Italian armies.[15] Brunt has argued that during 90 BC Rome had mobilized and deployed some 75,000 infantry and cavalry.[16] Archaeological remains in the form of sling shot found at Asculum reveal Roman legions numbering up to at least XV (IV, IX, XI and XV to be exact), though the number in Italy in total, but not at Asculum, may have been higher.[17]

With no major campaigns during the rest of 91 BC, the conduct of the war fell to the consuls of 90 BC, L. Iulius Caesar and P. Rutilius Lupus. Each consul seems to have been assigned to fight one of the two main Italian rebel groupings (the Marsi and Samnites), Caesar in central and southern Italy against the Samnites, and Lupus in the central and eastern Italy against the Marsi. Thus, despite the overarching title of Italian War or Social War traditionally given to this period and the nature of there being one overarching 'Italian Federation', the war was divided into two fronts – Marsic and Samnite – and two differing but interconnected campaigns.

2. The First Year of Campaigning (90 BC) – The Marsic Campaign

Given that the Marsic leader C. Poppaedius Silo already had 10,000 men under arms by mid-91 BC, we must assume that he took to the field immediately following the massacre at Asculum to set about securing the rebel territory in the region. The *Periochae* of Livy reports a siege of the Roman colony of Alba on the Via Valeria, leading from Rome to the rebel territories in eastern Italy (see Map 2). At the opening of the campaigning season for 90 BC, Poppaedius was faced by P. Rutilius Lupus, of whom we sadly know little (including any prior military experience). Nevertheless, given the importance of the campaign, it is clear that the Senate sent with him a body of experienced and talented legates to support his campaign, notably amongst them C. Marius himself and an up-and-coming Roman politician from Picenum named Cn. Pompeius Strabo.[18] Marius' inclusion and subordinate role is an interesting one. Plutarch's life of Marius barely dwells on this period, but it appears that Marius was selected to be one of Rutilius' legates due to family connections between the men, despite Marius' age of 66.

Again, we have little coherent narrative for the year that describes the campaigning as a whole. Orosius reports that Pompeius Strabo received senatorial orders to invade Picenum, the region from which his family came and in which it still maintained extensive estates.[19] More than anything else the Picentine campaign was of great symbolic value given that it was the place where the war had originated, with the massacre at Asculum, and taking that city would be of great symbolic importance.

Battle of Mount Falernus

At some point early in the campaigning season, the army of Pompeius encountered forces commanded by three Italian 'praetors', named by Appian as C. Vidacilius, T. Lafrenius and P. Vettius, commanding contingents of Picentes, Vestini, and Marsi respectively.[20] We have no details of the battle, other than it was by Mount Falernus and that Pompeius was defeated. Appian records that Pompeius retreated to the city of Firmum, where he was placed under siege by T. Lafrenius. Orosius also briefly mentions the defeat.[21]

Keaveney has argued that the defeats described by Appian and Orosius are separate ones, primarily based on the seemingly later position these events occupied in Appian's narrative of the year.[22] However, given the number of simultaneous campaigns ongoing at this point and the fact that Appian's text is not known for its strict adherence to chronology, there is no need to separate this defeat into two different ones.

Unnamed Battle

This first Roman defeat appears to have set the tone for the early Roman campaign throughout the region as a whole. Appian records that one of Rutilius' legates, C. Perperna, encountered the forces of P. Praesenteius, who it is argued was the commander of the Paeligni in central Italy.[23] Appian is the only source for this conflict:

> Publius Praesenteius defeated Perperna, who had 10,000 men under his command, killed 4,000 and captured the arms of the greater part of the others, for which reason the consul Rutilius deprived Perperna of his command and gave his division of the army to Caius Marius.[24]

Thus one of Rutilius' legates had met with defeat for a second time, this time losing the greater part of his army. The bulk of the main Roman army remained under the command of the consul Rutilius and his legates Q. Servilius Caepio and C. Marius. Orosius reports dissension between Lupus and Marius over which tactics to pursue, with Lupus pushing for a knock-out victory against Poppaedius and Marius advocating caution.[25] Again, we can see parallels to the Second Punic War, with disagreements over whether it was better to pursue the quick knock-out win or avoid the quick knock-out defeat. Nevertheless, under Lupus' command the main Roman army engaged a large Italian army at some point on the River Tolenus (see Map 2). They were faced by P. Vettius Scato, the Marsic 'praetor', and an army of unknown size.

Battle of River Tolenus

Both Appian and Orosius preserve accounts of what was the greatest battle of the war to date:

> The consul Rutilius and Caius Marius built bridges over the River Tolenus at no great distance from each other. Vettius Scato pitched his camp opposite them, but nearer to the bridge of Marius, and placed an ambush by night in some ravines around the bridge of Rutilius. Early in the morning, after he had allowed Rutilius to cross the bridge, he started up from ambush and killed a large number of the enemy on the dry land and drove many into the river. In this fight Rutilius himself was wounded in the head by a missile and died soon afterward. Marius was on the other bridge and when he guessed, from the bodies floating down stream, what had happened, he pushed away those in his front, crossed the river, and captured the camp of Scato, which was guarded by only a small force, so that Scato was obliged to spend the night where he had won his victory, and to retreat in the morning for want of provisions. The body of Rutilius and those of many other patricians were brought to Rome for burial. The corpses of the consul and his numerous comrades made a piteous spectacle and the mourning lasted many days. The Senate decreed from this time on that those who were killed in war should be buried where they fell, lest others should be deterred by the spectacle from entering the army.[26]
>
> In so much as Marius was constantly suggesting in private that a delay would prove beneficial to the conduct of the war and that the young recruits ought to be drilled in camp for a short time, Rutilius thought that the action of Marius was prompted by some hidden motive. He therefore made light of his advice and carelessly brought his army into an ambush set by the Marsi. There the consul himself and many nobles were killed and 8,000 Roman soldiers slaughtered. The Tolenus River carried the arms and bodies of the dead within sight of Marius, and thus furnished proof of the disaster. After quickly gathering together troops, Marius took the victors by surprise and slew 8,000 of these Marsi.[27]

Thus the largest engagement of the war to date had nearly resulted in a disastrous defeat for the Romans, with a consul and 8,000 men killed. If it were not for the quick actions of Marius (at the age of 66), this battle would have been a total disaster for the Romans. In terms of causalities, the battle was a draw, with 8,000 dead on both sides, but in propaganda terms, it was a significant Roman defeat, with the loss of a consul, and the commensurate effects on Roman morale. In effect, Rutilius had given the Marsi what they wanted, a clear victory for propaganda purposes, showing the vulnerability of Roman military might.

Thus in the three battles to date, the Romans had lost more than 12,000 men (4,000 against the Paeligni, 8,000 at Tolenus and an unknown number at Falernus) and more than 10,000 wounded. Tolenus highlighted two clear defects of the

Roman war effort: poor quality commanders and armies of fresh recruits. As seen earlier (Chapter 1), Rome was committed to a number of overseas wars, which, according to Brunt's estimates, were utilizing seven legions already.[28] The rapid mobilization of forces in Italy seems to have affected the quality of the troops in Rome's armies in Italy, with fresh recruits being thrown straight in at the deep end. Once again, Roman politics played a part, with untested military leaders in command, ignoring the advice of their vastly more experienced legates.[29]

Given the state of emergency, the Senate avoided holding an election to replace Rutilius as consul and took the expedient measure of appointing commanders in the field to take charge. Unfortunately, they choose to award command of Rutilius' army jointly to C. Marius and Q. Servilius Caepio. With hindsight, this decision seems strange, given the reputation and recent actions of Marius. Yet the *Periochae* of Livy preserves a notice that Caepio had recently distinguished himself in battle, though we have no further details: 'When Quintus Caepio, deputy of Rutilius, was besieged and successfully repelled his enemies, and was given equal powers to Caius Marius... .'[30]

There may also have been some lingering suspicion of Marius within the Senate itself and a desire to avoid appointing him in sole charge of an army once again, thus boosting his profile once more. Yet, if there were these political considerations, they should have come second to the military ones. Rome badly needed a morale-boosting victory in the Marsic campaign, and Marius was Rome's most experienced general. And, despite his age, he had shown that he had lost none of his instincts. It seems that the two commanders separated the remaining Roman forces and conducted their own campaigns.

Unnamed Battle

The *Periochae* of Livy preserves a note to an otherwise unattested battle between the Paeligni and a Roman commander named Sulpicius, who, it has been argued, was Ser. Sulpicius Galba.[31] The note simply states that Sulpicius routed the Paeligni.[32] This battle seems to have avenged the loss of C. Perperna (above) and formed the only Roman success in central Italy of this campaign.

Unnamed Battle

At some further point in the Roman campaign, Caepio encountered the forces of Poppaedius. Orosius briefly mentions this battle and adds that Poppaedius' army was made up of Marsi and Vestini.[33] Again, it is Appian who preserves an account of the battle:

> The opposing general, Q. Poppaedius, fled as a pretended deserter to this Caepio. He brought with him and gave as a pledge two slave babies, clad with the purple-bordered garments of free-born children, pretending that they were his own sons. As further confirmation of his good faith he brought masses of lead plated with gold and silver. He urged Caepio to follow him in all haste

with his army and capture the hostile army while destitute of a leader. Caepio was deceived and followed him. When they had arrived at a place where an ambush had been laid, Poppaedius ran up to the top of a hill as though he were searching for the enemy, and gave his own men a signal. The latter sprang out of their concealment and cut Caepio and most of his force in pieces. The Senate joined the rest of Caepio's army to that of Marius.[34]

Thus a second Roman general in succession had fallen to a Marsic ambush and met with a similar fate. Caepio may well have placed too much strength in the friendship he had with Poppaedius from before the war (see Chapter 1). Rome's Marsic campaign was now in disarray, with three successive defeats in central Italy, and casualty figures that must have exceeded 20,000 dead in this campaign alone (we have no figures for Caepio's defeat). Finally, the Senate affirmed what most Romans would have expected and appointed the six-time consul Marius in sole charge of what was left of the Marsic campaign for the remainder of the year. We have no clear idea of how many soldiers he had left under his command.

Unnamed Battle

It seems that Marius determined to restore Roman morale with a victory before the campaigning season was over and whilst his sole command lasted. He seems to have worked in concert with his old deputy and protégé L. Cornelius Sulla, despite the supposed enmity between the two men during this period. Again, details of this campaign are sketchy and we only have brief accounts, but it appears that Marius and Sulla, at an unknown location, met armies of the Marsi, who were led by an unknown commander, and the Marrucini, who were commanded by Herius Asinius. Interestingly, we do not know whether Poppaedius was in command of the Marsi at this battle. Again, Appian preserves a brief narrative of the battle:

> Cornelius Sulla and Caius Marius defeated the Marsi, who had attacked them. They pursued the enemy vigorously as far as the walls enclosing their vineyards. The Marsians scaled these walls with loss, but Marius and Sulla did not deem it wise to follow them farther. Cornelius Sulla was encamped on the other side of these enclosures and when he knew what had happened he came out to meet the Marsi, as they tried to escape, and killed a great number. More than 6,000 Marsi were slain that day, and the arms of a still greater number were captured by the Romans.[35]

The *Periochae* of Livy adds the detail that the Marrucinian commander Asinius was killed, whilst Orosius states that 7,000 were captured.[36] Thus, in his first battle in sole command of the Marsic campaign, Marius inflicted the first defeat on the Marsi and scored Rome's first major victory of the campaign. Following this victory, Sulla was dispatched back south to relieve the siege of Aesernia (see below).

The Marsi seemingly reformed under the command of Poppaedius and attempted to give battle once again, but Marius reverted to Fabian tactics and refused to give battle. Diodorus preserves an interesting fragment that details a meeting between Marius and Poppaedius and fraternization between their armies:

> As the armies came close to one another their grim belligerency gave way to peaceful feelings. For as they reached the point where features could be distinguished, the soldiers on both sides detected many personal friends, refreshed their memory of not a few former comrades in arms and identified numerous relatives and kinsmen.... . Seeing this Marius himself advanced from the battle line and when Poppaedius had done likewise they conversed with one another like kinsmen. When the commanders had discussed at length the question of peace and the longed for citizenship, in both armies a tide of joyous optimism surged up and the whole encounter lost its warlike air and took on a festive appearance.[37]

This extraordinary fragment of narrative, if true, throws into sharp relief the civil war element of this conflict, with soldiers in the opposing armies fighting friends, former comrades and kinsmen, with little personal rancour between them. At the soldiers' level, the war appears to have been fought as a matter of following orders, rather than any ideological or nationalistic aims. The meeting between the commanders also highlights the similarities between the two men and their armies. Both were Italian noblemen, one part of the Roman elite with close Italian ties, the other part of the Italian elite with close Roman ties. In the longer run, this meeting, at which Marius had consorted with the figurehead of the rebellion, would not have helped improve the Senate's view of the Roman commander, and may have led to the decision not to renew his imperium for the following year.[38]

Cicero actually reports a similar meeting between Pompeius Strabo and the Marsic general Vettius Scato, though we are not able to date the event. Again, we have a Roman general of Italian stock meeting his Marsic counterpart on friendly terms. Cicero reports a similar lack of rancour in the meeting:

> That conference was conducted with fairness: there was no fear, no suspicion, even their mutual hatred was not great, for the allies were not seeking to take our city from us, but to be themselves admitted to share the privileges of it.[39]

Battle of Firmum

Away from such encounters, events in the north-east showed a similar recovery. We have no idea of how long Pompeius Strabo had been under siege in Firmum, but Orosius has him breaking out of the siege following Marius' victory. Having been besieged in Firmum, Pompeius apparently bided his time and plotted his break out. Appian records the following engagement, though we have no details as to the time lapse between the two battles:

The latter [Pompeius] armed his remaining forces, but did not come to an engagement. Having learned that another army was approaching, he sent Sulpicius[40] around to take Lafrenius in the rear while he made a sally in front. Battle was joined and both sides were having a doubtful fight when Sulpicius set fire to the enemy's camp. When the latter saw this they fled to Asculum in disorder and without a general, for Lafrenius had fallen in the battle. Pompeius then advanced and laid siege to Asculum.[41]

Thus Pompeius had managed to turn a defeat into victory, killing one of the opposing commanders and clearing the Italian forces that were defending the route to Asculum. Orosius reports that upon this news the Senate ordered the restoration of dignified dress in Rome as a mark of the achievement.[42] It is possible that Asculum was under siege prior to Pompeius Strabo's arrival, as he preserves an interesting note on the activities of a Sex. Iulius Caesar (Cos. 91).[43] Unfortunately, Appian constantly mixes up the consuls of 91 and 90 BC, obscuring Sextus' role in this war.

Unnamed Battle
Nevertheless, Appian records that Sextus was successful in battle against an unknown opponent. All we have is the following statement from Appian:

> He attacked 20,000 of the enemy at some place while they were changing camping-places, killed about 8,000 of them, and captured the arms of a much larger number.[44]

Given the position in Appian's text, it is assumed that this clash took place in 90 BC. Appian goes on to state that Sextus died of disease whilst commanding the siege of Asculum, and was succeeded by C. Baebius. This whole reference is difficult to reconcile with the rest of the campaign narrative, and a number of modern commentators have attempted to amend the name and or the location of the command.[45] If we are to keep the reference as we have it, then we can only assume that Sextus, as proconsul was sent to besiege Asculum first, early in 90 BC, but that his death led to Pompeius being assigned command of the siege; what became of Baebius we do not know.

There are other scattered references to actions in this period though we have no dates to place them accurately in the campaign. Diodorus records the siege of the city of Pinna in the territory of the Vestini. The city remained loyal to Rome despite a massacre of the town's children by the Italian besieging forces.[46] Diodorus also records that the Picentines released a Cilician chief from prison, named Agamemnon, who assisted them by raiding Roman territory in a guerrilla campaign.[47]

Thus the first full year of campaigning in the Marsic campaign had seen Rome make a disastrous start, with a string of defeats, culminating in the deaths of the consul Rutilius and one of his replacements, Caepio. Roman losses must have exceeded 20,000 soldiers dead and a similar number wounded. Far exceeding the physical losses was the damage that these defeats had done to Rome's martial reputation. As the year progressed, the Italian Federation had shown itself to be militarily superior to the Romans, thus fulfilling their need for quick victories to show their viability as a viable alternative to Rome. As will be discussed below, this led to the rebellions against Rome spreading, further weakening Rome's war effort.

Rome's Marsic campaign only stabilized when Marius assumed command of the main Roman army with his two victories, at the end of the battle of Tolenus and at the unnamed battle later in the year. In this he was ably supported by Pompeius Strabo, who had turned defeat into victory and begun the symbolically important siege of Asculum. Nevertheless, as the year ended, Rome's military reputation had been dented, and despite the late rally, the year belonged to the Marsic alliance.

3. The First Year of Campaigning (90 BC) – The Samnite Campaign

Similarly, the Samnite campaign did not start well for Rome. Overall command fell to the consul L. Iulius Caesar, who also had a number of legates supporting him, including ex-consuls T. Didius (Cos. 98) and P. Licinius Crassus (Cos. 97), as well as L. Cornelius Sulla. As with the Marsic campaign, both sides spent the remainder of 91 BC mobilizing forces, though again we hear of attacks on Roman colonies that still held out and were now in rebel territory, most notably that of Aesernia in Samnium.[48] If anything, we have less details of this year's campaigning in the Samnite campaign than we do for the Marsic one. Nevertheless, as with the Marsic campaign, it seems that the consul was eager to engage the enemy, and early in the Samnite campaign Caesar faced a force of Samnites, led by Vettius Scato.[49]

Battle of Aesernia

We only have brief notes of this battle. Orosius places it at Aesernia, the Roman colony that was under siege. We must presume that Caesar was moving to relieve the siege when he encountered Vettius Scato. Both Appian and Orosius note that Caesar was defeated, but seem to differ on scale. Appian has 2,000 Romans killed, whilst Orosius refers to it as a slaughter, with Caesar needing to completely rebuild his army with a number of Gallic and African contingents. Orosius also adds the detail that Caesar was forced to flee the battle.[50]

Vettius then moved on to the siege of the city of Aesernia, which continued to hold out. With Caesar's army cleared from their path, the Samnites continued with this policy of reducing Roman cities, with Marius Egnatius capturing the nearby city of Venafrum. Appian ascribed this to treachery from within the city, which resulted in the slaughter of two Roman cohorts garrisoned there.[51] Such a slaughter seems to have been a common feature of the Samnite campaign, seemingly in stark contrast to the image given by Diodorus of the friendly meeting between the armies above, though it could simply be that we have fewer details on the sieges in the Marsic campaign.

The Samnite campaign appears to have continued in the same vein. A Samnite army led by C. Papius invaded Campania and attacked the Roman colonies there. Nola, on the Via Popilia, fell, also apparently through treachery. On this occasion the 2,000 strong defending garrison was offered a choice:

> Caius Papius captured Nola by treachery and offered to the 2,000 Roman soldiers in it the privilege of serving under him if they would change their allegiance. They did so, but as their officers refused the proposal, the latter were taken prisoners and starved to death by Papius.[52]

Thus we have the first recorded incident of the war in which Roman or allied soldiers deserted to the Italian Federation. With no opposition from Caesar, Papius continued his attacks on Roman and allied towns in the region, taking the cities of Stabiae, Surrentum and Salernum. The first two sat on Italy's western coast (on the Bay of Naples) and the latter on Via Popilia. Once again, we hear of defections to the rebels' side:

> The prisoners and the slaves from these places were taken into the military service. Then he plundered the entire country around Nuceria. The towns in the vicinity were struck with terror and submitted to him, and when he demanded military assistance they furnished him about 10,000 foot and 1,000 horse. With these Papius laid siege to Acerrae.[53]

Battle of Acerrae

It was only at this point that the consul Caesar appears to have been able to regroup his army, probably indicating that his losses were more severe than the 2,000 mentioned by Appian. Again, we have accounts in both Appian and Orosius of the battle:

> Caesar, with 10,000 Gallic foot and certain Numidian and Mauritanian horse and foot, advanced toward Acerrae. Papius took a son of Jugurtha, formerly king of Numidia, named Oxynta, who was under charge of a Roman guard at Venusia, led him out of that place, clothed him in royal purple, and showed him frequently to the Numidians who were in Caesar's army.[54] Many of them deserted, as if to their own king, so that Caesar was obliged to send the rest back to Africa, as they were not trustworthy. Papius attacked him rashly, and had already made a breach in his fortified camp when Caesar emerged with his horse through the other gates and slew about 6,000 of his men, after which Caesar withdrew from Acerrae.[55]

Orosius merely adds the detail that the rebel army was composed of both Samnites and Lucanians.[56] Thus Caesar, with his rebuilt army, was able to score his first victory of the Samnite campaign. He apparently wrote of his victory to the Senate, which received the news gratefully. Nevertheless, despite his 'victory', he was still forced to withdraw, perhaps due to the loss of the African contingent. In reality, we have to question how much of a victory this was. Although he had killed 6,000 of the enemy, he had been forced to withdraw once again and concede more territory to Papius, who had already received more troops than he lost from the Italian communities that had changed sides.

Battle of Taenum

Caesar, however, soon reduced the value of the limited victory even further when, on the march back from Acerrae, he appears to have fallen into an ambush. Only Appian preserves details of this battle:

> While Caesar was passing through a rocky defile with 30,000 foot and 5,000 horse, Marius Egnatius suddenly fell upon him and defeated him in it. He retreated on a litter, as he was sick, to a certain stream where there was only one bridge, and there he lost the greater part of his force and the arms of the survivors. He escaped to Teanum with difficulty and there he armed the remainder of his men as best he could. Reinforcements were sent to him speedily and he marched to the relief of Acerrae, which was still besieged by Papius, but when their camps were pitched opposite each other neither of them dared to attack the other.[57]

Thus Caesar managed to lose the second army of his campaign and ended his year of office as he started. As noted above with the consul Rutilius, although he was surrounded by wiser and more experienced commanders, the consul appears to have blundered from one disaster to another in the hopes of a quick victory, gifting the rebels the quick victories that they needed far more than the Romans. Away from Campania and Caesar, we have details of three more theatres of war in the Samnite campaign his year.

Unnamed Battle

The first was in Samnium itself, and was a clash involving the attempted relief of Aesernia by L. Cornelius Sulla, who had been sent with twenty-four cohorts to attempt to relieve the city. Frontinus preserves details of the battle, which is also mentioned by Orosius, though the two accounts differ considerably.

> Lucius Sulla was surprised in a defile near Aesernia by the army of the enemy under the command of Duillius, asked for a conference, but was unsuccessful in negotiating terms of peace. Noting, however, that the enemy were careless and off their guard as a result of the truce, he marched forth at night, leaving only

a trumpeter, with instructions to create the impression of the army's presence by sounding the watches, and to rejoin him when the fourth watch began. In this way he conducted his troops unharmed to a place of safety, with all their baggage and engines.[58]

Sulla was sent with twenty-four cohorts to Aesernia, where Roman citizens and soldiers were being hard pressed by a very close siege. He saved the city and its allies after he had fought a great battle and inflicted a terrific slaughter upon the enemy.[59]

Thus, on the face of it, we have two contradictory accounts. In Frontinus, Sulla walks into an ambush, which he skilfully manages to escape, whilst in Orosius he scores a great victory and saves Aesernia. The other problem we have with this is that the *Periochae* of Livy explicitly states that Aesernia fell after a long siege around this time: '...the colony at Aesernia, together with Marcus Marcellus, fell in the hands of the Samnites...'.[60]

It is possible that Sulla went on from extracting his forces from this ambush to scoring a notable victory over the forces of Duillius. Keaveney hypothesized that Sulla went on to lift the siege, but that the town later fell in a fresh siege.[61] No other source makes reference to anything other than a long drawn-out siege ending with the city being starved into submission, which the *Periochae* of Livy places in the same period as Sulla and Marius' victory against the Marsi. Given all this evidence, it seems unlikely that Sulla saved the city, though it is possible that he scored a victory against the Italian commander Duillius in the manner Orosius describes.

Battle of Grumentum

In Lucania, in southwestern Italy, operations were being commanded by the legate P. Licinius Crassus (Cos.97). However, experience proved to be no arbiter of success, as Crassus showed when he gave battle against the Lucanian commander M. Lamponius. Appian, Frontinus and Diodorus preserve short notes on this battle:

Marcus Lamponius destroyed some 800 of the forces under Licinius Crassus and drove the remainder into the town of Grumentum.[62]

When the camp of the Volscians had been pitched near bushes and woods, Camillus set fire to everything which could carry the flames, once started, up to the very fortifications. In this way he deprived the enemy of their camp. In the Social War Publius Crassus was cut off in almost the same way with all his troops.[63]

Lamponius rushed headlong at Crassus, for he believed that it was appropriate, not that the masses should fight on behalf of their leaders, but rather that their leaders should fight for the masses.[64]

Thus it seems that Crassus' camp was attacked by Lamponius, who set fire to the surrounding vegetation. Crassus, it seems, managed to escape with minimal casualties and seek refuge in the city of Grumentum. We hear no more of this threat during the year. In Apulia, Appian preserves a note detailing further Roman reverses:

> Canusium and Venusia and many other towns in Apulia sided with Vidacilius. Some that did not submit he besieged, and he put to death the principal Roman citizens in them, but the common people and the slaves he enrolled in his army.[65]

Thus, it can be argued that the Samnite campaign of 90 BC was an almost total disaster. The consul Caesar was heavily defeated on two occasions; the Samnites took a number of key Roman cities within their territory and conquered a series of Roman cities up to the Bay of Naples, and secured control of the Via Popilia. If this were not enough, Rome suffered reverses in Apulia and Lucania and saw a number of formerly allied cities defect to the Samnite alliance and supply them with fresh troops.

4. The Spread of the Rebellion – The Etruscan, Umbrian and Gallic Campaigns

In addition to the two major campaigns described above, of which we have some details, there are other perhaps more important campaigns of which we know next to nothing, but which were of vital importance to the war's outcome. Both the *Periochae* of Livy and Orosius refer to campaigns in Etruria and Umbria, which had apparently latterly risen in revolt:

> The Praetor Porcius Cato conquered the Etruscans and his legate Plotius conquered the Umbrians. Both victories entailed the most distressing hardships and much bloodshed.[66]
> Deputy Aulus Plotius defeated the Umbrians and praetor Lucius Porcius the Etruscans. Both nations had revolted.[67]

Appian also mentions the revolt, but not the military campaigns:

> While these events were transpiring on the Adriatic side of Italy, the inhabitants of Etruria and Umbria and other neighbouring peoples on the other side of Rome heard of them and all were excited to revolt.[68]

Regrettably, this is all that survives of two of the most important campaigns of the war. Central to the success of the Italian Federation's rebellion was to score quick victories over Rome, thereby showing her weakness and encouraging the other peoples of Italy to revolt. We know from the other sources that the Etruscans and Umbrians were not part of the original rebellion, and thus we can deduce that the Italians were indeed successful in encouraging key Roman allies to revolt. With Etruria and Umbria in revolt, and possibly allied to the Italian Federation, Rome would now be surrounded by hostile territory in Italy. We have no idea of how serious or widespread these revolts in Etruria and Umbria were, but Orosius does speak of hard-fought victories.[69] We can assume that if the Etruscans and Umbrians were wavering in 91 BC, the reported Roman losses during early 90 BC must have contributed to their decision.

The most interesting factor here is the apparent speed and ease with which these two peoples were defeated. Whilst Orosius labels them 'distressing and bloody', based on a more detailed Livian narrative, none of the other surviving sources mention these military campaigns. Both peoples seem to have been defeated by the end of 90 BC, which is surprising given the difficulties Rome was having in the two other major campaigns and the fact that they must have committed the bulk of their troops to the two consuls. Given both of these factors, we can only presume that these revolts were not as widespread as in the rest of Italy and only involved an isolated number of communities, which were relatively easy to isolate and defeat, albeit with a large amount of bloodshed. Aside from the swift military resolution to these revolts, the offer of citizenship to those who had not yet rebelled must have greatly aided the Romans in containing these fresh rebellions (see below).

Although we lack any details of the campaigns, the outcomes were important for two key reasons. Firstly, Rome had militarily prevented the rebellion from spreading and further undermining their position, thus neutralizing a key element in the Italian Federation's plans. If Rome could keep the rebellion isolated to just those two alliances, centred on the Marsi and Samnites, and prevent the war from spreading, then the war could be contained and effectively managed. Secondly, these additional rebellions, even if they were isolated, seem to have shocked the Senate into considering a political solution to accompany the military one (see below). Furthermore, the *Periochae* of Livy informs us that the Salluvii peoples of Transalpine Gaul also rebelled, perhaps indicating that these rebellions and defeats were having a wider impact on Rome's regional standing. Again, we only have the one reference to the campaigns: 'In Transalpine Gaul, Caius Caelius defeated the rebellious Salluvians.'[70]

5. A Political Solution: The Senate and the *Lex Iulia*

According to Appian, the revolts in Etruria and Umbria so alarmed the Senate that they agreed to a political solution to the crisis, and one which they had so voraciously opposed only a year earlier:

The Senate also voted that those Italians who had adhered to their alliance should be admitted to citizenship, which was the one thing they all desired most. They sent this decree around among the Etruscans, who gladly accepted the citizenship.[71]

This is one of the most important references in the ancient sources, as it details the extension of Roman citizenship. However, if we are not careful, it can also be one of the most misunderstood references. In Appian, this measure was unnamed, but the sources contain three other passing references to the granting of citizenship according to the Iulian Law, while one source refers to the discussions that took place:[72]

The general Gnaeus Pompeius, son of Sextus, for their valour made Spanish cavalrymen Roman citizens in camp at Asculum on November 17 in accordance with the Iulian Law.[73]

... the Latins have adopted whatever of them they have chosen; even by the Iulian law itself, by which the rights of citizenship were given to the allies and to the Latins, it was decreed that those people who did not ratify the law should not have the freedom of the city, which circumstance gave rise to a great contention ...[74]

... when citizenship was given to all Latium by the Iulian law ...[75]

... for example, if in the Italian War the Senate should deliberate whether or not to grant citizenship to the Allies.[76]

As it is commonly depicted, the law mentioned by Appian was the *Lex Iulia*, which was presumably passed by L. Iulius Caesar upon his return to Rome towards the end of his year in office. This seemed to grant Roman citizenship to all Italian and Latin communities that had not rebelled, thus supposedly meeting the main demand of the Italian communities, and thus preventing further rebellions.

Bispham provides the most concise and up-to-date summary of the arguments involved in the laws that extended Roman citizenship.[77] He argues that *Lex Iulia* was a rushed measure that had little in the way of detailed planning (hardly surprising given the nature of the crisis), and which allowed for allied communities who had not revolted to become citizens if they so chose. This measure was not a blanket enfranchisement of all Italy, but was an offer of citizenship for those allied communities who wanted it, thus isolating the moderates, who hoped for gain within the Roman system, from the radicals, who wanted outright independence from Rome, whether as part of a greater Italian federation or not.

As well as the *Lex Iulia*, the sources contain references to three other laws: the *Lex Plautia-Papiria*, the *Lex Calpurnia* and the *Lex Pompeia*. The first two are considerably obscure, both in terms of content, chronology and relationship to each other and to the *Lex Iulia*. Some have argued that the *Lex Plautia-Papiria* was a tribunician measure that extended citizenship to the rest of Italy, whilst others that it was limited to certain groups.[78] The only details of the law come from a speech of Cicero. Again, this measure seems to have been aimed solely at Rome's allies, and again, it was a voluntary measure.

> The freedom of the city was given him in accordance with the provisions of the law of Silvanus and Carbo. If any men had been enrolled as citizens of the confederate cities, and if, at the time that the law was passed, they had a residence in Italy, and if within sixty days they had made a return or themselves to the praetor.[79]
>
> Then the consuls [tribunes] Silvanus and Carbo passed a law, that anyone who belonged to an allied people could obtain Roman citizenship, if only he was living in Italy at the time that the law was passed, and if he made an application to the praetor within sixty days. Licinius Archias was unable to provide the necessary evidence that he was entitled to Roman citizenship ...[80]

The *Lex Calpurnia* is referenced only in one fragment of Sisenna and seems to be limited to granting citizenship to allied soldiers who had displayed bravery in the field. The *Lex Pompeia* is much easier to understand, being passed by Cn. Pompeius Strabo during 89 BC, and being concerned with the granting of Latin rights to Cisalpine Gaul, and was therefore a targeted measure to ensure that the Gauls in northern Italy did not join in with the rebellion.[81]

Thus, whilst the Romans conducted faltering and downright disastrous military campaigns against the Marsi and Samnites, they were considerably more successful in preventing the rebellion from expanding beyond their ability to deal with it militarily. By a combination of military campaigns and political concessions, Etruria, Umbria, Latium and the two Gauls were kept within Roman control, isolating the contagion to the Marsic and Samnite alliances. It was this, more than anything else, which brought victory to the Romans in this war. However, as with most legislation, the devil was in the detail, and as Appian states, these new citizens faced a key political restriction:

> The Romans did not enrol the new citizens in the thirty-five existing tribes, lest they should outvote the old ones in the elections, but incorporated them in ten new tribes, which voted last. So it often happened that their vote was useless, since a majority was obtained from the thirty-five tribes that voted first. This fact was either not noticed by the Italians at the time or they were satisfied with what they had gained, but it was observed later and became the source of a new conflict.[82]

Whether this measure was decided in the *Lex Iulia* is a matter of much scholarly debate. Bispham argues that given the rushed nature of the measure, this was a matter left for further legislation when the Senate had more time to work these matters out, and this author is inclined to agree with him.[83] Thus, by the back door, the Senate enacted a measure that allowed them to maintain control of the electoral system in Rome and negate the impact of these new voters. As Appian states, at the time this was of little issue, but it would become one the major issues in the years that followed, and a key catalyst for further conflicts.[84]

6. Military Reforms

Appian also refers to some military reforms that the Senate were forced to undertake due to the chronic manpower shortages they were suffering (with the Marsic, Samnite, Etrurian, Umbrian and Gallic campaigns, not to mention various overseas commitments):

> The Senate, fearing lest they should be surrounded by enemies for want of guards, garrisoned the sea-coast from Cumae to the city with freedmen, who were then for the first time enrolled in the army on account of the scarcity of soldiers.[85]

Thus for the second time in two decades Rome had, out of necessity, expanded the potential pool of military recruits, this time admitting freedmen.[86] Furthermore, the extension of Roman citizenship to the loyal allied communities meant that those who accepted it became liable for service in the Roman armies, rather than the allied contingents, thus again expanding the numbers available for Roman military service, albeit only after a period of time (enfanchsisment and census).

7. Political Backlash at Rome – The *Lex Varia*

Whilst the Roman nobility were spurred to political concessions towards the end of 90 BC, it seems that earlier in the year they had descended into a political witch-hunt. A tribune Q. Varius Severus Hybrida was persuaded by various factions to propose a law establishing a special tribunal to investigate and prosecute those who had 'encouraged the allies to revolt'; in other words, a McCarthy-style witch-hunt to seek out 'enemies' within the senatorial nobility itself.[87] In practice, this targeted the allies of Livius Drusus.[88]

This law was passed using violence in the face of the vetoes of his colleagues and set up a special court that tried and exiled a number of prominent Roman politicians. This desire to seek out internal enemies, previously seen during the Gracchan and Saturnine tumults, was to be a feature of the period 91–70 BC, which saw a number of Roman noblemen declared enemies of the state or exiled. The Varian court appears to have been a temporary madness, brought about by the shock of the Italian rebellion. The law was suspended the following year and Varius himself seems to have fallen foul of his own law and exiled.[89] Nevertheless, it was a sign that in times of extreme pressure the Roman elite were turning on themselves.

8. The Second Year of Campaigning (89 BC) – The Marsic Campaign

As the year 89 BC opened, Rome faced a mixed political and military situation. The campaigns against the Marsi and the Samnites had been disastrous to say the least, with a string of Roman defeats, and losses in excess of 50,000 men, caused by poor quality commanders, especially the two consuls of 90 BC. On the positive side, rebellions in Etruria, Umbria and Transalpine Gaul had been crushed and political concessions had been granted, which would separate the die-hard rebels from the moderates and prevent any but the most determined to rebel against Rome. With the war finely balanced, Rome's aims for the year will have been to gain ground militarily in both campaigns and avoid the disasters of the previous year. To those ends the consuls for 89 BC were both men with proven military experience in this war: Cn. Pompeius Strabo and L. Porcius Cato, two of the three Roman commanders (the other being Marius himself) with victories to their name the previous year. Interestingly, both consuls seem to have received commands in the Marsic campaign, with Pompeius returning to command the siege of Asculum and Cato the fight against the Marsi.

Marius was notable by his absence, as his command was not extended. Plutarch cites ill health, but given his performance the previous year and again in 87 BC, it seems more likely that various elements of the Senate did not want Marius to continue to show his military prowess and recover the position he once had, especially given his friendly meeting with the rebel figurehead Poppaedius.[90] Whilst this meeting may have been innocent, it would have been easily open to misinterpretation (perhaps deliberately so in some cases) in such paranoid times.

For the Italian rebels, the failure of the rebellions in Etruria and Umbria and the granting of political concessions would have been blows, but they would have been hoping to continue the military success of the previous year and continue the push into Roman-held territory, perhaps more determined that outright military victory was now their only choice.

This theatre of war saw both consuls of 89 active in the field, though it seems with each commanding a separate campaign. Pompeius appears to have been in command in the northern part of central Italy and Cato to the south.

Unnamed Battle

The first clash appears to have taken place over the winter of 90/89 when Pompeius intercepted an Italian relief force sent to aid the rebels in Etruria, unaware that the rebellion had already been crushed. Appian is the only source who mentions the battle and provides little detail other than that Pompeius attacked a force of 15,000 Italians, killing 5,000 of them, with another 7,500 perishing of starvation during the march home.[91] Pompeius then moved on to command the siege of Asculum.

His colleague Cato campaigned against the Marsi and received a limited amount of attention in the few surviving sources. Appian dismisses his campaigns with just a sentence,[92] whilst a fragment of Dio preserves an interesting and illuminating incident:

> Cato, the greater part of whose army came from the city and was rather too old for service, had little authority at best: and once, when he ventured to rebuke them because they were unwilling to work hard to obey orders readily, he came near to being buried under the shower of missiles which they hurled at him. … The man who began the mutiny, C. Titius, was arrested; he had been a loafer about the Forum, making his living in the courts and was excessively and shamelessly outspoken. He was sent to the city to the tribunes, but escaped punishment.[93]

Further light may be shed on this extraordinary incident by Orosius, who adds the detail that Cato was in command of the forces previously commanded by C. Marius, and appears to have had Marius' son amongst his legates. Thus Dio's description of them being from the city and old appears to refer to an army comprised mostly of Marius' veterans. It is entirely likely that Marius' army would not have taken kindly to him being replaced as commander.

This incident is important for a number of reasons. Firstly, it is extraordinary that a Roman army attempted to murder its own commander in the midst of a war of survival. Given the events that came in 88 and 87 BC (Chapters 3 and 4) it is tempting to see this event as a foretaste of things to come. Furthermore, many in the army, which must have been thrown together hastily in the emergency situation, seemed to feel more loyalty toward their former commander than the state and seemed to have placed their own interests ahead of those of the state, again perhaps foreshadowing the rise of client armies. Thus the extraordinary nature of the war seems to have had an affect on the quality and temperament of the soldiers that were rapidly mobilized, with less care being taken and less training and discipline being instilled in them than would have been expected under prior circumstances.

Just as interesting is the fact that the leader of the mutiny, Titius, was acquitted by the tribunes in Rome of attempting to murder the consul. Given the levels of paranoia in Rome seen under the Varian Commission the previous year this is highly surprising and perhaps more than a little suggestive. Under normal circumstances such an act of treason would have been punishable by death, yet given that the army was seemingly composed of a number of Marian veterans, it is probable that Titius himself was a client of Marius and thus may have received the protection of his patron, who was now back in Rome and most likely no friend of Cato. Nevertheless, despite this mutinous army, both the *Periochae* of Livy and Orosius refer to Cato winning a number of notable victories against the Marsi, though no details are given.[94]

Battle of Lake Fucinus

This string of victories culminated in a clash near Lake Fucinus in the centre of Marsic territory.[95] The *Periochae* of Livy states that once again Cato's forces were winning the encounter when Cato was killed whilst attacking the Marsic camp, which turned the tide against the Romans, culminating in a defeat.[96] Whilst a number of sources refer to Cato's death, only Orosius has the following extraordinary detail:

> The consul Porcius Cato, accompanied by the Marian forces, fought a number of hard battles. Indeed, he boasted that even C. Marius had not accomplished greater deeds. On account of this, when he was waging war against the Marsi at Lake Facinus, the son of C. Marius, as if an unknown champion, struck him down in the tumult of battle.[97]

Thus, according to Orosius, the accusation is made that Marius' son (who would figure prominently in the wars that followed), murdered Cato. This evidence ties in with the fragment of Dio quoted above. Whilst the younger Marius was judged harshly by Roman historians for his acts in the later period of the civil war, this is an extraordinary claim, which if true marks Cato as the first consular casualty to fall at Roman hands and emphasizes the earlier point about Roman armies in this period acting more as client armies, than armies of the state.[98] It must be pointed out that none of the other sources for Cato's death (Appian, Velleius, the *Periochae* of Livy, nor Eutropius) repeat this accusation, though only Velleius actually states that it was the enemy who killed him.[99] Although this may have been the first incident of a Roman commander being murdered by one of his own subordinates, it was far from the last (see Appendix III). We are not told who took over command of Cato's army in the immediate aftermath of Fucinus.

Whilst the Romans suffered a reversal against the Marsi, it seems that a number of Pompeius' legates were conducting highly successful campaigns of their own against the other rebel Italian peoples, as Pompeius continued the siege of Asculum.

Battle of Teanus River

Again, we only have short sentences from our surviving sources, which cover what must have been long campaigns. Several notable campaigns were conducted by Pompeius' legate Sulpicius, who defeated both the Marrucini and Vestini and pacified both regions.[100] Orosius refers to this, otherwise unattested, battle, which seems to have been a notable victory for Sulpicius:

> The attack of Sulpicius, Pompeius' legate, overwhelmed and destroyed the Marrucini and the Vestini. This same Sulpicius killed the Italian generals Popaedius and Obsidius in a frightful battle at the Teanus River.[101]

Following these victories, the Marrucini, Vestini and even the Paeligni all surrendered to Pompeius (as overall commander of the campaign). These capitulations brought a large swathe of central eastern Italy back under Roman control and cut Asculum off from the Marsic territories. Thus slowly and surely Pompeius and his legates were defeating the various rebel peoples, one at a time, and stripping the Italian Federation of support and crucially manpower, in a manner in which the Italians never managed with the Romans.

Unnamed Battle

Furthermore, we hear of another of Pompeius' legates defeating the Marsi themselves, though again we only have a single reference to these battles. This victory was won by L. Cornelius Cinna (who was to figure prominently in later events): 'The Marsi were broken in several battles by the deputies Lucius Cinna and Caecilius Pius.'[102]

Battle of Asculum

One of the most symbolic victories of the Marsic campaign came at some point in mid-to-late 89 BC when the Italians attempted to break the siege of Asculum. The two accounts we have of this battle vary slightly.

> Asculum was the native town of Vidacilius, and as he feared for its safety he hastened to its relief with eight cohorts. He sent word beforehand to the inhabitants that when they should see him advancing at a distance they should make a sally against the besiegers, so that the enemy should be attacked on both sides at once. The inhabitants were afraid to do so; nevertheless Vidacilius forced his way into the city through the midst of the enemy with what followers he could get, and upbraided the citizens for their cowardice and disobedience. As he despaired of saving the city he first put to death all of his enemies, who had been at variance with him before and who, out of jealousy, had prevented the people from obeying his recent orders. Then he erected a funeral pile in the temple and placed a couch upon it, and had a feast with his friends, and while the drinking-bout was at its height he swallowed poison, threw himself on the pile, and ordered his friends to set fire to it.[103]

> Had he [Pompeius] not first overcome and severely defeated the people who had rushed out on an open field, he would not have captured it. Eighteen thousand of the Marsi and their general Fraucus were slain in this battle and 3,000 captured. Four thousand Italians, fleeing from the slaughter, chanced to ascend the summit of a mountain with their column in close formation. Overwhelmed and weakened by the snows there, they suffered a miserable death from exposure.[104]

Velleius adds that on the day of the battle, across several engagements in the region, 70,000 Romans and 60,000 Italians met in battle.[105] This defeat precipitated the

fall of Asculum, which suffered Roman retribution for its role as the birthplace
of the Italian rebellion:

> Pompeius entered Asculum and had the prefects, centurions, and all the leading
> men beaten with rods and beheaded. He sold the slaves and all the booty at
> auction and ordered the remaining people to depart, free indeed, but stripped
> and destitute. Though the Senate expected that the proceeds of the booty would
> somewhat increase the public income, Pompeius did not contribute anything
> from it to the needy treasury.[106]

Thus by the end of 89 BC, the Marsic campaign had swung strongly in Rome's
favour. The Marrucini, Vestini and Paeligni had all been defeated and surrendered
to Pompeius, and the city of Asculum (the birthplace of the rebellion) had been
destroyed. It seems that it was only the Marsi themselves who continued to fight,
though they too had been defeated on several occasions, first by Cato and then
by Cinna. Their one notable victory had been the death of the consul Cato, but
he had been killed in a skirmish, and possibly by a Roman hand. Key to Rome's
success had been competent commanders methodically attacking and defeating
the various peoples that made up the Marsic alliance. This was made possible
by the failure of the rebellion to successfully spread to the other peoples of the
region. The Marsi had fallen to the same factors that had defeated Pyrrhus
and Hannibal in earlier centuries: namely that the core of the Roman system of
alliance and manpower remained intact, feeding the Roman armies a continuing
supply of troops, with which to grind down the rebel Italian peoples, one at a
time.

9. The Second Year of Campaigning (89 BC) – The Samnite Campaign

With both consuls holding command in the Marsic campaign, command against
the Samnites fell to a group of legates, the most notable of which were L. Cornelius
Sulla and T. Didius (Cos. 98). Following the death of Cato in combat with the
Marsi, it seems that Sulla was promoted to proconsular status for the rest of the
year.[107] He seems to have begun his campaign in Campania, where Caesar had
failed so spectacularly the year before, allowing the Samnites to capture a number
of formerly loyal Roman cities. During April of 89 BC, we find him destroying the
rebel city of Stabiae on the Bay of Naples.[108] This was soon followed by a siege of
the city of Pompeii. The siege is notable, not because of the city's later fame, but
because of a murder that took place during the siege. The man in question was A.
Postumius Albinus (Cos. 99) who was serving as legate of Sulla in charge of the
Roman naval detachment there. Orosius preserves the best account:

> The legate of L. Sulla, Postumius Albinus, a man of consular rank, at that time
> so aroused the hatred of all the soldiers against him by his insufferable arrogance

that they stoned him to death. The consul Sulla gave it as his opinion that civil bloodshed could be atoned for only by shedding the blood of the enemy.[109]

Thus once again a man of consular status had been murdered by Roman soldiers, the second time this year, and once again the murderers had gone unpunished. This again shows the poor discipline of the Roman troops under arms during this war and the tolerance that they were being shown by their commanders. In conjunction with Sulla's campaign, T. Didius retook the city of Herculaneum aided by a legion of loyal Hirpini.[110]

Battle of Nola

Following the siege of Pompeii, Sulla encountered a Samnite army led by L. Cluentius in the vicinity of Nola. Fortunately, Appian preserves a detailed account of the battle:

> While Sulla was encamped near the Pompeiian Mountains L. Cluentius pitched his camp in a contemptuous manner at a distance of only three stades from him, Sulla did not tolerate this insolence, but attacked Cluentius without waiting for his own foragers to come in. He was worsted and put to flight, but when he was reinforced by his foragers he turned and defeated Cluentius. The latter then moved his camp to a greater distance. Having received certain Gallic reinforcements he again drew near to Sulla and just as the two armies were coming to an engagement a Gaul of enormous size advanced and challenged any Roman to single combat. A Mauritanian soldier of short stature accepted the challenge and killed him, whereupon the Gauls became panic-stricken and fled. Cluentius' line of battle was thus broken and the remainder of his troops did not stand their ground, but fled, in disorder to Nola. Sulla followed them and killed 3,000 in the pursuit, and as the inhabitants of Nola received them by only one gate, lest the enemy should rush in with them, he killed about 20,000 more outside the walls and among them Cluentius himself, who fell fighting bravely.[111]

Thus Sulla scored the first notable victory in the war against the Samnites and drove them from Campania. One point of interest concerns the identity of the Gallic reinforcements that Cluentius received, given that they would have had to march through Roman territory to reach Nola, had they come from Gaul. It is likely that they were formerly in the service of Rome and had defected along with a number of other Roman allies of the region.

Thus Sulla had turned around the disastrous campaign of the previous year, recovered and punished a number of rebel cities in the region and driven the Samnites back into Samnium. This was swiftly followed by an attack on the rebel Hirpini, who lay between Campania and Samnium. In what seems to have been a lightning campaign, Sulla subdued the Hirpini, primarily through shock-

and-awe tactics.[112] In particular, he made an example of one particular town that had refused to surrender: Aeculanum. Having set fire to their walls, the town surrendered but was sacked anyway, setting an example for any town in the region that did not surrender immediately. Appian records that such an example brought about the swift surrender of the whole Hirpini.[113]

Unnamed Battle

With the Hirpini subdued, Sulla then invaded Samnium proper, evading a waiting Samnite army commanded by the general Mutilus. Appian provides the only description of the battle:

> Then Sulla moved against the Samnites, not where Mutilus, the Samnite general, guarded the roads, but by another circuitous route where his coming was not expected. He fell upon them suddenly, killed many, and scattered the rest in disorderly flight. Mutilus was wounded and took refuge with a few followers in Aesernia. Sulla destroyed his camp and moved against Bovianum, where the common council of the rebels was held.[114]

Thus, Sulla ambushed the Samnite army and routed them. As is usual for this war, we have no record of the numbers involved. Again, keeping the momentum, Sulla attacked and captured the Samnite city of Bovianum in a siege of just three hours, according to Appian.[115] Following this campaign, Appian reports that he returned to Rome to stand for the consulship. On the back of such a victorious campaign against an old Roman foe, it is hardly surprising that he was elected consul for 88 BC.

Thus, in less than a year, Sulla had turned around the Samnite campaign, driving the Samnite alliance forces from Campania, subduing the Hirpini, invading Samnium itself and defeating the Samnites on their own territory. The key to this victorious campaign seems to have been decisive leadership and avoiding the rash mistakes that had plagued the consul of 90, who continued to fall into Samnite ambushes. Having learnt his soldiering under the tutelage of Marius, this campaign saw Sulla step out of his former mentor's shadow.

Only one other fragment to this year's campaign survives and that comes from Ovid who records the death of T. Didius (Cos. 98), who had earlier been successful at the siege of Herculaneum. Ovid records that he fell in battle of 11 June, the same day as Rutilius the year previously, though we have no other details. If northing else, it records the death of another ex-consul and one of Rome's leading generals of the period.[116]

Battle of Canusium

Whilst Appian's focus is on Sulla's campaigns, we can find scattered references to the other Roman commanders operating in central and southern Italy against the Samnite alliance. In Apulia, on Italy's eastern coast, we find reference to the Roman praetor C. Cosconius. Appian records him being equally successful in capturing a string of rebel towns, such as Salapia and most notably Cannae, scene of the infamous Roman defeat over a century before. However, pushing southwards, his string of victories came to a halt at the city of Canusium where he encountered a Samnite army. Appian only provides a brief description of the battle, but it is clear that Cosconius was forced to withdraw with heavy casualties on both sides:

> He received the surrender of Cannae and laid siege to Canusium; then he had a severe fight with the Samnites, who came to its relief. After great slaughter on both sides Cosconius was beaten and retreated to Cannae.[117]

Battle of Aufidius River
In a battle that must have been poignant, with echoes of its more famous predecessor, Cosconius chose to make his stand close to Cannae:

> A river [the Aufidius] separated the two armies, and Trebatius sent word to Cosconius either to come over to his side and fight him, or to withdraw and let him cross. Cosconius withdrew, and while Trebatius was crossing attacked him and got the better of him, and, while he was flying toward the stream, killed 15,000 of his men. The remainder took refuge with Trebatius in Canusium.[118]

The *Periochae* of Livy also records these engagements, adding the detail that a notable Samnite victim was the commander Marius Egnatius, who fell in battle, most probably here at Aufidius. A fragment of Diodorus also refers to the victories of Cosconius.[119] With the Samnite army in Apulia destroyed, Appian records that Cosconius soon overran the remaining rebel towns in Apulia (Larinum, Venusia and Ausculum) and quickly subdued the Pediculi peoples.[120] Despite these notable victories, Cosconius disappears from our records following this campaign.[121]

Further to the southwest, in Lucania, we have references to two campaigns. The first was fought by the Roman commander A. Gabinius, who was meeting with equal success in capturing rebel towns when he was killed during the siege of a rebel camp.[122] The Roman campaign against the Lucanians appears to have been brought to a successful conclusion by a commander named Carbo, who is credited with its success, though no other details survive.[123]

Thus the year saw Roman forces wage successful campaigns in Campania, Samnium, Apulia and Lucania, at the end of which only the Samnites and Lucanians appeared to still be fighting in the Samnite alliance. The changes in Rome's military fortunes in just a year seem drastic. This year we see a number of Roman commanders operating independently and being successful on the field of battle, notably Sulla and Cosconius. Again, when one fell, namely Gabinius, it seems that another was able to take his place. Furthermore, there were no military disasters, as seen under Caesar the previous year.

Whilst we lack all but the most cursory of details, it seems that the Italians were unable to lure the Roman commanders into ambushes as they had done the previous year and appear to have been weakened by the need to defend key rebel towns; again an echo of one of Hannibal's failings more than a century before. Thus we see a number of Italian armies being drawn into fighting Roman forces in order to defend key towns. The Romans, with a series of commanders who appear to have ranged from the competent to the brilliant, were able to slowly pick off the rebel regions one by one, whilst their own territory remained intact. Once again, we can see the powerful effect that the failure of the rebellion to spread had on the Italian Federation. Whilst Rome was again able to call up increasing levels of manpower to cover its losses, the rebels were faced with a diminishing pool of manpower and territory in which to operate.

10. The Consequences of the War

Thus, in both theatres of war, the tide had turned completely in Rome's favour, with the few remaining rebel peoples being surrounded and cut off from each other. Yet whilst Rome was militarily successful, a war on her own doorstep had come at a high cost, some of which was not immediately visible.

Manpower Losses

The ancient sources all paint a picture of heavy Roman and Italian casualties. Velleius provides a high estimate of 300,000 in total, though modern commentators consider this to be too high.[124] Brunt estimates that the total may have been 50,000, thus denying the Romans a huge manpower resource to support their empire.[125] As noted above, in Italy, the Romans were so stretched that freedmen were admitted into military service. Not only did these losses deplete Rome of valuable military manpower, but the seeming collapse of Roman power and its near defeat in Italy had again shaken the myth of Roman invincibility for the second time in just over a decade.[126] To any outsiders, Rome must have looked weak, and Orosius does record a massive Thracian invasion of Roman Macedonia this year (see Chapter 3).[127] Into this equation came the figure of Mithridates VI of Pontus (see Chapter 1), who again seemed to take advantage of the Romans' loss of focus on their empire, threatening their power in Asia Minor (see Chapter 3).

The Financial Crisis and Murder in Rome

It is clear from the few surviving sources that the Marsic and Samnite campaigns devastated both the economy of Italy and the financial system of the Republic in a number of different ways. The first and most obvious of which must have been the devastation caused by the fighting in Italy itself, with upward of 300,000 men under arms at the peak of the war.[128] The war raged across the various regions of Italy devastating communities and local economies.

Aside from the devastation, was the need for Rome to be able to pay for having upward to 150,000 men under arms in Italy alone. Here the sources do shed some light on the desperate financial plight the Republican government faced. Orosius records the sale of state assets in Rome itself in a desperate bid to raise cash:

> The treasury at that time was thoroughly depleted and funds for the payment of grain were lacking. The public properties within the circuit of the Capitol, the ancient possessions of the pontifices, augur, decemvirs, and flamines, were therefore sold under the pressure of necessity. This brought enough money to relieve the deficit for the time being.[129]

As well as the sale of state assets, it is clear from the numismatic evidence that the Roman state relied upon the standard response of all governments throughout the ages, the printing (or in this case the minting) of more money. From the evidence of coin finds it is clear that there was a massive increase in the production of money in the 90–89 BC period.[130] Such a massive and rapid minting process could only have had the effect of debasing the quality of the precious metals used in the coins, with a consequent inflationary effect.

If this weren't enough, it is clear that there was a collapse of the credit system in Rome, an ancient credit crunch, brought about by the war in Italy. This much is clear from an incident related by Appian, who reveals a crisis in Rome in 89 BC between creditors and lenders.[131] Barlow provides an analysis of the underlying causes of this credit crisis.[132] The Roman system of credit was based on the use of land as collateral for the loan. Given that large tracts of land were devastated and others simply no longer accessible to the owners, the whole credit system was undermined, leading to a recall of loans, many of which would have defaulted due to a shortage of liquid cash, in a time of crisis.

As is always the case, this credit crisis soon turned into a political one, with the Urban Praetor A. Sempronius Asellio taking measures to protect debtors from their creditors, by means of resurrecting an ancient law that prohibited the charging of interest on loans.[133] Such an archaic law would naturally undermine the whole credit system further and ensured that all loans were thus referred to courts for judgment, preventing foreclosure. Whilst these actions may have provided temporary relief for Rome's debtors, it clearly exacerbated the credit crisis that the system faced.

This situation became worse still when the praetor Asellio was murdered at the hands of a lynch mob of money lenders in broad daylight on the streets of Rome. Asellio was attacked whilst attending to sacrificial duties at the Temple of Concord (ironically enough), and murdered. Appian and the *Periochae* of Livy place his death in the Forum, whilst Valerius Maximus states that he fled the Forum but was dragged from a shop he was hiding in and butchered.[134]

Aside from the disastrous consequences for Asellio himself, such an act was an ominous stage in the development of Roman political violence. The murder of Asellio is often overlooked or downplayed compared to the deaths that both preceded and succeeded it. Yet this was a whole new stage of political violence. The Gracchi and Saturninus and their followers had been murdered/executed by or on behalf of the state, in order (or so it was claimed) to save the state from sedition. The murder of Drusus was a political assassination, but had taken place at night and was the work of personal enemies. In this case, the urban praetor had been torn apart by an angry mob, probably in the Forum, in broad daylight whilst conducting a public sacrifice. Not only did no one come to his aid but the crime went unpunished as neither the offer of a reward nor immunity could induce any witnesses to come forward. This was the casual murder of a city official by political opponents who opposed his policies and wanted him removed. It was to be an ominous precedent.

It is clear that the credit crisis was not alleviated, perhaps beyond a temporary lull in proceedings (we hear no more of the Asellian measures themselves). By the next year, the issue was addressed by the consuls (L. Cornelius Sulla and Q. Pompeius Rufus) who seem to have either passed a fresh law or again resurrected an old one limiting the amount of interest that could be charged on loans and providing a partial cancellation of debts (probably a ten per cent reduction).[135]

Thus we can see that Rome faced a perilous financial situation due to the cost, both physical and financial, of fighting the war itself, but also the effects it had on undermining the Roman financial system, leading to a collapse of credit, which in turn led to political murder. This financial crisis was only worsened by the events that followed, notably the loss of Asia and its tax revenues.

The New Italian Question

Key to the Roman victory had been the offer of citizenship to those Italian peoples who had not yet rebelled, or possibly those who had lain down their arms. Whilst this was a crucial factor in the overall success in defusing the rebellion, it left Rome with the important and potentially dangerous task of fulfilling this promise and admitting these people into the citizenship. This would require the Senate to balance its own interests in ensuring the continued dominance of the senatorial aristocracy against the expectations of the new citizens and the fears of the existing citizens, who had always objected to any attempt to dilute their influence in the assemblies (such as it was). Such a potent mix, coming on the back of armed rebellion was always going to be a potentially explosive situation. As argued earlier, it seems more than likely that the initial legislation passed in 89 BC to offer the Italians citizenship did not contain specific provisions for the mechanics of how to do this, and this may account for the failure of the censors of 89 BC (P. Licinius Crassus and L. Iulius Caesar) to conduct a census.[136]

Victorious Commanders

Whilst this war had seen a range of incompetent Roman commanders, most notably the consuls Rutilius and Caesar, it had seen several key military leaders emerge. One in particular was Cn. Pompeius Strabo, who was elected consul for 89 BC on this record of earlier victories and repaid it with the capture of Asculum. Following a similar route was L. Cornelius Sulla, who was elected consul for 88, thanks to his victories against the Samnites the year before. Between them, the commanders had delivered a string of victories in Rome's wars against the Marsic and Samnite alliances, and both would have been hoping that this would lead to more 'honourable' and profitable campaigns overseas.

In addition to this pair was the ever-present figure of C. Marius, six-time consul and one-time saviour of Rome, who, despite being in his late sixties, had salvaged the Marsic campaign of 90 BC, thus showing that his military acumen remained as sharp as ever. His apparent subsequent fall from grace would not have aided his sense of injustice towards certain factions of the Senate, and it is likely that he would not have ruled out a last opportunity for military glory.[137]

Ill-disciplined Armies

Mention of Marius leads back to the death of the consul Cato, apparently murdered by a disloyal army of Marian veterans, led by Marius' own son, who seemingly had no compunction about murdering a commander to whom they objected. Such an act would have been unthinkable prior to this war, yet was mirrored by an element of Sulla's own army, who murdered the former consul Postumius Albinus. Both situations highlighted the increased ill-discipline of the Roman armies, probably caused by the rushed mobilization and limited time for training.

Furthermore, men such as Marius and perhaps Pompeius as well, seemingly raised armies, or significant contingents, from their adherents. The sources imply that Marius' army contained a number of his veterans, who objected to 'their' commander being replaced. Similarly, Pompeius' army seems to have contained a number of men from the Picentine region, where he had estates and notable family connections. Thus both armies seemed to contain a number of men who had a close personal link to the commander. The Cato incident in particular bore portents of what was to come, with an army attaching more loyalty to its commander than the state. The deaths of Cato and Albinus seem to have been a terrible precursor of the civil wars that followed.

Nevertheless, the year 89 BC had seen Rome reverse the disastrous losses of the previous year and stand on the cusp of victory in the opening conflicts of the civil war. However, the effects of the factors detailed above combined to create a situation that was just as dangerous to Rome as the one she had just overcome, and once again her survival was to be threatened.

From Crisis to Collapse

Chapter 3

Coups and Counter-coups in Rome (88 BC)

1. The Marsic and Samnite Campaigns

The reduced nature of the threat posed by the remaining Italian rebels can be seen in the fact that, of the two consuls of 88 BC (L. Cornelius Sulla and Q. Pompeius Rufus), one received an overseas command and one remained in Rome. Sulla received command in Asia against the threat of Mithridates VI (see below), which was a far more 'honourable' and financially rewarding campaign. Pompeius Rufus, however, appears to have remained in Rome, at some point being assigned command of Pompeius Strabo's army in central Italy. Strabo himself seems to have continued in command, mopping up the remaining members of the Marsic alliance, as proconsul, whilst Q. Caecilius Metellus Pius (son of the Metellus who was Marius' rival), took up a command in Apulia, replacing C. Cosconius.

The final stage of the Marsic campaign was fought either late in 89 BC or early in 88 BC (the sources are not clear), and we have conflicting accounts in Diodorus and Appian as to where the final battle took place and how the war ended. Appian has a brief sentence on the final Marsic campaign, with Metellus defeating the Marsic general Poppaedius Silo in battle and thus ending the war (before swiftly moving on to narrate events in Rome):

> Caecilius Metellus, his [Cosconius'] successor in the praetorship, attacked the Apulians and overcame them in battle. Poppaedius, one of the rebel generals, here lost his life. The survivors joined Metellus separately.[1]

However, a lengthy fragment of Diodorus paints a completely different picture, and throws into sharp focus the dangers of relying too heavily on brief accounts such as Appian's. According to Diodorus' account, the remaining Italian rebels consolidated their remaining forces under the leadership of Poppaedius Silo, the figurehead of the rebellion, which numbered 30,000 strong. They withdrew from Corfinum, the capital of the Italian Federation, and instead choose Aesernia as their new capital, a site in Samnium that had seen much fighting in 90 BC. Poppaedius seems to have supplemented this force by encouraging a large-scale slave insurrection in the region, which allowed him to amass an additional slave army of 20,000 men and 1,000 horse.[2]

With this newly enlarged army, it seems that Poppaedius went onto the offensive and recaptured the Samnite city of Bovianum, entering it in a triumphal procession.[3] Thus Poppaedius appears to have staged a last-gasp campaign that initially met with some success, partially overturning the victories of Sulla in the region the previous year. Faced with this renewed Italian counter-attack, a Roman army, led by a legate named Mam. Aemilianus, was dispatched to the city. The identity of this Roman commander is far from clear, although he is most commonly associated with Mam. Aemilius Lepidus (Cos. 77).[4] The two forces met in battle, with Obsequens placing it shortly after Poppaedius captured Bovianum.[5]

Unnamed Battle

Despite a lengthy build up, we only have a single sentence on Diodorus on the battle itself:

> Meeting in battle a Roman force under Mamercus, he [Poppaedius] slew a few Romans, but lost over 6,000 of his own men.[6]

He also mentions Metellus fighting in Apulia, besieging the city of Venusia:

> At about the same time Metellus took by siege Venusia in Apulia, an important city with many soldiers, and took more than 3,000 captives.[7]

Both the *Periochae* of Livy and the *de viris illustribus* also comment on this campaign:[8]

> After the Italians had been defeated again by deputy Aemilius Mamercus, the leader of the Marsi and ringleader of the affair, Poppaedius Silo, fell in battle.[9]
> As praetor in the Social War, he killed Q. Poppaedius, the leader of the Marsi.[10]

Thus Diodorus has the Marsic campaign ending with the defeat of Poppaedius in Samnium, in a location that must have been near Bovianum, whilst Appian has Poppaedius being defeated and killed in Apulia, most likely at the siege of Venusia. Livy mentions only Lepidus, whilst the *de viris illustribus* is a much later source and follows Appian. Given the wealth of detail in the Diodorus fragment and the brevity of Appian's note, and the fact that Diodorus states that the battles fought by Lepidus and Metellus were fought at the same time, it is more than likely that Poppaedius died in battle in Samnium in the battle that defeated the last major Italian army, and that Lepidus ended the Marsic campaign, not Metellus, with Appian mixing the two up.[11]

The defeat and death of Poppaedius and the victories in Apulia ended the Marsic campaign. However, remnants of the Samnite alliance continued their fighting throughout the year, with Samnite and Sabellian forces holding out at Nola in Campania. To the south the Lucanians also continued to fight on. However, these were just remnants of the Italian Federation, which just two years earlier had inflicted a series of defeats upon Rome that threatened her very existence. Diodorus even records an appeal from the remaining Italian rebels to Mithridates VI of Pontus to invade Italy, but even if such an appeal was made, at this stage it was nothing more than a flight of fancy.[12] At the time though, the outlook for the few remaining Italian forces seemed bleak.

2. The Thracian Wars

Rome's northern borders in Greece were notoriously difficult to defend and subject to frequent tribal incursions from mainland Europe. Little over a decade earlier, Greece and Macedonia had been invaded and devastated by the Scordisci.[13] The tribes of central Europe had little regard for Roman borders at the best of times. However, the consequences of the wars in Italy were felt throughout Rome's empire, with the implosion of the Roman system, which if not signalling the end of Roman military might, at least highlighted its weakening. Taken in conjunction with the massive tribal incursions of the Cimbri and Teutones into Roman territory, including Italy itself, just a decade earlier, the might of Rome and her ability to counter any attack must have been in question. Certainly, Rome in the period 89–88 BC suffered two major invasions of its territory, which may have been cases of co-incidental timing, but may equally have been facilitated (if not caused) by apparent Roman military distraction or weakness. The full scale of the war will be discussed later (Chapter 5), but Orosius provides some detail on the early stages:

> King Sothimus, accompanied by a large force of Thracian auxiliaries, invaded Greece and ravaged all the territory of Macedonia. The praetor C. Sentius finally defeated him and forced him to return to his own kingdom.[14]

The *Periochae* of Livy records the raids and plundering of the Thracians across several years, though we have no detailed chronology for the campaigns.[15] Dio raises the prospect that these Thracians were allied to Mithridates and following his orders in attacking Macedonia.[16] Though the sources are eager to place Mithridates' hand behind many events of the period, tribal incursions of Roman territory were a common feature of the period and a result of an ill-defined border and a laissez-faire Roman attitude to defending the European border of her territories. We have no details of Sentius' campaign against the Thracians, only that it was ultimately successful and that we still find him in Macedonia in 87 BC (see Chapter 4), indicating these tribal incursions continued for the next few years.

3. The First Mithridatic War

In the preceding decade Mithridates VI, the King of Pontus, had been slowly building up his powerbase in the Black Sea region. From his kingdom in Asia Minor he had annexed the Crimea, secured a marriage alliance with King Tigranes of Armenia and had friendly relations with a host of native tribes of mainland Europe and a range of the Hellenistic states in the east, including the Parthian Empire.[17] Such an expansionist policy was always going to make the Romans wary, given that their province of Asia (see Map 1) was a source of vast tax wealth to them. Whilst it would be going too far to speak of the Romans having a strategy for Asia Minor as a whole, their preference was for weak client kingdoms. Whilst Mithridates did not fit well in this mould, we would do well not to overstate his importance at the time. He remained a king of a middle sized Hellenistic kingdom in Asia Minor, but was sandwiched between the two great empires of the age: Rome to the west and Parthia to the east. His friendly relations with the other powers of the region were just that, and would not translate into active support if he took belligerent action against Rome, no matter how much they may have secretly wished for the collapse of Roman power.

Given the weakened state of the other kingdoms of Asia Minor, all with weak kings beholden to Rome, and given his avowed expansionist policies, some move against them was almost inevitable. The key to any policy, under normal circumstances, would have been to placate Rome, which, whilst protective of its province, only ever had limited interest in the events of Asia Minor.

During the 90s, Mithridates VI had, on two occasions, attempted to annex the neighbouring kingdom of Cappodocia, first by allying with Nicomedes III of Bithynia (who subsequently double crossed him), and then with Tigranes of Armenia. On each occasion puppet kings were installed on the Cappodocian throne, and on each occasion Rome intervened to restore a 'free' Cappodocia, the latter of which came at the hands of L. Cornelius Sulla himself.[18]

Whilst Rome's attention to the internal politics of Asia Minor was patchy at best, the outbreak of the Italian War and Rome's battle for her very survival naturally put other matters from her attention. Judging that the time was right to act, and that if Rome recovered it would be faced with a fait accompli, Mithridates, acting in concert with Tigranes, placed puppet rulers on the thrones of both Cappodocia and Bithynia. However, once again, Mithridates had underestimated the Senate, which in 89 BC sent a commission headed by M. Aquilius (Cos. 101), to restore the previous (pro-Roman) rulers. Once again, Mithridates and Tigranes backed down. However, perhaps to teach Mithridates a lesson, or in search of much needed monies for the war in Italy, the commissioners encouraged the newly restored puppet king of Cappodocia to launch raids on Mithridates' Pontic territories. When his protestations were rebuffed by the Roman commissioners, Mithridates, judging the local and overall Roman position to be weak, launched an invasion of Cappodocia, which was swiftly annexed.

The reaction from the Romans in Asia was swift, despite the fact that they had only one legion in the whole of Asia Minor. Aided by native contingents from the other client kingdoms, the Romans formed two armies, one headed by Aquilius and one by C. Cassius (the governor of Asia), and invaded Bithynia to counter Mithridates' advance, beginning the First Mithridatic War. Whilst the full scope of the war falls outside the remit of this present work, the consequences of the initial stages of the war were immense for Rome. The armies of both Cassius and Aquilius were crushed, with Aquilius being captured and executed. Mithridates adopted a blitzkrieg tactic and followed up with rapid invasions of the Roman province of Asia, accompanied by a massacre of all Romans and Italians in the province, which some sources say resulted in the murders of between 80,000 to 150,000 civilians.[19]

Mithridates then amazingly followed this with an invasion of mainland Greece itself, in many cases heartily welcomed as a liberator, including in Athens itself. Within a year, what had started as a squabble over a kingdom in Asia Minor between the regional Hellenistic kingdoms had resulted in a full-scale invasion of Roman territory and the annexation of her eastern empire. Aside from the startling loss of life and prestige, perhaps the greatest blow came to Rome in the form of lost revenue from her wealthiest province, exactly at a time of greatest financial need.

Nevertheless, once the shock of these invasions had been overcome, Rome found herself in a strong position. The close of 89 BC saw the Marsic and Samnite campaigns drawing to a successful conclusion, and Rome had huge numbers of battle-ready soldiers and battle-tested generals to fight off this invasion, all of whom would be eyeing the chance of a glorious and profitable eastern campaign against a new foe. The only issue was which of Rome's successful commanders would lead the campaign?

4. The Powderkeg – The Mithridatic and Italian Questions

In prime position for this command were the consuls, L. Cornelius Sulla and Q. Pompeius Rufus, and of the two, the one with the clear military pedigree was Sulla. As discussed earlier, the Samnite War had allowed him to emerge from his mentor's shadow and be hailed as a commander in his own right. He then strengthened his domestic political position by an alliance with Q. Pompeius Rufus and tied himself to the Metellan faction by marrying Metella, the daughter of L. Caecilius Metellus Dalmaticus (Cos. 119) and the recent widow of M. Aemilius Scaurus (Cos. 115). However, Plutarch (quoting Livy) records that the marriage was the subject of ridicule, given Sulla's low standing at the time, and having only just hastily divorced his third wife days prior to this marriage.[20]

Whilst Sulla is well known to us at this point, by contrast, we know little of Pompeius Rufus, which again tilts the narrative of events in Sulla's favour. Crucially, we do not know whether Sulla and Pompeius became allies only in the consulate or ran as a joint ticket. Certainly, we know that by the time of the events of 88 BC, Pompeius' son had married Sulla's daughter. Interestingly, what we do know of Pompeius marks him as more heavily involved in the intrigues of domestic politics in Rome than Sulla had been. Whereas Sulla is absent from the surviving narrative of the key events of the previous decade, notably centred on the tribunates of Saturninus and Livius Drusus, Pompeius' presence can be detected. In 99 BC he was one of the tribunes who jointly proposed the recall of Marius' opponent, Q. Caecilius Metellus 'Numidicus', from exile, a move that was blocked by pro-Marian tribunes.[21] In 91 BC we find him as urban praetor during the tribunate of Livius Drusus, though the sources are silent as to his role in or following Drusus' murder. Cicero goes further and names him as being a close friend of P. Sulpicius, who was part of the circle of Livius Drusus.[22] His praetorship was marked by the barring of a Q. Fabius Maximus from inheriting his father's estate due to a dissolute lifestyle, thus establishing his credentials as a supporter of traditional values.[23] During the Marsic and Samnite campaigns there is no surviving trace of any military activity on the part of Pompeius, but that does not rule out a position as a legate with one of the major commanders.

Therefore, of the two consuls, it is Pompeius who appears to be far more attuned to domestic politics, being involved on the fringes of the Saturnine and Drusan crises and marking himself out as an upholder of Roman traditions during his praetorship. Furthermore, as far as we can tell, he had no major military experience, yet was elected consul for 88 BC alongside Sulla, who had clearly benefited from his recent military record. If anything, the partnership, of a more military minded patrician and a more politically attuned plebeian seems to suggest a pre-planned partnership, borne out by Sulla gaining the overseas command and Pompeius remaining in Italy (although technically decided by lot). Certainly, we must move away from viewing Pompeius as a silent partner for Sulla in the consulship. If nothing else, it seems that the consuls of 88 BC represent a far more rounded partnership than is often portrayed.

Unsurprisingly, we find that of the two consuls the command against Mithridates fell to Sulla.[24] This represented the pinnacle of his career: a command against an eastern foe who had invaded Roman territory.

Yet, Roman domestic politics were occupied with a far more pressing issue than the Mithridatic command, namely the integration of the Italian and Latin communities into the Roman citizenship system. As detailed earlier, although offers of citizenship had been made to those Italian peoples who had not rebelled, it is unlikely that there was little detailed planning as to the mechanics of the integration process. Previously, when Rome had integrated new peoples to the citizenship, fresh voting tribes had been created, but no new tribes had been added since 242 BC, leaving the total at thirty-five voting tribes in the tribal assembly. Given the haphazard and piecemeal nature of their creation, these tribes had different numbers of peoples within each, and the existing citizenry were not evenly distributed amongst them. Furthermore, as elections were determined by a simple majority of the tribes, and they voted in order of precedence (creation), once eighteen tribes had voted the same way then the contest was over, regardless of whether the later tribes (those in the twenties and thirties) voted at all.

Thus, if new tribes were added to the thirty-five, their voting power would be severely restricted. The only other alternative was that the new citizens be evenly distributed amongst the existing thirty-five tribes. However, whichever of the two methods was chosen, there was a clear danger of angering a section of the citizenry. If new tribes were created, then the new citizens, especially the elites with the time to participate, would have had their voting power constrained and may have felt themselves designated as second-class once more, an act of perfidy on the part of the Roman oligarchy. However, if even distribution were to take place, the existing citizens, especially the urban ones, may have seen it as a diminution of their voting rights and power. Thus, whichever method was chosen there was a clear danger that sections of either the new or the old citizenry would be angered, with risk of further civil strife.

The exact chronology of the proposals made is now lost to us, but it seems that the Senate opted to restrict the new citizens to newly created tribes and we have several references to new voting tribes being established.[25] Velleius refers to the Italians being restricted to eight tribes, though he does not specify if these were new or not. Appian refers to ten new tribes being created, whilst a fragment of Sisenna refers to a *Lex Calpurnia*, which created two new tribes, around this period.[26] Thus it appears that those Italian communities who had chosen to become Roman citizens found themselves restricted to what seems to have been eight or ten new tribes, and thus had their voting power neutered. In terms of Roman domestic politics there was clear capital to be made from such dissent.

5. The Spark – Sulpicius, Marius and the Mithridatic and Italian Questions.

It was during the tribunate of a certain P. Sulpicius that these two major issues (of Mithridates and the Italians) became entangled, leading to bloodshed on the streets of Rome and ultimately military intervention. Cicero, who was a young man during this period, portrays Sulpicius as one of the finest orators of his age, a former ally of M. Livius Drusus and a close friend of the consul Q. Pompeius Rufus.[27] His early actions seemed to confirm this political affiliation when he proposed a law recalling the Varian political exiles back to Rome, many of whom were his friends and allies.[28]

Another incident of interest came when he and a colleague (P. Antistius) prevented C. Iulius Caesar Strabo from standing as consul (for either 88 or 87 BC), due to his lack of prior office, having only held the aedileship and not the praetorship. The details of this incident are far from clear, but such a clear proposed breach of the *cursus honorum* showed the interest that the Mithridatic command had generated and the lengths some aspiring aristocrats would go to.[29]

Despite the apparent obscurity of the issue, Asconius labels Sulpicius' clash with Caesar as one of the causes of the civil war, on account of the fact that both men started their dispute with legal means but soon moved on to violence, though we have no clear details.[30] In any event, Caesar was prevented from standing and fell the next year during the capture of Rome.

Sulpicius then moved on to proposing a series of laws. We do not have a clear picture of the chronology for all of the proposed laws, scattered as they are across a range of surviving sources, nor do we know whether they represent his sole thinking or the cumulative work of his affiliated faction. What is clear is that he proposed two laws, both involving key issues raised by the Marsic and Samnite campaigns. The lesser of the two was a law limiting senatorial debt to 2,000 *denarii*, which would not have gone down well with the senators. Whether this was a measure to gain popular acclaim in a credit crisis, or an attempt to reduce monies being spent in the pursuit of political office, we will never know.

The second was far more radical and far more in the mould of Livius Drusus, as Sulpicius proposed a measure to tackle the new 'Italian Problem' concerning the distribution of new citizens. This law proposed that all newly enfranchised citizens, and freedmen (who were now liable to military service, see Chapter 2), be distributed throughout all the pre-existing thirty-five tribes, thus giving them a theoretical majority in the Roman voting system.[31] Such a proposal disadvantaged the existing and long-established Roman citizens, at least in their own eyes, especially those in Rome itself, and it is not hard to see how antagonism between the two groups could soon flare up. This is especially the case given that it could also affect the existing patronage system that allowed the Roman nobles to win favour with the electorate. This is not to say that the nobles would not have adapted to the new situation and extended their circles of patronage, especially given their existing connections throughout Italy. Nonetheless, the proposal seems to have created resentment and tension amongst the existing Roman urban citizenry, who, rightly or wrongly, believed that they would lose out under the new system. Thus a fresh dimension was added to Roman politics: conflict between new and existing citizens.

Naturally enough, tensions rose as the vote on the law drew closer, with the inevitable clashes between groups, probably with fists at first and then sticks and stones. To date there was nothing unusual about this situation, especially given the background tensions. Yet the issues involved the very nature of the Roman voting system, and the last great unanswered question raised by the Italian rebellion seems to have raised the stakes. To reduce tension, the consuls suspended public business, postponing the key vote. Yet, the supporters of the proposed law, including all the new citizens could easily see this as something more sinister: another attempt to prevent them receiving full citizen rights. It is reported that Sulpicius took with him an armed mob (which in Plutarch's biography of Sulla, became a 3,000-strong body and went under the name of the 'Anti-Senate') and confronted the consuls to force them to rescind their suspension.[32] The confrontation soon turned violent with Q. Pompeius, the son of the consul (and son-in-law of Sulla), being murdered. The irony being that prior to them both winning office this year Pompeius and Sulpicius had been close friends. The consuls then fled for their lives, with Pompeius Rufus going into hiding, most probably in the city. Sulla interestingly ended up seeking refuge at the house of his old mentor; C. Marius.[33]

This is a highly interesting event and one that is only mentioned in Plutarch's biography of Sulla (which interestingly drew heavily on Sulla's own autobiography). For some commentators, this was due to Sulla being driven there by a mob under Marius' orders, while others suggest that Sulla sought out Marius as the shadowy mastermind behind Sulpicius, yet in most surviving narratives Marius is absent from these events until this point. Among the key questions to be asked are why Sulla went to Marius and what they discussed? Did Sulla go there to deal with the mastermind behind the events, as many would have us believe, or did he go to seek safety with his old mentor, the most prominent Italian-Roman citizen of the day, and seeking advice on defusing the situation? One thing is clear: he did defuse the situation, perhaps with Marius' help. The crowds were clearly quelled, and Sulla, with Pompeius Rufus still apparently in hiding, returned to the Forum and rescinded the suspension, allowing Sulpicius to call an assembly and vote on his proposal. Sulla then retired from Rome and joined his army of six legions at Nola, which was still continuing the siege (see above), prior to embarking for Greece.

6. The Marian-Sulpician 'Coup'

At this point, Sulpicius made two key decisions. With complete control of the assembly, he proposed two fresh laws: one deposing Pompeius Rufus of his consulship, the other transferring command of the Mithridatic campaign from Sulla to Marius. The deposition of Pompeius is a highly interesting one, as Sulla's consulship was left untouched. As noted above, of the two consuls, it was Pompeius who seemed to have the greater powerbase in domestic politics and it seems that he led the opposition to Sulpicius rather than Sulla, who, after meeting Marius, seemed in haste to abandon Rome to take up his provincial command and presumably leave Marius, Sulpicius and Pompeius to fight it out. Presumably his former mentor advised him to leave Rome and domestic politics behind and concentrate on the forthcoming campaign. Once again, this forces us to question just how much enmity there was between Marius and Sulla at this point.

However, with Sulla out of the way, Marius and Sulpicius appeared to pass radical measures, which when examined from one perspective could look like an attempted coup, albeit temporarily. With these two pieces of legislation, the only remaining consul in Rome would be deposed, whilst command of Rome's largest army, currently stationed in Italy, would be transferred to Marius himself.

An interesting question is whether, following the deposition of Pompeius, a suffect consul would have been elected? Whilst none of our surviving sources comment on this, it is interesting to speculate as to whether Marius had his own name in mind, chasing his prophesised seventh consulship, but this remains speculation only.[34] The act of a tribune deposing a consul was unheard of, although opposing the will of the people had been used as an argument in 133 BC for a tribune deposing another tribune.[35] As the will of the people via the assembly was sovereign, such a vote was technically legal, but was a major step in the use, or abuse, of tribunician power.[36]

That Marius coveted the Mithridatic command is hardly surprising. He was approaching his seventieth year and would have wanted one final glorious campaign to end his career on, especially following his decade of inactivity, albeit punctuated by an impressive cameo in the Marsic campaign in 90 BC. Furthermore, he seems to have been working towards a Mithridatic command since the late 90s (see Chapter 1). Whatever Marius and Sulla discussed in his home, it is inconceivable that it was these two pieces of legislation. At the very least it seems that Marius guaranteed Sulla his command, and Sulla seems not to have been unduly bothered about abandoning Pompeius to face Sulpicius and Marius alone.

However, once at Nola, Sulla found himself thoroughly betrayed by his old mentor and comprehensively outmanoeuvred. His colleague had been deposed and he had lost his command to Marius himself. His crowning achievement had ended in ignominy and all he could look forward to was a command finishing the Samnite War. The situation Pompeius faced was worse; his son had been murdered, his colleague had abandoned him and his consulship had been taken from him, all orchestrated by someone who had been a friend.

7. The Consular 'Counter-coup'

Whilst it is clear that Sulla and Pompeius grossly underestimated the ambition of Marius and Sulpicius and the lengths that they would go to, the same could be said in reverse. Faced with total humiliation and ruin, the consuls, denied a political solution through Sulpicius' control of the streets and the assembly, had violence as their only option and one that had precedents. In 133, 121 and 100 BC, tumultuous political situations had been ended through state-sponsored violence, whether legally sanctioned beforehand or not. However, on this occasion, it seems that Marius and Sulpicius had complete control of the city of Rome, though what the Senate made of this we are not told. Of the two consuls, Pompeius appears to have been in hiding in Rome and rendered powerless. Sulla, however, was at Nola with his six legions.

Facing personal ruin and stung by the betrayal of his old mentor, Sulla made one of the most momentous decisions in Roman history: to use his army to restore order in Rome, by marching a Roman army against Rome itself. We must presume that in his own mind the restoration of order was one of his highest duties as a consul, and that as those previous seditions had been crushed by force, he was acting in the interests of the state, and that the ends would justify the means. Whilst we no longer have Sulla's autobiography, we do know that later sources made use of it. Plutarch has Sulla's army spontaneously supporting him, whilst Appian refers to Sulla calling his army together and setting out the situation in Rome.[37]

Appian also makes the point that key in the minds of Sulla's army was the fact that Marius would more than likely have taken his own army (the one that had possibly murdered the consul Caesar in 89 BC) to Asia to fight Mithridates, leaving Sulla's men in Italy. Faced with the loss of what promised to be a highly lucrative war, with probably a generous amount of booty for all, Sulla's army backed its commander. Aside from greed and personal loyalty, Morstein-Marx has recently advanced an important argument, that the army was still a citizen one and that Sulla was still the duly elected representative of the Senate and People of Rome, and thus had legitimacy.[38]

It was undeniable that the city of Rome was in turmoil and that rioting and deaths had occurred. Thus we must not rule out the argument that the soldiers did believe they were following a legitimate order. Naturally, as Morstein-Marx himself points out, the counter-argument to this is that all of Sulla's senior officers bar one quaestor (usually identified as L. Licinius Lucullus[39]) refused to follow his orders, but this does not mean that the men, given to unquestioning obedience of a consul's orders, simply refused to think about the wider issues and did as ordered in the belief that it was right. Interestingly, we can see this in the Marsic and Samnite campaigns, where neighbours, friends and kinsmen fought each other as ordered.

Thus, when Marius' military tribunes arrived at Nola to take charge of the army, they were murdered on the spot – another example of a Roman army murdering Roman officers. Of the military tribunes, only M. Gratidius is named.[40] As mentioned above, all of Sulla's officers (bar possibly L. Licinius Lucullus) refused to join in his march on Rome and fled to the city. Again Morstein-Marx has argued that this meant senior officers, those of senatorial backgrounds, rather than the junior officers and centurions, allowing Sulla to maintain a disciplined army with a coherent command structure.[41] The arrival of Sulla's senior officers with news of the march naturally sparked alarm, not only in Marius and Sulpicius, but also the in Senate, which immediately dispatched praetors (M. Iunius Brutus and a Servilius) to stop Sulla from bringing the army to Rome.[42] Plutarch refers to friends of Sulla being murdered in Rome by supporters of Marius and Sulpicius, which if true added more bloodshed to the situation.[43]

When the praetors met Sulla, they were attacked by the army and fled back to the city. In Appian, when asked why he was marching his army against Rome, Sulla is purported to have replied 'to deliver her from tyrants'.[44] A second and a third embassy from the Senate met with similar responses. Sulla, meanwhile, had been joined by Pompeius Rufus, thus putting both elected consuls at the head of their army and lending the exercise even more legitimacy, as the consuls were now acting in unison rather than Sulla on his own. When they reached Pictae, a few miles to the south of Rome, they were met by a final embassy from the Senate, which according to Plutarch had voted that Sulla be restored to the Mithridatic command and presumably Pompeius to his consulship.[45] However, given that senatorial votes were nought but a professed opinion, no matter how much *auctoritas* it carried, it could not be passed into law without a vote of the people, and thus was little more than a gesture. With no corresponding movement from Marius and Sulpicius, the consuls ordered the attack on the city.

8. The Battle for Rome 88 BC

Unprepared for an actual attack on the city, the lightly defended walls and gates of Rome fell easily to a Sullan-Pompeian surprise attack. Both Plutarch and Appian provide short but detailed accounts of the assault (see Map 4):

> Sulla took possession of the Esquiline Gate and of the adjoining wall with one legion of soldiers, and Pompeius occupied the Colline Gate with another. A third advanced to the Sublician Bridge, and a fourth remained on guard in front of the walls. With the remainder Sulla entered the city, being in appearance and in fact an enemy. The inhabitants round about tried to fight him off by hurling missiles from the roofs until he threatened to burn the houses; then they desisted.[46]

Plutarch has a similar attack in his narrative, but has Sullan legates leading the assault:

> But no sooner were they gone than he sent forward Lucius [Minucius] Basillus and Caius Mummius, who seized for him the city-gate and the walls on the Esquiline Hill; then he himself followed hard after them with all speed. Basillus and his men burst into the city and were forcing their way along, when the unarmed multitude pelted them with stones and tiles from the roofs of the houses, stopped their further progress, and crowded them back to the wall. But by this time Sulla was at hand, and seeing what was going on, shouted orders to set fire to the houses, and seizing a blazing torch, led the way himself, and ordered his archers to use their fire-bolts and shoot them up at the roofs.[47]

Battle of the Esquiline

Resistance to the attack was led by Marius and Sulpicius, who rallied what forces they had, which must have been from the armed retinue that Sulpicius had assembled along with any hastily armed supporters they could find.[48] The two

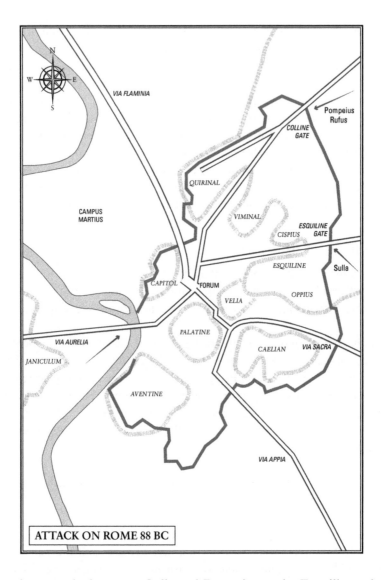

ATTACK ON ROME 88 BC

leaders then marched to meet Sulla and Pompeius at the Esquiline, where the first battle in Rome using military forces took place. Appian preserves an account of the battle:

> Sulla's forces were beginning to waver when Sulla seized a standard and exposed himself to danger in the foremost ranks. Out of regard for their general and fear of ignominy if they should abandon their standard, they rallied at once. Sulla ordered up fresh troops from his camp and sent others around by the so-called Suburran road to take the enemy in the rear. The Marians fought feebly against these new-comers, and as they feared lest they should be surrounded they called to their aid the other citizens who were still fighting from the houses, and

proclaimed freedom to slaves who would share their labours. As nobody came forward they fell into utter despair and fled at once out of the city, together with those of the nobility who had co-operated with them.'[49]

It is interesting to see that Sulla's soldiers, who must have outnumbered and outclassed the armed gangs they faced nearly broke, if we are to believe Appian's account. On the one hand, this may betray some lingering unease about fighting in Rome itself, whilst on the other, it may be that the heavily armed Roman soldiers were not as suited to fighting in street warfare. In the end though, it is clear that the more disciplined Roman soldiers won the day. With their forces scattered, it seems that Sulpicius and Marius fled, Marius to the Temple of Tellus on the Esquiline, where he issued a call for a slave insurrection in Rome itself. Unsurprisingly, given the presence of several Roman legions on the streets, this call fell on deaf ears. Sulpicius seems to have hidden within the city, whilst Marius fled from Rome.

Following their victory at the Esquiline, the consuls then marched up the Via Sacra to the Capitol, which they occupied.[50] Florus notes the irony of the Capitol, which held out against the Gauls, during the fourth century Gallic Sack, falling to an invading force.[51] In one short day, the battle for Rome was over and the consuls were once again in charge of the city, this time militarily.

9. An Uneasy Peace

Upon gaining, or should that be regaining, control of Rome, the consuls then set about solidifying their control and fully legitimizing their actions. Once again, we suffer from a lack of a good narrative source at this point. The *Periochae* of Livy is limited to a summary of the consuls' actions as 'establishing order or reordering the state' and sending out colonies.[52]

The most noted of the consuls' actions (again we must not forget that the consuls were working in concert, despite our sources' focus on Sulla) was the declaration of Marius and Sulpicius as *hostes*, or enemies of the people, to be executed upon sight. How exactly this declaration was made is unclear, but Florus, Plutarch and Valerius Maximus all favour a senatorial decree as the instrument.[53] Given the popularity of Marius and Sulpicius with the people, and the not-so-small matter of the consuls marching their army into Rome itself, the idea of a senatorial decree (possibly even the *senatus consultum ultimum*) is the more attractive.[54]

This is not to say that the Senate would have condoned the methods used by Sulla and Pompeius Rufus, and indeed Valerius Maximus preserves a story of the consuls surrounding the Senate house with soldiers to get the decree passed, with only Q. Mucius Scaevola opposing the measure, the adherents of Marius having most likely and sensibly departed Rome.[55] In any event, Marius, Sulpicius and around ten others were declared enemies of the people, though most had had time to flee Rome.[56] Once again, exile (this time with a death sentence) had been passed upon members of the Roman elite.

Marius famously was captured at Miturnae, though he escaped and made his way to his old powerbase of Africa, as did his son and a number of the other *hostes*.[57] Brutus was able to flee to Spain along with an unknown number of supporters. Sulpicius, however, was not so lucky, being betrayed by a slave, or in one version being hunted down by horsemen.[58] In any event, his murder added to the infamous list of tribunes murdered whilst in office.[59]

Clearly, the consuls took pains not only to legitimize their actions but to stabilize the situation, both in the short term and the long term. In addition to the murder of Sulpicius, his legislation, passed by force and against a consular moratorium, was annulled, with Pompeius restored to full office. We hear nothing more of these proposed colonies, though there were a number of legions to be demobilized after the Marsic and Samnite campaigns, and idle legions were the last thing that the consuls needed following their blatant use of military power in Rome itself. A fragment of Festus notes financial legislation passed by the pair to ease the credit crisis in Rome (as detailed above).[60]

The lengthiest account of their actions in this year comes from Appian, who lists a range of constitutional reforms that were enacted. These include a change to the voting system of the assemblies (by centuries rather than by tribes), restrictions on the office of the tribunate of plebs, the formalization of the tradition that all laws (whether *leges* or *plebiscita*) must first be approved by the Senate, and the addition of 300 new senators.[61] It has long been argued that Appian may be confusing these measures with ones passed by Sulla when he took control of Rome in 83/82 BC and ruled as dictator, with powers to amend the constitution (see Chapter 7). Given that no other surviving source places them at this point, and given the weak position the consuls found themselves in (with a hostile populace and Senate) and little support outside of Rome, full-scale constitutional reforms do not appear to be likely at this time.[62]

The next obvious step would be to secure further control of the military resources within Italy and favourable political office holders the following year. In military terms, Sulla once again received the command of the Mithridatic campaign, whilst Pompeius Rufus was granted command of the armies of the proconsul Cn. Pompeius Strabo in Italy. Furthermore, a certain P. Servilius Vatia celebrated a triumph in Rome.[63] Though we do not know the exact timing of this triumph, Servilius is most likely identified with a Servilius whom Sulla sponsored for the consulship of 87, thus securing a valuable (armed) ally and giving the people a spectacle to take their minds off the other Roman army that had recently paraded through Rome, though in far less favourable circumstances.[64]

This raises perhaps one of the most interesting points about this whole affair, namely the reaction, or lack thereof, of the other Roman commanders, both in Italy and abroad. In Italy, as detailed above, there were two other major forces still engaged in fighting: those of Cn. Pompeius Strabo and Q. Caecilius Metellus

Pius. Although we have no record of such, the consuls must have sent word to these other commanders detailing the reasons for their actions, and in both cases it is revealing that neither man sought to oppose them. Certainly, Metellus would have had no reason to aid Marius, given the bad blood between him and Metellus' father.[65] Pompeius Strabo, as will be detailed below, would probably have been weighing up what actions would bring him maximum advantage, and at this point opposing the consuls would not have been among them. In any case, both commanders were still engaged against Italian forces and neither would have been in an ideal position to break off. In both cases, it can be argued that their lack of action cannot be taken as support for the consuls, merely acquiescence. Even if their forces could disengage, the only option would be another march on Rome and one with far less legitimacy, as they would have been opposing the sitting consuls.

For those commanders overseas there would have been even less opportunity to intervene, especially given the lack of clear communication about the nature of events. The forces in Asia were engaged with Mithridates, and those in Macedon, under C. Sentius, fighting the Thracian invasion. Nearer to Italy, it is clear that the governor of Africa, Sextilius, adhered to the orders from Rome and treated Marius as an enemy of the state.[66] The governor of Sicily was a certain C. Norbanus, who would later oppose Sulla, but at the time seemingly kept Sicily neutral. As for Servilius Vatia, his province is unknown, but Sardinia has been suggested.[67] In any event, the offer of a triumph and a consulship for 87 BC quelled any qualms he may have had about the consuls' actions. In Nearer Spain we find C. Valerius Flaccus (Cos. 93) fighting a long campaign against Celtiberians and in no position to break off and concern himself with affairs in Rome. Thus we can see that the other forces in Italy were engaged in active campaigning and could not have opposed the consuls without escalating the situation even further into open warfare, whilst those overseas were either too far away, tied down in their own campaigns, or again unwilling to oppose the consuls and the 'legitimate' rule of law of Rome.

10. The Backlash

However, despite their efforts, it is clear, as it must have been then, that the efforts of the consuls to secure their position were failing. Firstly, Marius and, as far as we can tell, the other ten enemies of the state, had evaded death or capture, with Marius seeking refuge amongst old allies in Africa, including a number of his veteran colonies. In Rome, Sulla and Pompeius' choice for candidates for the consulship of 87, the aforementioned Servilius and a nephew of Sulla, named Nonius, were both rejected by the people.[68] The men elected as consuls were Cn. Octavius and L. Cornelius Cinna. Both Plutarch and Dio report that Sulla had Cinna swear some type of oath in support of Sulla and Pompeius.[69] It is not reported that Octavius was made to swear such an oath, but it is reasonable to assume that Sulla wanted an assurance from both men that they would support the consuls' actions in office and reverse neither the condemnation of Marius nor Sulla's command of the war against Mithridates. There is nothing to suggest that Octavius was a staunch Sullan supporter. In fact, Dio reports that one of Octavius' key attributes was his slowness in managing public business; thus at best he was someone who could be considered 'sound'.[70] Given all that Cinna and Sulla were to become enemies, there is no way of clearly ascertaining Cinna's attitude to the consuls upon his election. A number of the surviving sources paint Cinna as a staunch opponent of Sulla from the beginning, yet even if he was, it was in his interests to ensure that Sulla was gone from Rome, along with his forces.

Whether Sulla had any allies elected to the tribunate is far from clear, though several of the tribunes of 87 BC did flee to Sulla following the events of the next year. Whether this was from original Sullan loyalty or expediency will never be determined.[71] Certainly, one tribune, named M. Vergilius, immediately launched into an attack on Sulla for his actions during the year and ordered him to stand trial. Plutarch stated that this attempted impeachment was sponsored by Cinna, but there is no evidence that he was necessarily the instigator at this time.[72] Attacking Sulla, by then the sole surviving consul (see below), was an obvious choice for any tribune seeking popular acclaim. Sulla in turn ignored this impeachment and left Rome to resume his command in Asia.

The absence of Q. Pompeius Rufus in these latter events is a crucial factor. He had been granted command of the proconsular forces in Italy, replacing Cn. Pompeius Strabo. Strabo is an interesting figure, more commonly overlooked in favour of his more illustrious son, Cn. Pompeius Magnus (Pompey the Great). He had distinguished himself in the war in Italy, against the Marsic alliance, yet is notable by his absence in the events of 88 BC, apparently continuing his reduction of the remaining rebel strongholds (as detailed above). He clearly did not make any attempt to disengage and confront the consuls, and we have no detail of any communications between the consuls and himself, which must have accompanied their march on Rome.

What occurred next was a reflection of what had happened to Sulla himself, namely having his command stripped from him in favour of another, this time Pompeius Rufus. Given the consuls' own actions, we must question what they were expecting when they did the same to a man like Pompeius Strabo. What happened next is best described by Appian:

Q. Pompeius was given the command of Italy and of the army that went with the command, which was then commanded by Cn. Pompeius. When the latter learnt of this he was greatly displeased, but received the consul into his camp, and when, next day, the consul began to take over his duties, he gave way to him for a time as if relieved of command; but a little while later a crowd of soldiers that had collected around the consul, under pretence of listening to him, murdered him. After the guilty had fled, Strabo came to the camp in a high state of indignation over the illegal killing of the consul, but despite his displeasure resumed his command over them.[73]

Of the surviving sources, it is Paterculus who best sums the murder up:

In this year [88 BC] the hands of Roman soldiers were first stained with the blood of a consul. Q. Pompeius, the colleague of Sulla, was slain by the army of Cn. Pompeius, the proconsul, in a mutiny which their general himself had stirred up.[74]

This event was as much of a turning point as the march on Rome earlier in the year. The death of Sulpicius had been the murder of a serving tribune at the orders of the consuls and Senate, utilizing arguments for the preservation of order and the public good. The murder of a serving consul by his own army, at the instigation of the outgoing commander, had echoes of the deaths of L. Porcius Cato (Cos. 90) and A. Postumius Albinus (Cos. 99) the year before. Yet Rufus' death did not come during battle or the heat of war and had no arguments for the public good, merely the good of Pompeius Strabo, and marked another step along the road of individual generals using outright force for their own ends. For Rufus, it was a case of reaping what he had sown; for Sulla, it was a stark lesson in the forces that had been unleashed.

Ultimately, we must ask why Strabo's army did this? In the case of Sulla's army, they were following the commands of a serving consul, and the men faced at least the possibility that they would lose out on a profitable eastern campaign, especially attractive after fighting in Italy. In the case of Strabo's army, they had murdered a serving consul and would remain in Italy. It is possible that Strabo played upon the supposed illegality of the march on Rome or Pompeius Rufus' own deposition. In the end, though, it is clear that a new spirit had emerged amongst the Roman soldiers, perhaps engendered by years of fighting their own Italian kin, which destroyed the old certainties as to who the enemy was, so they relied upon the word of their commander. Clearly, a bond of loyalty and trust had been built up between the soldiers and their commander and not one that they wanted to be casually broken. This much the two armies of Sulla and Strabo shared.

Was this, as some claim, a result of landless men being recruited into the army? I find this unlikely. As I have argued elsewhere, the so-called 'Marian reforms' have long been overplayed by modern commentators.[75] Again, we can perhaps see the 'civil war by stages' argument being pertinent. The enemy was no longer clear; legion fought legion, Italian fought Italian, and Roman had fought Roman (actually in Rome itself). An enemy was no longer automatically a foreigner, as they had been for a century of more. An enemy could be anyone their commander decreed, whether they be an Italian community or a fellow Roman senator.

What I think we can see here is the result of the violence of the period 133–88 BC, in which inter-Italian and inter-Roman conflict had become casual. With their traditional value systems seemingly collapsing around them, the only thing that the legionnaires could trust was a commander they knew and respected; all other concerns were secondary. This, I believe, is key to the First Civil War and the ones that followed – local loyalty and shared bonds between soldiers and their commander replacing a wider loyalty to the state. The reaction of Sulla is an interesting one. Appian again provides us with a telling narrative:

> When the murder of Pompeius [Rufus] was reported in the city, Sulla became apprehensive for his own safety and was surrounded by friends wherever he went, and had them with him every night. He did not, however, remain long in the city, but went to the army at Capua and from thence to Asia.[76]

With Pompeius dead and Rome and Italy clearly slipping from his grasp, Sulla had little choice but to take up command in the east and hope that a glorious victory against a foreign enemy would cleanse his record. Even he could not have been prepared for the escalation of violence that would occur in his absence. When he left, Rome was at peace, albeit an uneasy one, but that peace was soon shattered, and by events that had little to do with Sulla.

Summary – A Civil War by Evolution

The consuls' act of deploying the army into a domestic dispute did not come out of the blue, nor was it solely reliant on the personality of one man. The Marsic and Samnite campaigns had seen Roman armies fighting battles in Italy and increasingly against men they knew – neighbours, friends and kinsmen – all for reasons of politics rather than survival or territory. This lack of a clear motive for military action, such as defending their own home or an overseas war of conquest, seems to have engendered a certain ambivalence in the soldiers of this period regarding who and why they were fighting. The norms of the last 200 years had seemingly been overturned, and in such circumstances, it is not surprising that with the bonds of state loyalty weakened, soldiers would turn increasingly to their generals for guidance. Army disloyalty had seemingly been responsible for the murders of one serving and one former consul during the Italian War. With the added incentive of financial reward, it is not difficult to see how the Roman soldiers would follow their general in moving on Rome itself, especially given that they were not following a rogue general, but the two serving consuls.

Thus the onus is thrown back onto Sulla and Pompeius for introducing the army into Roman politics. Usually, commentators let Pompeius off lightly, given that he is swiftly removed from the picture – the second serving consul to die at Roman hands in two years (see Appendix III). However, the two men presented a united front in this matter, and must bear equal responsibility. Yet both men had themselves been conditioned by the background of Roman political life in the last generation. State sanctioned violence had been seen in 133, 121 and 100 BC, all aimed at ending supposedly seditious tribunes. Seen against this backdrop, using the only forces they had available (the army) to restore order, was not such a radical step. Condemning fellow Romans to death for sedition had occurred just over a decade previously, following the Saturnine tumult (in 100 BC), and leading Romans had been exiled under the Varian Commission just two years earlier.

Thus, both the army and the politicians had been conditioned by political evolution into accepting this act as a logical step, rather than something out of the blue. This is not to rule out the personal decisions involved. All four men – Pompeius and Sulla, Marius and Sulpicius – had taken radical steps in pursuing their aims and continuing the trend of Roman politicians putting their own good ahead of the state, examples of which, quite frankly, can be found from the earliest days of the Republic, from the Scipios through to the Gracchi. Hölkeskamp has recently spoken of the increasing need for Roman politicians to live up to the glorious deeds of their ancestors, but as their ancestors' deeds had become increasingly glorious, they then became locked in a vicious spiral, with an increasing urgency to achieve personal and familial glory regardless of the good of the state.[77]

Yet, despite the fact that all four individuals had clearly all gone to extreme lengths for personal success, all of which could, at least to themselves, have been classed as acting in the good of the state, this did not mean that the Republic was now doomed to fail. In fact, the recent record had shown that bouts of extreme violence (133, 121 and 100 BC) had all been followed by a collective pulling together of the Roman oligarchy. There were foreign wars aplenty to occupy their minds, and nothing creates internal cohesion like a foreign threat. By the end of 88 BC, with Sulpicius and Pompeius dead, and Marius and Sulla out of Italy, many would have been hoping that the worst was behind them and that the Republic had proved strong enough to survive these few tumultuous years. Unfortunately, this violence had not solved the underlying problems, such as the Italian question, and whilst the individuals may have been removed from Rome, their precedents remained: consular deposition and turning to the military. In the end, it was these factors that proved far more potent than the individuals themselves.

Chapter 4

The Consuls at War (87 BC)

With the election of fresh consuls and the departure of Sulla to Greece, the start of the year may have seemed to bring fresh hope after the tumultuous events of 88 BC. Certainly, the war against the remnants of the rebel Italian armies continued and there was a full-blown invasion of Rome's eastern empire to deal with, but the crisis caused by the consular march on Rome appeared to have abated. Indeed, there was nothing inevitable about there being further bloodshed amongst the Roman elite. Political solutions could have been found for the Italian question and economic ones for the financial crisis. Sulla could have defeated Mithridates, restored the eastern empire and returned home triumphant. Pompeius Strabo's ambitions could have been accommodated, and Marius, who was an old man, could have easily died in exile. As it happened, none of these events came to pass and the issues that lay unresolved by the events of 88 BC were exacerbated by the events of this year, not ameliorated.

Interestingly, the year seemed to contain a number of omens and portents. Most famously, Halley's Comet passed through the skies of the ancient world towards the end of this year.[1] Plutarch and a fragment of Livy (who also quotes Diodorus) all report that a group of Etruscan soothsayers determined that one of the eight ages of man was coming to an end in this period, which would usher in a new race and a new era.[2] Cicero, who was contemporaneous with the period, reports that a certain Cornelius Culleolus, a man of senatorial background, also made a number of prophesies of doom this year.[3] To a modern audience, such portents can be too easily dismissed, yet we must never forget the effect they may have had on the background social and political atmosphere at the time.

1. The Samnite Campaign

With the Marsic campaign ended, only the remnants of the Samnite alliance continued fighting, in particular the Samnites and Lucanians. Metellus Pius continued in his pro-magisterial command against the Samnites, though we have no details of any military engagements, other than a fragment of Dio that refers to the Samnites still ravaging Campania.[4] When leaving for Greece, Sulla had left one legion to continue the siege of Nola, possibly commanded by Ap. Claudius Pulcher.[5]

However, thanks to a fragment of Diodorus, we hear of one last bold move by a number of the surviving Italian leaders to open up a fresh front of the war, namely an invasion of Sicily. The island had been the scene of the two largest slave revolts in Rome's empire to date, but had been quiet during the Marsic and Samnite campaigns, most likely due to its pacification only a decade earlier.[6]

> M. Lamponius, Ti. Clepitius and also Pontius [Telesinus], the generals of the Italian remnant, who were now in Bruttium, laid siege for a long time to Isiae [Tisia], a strongly fortified city. They did not succeed in capturing it, but, leaving a part of their army to continue the siege, strongly attacked Rhegium with the rest of their forces, expecting that if they succeeded they would be able to transport their armies to Sicily with ease, and win control of the richest island under the sun. But C. Norbanus, the governor of Sicily, by prompt use of his large army and military sources, struck fear into the Italians by the magnitude of his preparations and rescued the people of Rhegium.[7]

Though this fragment is light on military detail, it seems that the prompt actions of the Roman governor of Sicily, C. Norbanus, prevented the capture of Rhegium by the Italians and prevented an invasion of Sicily. With escape from Italy denied them, the rebel forces were now trapped in Italy, though again we have no detail as to the size of their forces. What this incident does show us, however, is that the rebel Italian forces could still muster enough strength to attack Roman cities and were not completely defeated yet.

2. The Thracian Wars

Outside of Italy, Rome still faced a full-scale invasion of Greece and Macedonia by an assortment of Thracian tribes. Again, this war will be covered in more detail later (Chapter 5). The governor of Macedonia at the time was C. Sentius, but as detailed below, his defence of the region was undermined by a second invasion of Greece, this time from the east, which he judged to be the greater threat, seemingly leaving the tribes to plunder at will.

3. The First Mithridatic War

The full details of the First Mithridatic War fall outside the scope of this present work, yet the course the war took did have an important impact on events in the civil war. Mithridates had taken full advantage of the chaos in Rome to launch a full scale-invasion of Asia, Rome's richest province, accompanied by the mass slaughter of the Roman and Italian citizens living there (see Chapter 2). Meeting no serious opposition, his armies then crossed from Asia and invaded Greece and Macedonia. Not only was this the first invasion of Greece from the east in over a century, but it is clear that a number of the Greeks defected to Mithridates' side, welcoming him as a liberator, an ironic reversal from the situation in the previous century. The most notable of all these defections was the city of Athens itself. Thus 100 years of expansion had been thrown into reverse and Greece, Macedonia and Asia had fallen from Roman control within the space of a year. Overall, in the space of just four years, a large number of both Italian and Greek subject peoples had revolted against Roman rule, marking what must have seemed to many at the time, as the collapse of the Rome's empire. Map 6 represents this reversal of fortune and shows the extent of the Mithridatic Empire at its height.

Furthermore, aside from the military defeats and the defections, there were worrying signs that Roman forces were not co-operating with each other. In the absence of reinforcements from Italy, the governor of Macedonia, C. Sestius, sent his forces (commanded by his legate C. Bruttius Sura) into Greece to try to block Mithridates' invasion by both land and sea. Again, we are hampered by a lack of clear narrative sources with regard to the campaigns of Bruttius, but we do possess some interesting details. There are two surviving sources, Appian's *Mithridatic Wars* and Plutarch's biography of Sulla:

> Bruttius advanced against him [Metrophanes] with a small force from Macedonia, fought a naval battle against him, sinking one ship and one hemiolia, and killed all who were in them while Metrophanes looked on. The latter fled in terror, and, as he had a favourable wind, Bruttius could not overtake him, but stormed Sciathos, which was a storehouse of plunder for the barbarians, crucified some of them who were slaves, and cut off the hands of the freemen. Then he turned against Boeotia, having received reinforcements of 1,000 foot and horse from Macedonia. Near Chaeronea he was engaged in a battle of three days' duration with Archelaus and Aristion [two more of Mithridates' allies], the battle being evenly contested throughout. But when the Lacedaemonians and Achaeans came to the aid of Archelaus and Aristion, Bruttius thought that he was not a match for all of them together and withdrew to the Piraeus.[8]

Plutarch's biography of Sulla, however, paints a different slant on the campaigns of Bruttius:

> For here he [Archelaus] was confronted by Bruttius Sura, who was a lieutenant of Sentius, the praetor of Macedonia, and a man of superior courage and prudence. This man, as Archelaus came rushing like a torrent through Boeotia, opposed him most fiercely, and after giving battle at Chaeronea, repulsed him, and drove him back to the sea. But when Lucius Lucullus ordered him to give way to Sulla, who was due to arrive, and to leave the conduct of the war to him, as the Senate had voted, he at once abandoned Boeotia and marched back to Sentius, although his efforts were proving successful beyond hope, and although the nobility of his bearing was making Greece well disposed towards a change of allegiance. However, these were the most brilliant achievements of Bruttius.[9]

Here we have some important differences between the two accounts, though both agree on the military pedigree of Bruttius, who does not appear elsewhere in our sources after this campaign, which is both interesting and unfortunate. In Appian, the battle of Chaeronea is a stalemate, with Bruttius being forced to withdraw when outnumbered. In Plutarch, the battle of Chaeronea is a Roman victory, but one that was wasted when the Roman commanders disagreed with each other and lost the momentum of the campaign. It is interesting that blame seems to be evenly attached to both Bruttius and Lucullus. Lucullus was technically correct that the command against Mithridates had been (re)awarded to Sulla by the Senate, but only after the armed intervention in Rome. Nevertheless, if Bruttius' campaign had been as successful as Plutarch relates, the truth of which we will never know, then it has hardly the time to pull rank and disrupt a successful defence against Mithridates' forces. Thus it appears, at least to Plutarch, that the Roman defence of their empire was being undermined by disunity between Roman commanders in the field, caused in great part by the events in Rome of 88 BC.

4. Unresolved Questions in Rome

Aside from the ongoing wars in Italy and Greece, there were a number of unresolved issues in Rome that still dominated the domestic political agenda. The first and most obvious was the legacy of the consular interventions of 88 BC. Of the four key men involved in clashes of the previous year, two lay dead (P. Sulpicius and Q. Pompeius Rufus), yet C. Marius was still alive and in exile in northern Africa and L. Cornelius Sulla was now engaged in fighting Mithridates' forces in Greece. Whilst there would have surely been many in Rome who hoped neither man would return, the reality must have been that both men could, sooner or later, be making bids to return home and re-establish a dominance they once held. Certainly, both men still had a number of supporters in Rome, though the key Marian allies had been exiled and key Sullan ones would have accompanied him to Greece. By far the majority of Romans, including those in the Senate, would not have been close adherents of either man, but would have been hoping for a return to calm after the events of 88 BC and would certainly have wanted to avoid any repetition.

Aside from Marius himself, there were up to eleven other men who had been outlawed with him. Whilst Sulpicius was dead, the majority, some of whom are not clearly identified, would have also been in exile, most likely in northern Africa with Marius or Spain with Brutus. In addition, there were still a number of exiles from the Varian Commission of 90 BC (see Chapter 2). Both groups would have had supporters in Rome pushing for their respective exiles to be overturned.

Domestic politics in Rome would have been governed by the new constitutional settlement that the consuls of 88 BC had enacted, details of which will forever be open to question, but which may have involved limitations of the power of the tribunate and of the tribal assemblies (see Chapter 3). Certainly, the people, and no doubt a number of ambitious politicians, would have been agitating for the reversal of these measures, passed as they were following an armed occupation of the city.

As detailed earlier, the war in Italy had already devastated Rome's economy and finances, with a full-blown credit crisis, leading to the murder of a praetor on the streets of Rome by enraged creditors. This was compounded by the loss of Asia, the richest province in Rome's empire and the source of considerable tax revenue, which can only have made the financial crisis even worse for Rome.

Although the war against the Italian rebels was virtually over, with only the Samnite campaign ongoing, the question over how to integrate all of these new Roman citizens still remained unanswered. Sulpicius' law to enrol them evenly across all the thirty-five tribes had been annulled by the consuls during the previous year. This meant that there were a huge number of newly enfranchised citizens still with no firm idea over where they would be in the Roman electoral system. Whilst this may not have bothered the vast majority of Italian peasants, who lived far from Rome, for the provincial elites, who wanted to be a part of the system, this would have been a continuing grievance.

The previous year had shown the political dangers of armies operating on the Italian peninsula; that they could be used to settle domestic political disputes in Rome itself. Whilst Metellus was still engaged with the Samnite War, there were at least two other armies still in Italy, which seem to have been under-utilized and still represented a potential danger. One lay under the command of the proconsul Cn. Pompeius Strabo and had been responsible for the murder of one of the consuls of the previous year. The other was under the command of an Ap. Claudius and was at Capua or Nola (the sources disagree on which).[10] Again, we are not told whether it was actively involved in combat or merely mopping-up activities. Given that Appian stated that Sulla's army set out from Capua, it is likely that the remaining forces were ones that Sulla himself had left behind.[11]

Thus there were a number of elements that overshadowed the start of the new consular year. Yet despite all these, there was still no inevitability about the events that befell Rome this year. The crisis of 88 BC had passed and its key players dispersed, and Rome's ruling elite had it within their ability to ensure the year passed peacefully and to resolve the key issues that were affecting the Republic, as they had done so many times before. Yet as we shall see, as with 88 BC, there were key individuals whose actions provided the spark to the powderkeg that has been described above.

5. Conflict on the Streets of Rome

Whilst the armed struggles of 88 BC were caused by the two consuls acting in unison against a tribune, those of 87 BC were caused by the two consuls going to war with each other (a first) and were of a far higher magnitude. As far as we are concerned, the two consuls of 87 BC arrive on the scene as unknown quantities. We must quickly discard any notions that one was a 'Sullan' and the other a 'Marian'. We do know that the Sullan-Pompeian ticket for this year had been rejected by the electorate and that Sulla, as the surviving consul, had sworn at least one, if not both, of his successors to uphold the Pompeian-Sullan settlement: constitutional reforms and the annulment of Sulpicius' legislation, especially where Sulla's command against Mithridates was concerned.

The two new consuls were Cn. Octavius, from a leading plebeian family, and L. Cornelius Cinna, who came from an obscure patrician family. Prior to his consulship, we have two fleeting references to Cinna's military service in the Italian Wars, as a praetorian commander who along with Metellus helped defeat the Marsi in 89 BC (see Chapter 2).[12]

Again, we have no clear timeline for the year, but it soon became apparent that the two consuls had diametrically opposing views with regard to one of the key political issues in Rome: the Italian question. It was Cinna who once again revived the Sulpician plan to distribute all new citizens throughout all the existing tribes rather than just create new ones who would vote last and thus be marginalized. Florus, however, makes no mention of the citizenship issue and solely relates a Cinnan proposal to recall the Marian (and possibly Varian) exiles.[13]

Ultimately, we will never know Cinna's motivation in proposing the full distribution of new citizens, but it is futile to divide the consuls up into *optimate* and *populares* camps, as it is far too simplistic. One of the key factors in winning the war against the Italian Federation had been the vast swathes of Italian peoples that had not joined the rebellion, having been offered full citizenship. If this bribe turned out to be worth less than initially thought, then there was a clear danger the rebellion could flare up once more, this time with previously loyal communities involved. Naturally enough, the Roman politician who achieved this even distribution of new citizens would have been able to count on the support of a number of them, but equally, he knew that he would be opposed by many of the existing ones, especially those in Rome.

This is what we see happening in Rome in 87 BC: a clash between new and old citizens. However, unlike the previous year, when the new citizens were championed by Sulpicius and ultimately Marius, and the old by the consuls, this time the two groups of citizens had one consul each as their champion, thus splitting the Roman state into two; three if we include the neutrals who wanted to maintain peace and order in Rome.

Battle of the Forum

Once again, we see Roman domestic politics turning violent. Appian, Plutarch and Exsuperantius all refer to a major conflict on the streets of Rome:

> While Octavius was still at home awaiting the result, the news was brought to him that the majority of the tribunes had vetoed the proposed action, but that the new citizens had started a riot, drawn their daggers on the street and

assaulted the opposing tribunes on the *rostra*.[14] When Octavius heard this he ran down through the Via Sacra with a large number of men, burst into the Forum like a torrent, pushed through the middle of a crowd, and separated them. He struck terror into them, went onto the Temple of Castor and Pollux and drove Cinna away; while his companions fell upon the new citizens without orders, killed many of them, put the rest to flight and pursued them to the city gate.[15]

For this reason Octavius was aroused to put an end to the dissension, and with the approval of the old citizens he took us arms, depending on the support of Sulla's forces, and forced his colleague Cinna into exile. In the course of these events, a large number of citizens were killed on both sides.[16]

A great battle was fought in the forum between the consuls, in which Octavius was victorious, and Cinna and Sertorius took to flight, after losing almost 10,000 men …[17]

On the face of it, we again have a battle between the new and old citizens on the streets of Rome, with both consuls losing control of their supporters and ending with a massacre. Yet the scale of this conflict appears to have been unlike anything Rome had seen before, especially if we turn to Plutarch's account, which has 10,000 men killed in Rome itself, and paints the conflict as more of a military battle than an urban riot. As well as higher casualties than any previous clash in Rome (even if we consider the 10,000 figure to be an exaggeration), the intensity of the conflict seems to have led to another act by Cinna. Rather than accept a defeat, both politically and on the streets, Cinna apparently appealed to the slaves of Rome to rise up and aid him in return for his freedom, though this may be a corruption of the slave force used later in the year.[18] If true, this would be the second year in a row that a senior Roman politician had called on slaves of Rome to rise up (the other being Marius). What is clear is that Cinna then fled the city along with a number of supporters, including Sertorius and six of the ten tribunes. In response, the Senate took the unprecedented step of having verses from the Sibylline books read aloud in public for the first time, which was used to justify sentences of exile on a serving consul and six serving tribunes.

Whilst violence in a legislative assembly was not new, the scale of the massacre seems to have spurred Cinna to take a fateful step in fleeing the city, following Sulla's example, though the call for a slave insurrection, if accurate, again highlights the increased intensity of the clashes. We will never know whether this flight was due to Cinna being in fear of his life or a calculated move to escalate the situation. However, it soon became clear that Cinna was attempting to ferment the rebellion that his very measure was attempting to avoid.

6. The Formation of the Duumvirate of Cinna and Marius

Cinna and his supporters toured the nearby Italian towns (all now eligible for Roman citizenship), in an attempt to stir up a fresh rebellion against his own state.

Taking a leaf out of Sulla's book he apparently determined that his only course of action was to return to Rome at the head of an army. Whilst he may have had the Sullan-Pompeian model in mind, the circumstances were much different. Rather than the consuls using military force to quash a 'seditious tribune', he would be opposed by his consular colleague, opening the way to Rome's full-blown consular civil war.

Cinna raised soldiers from two sources: firstly, from the newly enfranchised Italian states, all fearful for their newly won status; and secondly, by visiting the Roman army at Nola/Capua under the command of Ap. Claudius and winning them over to his cause, just as Sulla had done a year previously (by appearing as a consul of Rome trying to restore order to his city). Again, we can return to Morstein-Marx's argument over how citizen soldiers viewed consular legitimacy; the big difference on this occasion being a clash between equally legitimate consuls.

Velleius states that he soon raised thirty legions, a figure treated with justified scepticism by modern commentators.[19] Nevertheless, it would have been a significant body of men. During the Marsic and Samnite campaigns, Rome and her loyal Italian allies fought rebel Italians. In the war of 88 BC, Roman fought Roman for control of Rome. Now Romans and Italians fought together against other Romans and Italians for control of Rome, with all sense of loyalist and rebel abandoned.

With one of the consuls in open insurrection, it was not long before Marius and his allies appeared back in Italy, landing in Etruria and recruiting 6,000 Etrurians to his cause. Fentress has argued that Marius in the period 88–87 BC had organized a coup in Numidia and placed a Gaetulian pretender Iarbas on the throne.[20] Granius Licinianus states that Marius landed in Italy with 1,000 men (a mixture of Italian exiles and Mauri cavalry[21]), where he was soon joined by M. Iunius Brutus, another of the twelve *hostes*, who had fled to Spain, along with a number of the other exiles.[22] This was a major boost to Cinna's cause, not only in terms of manpower, but because it brought him a figurehead and established military leader in the form of Marius – six-time consul, saviour of Rome, with an impeccable Italian heritage. Thus was formed a duumvirate, between Marius and Cinna, unifying two previous separate disputes, and two sets of supporters. As Florus states, with Marius as figurehead, recruits flocked to his banner, many of whom must have been his veterans from the Jugurthine and Northern Wars over a decade previously.[23] Furthermore, we are told that Marius recruited slaves and convicts to bolster his forces.[24]

Back in Rome, the Senate and the remaining consul, Octavius, had Cinna stripped of his office (the second consecutive year that this had happened), ostensibly for attempting to ferment slave insurrection in Rome. In his place, L. Cornelius Merula was elected as consul. Merula was *Flamen Dialis* (high priest of Jupiter), whose role prevented him from engaging in military activity or even leaving the city and thus proved to be a silent partner for Octavius.[25]

In military terms, Cinna, and now Marius, had achieved what Sulla had the year before: a sudden tactical advantage and military superiority. The difference lay in the fact that Rome was held by a serving consul who had the imperium to call upon military forces to support his own cause. Furthermore, Cinna and Marius had to assemble and combine their forces rather than march straight on Rome, as Sulla and Pompeius Rufus had done. Although this gave the faction in Rome time to defend the city, the initiative still clearly lay with the duumvirs.

Octavius and the Senate had a limited amount of time to marshal a defence of the city before any move was made by the duumviral forces. In terms of manpower, they had two options: to raise fresh troops from Rome and the surrounding areas and/or summon back the remaining armies in Italy. To this end, we are told they levied troops from the environs of Rome and as far away as Cisalpine Gaul, and summoned the armies of Cn. Pompeius Strabo and Q. Caecilius Metellus Pius. Of the two commanders, Metellus came willingly, but had to first extricate himself from the ongoing Samnite campaign. Metellus was ordered to make peace with the Samnites as best he could and return to Rome at all costs. Unfortunately for him, he was bargaining from a position of weakness and the Samnites knew this. Fragments of both Dio and Granius Licinianus preserve these negotiations:

> [Octavius and the Senate] sent for Metellus, bidding him to come to terms with the Samnites as best as he might; for at the time they alone were still ravaging Campania and the district beyond it. Nevertheless, he did not conclude a truce with them, since they demanded that citizenship be not only given to them, but also to those who had deserted to their side. They refused to give up any of the booty which they had and demanded back all the captives and deserters from their own ranks. As a result, even the senators no longer chose to make peace with them on these terms.[26]
>
> The Senate was asked by the envoys of Metellus to decide about the allegiance of the Samnites, who said that they would not agree to peace except on condition that they and all the deserters should receive the citizenship, and have their property returned. The Senate refused, wishing to preserve the ancient dignity of the Roman people. When Cinna heard about this, with the help of Flavius Fimbria he enlisted the Samnites on the terms which they requested, and joined their forces to his.[27]

With no other option, Metellus withdrew from the campaign and returned to defend Rome. Not only had the Samnites benefited from a Roman withdrawal, but Marius and Cinna soon concluded an alliance with them against Rome, most likely on the terms they demanded. Thus, from the brink of defeat the Samnites had now gone onto the offensive against Rome, albeit on one side of a Roman civil war.

The recall of Cn. Pompeius Strabo proved to be equally troublesome, even though he was not apparently involved in an active campaign. Having connived at the murder of a consul the previous year, Strabo had a clear track record of looking after his own interests first and promptly opened negotiations with both sides. Velleius best sums the situation up:

> Foiled in his hope of a second consulship, he maintained a doubtful and neutral attitude as between the two parties, so that he seemed to be acting entirely in his own interest and to be watching his chance, turning with his army now to one side then another, according to each offer of greater promise of power for himself.[28]

In the end he camped outside of Rome, most likely at the Colline Gate, ostensibly on the side of Octavius and the Senate. Thus the Senate could call upon the forces of Metellus (of unknown size), the fresh levies they had raised, and possibly the armies of Pompeius Strabo. The surviving sources preserve no clear idea of the numbers on Octavius' side, but Brunt estimates that it cannot have been more than 60,000 and that they were outnumbered two to one by the duumvirate.[29] With no other option, Octavius and the Senate fortified Rome and prepared for the first siege of Rome in over 300 years. Walls were repaired, trenches dug and siege engines placed on the walls.

7. The Siege of Rome – 87 BC

For Cinna and Marius, whilst their motivations may have been different, the taking of Rome would allow them to legitimize their actions, as Sulla and Pompeius had done the year previously, through a cowed Senate and People. For Cinna, as serving consul, he could claim to be acting in defence of the Republic and restoring order to a city seized by a mob. How much he truly believed this, we will never know. What is clear is that Cinna, like his estranged colleague Octavius and their predecessors Sulla and Pompeius before them, appears to have been totally convinced that his actions were justified and that only he knew how to 'save' the Republic from its enemies, even when one was his fellow consul. Years of warfare and bloodshed on their own doorstep appear to have hardened certain of the Roman elites, especially those who had fought in the Italian War. Apparently, compromise was not an option, only establishing the superiority of their own views and programmes.

The chronology of the battle for Rome is confused by the large number of fragmentary and sometimes contradictory accounts. Added to which is the fact that that there may have been up to four Marii fighting in them: the elder C. Marius, his son C. Marius (the Younger), a nephew of the elder Marius named M. Marius Gratidianus, and another M. Marius, who is an unknown relation (possibly another nephew).[30] Nevertheless, we have a good surviving account in

Appian, which provides us with the outline of the campaign and the key events, supplemented by a number of additional snippets from the surviving sources, most notably Granius Licinianus, which though fragmentary contain significant amount of detail.

Whilst we have few details on the size of the armies involved, we can recreate the key dispositions and tactics of the two sides. The duumviral army was divided into three or four parts (the sources are divided on which), headed by Marius, Cinna, Q. Sertorius and Cn. Papirius Carbo (another key Cinnan lieutenant). Orosius tells us that Marius had three legions; the rest are of unknown size. Whilst they were still organizing their armies, it appears that Marius ordered a cavalry detachment to advance upon Rome under the command of a Milonius, expecting to find the city undefended.[31] However, this apparently came to nought, as he obviously found the city guarded and prepared.

The key strategy that was adopted in the early phase of the siege appears to have been one of encirclement, cutting off Rome's food supply and any reinforcements. To these ends, Marius took his forces to lay siege to Ostia, Rome's port and vital connection to the sea, whilst attacking a number of coastal cities loyal to Rome, with a fleet of ships.[32] Bridges were erected across the Tiber to cut Rome off from Ostia and the sea, but Ostia fell quickly, having been betrayed to him by a Valerius.[33] Setting an ominous precedent, Marius then proceeded to sack the city, butchering a number of the inhabitants, and plundering the property – an unfortunate first in Roman history. With the loss of Ostia and access to fresh quantities of grain, Rome faced starvation. This tactic foreshadowed the various sieges of Rome that took place throughout later history and highlights the city's vulnerable geographic position.[34]

> This process of encirclement was reinforced by the other duumviral armies, with Sertorius positioning himself to the northwest of the city, by the Janiculum Hill, and throwing up bridges across the Tiber to the north (see Map 5). Cinna (and Carbo) occupied the east of the city and not only bottled up the senatorial forces in the city, but set about reducing the various neighbouring cities that still remained loyal to Rome, notably Ariminum and Placentia.[35]

Granius Licinianus records a clash between a Marius and a Servilius at Ariminum: 'Marius routed Servilius at Ariminum; he killed a few of his men, and accepted the surrender of the rest, whose loyalty he had undermined.'[36] Unfortunately, neither commander's identity can be confirmed, but as Cinna was in overall command of this campaign we must assume that it was not C. Marius himself. The Servilius is most often associated with P. Servilius Vatia, but this remains speculation.[37] In any event, it shows that the war was being fought on a wider scale than just the siege of Rome and that again armies were rebelling against their commanders.

Facing the duumvirate were the key senatorial commanders: Octavius within the city, aided by P. Licinius Crassus, with Pompeius Strabo camped outside of Rome (initially by the Colline Gate), and Metellus Pius, who may still have been marching towards the city. Having encircled the city and cut off its food supply, the first major clash of arms came to the west of the city and was fought for control of the strategic Janiculum Hill, which guarded the vital river crossing points into the city (see Map 5).[38] Here we have some confusion as to who took part in the Battle of the Janiculum, with a number of differing scenarios.

Battle of the Janiculum

The two clearest accounts come from Appian and Granius Licinianus:

> Ap. Claudius, a military tribune, who had command of the defences of Rome at the Janiculum Hill, had once received a favour from Marius of which the latter now reminded him, as a result of which he admitted him into the city, opening a gate for him at daybreak. Marius then admitted Cinna. They were at once thrust out by Octavius and Pompeius, who attacked them together, but a severe thunderstorm broke upon the camp of Pompeius and he was killed by lightning together with others of the nobility.[39]
>
> Marius with his supporters gained control of the Janiculum, after killing many of his opponents, who were captured and slaughtered on Marius' orders. Octavius received six cohorts from Pompeius, and crossed the Tiber. Milonius was killed, and the other soldiers whom Sertorius sent to help Milonius were driven back. ... thousands of Octavius' men were killed, including a senator, Aebutius, and 7,000 of their enemies. The Janiculum could have been captured the same day, but Pompeius would not allow Octavius to advance any further, and forced him to recall Crassus. He did not want the fighting to stop before the elections, so that he himself could obtain a formidable office. The two Catuli and Antonius went as envoys of the Senate to beg Metellus, whose camp was situated nearby, to come to the aid of his fatherland.

During the fighting between Pompeius and Sertorius, a common soldier from Pompeius' army, while he was stripping the body of an enemy, recognized that it was his brother. He built a pyre for his brother and in the middle of the funeral rites, after uttering many curses, he slew himself with his sword. This incident struck everyone as a great condemnation of the civil war and changed their attitudes. Nobody was able to refrain from tears.[40]

The story of the two brothers occurs throughout a number of the sources and was used by a range of commentators to address the evils of civil war, and is a familiar dramatic twist in tales of civil wars ever since. There are lesser accounts of the battle in Velleius, Orosius, Tacitus, Plutarch and the *Periochae* of Livy:

> In the end, however, he [Pompeius] fought against Cinna in a great and bloody battle. Words almost fail to express how disastrous to combatants and spectators alike was the issue of this battle, which began and ended beneath the walls and close to the hearts of Rome.[41]

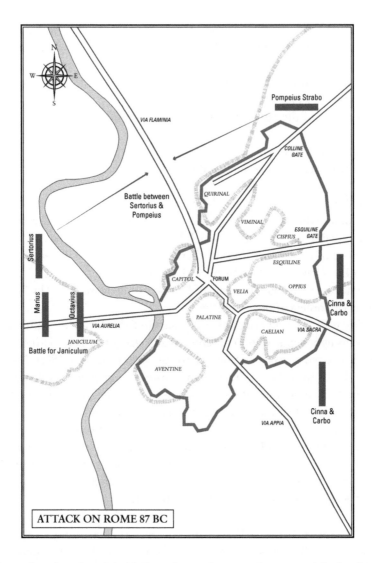

ATTACK ON ROME 87 BC

Pompeius therefore joined Octavius and promptly engaged in battle with Sertorius. Night ended the unfortunate conflict in which 600 soldiers on each side were slain.[42]

In the struggle against Cinna on the Janiculum, as Sisenna relates, one of Pompeius' soldiers killed his own brother and then on realizing his crime, committed suicide.[43]

Then he [Marius] set out and marched with his army towards the Janiculum.[44]

Cinna and Marius, together with Carbo and Sertorius, attacked the Janiculum, but were routed by consul Octavius and retreated.[45]

As can be seen, there are a number of key differences between the sources on the details of the battle and the identities of the combatants, which has led to speculation over whether there was more than one battle.[46] Whilst the accounts of Appian and Licinianus are clear that Marius gained entry into the Janiculum, possibly through treachery once more, he was apparently beaten back by a combined effort of the forces of Octavius and Pompeius Strabo, crossing the Tiber from the city. Appian has Marius acting in concert with Cinna, whilst Licinianus has Sertorius there (which positionally makes more sense, given that Cinna was meant to be on the east of Rome and Sertorius the northwest).

Velleius' account makes it clear that the battle took place within sight of the city walls. Tacitus only has a sentence on the battle but is quoting Sisenna, one of the key historians of the First Civil War, and only has Pompeius and Cinna involved, which is supported by Velleius. Orosius has Pompeius and Octavius fighting Sertorius in a light skirmish (600 dead on both sides), whilst the *Periochae* of Livy has all four commanders attacking Rome. So what are we to make of it?

The fragments of Licinianus, which preserves the most detail, indicates that there was indeed more than one battle and that the other sources have conflated the different battles into one. As well as his account of the Battle of the Janiculum he has an account of a battle between Pompeius and Sertorius, which is generally placed before the account of the Battle of the Janiculum:

> Pompeius no longer put off war with Sertorius, and openly fought against him. Envoys were sent to both sides, but achieved nothing, because Cinna believed that he had the upper hand.[47]

This would fit in with Orosius' account of a light skirmish between the two sides. Thus, whilst Marius was besieging Ostia and the coastal towns, we have an early skirmish between the forces in the north of Rome, (Sertorius and Pompeius Strabo), which need not necessarily have been on the Janiculum, but may have been anywhere in the northwest of Rome. Both sides seem to have withdrawn after light casualties and this can have been nothing more than a probing of defences, and in Pompeius' case his resolve to defend the city.

This only leaves the role of Cinna in the fighting. Appian clearly has him with Marius, as does Tacitus (quoting Sisenna).[48] It is possible that Cinna worked his way round the south of Rome and joined Marius for an attack on the Janiculum, possibly leaving Carbo in charge of the duumviral forces to the east of the city. It is also possible that the sources place both men there as they were joint commanders.

We cannot be clear that Pompeius himself was there in person; Licinianus speaks of Pompeius sending forces to help Octavius, not actually taking part in the fighting himself, which appears to have involved Octavius and Crassus on the defending side.[49]

Two interesting points arise from Appian's story of Marius gaining admission into the city by treachery. The first is that, although this could be a dramatic flourish, there would have been a number of commanders and soldiers on the defending side who had served under Marius previously, which means that all defending forces must have had the potential for traitors in their ranks. The second comes from the naming of Ap. Claudius as the traitor, as this was the same name given for the commander of the Sullan forces that turned to Cinna earlier in the year.[50] We have no way of knowing whether these acts of treachery have been interchanged, whether it was the same person, or whether there was more than one Ap. Claudius engaged in treachery.

Following the Battle of the Janiculum, it seems clear that the besieging side abandoned the idea of taking Rome by force and continued with the slow strangulation of the city. Appian reports that Marius moved inland and attacked the cities of Antium, Aricia and Lanuvium, which were listed as being depositories of grain for Rome. Orosius adds that each city was accompanied by a slaughter of the inhabitants.[51]

For the defenders of Rome, the victory at the Janiculum proved to be a high point in their campaign. It was shortly after this that a pestilence struck the defending armies, killing thousands of soldiers (and presumably civilians, though we are not told of this). Licinianus provides a figure of 17,000 dead amongst the defending forces alone.[52] The most notable casualty was Pompeius Strabo himself, who, according to Licinianus, was also struck by lightning as he lay dying on his sick bed.[53] C. Cassius was sent to take over the remnants of his forces.

Aside from the death of Pompeius Strabo and the massive loss of defending forces, there was the issue of Metellus Pius. The sources do not confirm when Metellus was able to disengage from the Samnite campaign (leaving them to ravage Roman Italy) and return to Rome. Again, the best source is Licinianus, who has Metellus camped outside of Rome during the Battle of the Janiculum, though we are not told where:

> The two Catuli and Antonius went as envoys of the Senate to beg Metellus, whose camp was situated nearby, to come to the aid of his fatherland.

Aside from a conspicuous lack of involvement in the fighting, once in Rome, what is clear is that Metellus' alliance with Octavius was not a solid one. Plutarch reports that the defending forces demanded that he be named commander rather than Octavius, an impossibility given that Octavius was a serving consul. However, this does perhaps indicate a lack of faith in Octavius, who is most commonly described as lacking in military skills. This is perhaps an unfair description given his apparent leading role in defeating Marius at the Battle of the Janiculum. Nevertheless, the defending forces had lost Pompeius, a large number of troops and had dissension in their command structure.

It appears that both sides then lifted the siege of Rome temporarily. Appian reports that having reduced Rome's food supplies further, Marius advanced up the Appian Way (to the south of Rome) and met up with the other three rebel commanders at a distance of 100 stades (approximately 12/13 miles) from Rome.

He also reports that the three surviving key senatorial commanders – Octavius, Crassus and Metellus Pius – had withdrawn to the Alban Hills.[54] The rebels then set up camp near the Alban Mount and offered battle, which Octavius was apparently unwilling to commit to.

The most interesting aspect of this is that both sides appear to have abandoned Rome and moved to the Alban Mount. For both sides, this seems an odd move; the defenders had successfully fought off an attack on the city and the attackers were conducting a comprehensive stranglehold on the city, cutting off its food supply. Two possibilities come immediately to mind. First, there was the issue of the pestilence and the defenders wanting to avoid being trapped in a starving and plague-ridden city. The counter argument to this is to ask why the besieging forces would want to let them leave. The second possibility is that they left to give battle, sparing the city more damage and destruction, on top of the starvation and pestilence. Another fragment of Licinianus may shed some light on this:

> Octavius brought Pompeius' soldiers into his own camp. Metellus led his army against Cinna, but his soldiers suddenly seized all the standards and with a loud cry greeted the army of Cinna, who greeted them back. Alarmed by this turn of events, Metellus led his army away, and was amongst the first to say that an envoy should be sent to Cinna to discuss peace. On his return, Crassus pressed for a battle, and advised Metellus that he ... should seek out Cinna with no further delay ... engaging in battle with Fimbria, he was miserably defeated but not killed, when Metellus ...[55]

This fragment sheds some important light on events after Janiculum. It is the only source that reports that Metellus attempted to engage in battle during this period, but could not do so because of the treachery of his army, which clearly indicates that the defenders believed that the tide of the war had turned against them. Thus, with a military solution seemingly out of the question, the issue of a negotiated peace appears to have been raised. This may explain the removal of the defending forces from the city, so that the Senate could negotiate with Cinna (and Marius) from a neutral stand point. What is clear is that the besieging forces allowed the defending forces to settle on the Alban Mount and then confront them there, rather than attempt to stop them leaving Rome.

Appian reports that the Senate did indeed send envoys to Cinna to negotiate an end to the war. This is hardly a surprise, given the stranglehold that the besieging forces had laid on the city, with the accompanying onset of pestilence and starvation, the lack of a decisive military victory and the absence of any additional forces to raise the siege. In addition to this, we are told that representatives from Cinna, and most likely Marius too, went about the city stirring up the slaves to rebel in return from their freedom (the third occasion such an uprising had been encouraged in two years). On this occasion, it seems that the call was far more successful and a large number of slaves did rise up and desert Rome, with a number ending up as a personal bodyguard to Marius himself.

This initial senatorial approach to Cinna was, however, rebuffed when he raised the issue of his deposition as consul, apparently asking them whether they came to him as a consul or as a private citizen. As the envoys could not answer this question on their own authority, they returned to the Senate to seek clarification. We are told that as these negotiations were continuing, the slaves were not the only people in Rome to see which way the wind was blowing, with large numbers of citizens leaving the city and flocking to the duumvirate. It also seems that Cinna moved his forces closer to Rome to make the point more forcefully.

Octavius and his colleagues were apparently still on the Alban Mount during these negotiations, suffering from desertions themselves, the most notable of which seems to have been Metellus Pius. Diodorus reports that whilst the senatorial envoys did not recognize Cinna as consul, Metellus left the Alban Mount and approached Cinna's camp, with the remnants of his forces, and was the first to recognize him as consul. Diodorus also reports that both men were reproached by their allies for such a move, with Marius remonstrating with Cinna not to tempt fate by jumping the gun and Metellus quarrelling violently with Octavius on his return to camp, being denounced as a traitor to his county.[56] For Metellus, it seems to have been the last straw, and he soon left Octavius' camp and made his way to Roman northern Africa. Despite the rapprochement between himself and Cinna, there would be no doubting the enmity between him and Marius, given the history between the two men (see Chapter 1). Ultimately, it proved to be a wise decision.

It was apparent that the key stumbling block to a negotiated peace was the fact that Rome now had three consuls: Octavius, Cinna and Merula. Both the Senate and Merula agreed that he should stand down and Cinna was reinstated as consul. With this agreed, the Senate once again sent envoys to Cinna and Marius to discuss the surrender of the city to them. Both Appian and Plutarch report that Cinna received them whilst seated on a curule chair, in his role as consul, but refused to swear an oath not to commit bloodshed upon entering the city. Marius apparently stood by his side without speaking, but with a face and manner that spoke volumes.[57] Nonetheless, given the deteriorating situation, there was little the Senate could do except make a humiliating peace and hope for the best. Thus, the Senate bade Cinna and Marius to return to the city; Rome had fallen to an attacking force for the first time in 300 years.

8. The Sack of Rome – 87 BC

With peace terms agreed (albeit one-sided), we are told that both sides returned to the city. Appian tells us that Octavius, with some remaining troops, returned to Rome (from the Alban Mount) from the opposite side of the city to Marius and Cinna.[58] Apparently, Crassus did as well, as we find him in the city when Marius and Cinna arrive. For Octavius, this act seems to have been a mixture of religious belief and the determination to maintain his honour and not yield to Cinna. Diodorus tell us that he had a plan to commit suicide by burning his house down with himself in it rather than lose his honour and his liberty.[59] Plutarch states that again Octavius had put his faith in Chaldaean soothsayers and the priests who interpreted the Sibylline Books, both of whom assured him that he would be safe.[60] As for Crassus, we have no details, but we do know that he too had a small force of troops with him. He must have assumed that there would be little personal danger in it for him, having not been part of the original Cinnan/Octavian quarrel or even the Sullan/Marian one the previous year. As they soon found out, both men had made a fatal miscalculation.

We are told that Cinna and Marius approached the city together, with their bodyguards, but that Marius halted at the gates stating that as an exile he was not allowed to legally enter the city. This was soon remedied at a hastily arranged assembly, with the tribunes proposing the overturn of the Sullan law declaring Marius and the eleven others as enemies of the state and rescinding their banishment. Both Cinna and Marius, now both reinstated, entered Rome as victors, along with their bodyguards. Octavius, displaying a greater degree of self-preservation, retired from the Forum to the Janiculum, the site of his earlier triumph, with the remnants of his forces and a number of supporters, and awaited Cinna and Marius. He too, occupied a curule chair, wearing his robes of office and attended by his lictors.

Thus Cinna and Marius, accompanied by their retinue of bodyguards and a force of cavalry, entered Rome with their honour restored. The city had not fallen to a bloody siege, but had been won through negotiation, having been placed in a stranglehold. It was clear that both Cinna and Marius were the victors, both now restored to their rightful places in Roman society. Yet it is equally clear that both men were not going to take winning gracefully. Almost immediately, two forces were dispatched to hunt down the two key opposition commanders, Octavius and Crassus.

The first detachment was commanded by (C. Marcius) Censorinus, who attacked Octavius and his retinue on the Janiculum. Appian tells us that, despite a valiant effort from his friends and soldiers in defending him, Octavius refused to flee, and even refused to rise from his chair and was murdered where he sat, despite the gods' protection.[61] Censorinus hacked off his head and presented it to Cinna, who had it placed in front of the Rostra in the Forum. The second detachment was commanded by (C. Flavius) Fimbria, who hunted down P. Licinius Crassus. Again, a fragment of Granius Licinianus preserves a note of a battle (more a skirmish) between Crassus and Fimbria, though the location in the city is not noted: '... engaging in battle with Fimbria, he was miserably defeated but not killed.'[62]

Crassus was clearly defeated, but survived the encounter, though he was pursued by Fimbria's cavalry. The pursuit ended in both his death and that of his eldest son, though the sources disagree as to whether it was by his own hand or those of Fimbria's cavalry.[63] Crassus' younger son, M. Licinius Crassus, had already fled the city for the safety of Spain, and would return to play a leading role in both the later stages of the civil war and the subsequent history of the Republic.

However, the deaths of Octavius and Crassus were but the first of many, as Cinna and Marius committed themselves to a wholesale purge of their enemies amongst the senatorial and equestrian orders, filling the Forum with the severed heads of their enemies. We will probably never know the reasons for the murders of the majority of the men whose names we have, but we can assume that they had sided with either man's enemies in the clashes of 88 and 87 BC. We will also never know the full death toll, but we are given the names of a range of prominent senators and ex-consuls (see Appendix III).

There was no escape for those nobles that had wisely chosen to flee Rome in advance of Marius and Cinna taking the city. M. Antonius, the celebrated orator and consul of 99 BC was tracked down to his country villa and murdered there. After the initial round of murders, judicial proceedings were begun against those men who Marius and Cinna wanted rid of, but who either had a position that meant outright murder in the streets would be frowned upon or had only tenuous connections with the events of 88 or 87 BC. Notable victims included L. Cornelius Merula, who had replaced Cinna as consul that year and had stood down to facilitate the peace. As a flamen, he held a sacred post that meant outright murder would be sacrilege. Another was Marius' old colleague Q. Lutatius Catulus, who was co-consul with Marius in 102 BC and had helped defeat the Cimbri at the Battle of Raudine Plain (Vercellae).[64] Both men chose suicide over execution, Merula by opening his veins, Catulus by suffocation via burning coals in a freshly plastered room. Appian reports that there were a range of non-fatal sentences carried out, including banishments, confiscations of property and depositions from office.[65] As you would assume, Marius made a special effort to avenge himself on Sulla, even though the man himself was absent:

> All of Sulla's friends were put to death, his house was razed to the ground, his property confiscated, and himself made a public enemy. A search was made for his wife and children, but they had already escaped.[66]

Thus, by the close of the year, the only senior Roman nobles left in Rome or Italy were close supporters of either Marius or Cinna, or were neutrals who could be of use to them. Any opponents were either dead or scattered throughout Rome's empire. The slaughter was not confined to the upper classes, because although the army of Cinna and Marius had not entered the city in great numbers, they were accompanied by a 4,000-strong bodyguard of ex-slaves, those who had answered Marius and Cinna's call for them to rebel. Whether by intent or not these ex-slaves, usually referred to as the Bardyaei, went on a rampage throughout the city plundering, raping and murdering all they came across. Most ancient sources put the blame for this squarely on Marius' shoulders, arguing that he had a desire to make the citizenry suffer.[67] Appian, however, states that it was Cinna's responsibility, and that he could not control them.[68] Whatever the intention, the Roman citizenry that had endured starvation and pestilence now had an enemy force looting their city. However, due to the scale of the slaughter, even Marius and Cinna were prompted into action, and the Bardyaei were murdered in their own camp. Most sources attribute this act to Sertorius, but Appian has Cinna undertake it with a contingent of Gallic troops, which is the first mention of Gallic forces in the duumvirate's army.[69]

With Rome and Italy under their firm control and their immediate enemies disposed of, Marius and Cinna turned to the future. The laws that had been passed by Sulla and Pompeius Rufus in 88 BC were annulled. This probably meant that the new constitutional arrangements were overturned, as was Sulla's annulment of the Sulpician laws, though these may have been passed once again, the most notable of which was Marius being given command of the Mithridatic campaign once again. In an ironic reversal of 88 BC, it was Sulla's turn to be declared *hostis*, or enemy of the state. Finally, both men had themselves elected consuls for the following year, Marius for the seventh time, Cinna for the second. After two years of bloodshed and civil warfare, Rome and Italy were firmly controlled by the duumvirate of Marius and Cinna, Rome's twin rulers.

9. The Samnite Campaign

Away from Rome, this conflict is also noted for a blurring of the lines between ally and enemy and an intermixing of the various conflicts of the period. For four years, the Samnite alliance had been fighting a war against Rome, and just when they were on the verge of defeat they became allies of what was to become the new ruling faction of Rome. Aside from supporting Cinna and Marius with men, we posses a few surviving references to the Samnites taking to the field themselves once more and attacking Roman forces and towns in the region.

Unnamed Battle
The *Periochae* of Livy has the only reference to a battle between Roman and Samnite forces away from Rome:

> The Samnites, the only ones to take up arms again, sided with Cinna and Marius.
> They defeated deputy Plautius and his army.[70]

Although we have no other details of the encounter, it has been suggested that Plautius was a legate of Metellus.[71] Granius Licinianus also adds an interesting detail of the Samnite campaign: 'The inhabitants of Nola advanced against the town of Abella, and burnt it down.'

It is interesting that Licinianus states that the residents of Nola attacked Abella, rather than naming a rebel Roman army or commander. Nola had fallen to the Samnites earlier in the Samnite campaign and it is seems clear that, since they were now allied to Marius and Cinna, the Samnites were keen to recover their losses in the earlier fighting.

With the success of Marius and Cinna in Rome, we must assume that the Samnites made their peace with the new Roman regime, upon their own terms. Those who wanted Roman citizenship would have it, and prisoners and booty would be restored. The key unanswered question is what status the Samnite alliance had in the Roman system after 87 BC. Whilst Samnites took up Roman citizenship and were assigned to a tribe (Voltinia), some have argued that they used their position of strength to gain a greater degree of autonomy from Rome.[72] Thus we can see the continuation of the Italian War in this year and the two conflicts becoming entwined; it is clear that in 87 BC, the fighting in Italy was not confined to the siege of Rome, but was more widespread than the sources usually report.

10. The Senate & Citizenship

There is another interesting statement found in the *Periochae* of Livy for this year: 'Citizenship was given to the Italian nations by the Senate.'[73] In the *Periochae*, this is placed in the middle of the siege of Rome. It has been argued that this could well mean that the Senate, desperate for additional assistance against the duumvirate's onslaught, offered or granted citizenship more widely throughout Italy, rather than just to those who had not taken up arms against Rome.

The sentence from the *Periochae* highlights two key issues. The first is that possibly one of the key stages of the enrolment of Italians into the citizenship is known to us by only one line from a summary of Livy, showing how little we really know about this period. The second aspect is that, if correct, the Senate had seemingly managed to snatch defeat from the jaws of victory. By the end of 89 BC, the Senate had offered citizenship to those rebels who either did not actively take up arms against Rome or immediately stopped fighting. In either case, it was a limited offer, which still seemed to maintain the Senate's tight grip on who was admitted into full citizenship. Yet within just two years, the Senate had seemingly been reduced to offering citizenship to all Italians in the desperate hope that their former enemies would now come to their aid in the face of an even greater threat: other Romans. Thus, in many respects the hard-won gains of the Italian Wars had been negated by the outbreak of civil war amongst the Roman oligarchy.

Chapter 5

Peace in Italy – a World at War (86–84 BC)

1. From Duumvirate to Coalition

The year opened with Rome's ruling duumvirate, the consuls L. Cornelius Cinna and C. Marius, facing a number of challenges. Although they had secured military control of Rome and Italy and eliminated all domestic opposition, they still faced formidable hurdles at home and abroad. At home there were still two key issues: the Italian question and the financial crisis, both of which had been exacerbated by the fighting in 87 BC. Promises made to the Italian communities now had to be honoured and opposition from the existing citizenry still had to be overcome. The economic and financial crisis would have been exacerbated by the siege of Rome and the slaughter that accompanied it. Whilst some exiles had been recalled a greater number now lay scattered throughout the empire. The constitution had nominally been restored, with the Sullan–Pompeian legislation annulled, but Rome was now ruled by what were in effect two military dictators (in the modern sense of the word rather than the technical Roman official sense).

Outside of Rome, the duumvirate only had firm control of Italy itself; the rest of the empire lay in the hands of the various governors, who would not automatically support them. A number of notable exiles were scattered throughout the empire, from Metellus Pius in Africa, to M. Licinius Crassus in Spain. The war with Mithridates was still ongoing and Greece and Asia were still under Mithridatic control. Added to this, piracy in the Mediterranean was on the increase, being encouraged and supported by Mithridates. Finally, there was the matter of Sulla himself, currently fighting Mithridates' generals in Greece and now an enemy of the state. With Marius now formally in command of the war against Mithridates, and preparing to cross into Greece, a military confrontation between the two enemies seemed inevitable. Thus the duumvirate ruling Rome faced some formidable tasks.

Marius started his year in office in typically forthright fashion. We are told that on his first day of his office he ordered one of the new tribunes (P. Popillius Laenas) to throw one of his predecessors (Sex. Licinius/Lucilus) off the Tarpeian Rock, the traditional means of execution for traitors. Interestingly, a fragment of Dio ascribes this act to Marius' son, C. Marius, who also decapitated another ex-tribune and exiled two ex-praetors.[1]

However, Marius' reign as consul and partner in the ruling duumvirate was cut short after only seventeen days, when, on the Ides of January, he fell ill and died peacefully in his sleep at the age of seventy. In retrospect, given the exertions of the previous two years, including his escape from Rome, his command of a besieging army, the sacking of Ostia and the attack on Rome, all in his late sixties, his death is hardly surprising. However, it seems to have been something of a surprise at the time, with Marius preparing to invade Greece and fight the forces of both Mithridates and Sulla. It was an encounter that never happened, leaving the score between Sulla and Marius unsettled.

Thus, one of the principal architects of Rome's First Civil War died peacefully in his own bed; it was a fate that few other men of this time shared (see Appendix III). Of all the obituaries of the man, perhaps the simplest and most succinct comes from the *Periochae* of Livy:

> When we take everything into account, he had been a man about whom it was not easy to say whether he was more excellent in times of war than he was dangerous in times of peace. It can therefore be said that as much as he saved the state as a soldier, so much he damaged it as a citizen – first by his tricks, later by his revolutionary actions.[2]

Marius' death ended the duumvirate that had been formed in 87 BC. In its place, Rome had one clear leader, L. Cornelius Cinna, but he ruled as the head of a coalition of men either loyal to him or to Marius. For the next three years, he guided the state by means of repeated consecutive consulships. Given the scant surviving sources for this period, it is not surprising that we have no clear idea of what type of rule Cinna exercised in the years 86–84 BC.[3] Like Sulla, Cinna had seized control of Rome by the use of military force as part of a partnership and soon found himself bereft of a colleague. However, whereas Sulla's position was precarious, with a hostile Senate and People and rivals in the wings, Cinna's appears to have been more secure. It is clear that he had a good deal of support amongst the people, especially from the new citizens and the Italian peoples, and in 87 BC he had secured the support of a number of tribunes. We can assume that this was repeated throughout the years 86–84 BC, aided by the repeal of the Sullan–Pompeian constitutional reforms. Added to which, all of his opponents in the Senate had been slaughtered or exiled, ensuring a compliant Senate of nominal allies.

This does not mean that Cinna was a tyrant, in any sense of the word. In many ways, his period foreshadowed that of Octavius, with repeated consulships, a tame Senate and tribunes, and support of the new citizenry. Furthermore, at the time, he would have promised to bring about peace, both within Rome and Italy, and an end to the bloodshed. This alone would have earned him the temporary support of those people and senators in Rome who were not staunch allies, but who would lend their support to anyone who could establish peace and promote recovery after four apocalyptic years. To keep this support, he had to avoid a tyranny and deliver on his promises.

To replace Marius, he selected L. Valerius Flaccus as suffect consul. Flaccus had been a governor of Asia in the late 90s BC and was the younger brother of C. Valerius Flaccus (Cos. 93 BC) who was currently serving as governor of the Gallic and Spanish provinces (see below), and whose absence from the wars of 88 and 87 BC is an interesting topic in itself. The senior member of the family in Rome was another L. Valerius Flaccus, who had been co-consul with Marius in 100 BC and was appointed *princeps senatus* this year. Thus the Valerii Flaccii were at the centre of the ruling coalition, aided greatly no doubt by the presence of C. Valerius Flaccus in Gaul with his army, always a good guarantor for his family's elevation in this period. The younger L. Valerius Flaccus also replaced Marius in the Mithridatic command, and was charged with taking an army to Greece to fight Mithridates, and if necessary Sulla himself. The coalition was now faced with the two key issues of the Italian question and the economic and financial crises, not to mention ensuring that this year did not follow the two previous ones and descend in bloodshed and warfare.

2. Roman Domestic Affairs During the Cinnan Regime (86–84 BC)

The Economic and Financial Crises

It appears that the new regime quickly attempted to resolve the financial crisis. Prior to his departure, the consul Valerius Flaccus passed a measure of debt relief, which allowed all private debts to be settled for a quarter of their value, with the rest written off. Barlow provides a good analysis of the possible wider financial motivations behind the *Lex Valeria*, which may have brought debts back into line with land prices, which had collapsed during the previous years of warfare.[4] As land was the primary source of debt security, both debts and security values may have now been balanced and stability restored to the credit system, with debts and land values equal. Thus stability may have been brought to the credit system, though given the paucity of the sources this will never be known for sure.

Whilst the debt relief would have been welcome to the populace, the state's finances would still have been in terrible shape. In terms of income, the government in Rome could not draw upon the tax revenues of Asia, and piracy was a major disruption to Mediterranean trade. Nevertheless, the government could still raise revenues from the western provinces, notably Spain and Gaul, which lay in their sphere of influence (see below). In terms of expenditure, the forces raised during 87 BC had to be paid off, whilst still maintaining strong enough forces to equip another army to fight Mithridates and support campaigns in Gaul. On a positive note, peace in Italy would have greatly helped both income and expenditure levels. In 87 BC, Cinna had been funded by the Italian cities (not affected by the war), and we again hear of this in 85 BC when the regime was raising forces to fight Sulla. Thus state expenditure in this period had to be of a more limited nature than in previous years.

Whilst the credit system may have been rebalanced and the state expenditure reduced, it is clear that there were serious issues with Rome's currency, either through hoarding or debasement, which seems to have continued to undermine the economy with an unstable currency. In 86 or 85 BC, in a testament to the serious nature of the problem, the praetors and tribunes jointly agreed a proposal to re-establish Rome's currency on a firmer footing. This joint proposal was promptly stolen by one of their number, a praetor named M. Marius Gratidianus, who was a nephew of C. Marius, and who promptly took all the credit for the reforms. The measure of the law's success can be seen by the huge amount of adulation that Marius received, with Pliny telling us that the populace raised statues of him across the city.[5] We can assume that his betrayed colleagues did not hold him in such high esteem. The nature of the proposal is less clear than its outcome, but it appears to have centred on a new system for testing the purity of coins, thus enabling a crackdown on counterfeiters. It may also have set an official exchange rate, to counter inflation. Overall, it seems that the Marian measure did indeed stabilize Rome's currency in this period.

Thus, throughout this period, the Cinnan regime made strenuous efforts to rebuild or at least stabilize Rome's finances, through reduced state expenditure and attempts to stabilize the debt system and the currency. Nevertheless, we must not underestimate the poor state of Rome's finances throughout this period, which in turn affected the nature of the military expenditure in this period.

It is interesting that both the laws introduced by Valerius and Marius Gratidianus were not sponsored personally by Cinna. In fact, the currency measure was originally meant to be jointly issued by the praetors and tribunes combined. This perhaps allows us to see the style of Cinna's government, with Cinna appearing to take a step back from issuing laws himself and allowing colleagues to propose them. As well as gaining their support for allowing them to take the credit, it allowed him, much as Octavian was to later do, to remain in the background and avoid looking like he was actively governing Rome, and thus avoid the impression of being a tyrant. Consensus amongst the ruling elite (what was left of it in Rome) appears to have been very much the order of the day for the Cinnan regime.

The Italian Question

This approach appears to have been used in the efforts to resolve the ongoing Italian question. By 86 BC, it is believed that the majority of the three groups of Italians – those who had not rebelled, those who had surrendered, and those still fighting – had been granted citizenship, whether through the *Lex Iulia* of 90 BC, the senatorial grants of 87 BC, or the alliance with Cinna and Marius. Yet despite this technical grant of citizenship, there were a number of practical matters to be resolved, centred upon their formal registration in a census and their distribution to voting tribes, the latter of which issues had caused the riots in Rome in both 88 and 87 BC that were the sparks of all the bloodshed that followed.

Again, due to the fragmentary nature of our sources, we have no clear narrative for events of the Cinnan regime. But what is clear is that special censors were elected in 86 BC, only three years after the appointment of the previous ones, thus breaking the five year rule for censorial elections. The men elected were two of the only surviving former consuls in Rome, L. Marcius Philippus (Cos. 91) and M. Perperna (Cos. 92), neither of whom could be labelled as died-in-the-wool Cinnan supporters.[6] However, despite this extraordinary census, the citizen list remained constant, registering 463,000 Roman citizens. We have no accurate figures for the period between the census of 115/114 and that of 86/85 BC, including the crucial census of 89/88 BC, but we know that the number of citizens given for 115/114 BC was 394,000. Thus, we only have a slight increase in the course of a generation, and certainly no mass enfranchisement of Italians. In the census of 70/69 BC, the total number of Roman citizens was over 900,000, and that was after another fifteen years of bloodshed. Thus it seems that the central tenet of Cinna's programme of 87 was not carried out. This has naturally puzzled modern historians.[7] The easiest explanation given is that the figure of 463,000 has been wrongly transmitted, and it was in fact 963,000, but this is pure conjecture.[8]

Furthermore, the *Periochae* of Livy states that c.84 BC,[9] the Senate passed a decree granting citizenship to Italians, and that freedmen were distributed equally amongst the thirty-five tribes.[10] Therefore, it seems that both Italians and freedmen were enrolled as Roman citizens in this census, thus fulfilling the central plank of Cinna's programme and bolstering his support. As Lovano points out, it is barely conceivable that given the importance of the Italian question to Cinna, and his position of dominance, he failed to have this enacted. Furthermore, the evidence of Sulla's promises to the Italians when he returned to Italy in 83 BC also lends weight to this interpretation.[11] This still leaves us with the Jerome figure of 463,000, but it is possible that this represented a two-stage census: first, a tally of the existing Roman citizens before the additional ones were enfranchised; and second, an enfranchisement of the new citizens. Such a move is without precedent, but then so was an additional census, and such a set of circumstances – the mass enfranchisement of Italy – was without precedent too.

We certainly hear nothing of any further disturbances in Rome in this period, and the mass enfranchisement of the new citizens appears to have been conducted without further bloodshed. Given that there were no leading opponents of Cinna left in Rome in this period (certainly none that would risk their lives in a public display of opposition), and that all magistrates would have been carefully selected, the old citizens would have been left leaderless. Furthermore, given the levels of violence used by Cinna the year before, any opponents of enfranchisement would have clearly thought twice about publicly opposing such a move.

Such an extraordinary census would probably have also been needed to rebuild the Senate, whose numbers must have been thinned given the slaughter of 87 BC and those who fled Italy. This would have given Cinna the opportunity to have the Senate re-stocked with men who would, in theory, owe him their elevation. It would also allow for the removal of any surviving senators whose loyalties were suspect, whether they were in exile or in Italy. Cicero confirms this when he tells us of the case of Ap. Claudius Pulcher, uncle of one of the censors (L. Marcius Philippus), who was removed as a senator whilst in exile.[12] It must be stressed, however, that this does not mean that the Senate was a rubber stamp for Cinna, in the way it became under the emperors; a number of those remaining senators were at best temporary supporters of Cinna, and even the new ones would soon forget their gratitude when it came to their own future survival. The elevation of the Valerii Flacci was confirmed by the appointment of the L. Valerius Flaccus (Cos. 100) as *princeps senatus*. His kinsmen, L. Valerius Flaccus and C. Valerius Flaccus, were serving as consul and proconsul respectively, and had control of a significant portion of Rome's military forces. Thus, the Cinnan regime appears to have resolved the long standing Italian question, with full enfranchisement being offered to the Latin and Italian communities, even those that had rebelled and not been defeated, such as the Samnites and Lucanians.

Peace in Rome and Italy

The case of the Samnites and Lucanians is an interesting one. Despite the perilous military position in which they found themselves, by the year 87 BC, thanks to events in Rome, they were able to negotiate a peace settlement from a position of strength. C. Flavius Fimbria, negotiating on behalf of Marius and Cinna, and desperate for additional manpower and resources, appears to have granted all of the Samnites terms. We can include the Lucanians in this peace treaty, as Appian refers to the two peoples receiving the citizenship together, later than the rest of the Italian peoples.[13] Thus, almost by default, the last of the Italian Wars, which had been waged for the last four years across the Italian peninsula, and had done so much to weaken Rome, came to an end, not with outright Roman military victory, but by a hastily arranged peace treaty, having been overtaken by wider events.

Salmon is right to argue that this treaty would have led to the demobilization of forces throughout Italy, by both sides, although the Samnites later re-mobilized to face Sulla (see Chapter 6). Cicero describes these years (86–84 BC) as Rome being free from the threat of arms.[14] Such an outbreak of peace would have helped the Cinnan regime, providing a period of military and financial recovery, but also allowing Cinna to portray himself as the bringer of peace and stability to Rome.

On a similar note, after two years of street warfare, we hear nothing more of fighting on the streets of Rome, with the full enfranchisement of the Italians passing through the assembly without the bloodshed that had accompanied previous attempts. Given the bloodletting of previous years and the absence of any visible opposition to the regime, this is hardly surprising, but again, it would have allowed the regime to reap the benefits of the restoration of peace and security.

3. Roman Foreign Affairs During the Cinnan Regime (86–84 BC)

The years 91–87 BC are notable for the absence of the spreading of the civil war to the rest of Rome's empire, though the east was invaded by external enemies. Yet, simply because the focus of our surviving narrative sources is on events in Italy, Greece and Asia, we must not forget the rest of the empire; we must appreciate how far the writ of the Cinnan regime in Rome ran.[15]

Sicily, Sardinia and Corsica

Throughout this period, Sicily appears to have avoided the fallout of both the Italian and Roman civil wars. As we saw earlier, the nearest the fighting came was in 87 BC when the governor, C. Norbanus, intervened on the mainland to prevent the remnants of the Italian rebels from seizing Rhegium and spreading the war to Sicily (see Chapter 4). We have no clear idea of when his governorship started, but Cicero indicates that Norbanus was there for the duration of the war in Italy. Badian has argued that Norbanus was a follower of C. Marius, which would have placed Sicily at odds with Rome during 88 BC, though it seems that Norbanus wisely kept out of events in Rome. The same can be said of 87 BC, with no record of Norbanus' support for the duumvirate. Norbanus did return to Rome to successfully run for the consulship of 83 BC, which placed him at the forefront of the post-Cinnan coalition government. His replacement appears to have been M. Perperna, a praetor and kinsman of the censor of 86/85 BC. Thus, throughout this period, Sicily was firmly in the coalition orbit.

We know even less about the governance of Sardinia and Corsica during this period. Badian suggested that P. Servilius Vatia, who returned to Rome in 88 BC to celebrate a triumph and was endorsed by Sulla as one of his preferred candidates for the consulship of 87 BC, was governor of Sardinia during the Italian War. We have no record of which province he triumphed over, leading to the speculation that it was not a major province and there are few viable provincial commands he could have filled.[16] Again, this is speculation, albeit highly informed. What we do know for certain is that by 82 BC the province was securely in the hands of the coalition government and that C. Antonius Balbus was in charge. We can assume that if the two islands were not held by duumviral supporters in 87 BC, they soon were brought under the control of the coalition government.

Farther and Nearer Spain

It seems that throughout the first decade of the civil war, the bulk of Rome's western empire fell under the control of one man: C. Valerius Flaccus. He has rightly been identified as one of the great enigmas of the First Civil War. Throughout the early periods of fighting he remained quiescent, remaining in his provinces with his forces. During the Cinnan regime his brother was appointed suffect consul for Marius and given command of the regime's eastern armies, and his kinsman was appointed *princeps senatus*. Yet by 81/80 BC, he was welcomed back in Rome and celebrated a triumph over the Celtiberians and Gauls. It is only this triumph that gives us an indication of the range of his command, which Badian argues must have originally been one or both of the Spanish provinces, with Gaul (most likely Transalpine Gaul) added later.[17] Appian briefly mentions that Flaccus was engaged in fighting a Celtiberian revolt in Spain and killed 20,000 of them, though we have little detail and no chronology for the war.[18]

This was the second Celtiberian revolt within the decade, and it seems to have provided a safe haven for refugees and exiles from Rome. We hear of a number of exiles from across the various conflicts seeking refuge in Spain, whether it be Brutus fleeing Sulla in 88, Crassus fleeing Cinna in 87, or the younger L. Valerius Flaccus fleeing Fimbria in 86.[19] Exiles from all sides of the civil war appear to have found refuge in Spain, indicating either a policy of neutrality or a tenuous grasp of such a large fiefdom – or a combination of the two. Crassus himself was able to raise an army (2,500 strong) to support his cause and crossed to Africa to join Metellus' uprising (see below). Despite this, given the resources at his disposal, Flaccus must have been one of the most powerful men of the period, and this period of semi-autonomous rule way from Rome must have helped lay the foundations for the greater independence from Rome that the region exerted during the 70s, under Sertorius (see Chapters 8 to 10).

Transalpine and Cisalpine Gaul

As noted above, ultimately, Transalpine Gaul found itself under the command of C. Valerius Flaccus and was most likely added to his commands in Spain, creating an extraordinary provincial command, in both size and tenure. We do not know the circumstances of his taking command in Transalpine Gaul; we only have knowledge of one commander in Gaul shortly before him, a C. Coelius (possibly the consul of 94 BC, who in 90 BC crushed a rebellion of the Salluvii against Rome, inspired no doubt by the Italian War.[20] The only reference we have to this comes from the *Periochae* of Livy, which states that Caelius defeated the Salluvii.[21] Badian argues that Coelius had command of both Gallic provinces (as was common) during the period 91–87 BC, with a prolonged command for the period of the Italian Wars.[22] Interestingly, we find a mention of a possible kinsman, P. Coelius, being appointed prefect of Placentia by Octavius in 87 BC and committing suicide when captured by Cinnan forces.[23] Thus Badian argues that C. Coelius supported the Octavian regime in 87 BC, holding the vital provinces of the Two Gauls.[24] Given that C. Coelius disappears from history and that by 85 we find C. Valerius Flaccus in command in at least Transalpine Gaul, Badian takes the argument to the logical conclusion, namely that the Cinnan regime had Flaccus take charge of the Gallic provinces and secure them for the regime, though sadly we lack any detail of this process. Thus we can see that the silence of the sources may well be masking a wider expansion of the civil war to the provinces as the Cinnan regime fought to secure control, however tenuous, of Rome's empire.

Africa

Africa too proved to be a popular destination for Roman exiles, the most famous being C. Marius in 88 BC, which is hardly surprising given his strong links with the region from the Jugurthine War, two decades earlier. The governor at the time was a P. Sextilius who is assumed to have been governor of the Roman province of Africa throughout the wars in Italy.[25] Sextilius appears to have observed a policy of strict neutrality in the civil wars of 88 and 87 BC, with Plutarch describing him as a man who was neither a supporter nor an opponent of Marius, but merely an official enforcing Rome's edicts, and who opposed Marius' landing and denied him refuge in Roman northern Africa.[26] When Marius found refuge in one of his veteran colonies, he apparently made no move against him, nor prevented him crossing back to Rome in 87 BC, as far as the silence of our meagre sources allows us to postulate.

The Jugurthine War connection again came to the fore in 87 BC when, anticipating the fall of Rome to the duumvirate, Q. Caecilius Metellus Pius (son of Numidicus) took refuge there. This time we hear nothing from Sextilius, who disappears from our sources. Metellus' role in Africa between 87 and 84 is unclear, with most commentators assuming that he acted as de-facto governor.[27] However, the *Periochae* of Livy has for the year 84 BC an entry stating that Metellus provoked a war in Africa, which forced the Cinnan regime to send a Praetor C. Fabius Hadrianus to dislodge him and restore Roman (Cinnan) control. Thus it seems more logical that Metellus stayed in hiding in the province from 87 to c.84 BC and then attempted to seize it, most likely as a strategic asset for Sulla.[28] Control of Africa would be an important stepping stone for Sulla, through whether he ordered this move or it came from Metellus' own initiative we will never know.

Plutarch sheds some further light on this, as he reports that M. Licinius Crassus, the son of the murdered senatorial commander in 87 BC (and future triumvir), came out of exile in Spain with a force of 2,500 men and joined Metellus, who apparently had amassed a considerable army, but we are not told its size.[29] Crassus, it appears, soon fell out with Metellus and left to join Sulla in Greece. In any event, Fabius arrived from Italy with fresh forces and defeated Metellus, forcing him to flee to northern Italy (Liguria), restoring Cinnan control over the province. Hadrianus maintained control of Africa for the next few years (see Chapter 7). Thus its seems that Metellus' aborted rebellion in Africa attracted wider support amongst the anti-Cinnan exiles, and may have been more serious than the meagre surviving references portray. Interestingly, the *Periochae* of Livy has the following entry for the aftermath of the African War:

> [After Metellus] had been defeated by praetor C. Fabius, the faction of Carbo and the adherents of Marius passed a senatorial decree that all armies everywhere ought to be disbanded.[30]

Thus it seems that the African War had alarmed the Senate to a considerable degree, and also demonstrated how fragile their control of the western empire was and how fearful they were of other Roman commanders and their armies. Whether this decree was acted on is not known, though C. Valerius Flaccus certainly retained his forces.

In terms of the wider Roman sphere of influence in Africa, we can see that the Roman allied states, such as Numidia, placed obedience to Rome (whoever was in charge) above personal ties. Plutarch relates the story of the Younger Marius fleeing to the Numidian court in 88 BC following Pompeius and Sulla's seizure of Rome, exploiting his father's close connection with the Numidian royal family, the current branch of which owed the throne to his efforts in the Jugurthine War.[31] However, despite these ties, Plutarch reports that the king of Numidia, Hiempsal II, was planning to size Marius and hand him over to the Romans.[32] If true, this gives us an insight into the allied attitude to the apparently perplexing events in Rome, namely obedience to the Senate and its representatives, regardless of who had control of Rome at the time.

Other States of the Eastern Mediterranean

For states of the eastern Mediterranean, however, choices were made more difficult by the presence of the army of Sulla in Greece and the forces of the Pontic King Mithridates, who was busily carving out a Mediterranean empire of his own (see Map 6). For them, edicts issued by Rome would have had less force than the dangers posed by the Sullan/Mithridatic conflicts raging in Greece and the Mediterranean. For some, it was a case for balancing Rome against Mithridates and not wanting to choose one side or the other for fear of making the wrong choice. For others, such as Rhodes, allegiance to Rome was the priority, regardless of divisions between the Romans themselves. Rhodes notably defeated a Mithridatic invasion fleet in 88 BC.

The Ptolemaic Empire

For other key states in the region, matters were complicated further by their own internal problems, and this period sees a spate of civil wars breaking out amongst the remaining powers of the east. Egypt in particular would have been crucial to all three of the main protagonists in this period, being the ancient world's richest state and the source of much of its grain supply. As Rome collapsed into a bout of internal bloodletting in 88 BC, so did Alexandria, with the populace rising up and forcing out Pharaoh Ptolemy X in favour of his elder brother Ptolemy IX. Ptolemy X fled to Egyptian controlled Cyprus, dying in battle there against the forces of his brother. His son (the future Ptolemy XI), was first handed over to Mithridates as a captive and then managed to escape and find his way to the army of Sulla, by 84 BC. It seems that the reigning Pharaoh Ptolemy IX also took a policy of (three-way) neutrality between Rome, Sulla and Mithridates.

In 86 BC, Sulla sent a legate, L. Licinius Lucullus, around a number of the largest allied states of the east to raise fresh naval forces, but Lucullus, whilst receiving an honoured welcome, found the support lukewarm. Again, we can perhaps see loyalty to the Senate overriding all other considerations, though we hear nothing of Ptolemy IX's relations with the Cinnan regime.

In Cyrene (modern eastern Libya), however, Lucullus had greater success. Historically, the kingdom was part of the Ptolemaic Empire, but had apparently been bequeathed to Rome in 96 BC, though the bequest had never been taken up (see Appendix I). It seems that between then and 86 BC, the kingdom had collapsed under a series of short-lived tyrannies. Both Plutarch and Josephus report that Lucullus pacified the region and gave it a stable government, also converting it to the Sullan cause. Plutarch also reports that he won Crete over to the Sullan cause, though we are not told what method he employed.[33]

The Parthian and Seleucid Empires

The theme of civil war is one which continues across the east in this period, with both the rump of the Seleucid Empire (Syria) and the Parthian Empire collapsing into civil wars of their own as well, which merely added to the general instability of the eastern Mediterranean. In practical terms, it meant that the rising power of Parthia was not able to capitalize on Rome's misfortunes in this period and ultimately allowed the rise, albeit temporary, of the Armenian Empire of Tigranes (the Great). During the following decade, Tigranes, allied to Mithridates, was able to take advantage of the Parthian and Seleucid Empires' weaknesses and annex large swathes of Parthian and Seleucid territory, extending the Armenian Empire from the Caspian to the Mediterranean itself. This soon brought him into conflict with a resurgent Rome in the 60s BC (see Appendix I).

Interestingly, Velleius records that in c. 85/84 BC, following the Peace of Dardanus (see below), Sulla once again met with a Parthian ambassador, establishing cordial relations between the two empires, both of whom were suffering from civil wars and the rise of the new regional powers of Pontus and Armenia. No details are recorded as to what was discussed.[34]

Macedon and Illyria

As noted earlier (Chapter 1) the Macedonian borders were again being threatened by what seems to have been an alliance of Thracians tribes, with C. Sentius being defeated by the Maedi.[35] The scale of the war is clear from the snippets of information that our meagre surviving sources provide:

> Against the Denseletti, a tribe which has always been submissive to the empire and which even at the general rising of the barbarians preserved Macedonia when C. Sentius was praetor, you waged an abominable and cruel war.[36]
>
> The Thracians, at the instigation of Mithridates, overran Epirus and the rest of the country as far as Dodona, going even to the point of plundering the Temple of Zeus.[37]
>
> The Scordisci, the Maedi and the Dardani again invaded Macedonia and Greece simultaneously, and plundered many temples, including that of Delphi.[38]

Although the Thracian War had predated the Mithridatic War, the Thracian tribes usually needed little encouragement to raid Roman territory, though they may have been spurred on by the seeming Roman collapse in this region, similar to those conflicts in Gaul and Spain. It is interesting that Cicero speaks of a general tribal uprising whilst the *Periochae* of Livy still speaks of raids.[39]

Again, our few sources seem to be confused. Orosius states that the Romans defeated the Maedi quite early on (c. 87 BC) when the governor of Macedonia, C. Sentius, was able to defeat the Maedian King Sothiumus, decisively driving him back into Thrace.[40] However, it seems that the Thracian raids continued into 85/84 BC.

Sentius' victory proved to be short lived in another way, as in 86 BC, one of Mithridates' sons, Arcathias, invaded Macedonia and conquered the province, adding it to the Mithridatic Empire (albeit briefly). At the time, Sulla was engaged in the siege of Athens, and Flaccus and Fimbria were in Asia (see below). We hear nothing more of Sentius or his legate Bruttius after these events, and it is highly likely that they were killed defending the province. Appian has but a brief note on the invasion:

> At the same time Arcathias, the son of Mithridates, with another army invaded Macedonia and without difficulty overcame the small Roman force there, subjugated the whole country, appointed satraps to govern it ...[41]

Memnon has the Mithridatic general Taxiles capturing Macedonia, most of which joined large parts of Greece in defecting to the Mithridatic side:

> They would have been in desperate trouble, if Taxiles had not captured Amphipolis, after which the rest of Macedonia went over to his side, and he was able to provide plentiful supplies.[42]

Thus Macedonia, which had seen another protracted war against the Thracian tribes, was annexed (albeit temporarily) to the Mithridatic Empire (see Map 6). Appian preserves details of a campaign against these tribes by a certain L. Scipio (who may be L. Cornelius Scipio Asiaticus), which appears to date from this period. According to Appian, Scipio was able to decisively defeat the Scordisci and drive them back across the Danube. The Maedi and Dardani then made peace with Scipio and handed over the looted Delphic treasures to him (as a bribe, according to Appian), which he then apparently used in the later stages of the civil war. Where exactly these campaigns took place is not stated, though it seems that Macedonia was still under (nominal) Mithridatic control, though this is not mentioned by Appian in this narrative.[43]

However, it seems that although Scipio had destroyed the Scordisci, the Maedi and Dardani remained a problem for the province. Scipio appears to have returned to Italy, complete with the treasure, where he ran for and won a consulship for 83 BC. In late 85 and early 84 BC, having secured control of Greece, Sulla sent a large force into Macedonia. Primarily, this would have been to restore Roman control, and eliminate any Mithridatic garrisons there may have been. However, Eutropius and a fragment of Granius Licinianus record campaigns by Sulla's legate Hortensius and then Sulla himself against these Thracian tribes:

> In the meantime Sulla also reduced part of the Dardanians, Scordisci, Dalmatians, and Moedians, and granted terms of alliance to the rest.[44]
>
> While the terms of the treaty (of Dardanus) were being negotiated, Sulla's officer Hortensius routed the Maedi and Dardani, who were harassing the allies. Sulla himself had led an army into the territory of the Maedi, before he crossed over to Asia for the talks. After the slaughter of the enemy forces who were harassing Macedonia, he received the surrender of the Dardani and Denselatae.[45]

Thus, by the end of 85 BC, after the campaigns of Sentius, Scipio and Sulla, Macedonia was finally recovered and secured to Rome, albeit in the form of Sulla, rather than the Senate.

Greece

Throughout the civil war of 87 BC, Sulla was engaged in the war in Greece against the generals of Mithridates. Although the details of this war fall outside the remit of this work, a short overview of the campaigns will be of use. Central to Sulla's campaign was the capture of Athens, which had become headquarters of the Mithridatic forces and a symbol of the Greek rebellion. He laid siege to the city throughout 87 BC, eventually taking it by storm in March 86 BC.[46] Thus both Rome and Athens fell to Roman sieges within a year of each other.

Interestingly, Memnon reports that during 86 BC Sulla received reinforcements from Italy, in the shape of 6,000 men commanded by L. Hortensius.[47] Although we have no further details, it is an important note, as its shows that, despite being an official enemy of the Roman state, Sulla still had supporters in Italy who were capable of mustering additional forces to help his fight against Mithridates.

Sulla followed the capture of Athens with major victories over Mithridatic forces at the Battles of Chaeronea and Orchomenos. Appian and Orosius report that Sulla killed 110,000 of the Mithridatic forces at Chaeronea, with only 10,000 escaping.[48] Faced with the loss of Greece, Mithridates, who was in Asia, sent another 50,000 reinforcements to Greece, only to see them destroyed at the Battle of Orchomenos. With these two stunning victories, the Mithridatic forces in Greece were destroyed and Greece was restored to Roman control. Furthermore, it sparked a series of revolts in the Greek cities of Asia Minor against Mithridatic rule. By 85 BC Sulla was moving against Mithridates in Asia, who was forced to start negotiations with him.

Sulla, however, was the not the only Roman commander appointed to the war with Mithridates. L. Valerius Flaccus (Cos. 86) had been appointed by the Senate to replace Marius. With Sulla in Greece, Flaccus appears to have chosen to transport his army from Italy to Asia to take the fight to Mithridates directly, despite only having two legions. Unfortunately for him, he lost a large part of his army in the crossing. Appian reports that a portion of his army crossed Thessaly heading toward Asia.[49] Plutarch reports that Sulla's intention was to intercept Flaccus' army as it crossed Thessaly, following the Battle of Chaeronea, but that the arrival of the Mithridatic reinforcements from Asia prevented him.[50] In any event, Appian reports that a portion of Flaccus' army did defect to Sulla when crossing Thessaly. The rest passed into Asia to prosecute the war there.[51]

Asia Minor

For Flaccus, the Asian campaign went from bad to worse. Following the losses at sea (from both storms and Mithridatic forces) and the defection of parts of his army to Sulla, he managed to assemble his army at Byzantium and crossed into Asia, by late 86 BC. It seems, however, that Flaccus fell into a dispute with one of his legates, C. Flavius Fimbria. Fimbria was a follower of Marius who had been one of the commanders at the storming of Rome in 87 BC and had commanded the force that killed P. Licinius Crassus. At Marius' funeral in early 86 BC, he attempted to murder one of his rivals, Q. (Mucius) Scaevola, but only wounded him. He followed this attempted assassination by prosecuting Scaevola on a trumped-up charge. Despite this, he appears to have been popular with the army, whereas Flaccus was not.

Following a series of arguments between the two men, which led to Flaccus threatening to have Fimbria sent back to Rome, Flaccus himself was murdered. The sources disagree as to how this occurred. Whilst all agree that Fimbria inspired the act, they disagree as to whether he struck the blow himself. Memnon and Appian preserve the best two variant traditions:

While Flaccus was bitterly rebuking Fimbria and the most distinguished soldiers, two of them, who were roused to greater fury than the others, murdered him. The Senate was angry with Fimbria for this; but it disguised its anger, and arranged for him to be elected [pro] consul. Fimbria, thus becoming commander of the whole force, won over some cities by agreement and captured others by force.[52]

Fimbria watched his opportunity, and when Flaccus had sailed for Chalcedon he first took the *fasces* away from Thermus, whom Flaccus had left as his praetor, as though the army had conferred the command upon himself, and when Flaccus returned soon afterward and was angry with him, Fimbria compelled him to fly. Flaccus took refuge in a certain house and in the night-time climbed over the wall and fled first to Chalcedon and afterward to Nicomedia, and closed the gates of the city. Fimbria overcame the place, found him concealed in a well, and killed him, although he was a Roman consul and the commanding officer of this war, and Fimbria himself was only a private citizen who had gone with him as an invited friend. Fimbria cut off his head and flung it into the sea, and left the remainder of his body unburied. Then he appointed himself commander of the army.[53]

Thus we have the two clear divergent stories. Either Fimbria murdered Flaccus himself and took over command of his army or Flaccus was murdered by mutinous elements in his army and Fimbria stepped into the position, with the Senate's grudging blessing. The common ground between the two versions is that one may have reflected reality and one may have been the story that the Senate was told; Fimbria could hardly have admitted to the Senate that he murdered Flaccus. However, once again, a Roman consul had been murdered by his own army (see Appendix III).

In terms of the Asian campaign, it seems that, despite his underhand method of becoming commander, Fimbria proved to be a very able general, and throughout 85 BC he enjoyed military success, defeating one of Mithridates' sons at the Battle of Miletoplis and slaughtering a much larger army. He followed this up by driving Mithridates from Pergammum and sacking the pro-Mithridatic cities of Cyzicus and Ilium, each accompanied by great bloodshed. The latter was a notable and somewhat unusual action, given that Ilium claimed to be the site of ancient Troy, the ancestral homeland of the Romans.[54] Nevertheless, his actions proved to be successful in military terms, as the cities of Asia soon defected from Mithridates back to Rome to avoid a similar fate.

Fimbria also came close to ending the Mithridatic War with the capture of Mithridates himself. He drove Mithridates to seek refuge in the city of Pitane and laid siege to it. To trap him in the city, he contacted Sulla's legate Lucullus, who was in charge of the only Roman naval force in the eastern Mediterranean, seeking his assistance. However, it was here that the enmities between the various Roman factions in the civil war came to the fore, and Lucullus refused to help Fimbria, allowing Mithridates to escape by sea. Thus, in one incident, we can see the damage that Rome's civil wars were causing to its wider military activities.

Rather than allow Fimbria to end the Mithridatic War, Lucullus was happy for Mithridates to escape (and plague Rome for another fifteen years).

With Mithridates fled, Fimbria continued to restore Roman control of Asia, but he was now confronted by Sulla, who moved his forces from Greece to Asia. Full-blown military conflict was only averted when Fimbria's army deserted him and defected en-masse to Sulla, their second betrayal of a commander in two years. Faced with the loss of his army, Fimbria fled to Pergammum, where he committed suicide. Two of Fimbria's legates, L. Magius and L. Fannius, remained loyal to the coalition and fled, finding safe haven at the court of Mithridates.

With his forces driven from Greece, Macedonia and Asia, Mithridates had clearly lost the war with Rome. He was only able to escape Asia thanks to the divisions caused between the Romans by the civil war. At any other time, Mithridates would have paid the ultimate price for invading Roman territory and slaughtering its citizens. However, once again, civil war took precedence over a foreign war, and Sulla, rather than prosecute the war to its logical conclusion (the destruction of Mithridates and Pontus), chose to negotiate a peace treaty, which allowed him to concentrate on the civil war.

4. The Approaching Storm

The outcome of negotiations between Mithridates and Sulla was the Treaty of Dardanus, one of the most extraordinary peace treaties made by a Roman. Despite waging war on the Romans, invading Asia and Greece and slaughtering tens of thousands of Roman citizens and allies, Sulla confirmed Mithridates as an ally of the Roman people and confirmed him as ruler of Pontus and its original territories. In return, Mithridates was to vacate all the territory he had conquered, restore the kings to the thrones of Bithynia and Cappodocia, return all prisoners he had taken, and all Roman deserters and – most importantly – pay Sulla a war indemnity of 2,000 talents and provide seventy triremes to support any military action. Thus, from a position of total military defeat, in both Greece and Asia, Mithridates found a way to avoid Roman retribution and keep his kingdom intact, as it was before the war started – a clear case of snatching victory (or at least a draw) from the jaws of defeat. The price was the funding of an attack on Italy by a Roman general, which was itself a bonus for Mithridates, as Rome collapsing into civil war once more would give him a freer hand in Asia Minor.

Thus, with the war in the east complete and Roman territory restored, Sulla turned his attention to Rome and returning from exile and still being an enemy of the state. Whilst he was clearly preparing for a military invasion of Italy, it is clear also that his preferred solution was a negotiated one. His and Pompeius' move on Rome in 88 BC had at least a veneer of legitimacy, as consuls restoring order, though whether anybody believed that is another matter. However, a full-scale invasion of Italy could not be legitimized in such a manner. It also seems that a negotiated settlement was the preferred choice of the neutrals in the Senate, of which there must have been a sizeable number. The *Periochae* of Livy records that L. Valerius Flaccus, the *princeps senatus*, led the calls for a negotiated settlement and ensured that the Senate dispatched envoys to Sulla to discuss a peaceful return.[55] This dialogue was facilitated by the presence of a number of senators who had been forced out of Rome by Cinna and had found refuge in Greece with Sulla.

However, whilst various elements in the Senate may have wished for a bloodless return to Rome, neither Sulla nor Rome's consuls, Cinna and Carbo, seem to go out of their way to find a negotiated settlement. Sulla in particular, although he may have wanted a peaceful return to Rome, certainly did not seem to intend to keep the peace once he arrived, and did not help his cause by threatening bloody vengeance against his nemeses (those who had hounded his supporters) in a letter read to the Senate.[56] Whilst the Senate ordered the consuls to desist from mobilizing an army, including the recruitment of fresh forces from across Italy, Cinna and Carbo ignored them and went a stage further by having themselves declared consuls for 84 BC without even the pretence of an election.

Having recruited a fresh army of an unknown size, in early 84 BC, the consuls made preparations to transport them to Illyria. Here we are not clear on whether they intended a preparatory campaign against the tribes of the region, to give their forces combat experience, or whether they intended to fight the war in Greece, rather than Italy. Whilst the first detachment of troops landed safely, the second were hit by a storm, and a number of those that survived the crossing apparently deserted. The troops who remained in Italy then apparently mutinied at the prospect of being sent overseas. Appian preserves a detailed account of the event:

> When the rest learned this they refused to cross to Liburnia. Cinna was indignant and called them to an assembly in order to coerce them and they assembled, angry also and ready to defend themselves. One of the lictors, who was clearing the road for Cinna, struck somebody who was in the way and one of the soldiers struck the lictor. Cinna ordered the arrest of the offender, whereupon a clamour rose on all sides, stones were thrown at him, and those who were near him drew their swords and stabbed him.[57]

Carbo, now sole consul, ordered the withdrawal of the sections of the army already in Illyria and changed tactics, preparing a defence of Italy. Delaying his return to Rome until threatened with deposition by the tribunes, he eventually held fresh elections for a suffect consul, but a lightning strike on a temple led to a postponement of the election due to unfavourable omens. Conveniently, augurs were found to interpret this omen in such a manner that no elections for a suffect consul were held that year, allowing Carbo to rule Rome throughout the majority of 84, as sole consul and new leader of the coalition. The rest of the year passed without notable incident, with Carbo mobilizing armies to defend Italy and Sulla returning from Asia to Greece to likewise prepare for an invasion of Italy.

Thus, without a shot being fired, Sulla had gained a considerable strategic advantage. The leader and driving force of the coalition had been murdered, throwing the coalition forces into chaos and stopping them from fighting the war in Greece. Given the monumental consequences of this event and Sulla's track record of subverting opposing armies, one has to wonder whether this was a Sullan plot or one of those coincidences. As has been seen throughout this period, Roman armies were notoriously poor in terms of discipline. Despite Cinna's death, and the Senate's wavering, the coalition still had enough supporters to mobilize a far larger army to defend Italy than the one Sulla had to invade it. Added to this was the support of the majority of the Italian peoples and new citizens, many of whom had no love for Sulla. Nevertheless, the civil war was about to enter a new phase, with an invasion of Italy by a Roman general and the prospect of another peninsula-wide conflict, the second within the decade.

Total Civil War

Chapter 6

The War for Italy (83–82 BC)

1. The Various Factions on the Eve of War

The Coalition (Rome's West)

With the death of Cinna, the coalition that ruled Rome, Italy and the western part of the empire was robbed of its last major figurehead from the year 87 BC. However, the two junior partners of that coalition, Cn. Papirius Carbo and Q. Sertorius, were still active. Of the two, it seems that Sertorius was the better general and Carbo the better politician. Certainly, Carbo's career had flourished under Cinna, with consulships in 85 and 84 (the latter being a sole consulship for most of the year), whilst Sertorius had seen no such obvious advancement. For 83 BC, neither man took the consulship. Carbo stepped down after two consecutive years to focus on the command of the forthcoming war in Italy, via a proconsulship of Italy and Cisalpine Gaul. Sertorius had been appointed to a command in Nearer Spain. Between them, they controlled some of the key military regions of the western half of the empire. The other regions were Transalpine Gaul and possibly one of the Spains under C. Valerius Flaccus (see Chapter 5 and below), Africa under C. Fabius Hadrianus (see Chapter 7) and Sicily under M. Perperna.

Fresh consuls were elected for 83 BC, in the form of C. Norbanus, the former governor of Sicily, and L. Cornelius Scipio 'Asiaticus', who had returned from his command in Illyria, both with good (if not spectacular) recent military records (see Chapters 4 and 5 respectively). In addition, the son of C. Marius, another C. Marius, aged only in his mid-twenties, was in Rome, obviously acting as a figurehead for the former supporters of his father.[1] The preparations for the impending invasion of Italy continued throughout 83 BC, with the coalition apparently being able to field over 100,000 men, according to Appian.[2] Appian also states that the coalition government benefited greatly from being seen as the legitimate government of Rome at a time when Italy was faced with an invasion, even if it was by another Roman general.[3]

However, despite this apparent position of strength, there were a number of potential flaws in the coalition strategy. The initial plan adopted by Cinna appears to have been to confront Sulla in Greece, rather than Italy. As had been shown in both 88 and 87 BC, control of Rome, and the legitimacy it granted, was the key objective in these civil wars, and fighting in Greece denied Sulla that advantage.

Allowing him to cross, seemingly unopposed, into Italy, put Sulla in striking distance of Rome itself. An invasion would also test the strength and resolve of the coalition and just how firm a grip it had on Rome and Italy. As we have seen, the deaths of Marius and Cinna robbed the coalition of their key figureheads and the personal ties that would have ensured the support of a number of the Senate and People of Rome and the wider Italian communities. None of these constituencies would be guaranteed to support the new leaders of the coalition. Whilst a number of the Italian communities supported the coalition in 87 BC, they had now received full citizenship, and unless they could be convinced that Sulla would remove these newly won rights, their active support may have turned into neutrality.

In military terms, whilst all the key coalition leaders (Carbo, Sertorius, Scipio and Norbanus) had military experience, none of them had the experience to match Sulla, and their forces were mostly freshly raised troops, who would be pitted against Sulla's battle-hardened veterans. Furthermore, there was no one clear figurehead who could take overall control of the military effort. Whilst Carbo was technically the most senior figure in the coalition, it was only by default, having been Cinna's deputy during the 87–84 BC period. Whilst on paper he was a two-time consul, he had little of the overriding *dignitas* to match his former mentor and could not be guaranteed to keep the coalition forces and their generals in step.

The Sullan Faction (Rome's East)
By contrast, Sulla had a far smaller army at his disposal, the highest estimate for which comes from Appian, who puts it at just over 40,000 soldiers and cavalry.[4] However, his forces had two key advantages over the coalition: experience and a clear command structure. In terms of experience, this army had defeated the forces of Mithridates in two separate battles and driven them from Greece, also recapturing Athens after a protracted siege. This had been followed by a campaign in Macedon to drive out the invading Thracian tribes and any remaining Mithridatic garrisons. Thus they were an experienced and battle-hardened army. Furthermore, they were led by Rome's foremost surviving general, who was in total command of the campaign, despite having allies commanding portions of his force, most notably M. Licinius Crassus, fresh from the aborted African campaign.

Furthermore, the death of Cinna had removed the prospect of a coalition invasion of Greece, which handed Sulla the initiative. In terms of strategy, the campaign objectives were clear: invade Italy, fight his way to Rome and capture the city. With the Senate and assemblies under his control, he could change status from renegade to legitimate proconsul, overturn his *hostes* status and become the 'legitimate' representative of the Senate and People of Rome once more. For the time being, he had control of Rome's eastern empire and an alliance with Mithridates, none of which could be relied upon if he failed in his invasion of Italy.

The Neutrals

Whilst we may have analyzed the two key sides in the forthcoming conflict, we must not forget that the vast majority of the Roman people, old and new citizens alike, whether in Rome, Italy or the wider empire, did not fall into either camp, but would remain neutral, as they had done in 88 and 87 BC, either until the war was over or a clear winner began to emerge. Crucially, in both 88 and 87 BC, the forces that gained the initiative had been victorious, whilst the defending, or reactive, forces had been defeated. For the majority, the crucial objective was not victory, but survival and ultimately a restoration of peace and normalcy in Rome and Italy. For the client kingdoms, a continuation of neutrality and obedience to the Senate (whoever was in charge of it) was the wisest course. For Rome's enemies, both within the empire and without, a long-drawn-out struggle between the two warring sides would further weaken Rome and provide them with the opportunity to escape, or avoid, the Roman yoke.

One of the key neutrals in this conflict was C. Valerius Flaccus, who continued to command a large army in Spain and Gaul in this period without apparently declaring for either side. He apparently took no part in the eighteen months of conflict that followed, remaining in the north and not returning to Rome until the war had ended and then only to lay down his command. In this period of conflict such studious neutrality marks him down as a fascinating, albeit shadowy, figure. What is also interesting is that his kinsman, L. Valerius Flaccus (Cos. 100), was the *princeps senatus* in Rome throughout the civil war period and interestingly passed through every change of government unharmed. Between them, the Valerii Flacii represented a powerful, perhaps the most powerful, neutral faction in Rome during this period.

2. The Invasion of Italy

Thus 83 BC saw the first invasion of Italy from Greece since the time of Pyrrhus, some 200 years earlier, and the second invasion in a generation (the first being the Cimbri in 101 BC from the north). Ironically, in 88 BC, the fear (however genuine) had been that it would be Mithridates invading Italy, but now the invader of Italy was the general the Senate had sent to defeat Mithridates, though it is doubtful the citizenry appreciated the irony of the situation. Backed by the resources of the eastern empire and his Mithridatic alliance, Sulla had amassed a force of 1,600 ships with which to make the short but potentially dangerous crossing, choosing to cross from Dyrrhachium in Illyria (modern Durazzo), to Brundisium.[5]

The lessons of the war of 87 BC would not have been lost on Sulla, and it is clear that the key element to his strategy was to isolate the hardcore anti-Sullans amongst the supporters of Marius and Cinna, and deny them the support of the majority of the people of Rome and Italy. This could be accomplished in two ways: military victories to quickly establish his image as the clear favourite to win the war; and propaganda to ensure that the peoples of Italy did not see him as their enemy and this war a continuation of the Italian rebellion, merely another bloody squabble amongst the Romans. To these ends, we hear of messages being sent out to the Italian peoples stating that he would not overturn their newly won citizen rights, thus removing their motivation for supporting his enemies. In many ways, these tactics draw a superficial comparison to those of Hannibal, a century and a half earlier, who also needed quick victories and the support of the Italian communities.

Whether through fear, apathy, successful propaganda or outright bribery, Sulla was able to make an unopposed landing at Brundisium. In recognition of this, Brundisium was granted permanent exemption from custom duties, an arrangement that appears to have lasted well into the Imperial period. Given the presence of Sullan emissaries in Brundisium in 84 BC, we may speculate that this deal was worked out in advance with the relevant town authorities. With his army safely in Italy, he fanned out from Brundisium, passing into Campania apparently without any opposition (or at least none that survives in our sources). In fact, Velleius points out that Sulla went out of his way not to arouse the hostility of the regions he passed through:

> One would think that Sulla had come to Italy not as the champion of war but as the establisher of peace, so quietly did he lead his army through Calabria and Apulia and into Campania, taking unusual care not to inflict damage on crops, fields, men or cities ...[6]

Thus Sulla appears to have made an initial ploy of portraying himself to the Italians as a man who wanted to avoid a repeat of the bloodshed of 91–87 BC, and that he was not in Italy as a conqueror but as a returning Roman general. How successful this was we can never know, but it seems clear that the Italian communities had no desire to start a fight unnecessarily, especially with a man in command of 40,000 plus battle hardened veterans.

It seems that the coalition policy was to allow Sulla to land, progress inland and then meet him head on, with two consular armies (Norbanus and Scipio) seeming to converge in the vicinity of Capua. Thus the coalition held northern and central Italy and Sulla in the south. An interesting passage in the fourth century AD writer Iulius Exsuperantius, based upon Sallust, preserves the following:

> ... Sertorius forestalled the anger of the Senate at the public suffering, which the fighting between the leaders would cause, by passing a resolution that 'the consuls should see to it that the state received no harm.' This resolution of the Senate prompted the consuls to prepare defences of every kind against Sulla, who was advancing against them and threatening everyone with destruction; and they chose suitable generals, including Sertorius, who would direct the war energetically. After preparing a very strong army, the consuls marched out and

in spite of Sertorius' objections they agreed to discussions between their army and Sulla's army.[7]

This interesting passage has a distinctly pro-Sertorian tinge and details that we do not find even in Plutarch's biography of Sertorius. It also illustrates the obvious unease amongst the Senate and People of Rome about the oncoming war and gave the coalition a clear legal mandate to go to war with Sulla.

The consuls marched towards Sulla with a combined force of 200 cohorts of 500 men (100,000 men in total), though we are not told the disposition of the two armies. We are told that Scipio was accompanied by Sertorius, whilst Norbanus had the younger Marius on his command staff.[8] We also know that the two armies did not meet up before the first encounter with Sulla, though this may well have been their plan. The first battle of the war of 83/82 BC occurred between the armies of Sulla and Metellus on the one hand and Norbanus and Marius on the other.

Battle of Mount Tifata (Casilinum)[9]

The two forces met to the east of Capua, on the foothills of Mount Tifata. The exact location is unknown, but Velleius states that it was by the River Vulturnus (the modern Volturno), which runs past the mountain. What we do not know are the circumstances of this encounter. Velleius has Sulla ascending the mountain with his forces when Norbanus' forces attacked. The key question is what was Sulla doing there? Both Velleius and Plutarch link the mountain to religious factors, with Velleius mentioning the Temple of Diana on the mountain and Plutarch reporting that there was an apparition of two male goats, which was meant to be emblematic of the war.[10] Aside from the spiritual aspect, Mount Tifata overlooks the city of Capua and the plain to its west. Thus we can ask whether Sulla was moving to occupy the city of Capua when Norbanus attacked. This situation is further complicated by the presence of the other coalition army under Scipio, which was also in the region. If Sulla was moving towards Capua why did Norbanus not wait until Scipio's army joined him to deliver a knock-out blow? Furthermore, both Plutarch and Florus speak of Sulla immediately attacking the forces of Norbanus and immediately routing them:

> Sulla, without either giving out an order of battle or forming his own army in companies, but taking advantage of a vigorous general alacrity and a transport of courage in them, routed the enemy and shut Norbanus up in the city of Capua, after slaying 7,000 of his men.[11]
>
> … The whole army of Norbanus was immediately routed …[12]

Unfortunately, that is all the narrative we have for the battle itself, though Orosius and Eutropius provide some additional detail on the casualty figures:

Sulla's men slew 7,000 other Romans and captured 6,000; Sulla's losses amounted to 124 killed.[13]

In the first battle he engaged with Norbanus not far from Capua, when he killed 7,000 of his men, and took 6,000 prisoners, losing only 124 of his own army.[14]

Despite these meagre details, the few surviving sources do give us two highly suggestive elements to consider. Firstly, Sulla managed to attack first and seemingly caught Norbanus' forces by surprise. This is backed up by the one-sided casualty figures, with large numbers of Norbanus' men killed or captured. Secondly, despite this apparent surprise attack, Norbanus was able to retreat into the city of Capua unopposed, which indicates that at the very least he was between the city and Sulla's forces.

The first would suggest that it was Sulla who ambushed Norbanus and the second that Sulla had not entered the city of Capua, nor was laying siege to it. Taken together, this suggests that Norbanus was camped outside the city of Capua, perhaps awaiting Scipio's army, when Sulla took the initiative and attacked first, thus preventing the joining of the two armies and having to face overwhelming numbers. Thus Sulla would have been able to disrupt the coalition strategy and pick off each army at his own pace. Whatever the manoeuvres which led to the battle, it was clear that first blood had gone to Sulla, and with Norbanus and the remnants of his army holed up in Capua, Sulla was free to face Scipio.

Sulla, Scipio and the Battle that Never Was

Leaving Norbanus in Capua, it seems that Sulla and Metellus took their forces into the field and settled near the town of Teanum (modern Teano), which occupied an important strategic position on the Via Latina. They also seem to have secured the nearby town of Suessa. Obviously, having heard of the defeat at Tifata, Scipio (and Sertorius) moved their army to Teanum to engage Sulla, but were met by a Sullan offer of a negotiated peace, which, whilst it was opposed by Sertorius, seems to have found favour with Scipio at least. Appian provides full narrative details of the situation:

Next, while Sulla and Metellus were near Teanum, L. Scipio advanced against them with another army, which was very downhearted and longed for peace. The Sullan faction knew this and sent envoys to Scipio to negotiate, not because they hoped for or desired to come to an arrangement, but because they expected to create dissension in Scipio's army, which was in a state of dejection. In this they succeeded. Scipio took hostages for the conference and marched down to the plain. Only three from each side conferred, so that what passed between them is not known. It seems, however, that during the armistice Scipio sent Sertorius to his colleague Norbanus, to communicate with him the ongoing negotiations, whilst there was a cessation of hostilities. Sertorius on his way [to

Capua] captured the town of Suessa, which had joined the side of Sulla, and Sulla made a compliant of this to Scipio. The latter, either because he was privy to the affair or because he did not know what answer to make concerning the strange act of Sertorius, sent back Sulla's hostages. His army blamed the consul for the unjustifiable seizure of Suessa during the armistice and for the surrender of the hostages, who were not demanded back and made secret agreement with Sulla to defect, if he drew nearer. This he did and straight away they all went over en masse, so that the consul Scipio, and his son, Lucius, alone of the whole army were left not knowing what to do, in their tent when they were captured by Sulla.[15]

The account is supported by that of Plutarch, but contains some important differences:

[Sulla] invited Scipio to make terms of peace. He [Scipio] accepted the offer and several meetings were held; but Sulla continually interposed some pretext for gaining time, and gradually corrupted Scipio's soldiers by means of his own [soldiers], who were practiced in deceit and every kind of trickery, like their general himself. For they entered the camp of their enemies, mingled freely with them and gradually won them over to Sulla's cause, some at once with money, others with promises and others still with persuasive flatteries. And finally, when Sulla drew near with twenty cohorts, men greeted those of Scipio who answered their greetings and went over to them. Scipio who was left alone, was taken in his tent, but dismissed, while Sulla, who had used his twenty cohorts as decoy birds to catch the forty cohorts of the enemy led them all back to his camp. It was on this occasion that Carbo is said to have remarked that in making war upon the fox and the lion in Sulla, he was more annoyed by the fox.[16]

Thus Sulla was able to defeat a second consular army in a row, this time without a single clash of swords. For the second time in a few years he had managed to subvert an opposing army to his cause, resulting in a wholesale defection, the other being that of Fimbria in 85 BC. Not only did he defeat a second consul, but he added the consular forces to his own, more than doubling his strength.

Aside from the result, perhaps the most interesting feature of this episode concerns the role of Sertorius. Three further sources touch on Sertorius' role in this affair. Plutarch in his biography of Sertorius dismisses the affair with a few lines, stating that Sertorius warned Scipio of what would happen but that Scipio ignored him.[17] This is the line taken by Exsuperantius (and thus possibly Sallust).[18] Plutarch's account of the incident in his biography of Sulla makes no mention at all of Sertorius; he mentions neither the Suessa affair nor Sertorius' role in breaking the armistice.[19] Velleius takes this silence in Plutarch one stage further by reporting that Sulla captured Sertorius along with Scipio and his command staff, all of whom were later released.[20]

Velleius' statement is the only one to survive in the ancient sources concerning Sertorius' capture, and Spann dismisses it as being a Sullan fabrication, most likely from his memoirs.[21] Plutarch seems to ignore a number of aspects of this incident, which painted Sertorius in a poor light, as apparently did Sallust or at least his epitomator Exsuperantius. Unless Sertorius had orders from Scipio (which seems unlikely, given the present evidence), his actions were a remarkable breach of military discipline and a clear attempt to force an end to the negotiations and avoid Scipio being suckered in by the proffered peace process. If this was the case, it seems at best to have been too little too late, and at worst counter productive.

What can we say about the capture of Sertorius? Initially, this depends upon whether Sertorius returned to Scipio after taking Suessa and meeting Norbanus at Capua. To return to his commander after so flagrant a breach of an armistice would have been a bold act in itself, even more so if he suspected Scipio's army of treachery. Furthermore, if he did return and was captured, would Sulla have so easily forgiven him? Velleius himself marks this out as an unusual move for Sulla, given his notorious low threshold for forgiving enemies, especially as the two had clashed in 88 BC,[22] and puts it down to 'a notable example of a double and utterly contradictory personality in one and the same man.'[23]

All that we know of Sertorius is that he returned from Campania and was sent to Etruria to recruit fresh troops for the war effort, prior to leaving for Spain, where he had been appointed governor of Nearer Spain. Plutarch again misses out the Etrurian role and has him heading off to Spain in disgust at Scipio's incompetence; seeing the 'writing on the wall', he wished to distance himself from the coalition and their seeming defeat.[24] Yet given the Suessa incident, both Etruria and Spain (which were minor, non-combat roles) could have been a sign of his fall from grace and punishment for his appalling lack of discipline. His military record at that time was a solid but unspectacular one, and now it was blighted by Suessa. Exsuperantius states that he was sent to Spain because the coalition needed a competent commander in that province and to be rid of a nuisance.[25]

We do know that Sulla released Scipio and his son, after failing to convince him to join his side. But then Scipio was a serving consul and had shown himself to be utterly inept at military matters, and so releasing him was not necessarily aiding his opponents, and in fact may have had the opposite effect. Sulla provided him with a cavalry escort and safe conduct to any city he chose. It seems that he chose to return to Rome to continue as consul, and according to Diodorus, was once again put in command of an army.[26]

Thus Sulla had achieved the two quick victories he needed to confirm his credentials as the likely winner in this war, and he increased his forces at the same time. For the coalition, the defection of a whole army (for the second time) must have been as hard a blow as the defeat at Mount Tifata, highlighting their weak position for all to see.

3. Stalemate in Italy

Despite the apparent weakness of the coalition, it appears that Sulla was unable to capitalize on these victories to bring the war to a swift conclusion. Whilst the capture of Scipio was a victory, he failed to convince the serving consul to join his side, which would have been a boost to Sulla's official position, if not his military capacity. With a captive Scipio proving to be of little intrinsic value, he therefore seems to have chosen the lesser of two evils and released the man, possibly with Scipio's other commanders, in a show of clemency. This may also have been related to his opening negotiations with the other consul, C. Norbanus, who was still based in Capua. Sulla apparently had neither the men nor the time to engage in a siege of the city. In fact, despite the 13,000 men lost or captured, Norbanus would still have had a considerable force at his disposal.

Appian reports that Sulla attempted to play the same trick on Norbanus that he had pulled on Scipio, but to no avail; Sulla's envoys got no response, as Norbanus was determined to continue the war.[27] Thus, despite the two victories over the consuls, neither could be convinced to sue for peace, and so the war continued. Appian reports that both Sulla and Norbanus went on the offensive in the Campania, with both sides attacking the allies of the other in the region, and destroying anything that could be of use to the enemy.[28] However, it does seem that Norbanus had learnt his lesson and he avoided another full-scale battle, but both armies continued to harry the other. Thus again we have echoes of Hannibal, with Norbanus shadowing Sulla with a large army, whilst apparently refusing to give battle, and thus avoiding handing Sulla the further advantage of another victory.

Whilst the consuls were seemingly determined to continue the war, it seems that this view was not shared by all the senatorial oligarchy. The *Periochae* of Livy reports that a large number of defections took place among the leading men of Rome.[29] Of these leading men, only one is known of for sure: the Cornelius Cethegus who was one of the twelve *hostes* of 88 BC, along with Marius and Sulpicius. This marked him as one of the close adherents of the elder Marius, and his defection would have been a propaganda coup for Sulla, who promptly pardoned Cethegus. We have no other details of senatorial defections, but the *Periochae* of Livy describes Rome as seeming abandoned, though this may refer to a general abandonment of the city by a populace who expected an attack from Sulla any day.

As a matter of fact, it seems that senatorial and city business continued as normal. However, the number of physical defections to Sulla's camp must have been matched by the number of the neutrals in the Senate who wanted a negotiated peace. It seems that the situation was only salvaged for the coalition by the actions of Carbo, who swiftly returned to Rome and re-imposed coalition control of the Senate. Appian reports that he had the assemblies pass a motion declaring as enemies of the state Metellus and all those who had defected to

Sulla.[30] This must have meant that Cethegus earned the dubious distinction of being declared an enemy of state by both principal factions.

4. The Capitol Fire

Rome itself suffered in this year, though not through the expected Sullan siege. Midway through the year, on 6 July, the Capitol of Rome caught fire, with the resulting destruction of all the original buildings on the Capitol, many dating back to the early days of the Republic.[31] Thus the buildings on the Capitol that had survived the Sack of Rome in c.390 BC did not survive Rome's First Civil War. Apparently, a number of people at the time put this fire down to divine providence, a warning of the consequences of Roman fighting Roman. A number of others claimed it was the work of human agents, though opinion was divided on whether they were acting on Sulla's orders or Carbo's. Appian summed the situation up the best:

> It was at this time that the Capitol was burned. Some attributed this deed to Carbo, others to the consuls, others to agents of Sulla; but of the exact facts there was no evidence; nor am I able to now conjecture what caused the fire.[32]

One could see why the coalition would want to attribute this disaster to human hands, especially Sulla's, if only to avoid the charge of being disfavoured by the Gods. History has a more famous example of a Roman fire being blamed on scapegoats, but this does not turn Carbo into a new Nero. If it was an accident, the timing (during a period of open civil warfare) does seem coincidental, but this may have been just one of those quirks of history. In practical terms, the destruction of the most ancient part of the city, and its religious heart, would have been a blow to the Roman government and people.

5. Preparations for Renewed Warfare – The Revolt of Cn. Pompeius

Thus it seems that on both the military and political fronts, the coalition managed to salvage the situation and avert full-scale disaster. Through his use of harrying tactics and refusal to give battle, Norbanus managed to stabilize the military situation and keep Sulla confined to southern Italy. By his swift and decisive actions in Rome, it seems that Carbo managed to stabilize the political situation. Therefore, with both a swift military resolution and a negotiated settlement ruled out, both sides set about rearming and equipping for the war ahead, which seems to have taken the rest of 83 BC.

For Sulla, the most notable reinforcements arrived in the shape of a legion commanded by the twenty-three-year-old son of Cn. Pompeius Strabo (Cos. 89), one of the key figures in the war of 87 BC. The young man's name was Cn. Pompeius, soon to be known as Magnus (the Great). He had spent the years between his father's death and Sulla's invasion in Rome on the edges of the Cinnan regime. By 83 BC, he had made his way to Picenum on the Adriatic coast and his father's estates. Seeing the way the war was going and having no intention of turning up in Sulla's camp empty handed, he raised an army from his father's veterans and family supporters in the Picentine region and declared for Sulla. The sources differ on the size of his army; Plutarch states that it was three legions, whilst Appian has him raising just one in Picenum and a further two after he had joined Sulla.[33]

Pompeius then proceeded to seize the city of Auximum (modern Osimo) from the supporters of Carbo, and then marched from Picenum towards southern Italy with the intent of stirring up rebellion from coalition rule as he went. Naturally enough, the coalition did not tolerate such open rebellion and three junior officers were dispatched to deal with Pompeius: L. Iunius Brutus Damasippus, C. Carrinas and a Cloelius, each with their own forces, though no figures are given for their respective sizes.[34]

Unnamed Battle

Plutarch reports that the three coalition forces attempted to surround Pompeius' army, but that Pompeius took the offensive and attacked the nearest one, commanded by Iunius Brutus:

> Pompeius, however, was not alarmed, but collected all his forces into one body and hastened to attack one of the approaching armies, that of Brutus, putting his cavalry, amongst whom he himself rode, at the forefront. When the Celtic horsemen rode out from the enemy's cavalry against him, he promptly attacked the nearest and sturdiest amongst them, attacked him with his spear, and brought him down. The rest then turned and fled and threw their infantry into confusion so that there was a general rout. The opposing commanders fell out with each other and then retired, each as best they could'.[35]

Thus the young Pompeius had won his first battle, admittedly against other junior officers. Plutarch goes on to list two more battles that Pompeius fought as he marched across Italy to reach Sulla, the first apparently against the consul Scipio.

Unnamed Battle

According to Plutarch, Scipio marched out against Pompeius, though we must treat the account carefully:

> Next, Scipio the consul came up against him, but before the lines of battle were within reach of each other's javelins, Scipio's soldiers saluted Pompeius' and came over to their side and Scipio took flight.[36]

Thus we apparently have Scipio losing yet another army to defection. This has naturally led many commentators to assume that Plutarch is confusing the Sullan incident against Scipio with the Pompeian one. And certainly, we cannot dismiss the chance of their being a clash between Scipio and Pompeius. A fragment of Diodorus mentions that Scipio did indeed take up a fresh command, and we have no clear timescale for Pompeius' campaigns in relation to those of Sulla.[37] In point of fact, most ancient sources seem to have Pompeius meeting Sulla almost as soon as he landed, allowing no time for the amassing and equipping of an army, or the battles Plutarch describes, never mind the march itself. Furthermore, crushing the rebellion of a young man with little military experience, as they would have seen it, would have been the perfect opportunity for Scipio to contribute something to the war effort without being out of his depth (as he was against Sulla). It seems, however, that this was not the case, and that Scipio's military ability was well below the mark for a Roman general, especially one who bore such an illustrious name. Thus it is perfectly possible that Scipio was defeated once again, this time by Pompeius.

Battle of the River Arsis

The third clash took place between the forces of Pompeius and a large force of cavalry sent out by Carbo himself, though he does not seem to have been present. Again, as with his first battle, Pompeius seems to have attacked the enemy first and routed them. He then pursued them onto rough ground that was unsuitable for cavalry and forced them to surrender, probably adding them to his growing army.

Thus Pompeius fought his way through central Italy to meet up with Sulla's army at some point in mid to late 83 BC. Famously, when the two men met, Pompeius hailed Sulla as *imperator*, an acknowledgment of his imperium, but Sulla apparently returned the greeting, hailing Pompeius as *imperator* also, an acknowledgement of his practical power though, rather than an official position. Given the young man's undoubted abilities, Sulla must have assumed that it was better to keep him close and use him as a legate rather than stand on ceremony about his youth and inability to command troops under the formal *cursus honorum*. Furthermore, given the youth's uncanny ability to command an army and his lineage (his father being as unscrupulous as they come, with an uncanny ability to manipulate armed forces for his own ends), it must have been expedient for Sulla to keep Pompeius onside and deal with him later, when the war was won. As events turned out, this was more easily said than done. We must also not forget that it was Pompeius' father who had had Q. Pompeius Rufus, Sulla's consular colleague in 88 BC, murdered (see Chapter 3).

6. In the Shadow of Pompeius – M. Licinius Crassus

We are told, by a fragment of Diodorus, that Pompeius' actions were used by Sulla to berate a number of his allies, especially the senators who had recently arrived in his camp, as they had come empty handed and Pompeius brought legions and victories. Certainly, Pompeius would not have been welcomed by many in Sulla's camp, especially those older commanders who had been with Sulla for a number of years.

Furthermore, the case of Pompeius should remind us of that of M. Licinius Crassus, the youngest and only surviving son of P. Licinius Crassus (Cos. 97), who had helped to defend Rome in 87 BC against Marius and Cinna (see Chapter 3). The younger Crassus had fled the city, most likely before it capitulated, and fled to family friends in Spain. He too declared for Sulla, but in c.84 BC also raised his own army, fighting first in Spain, albeit briefly, and then crossing to Africa to take part in the Metellan uprising of 84 BC (see Chapter 5). When this uprising failed, he then transported the reminder of his forces to Greece, to join up with Sulla, who also apparently greeted him warmly, with Plutarch stating that Crassus stood in 'a position of special honour'.[38] This position of precocious and talented youth appears to have been taken by Pompeius, who was only a few years his junior.[39] Thus we can see the clear parallels between the two men. This was a rivalry that came to define both the latter stages of the First Civil War and the late Republic as a whole.

Crassus does not seem to have played a major part in the early stages of the Sullan campaign, and it cannot have helped that Metellus had rejoined Sulla in Italy and become his de-facto deputy, given the clashes the two men had had during the failed Metellan uprising in Africa. We are told that once in Italy, Sulla sent Crassus on a recruitment drive amongst the Marsi, which is interesting in itself, given their role and Sulla's in the Italian War. Plutarch also specifically records a clash between Sulla and Crassus, and that Sulla expressed doubts about his character, though how much of this was tainted by his later years is impossible to judge.[40] Thus, as one star rose, another seemed to fade.

Both Plutarch and Appian record some of the general activities that Sulla undertook to bolster his forces in this period. They both record that Sulla sent emissaries (mostly his younger legates, such as Crassus), to all the regions of Italy, to raise fresh troops, whether by alliance, threats or bribes, though again we are unable to accurately judge the levels of success. However, we are told on a number of occasions that the Italian communities stayed loyal to the coalition, a fact that would have hampered Sullan recruitment.[41]

7. The Coalition Forces – The Rise of C. Marius

Sulla was not alone in the promotion of talented youth. Whilst he had both Pompeius and Crassus to call upon, the coalition chose to promote a new figurehead, C. Marius, son of the seven-time consul. At the age of twenty-six, he surpassed both Pompeius and Crassus to become the youngest consul Rome had ever seen, being some sixteen years short of the mandatory age.[42] However, it seems that the election of one so young to the consulship did not pass smoothly, with the *Periochae* of Livy recording that he was only elected following violence, though again we have no further details.[43]

His fellow consul was none other than Cn. Papirius Carbo, who took his third consulship in four years. It is clear from this that Carbo had tired of the previous year's experiment with fresh consuls, given that Norbanus had been easily defeated in battle and Scipio had been stripped of his army at least once, possibly twice, including by the twenty-three-year-old Pompeius. Carbo was undoubtedly the senior surviving figure in the coalition and needed to take total control of the war for the crucial year ahead, which both sides hoped would be decisive. Despite his young age, having the son of the great Marius as consul would be a major boost to shoring up any wavering Marian supporters and would give the coalition a new figurehead who could tap into a glorious past, unlike himself. The major issue would be his military inexperience. Thus the civil war saw a twenty-six-year-old leader on one side and a twenty-three-year-old one on the other.

Norbanus seems to have received a proconsulship and was dispatched to Cisalpine Gaul, with Carbo and Marius taking command against Sulla in the south. Wisely, it appears that Scipio was removed from the military side of operations and left in Rome. Sertorius, another figure from the early years of the coalition, was chosen as praetor for Nearer Spain, and after conducting a recruitment drive in Etruria (see above) he was dispatched to his province. According to Iulius Exsuperantius, he also had orders to settle affairs in Transalpine Gaul, province of C. Valerius Flaccus (see above), but again we have no further details.[44] L. Iunius Brutus and C. Carrinas, two of the young officers who had faced Pompeius in 83 BC, also were elected to the praetorship, with Carrinas heading south to join the fight against Sulla and Iunius Brutus staying in Rome as urban praetor. Given the lineage of the Iunii Brutii, as defenders of the Republic and tyrant-slayers, this was a good propaganda move.

With new and perhaps more robust commanders in place for the coming year, the coalition set about building up fresh forces, even though they already had a numerical advantage over Sulla. Appian records the following:

> In the meantime, the forces of the consuls were constantly increasing from the major part of Italy, which still adhered to them, and also from neighbouring Gauls on the Po.[45]

Thanks to Iulius Exsuperantius, we have more detail on this recruitment from central and northern Italy:

But the Etruscans were faithful supporters of Marius' party, because they had received from them the Roman citizenship, which they did not possess before. They were afraid that Sulla would revoke the grant of this dignity, given to them by Marius' party, if his enemies were completely destroyed. So they joined Sertorius and the other leaders of that party, promising that they would do everything which was commanded without demur. And so it happened that a strong army of forty cohorts was again assembled; and many soldiers, who had surrendered to Sulla on his arrival, returned to the camp of their former generals, whom they had betrayed, because their hopes of an agreement had been dashed.[46]

Thus we can see that despite Sulla's early victories, the bulk of the Italians did not appear to have gone over to him, or even remained neutral as he may have hoped. The coalition, especially with a Marius in command, could claim the success for the full awarding of citizenship to the Italian communities, whereas Sulla, who in 88 BC had ordered the murder of the men who supported this, would find it hard to shake off his old image, no matter how well he treated the locals. Furthermore, he was restricted to southern Italy, whilst the coalition had access to the manpower of central and northern Italy, as well as both Gauls and both Spains.

One crucial aspect is how these forces were paid for. We have already noted the difficult financial and economic climate in which the Roman state operated during this period (see Chapter 5). Brunt estimates the total number of troops the coalition had in the field at over 100,000.[47] Whilst the years of peace (in Italy at least) from 86 BC to 84 BC must have helped embed the financial reforms of 86 BC and give the state a breathing space financially, they were still without the revenues of the eastern empire. Both Pliny and Valerius Maximus record that Marius used the temple treasures, including those saved from the fire, to finance his campaigns, apparently authorized by senatorial decree, the total weight of it being 13,000 pounds.[48] It also appears that the government once again took to the minting of more and more coinage to pay for the increased military expenditure, wrecking the balanced financial settlement achieved only a few years before.[49]

8. The War for Eastern Italy

We have no details of where Sulla spent the winter of 83/82 BC, but Appian reports that it was a harsh winter, which prevented any thought of further campaigning.[50] At some point, either during the winter or in early spring, the Sullan forces made a coordinated thrust northwards into central Italy, with Sulla on the west of Italy and Metellus the eastern coast (see Map 7), commanding an army of unknown size. His advance was met by the coalition forces led by the praetor C. Carrinas.

Battle of the River Aesis

Again, we have no details as to the size of the forces involved, but in what Appian indicates to be a major encounter, the forces of Carrinas were heavily defeated by those of Metellus, with Carrinas routed and his camp captured.[51] Following the battle, Appian reports that the region defected to the Sullan cause. Plutarch does record that Crassus captured the city of Tuder in Umbria, though no other details are given.[52]

Again, this placed the coalition on the back foot and Carbo himself moved to intercept Metellus. It seems that Carbo had greater success against Metellus and had him besieged, though we are not told where. We are also in the dark as to whether Metellus retreated in the face of superior coalition numbers in the form of Carbo's army or whether he was defeated and forced to withdraw. What we do know is that Sulla dispatched reinforcements to relieve Metellus, whose forces were being pinned down by those of Carbo.

Appian reports that upon hearing the news of the defeat at Sacriportus (see below), Carbo broke off his engagement and retreated to Ariminum, being harried by Pompeius' forces as he went.[53] Orosius, however, has Carbo's camp being overrun by Pompeius' forces, as he was withdrawing, which makes Pompeius' arrival, rather than the news of Sacriportus, the key factor in Carbo's retreat.[54] Whilst the exact chronology is now lost to us, it appears that Carbo regrouped his forces, as did Metellus, with two further key battles being fought.

Unnamed Battle

The larger of the two battles appears to have been between the forces of Carbo and those of Metellus. As is common, we have few details other than the fact that Metellus was victorious and that, again, a number of the coalition forces changed sides during the battle – five cohorts, according to Appian.[55] Such an occurrence can signal one of two key factors, if we are to believe our sources. The first one is that the bonds of loyalty were weak amongst the coalition forces, which were all freshly levied. This was no doubt aided by the nature of the conflict: Roman vs. Roman, with both sides guaranteeing the new citizen rights. Second, it would have been increasingly clear that Sulla was winning the war, with victories over three consuls in a row: Norbanus, Scipio and now the younger Marius.

Battle of Senae

The second clash took place between the junior commanders, who must have been in command of smaller forces, though again, we do not know their size. Here Pompeius faced the force of Carbo's legate, C. Marcius, and emerged victorious, though again, we have no details of the encounter, not even from Plutarch's life of Pompeius.[56]

The War for Western Italy

As Metellus thrust into central Italy, it seems that Sulla mirrored his move with a thrust into Latium itself. Sulla advanced towards the city of Praeneste (modern Palestrina), Marius being camped in the vicinity. Following his capture of the town of Setia, the two forces engaged in battle.

Battle of Sacriportus
Appian and Plutarch preserve accounts of the battle:

> After this, at Signia [Setia], Marius, with eighty-five cohorts, challenged Sulla to battle. Now Sulla was very eager to have the issue settled on that day, for he had seen a vision in his dreams, as follows. He thought he saw the elder Marius, who was long since dead, advising his son Marius to beware of the ensuing day, since it would bring him a great calamity. For this reason, then, Sulla was eager to fight a battle, and was trying to get Dolabella, who was encamped at some distance, to join him. But the enemy beset the roads and hemmed Sulla in, and his soldiers were worn out with fighting to open a passage.
>
> Much rain also came upon them while they were at work and added to their distress. The tribunes therefore came to Sulla and begged him to defer the battle, showing him the soldiers prostrated with weariness and resting on their shields, which they had laid upon the ground.
>
> Sulla yielded reluctantly, and gave orders to pitch a camp, but just as his men were beginning to dig a trench and throw the rampart before it, Marius attacked them confidently, riding ahead of his lines, and hoping to scatter his enemies while they were in disorder and confusion. There the Deity fulfilled the words which Sulla had heard in his dreams. For Sulla's rage imparted itself to his soldiers, and leaving off their work, they planted their javelins in the trench, drew their swords, and with a general shout came to close quarters with their enemies. These did not hold their ground long, but took to flight, and were slain in great numbers.
>
> Marius fled to Praeneste, but found the gate already closed. A rope was thrown down to him, however, and after fastening this around his waist, he was hoisted to the top of the wall. But there are some who say, and Fenestella is one of these, that Marius knew nothing of the battle, but was forced by loss of sleep and weariness to cast himself upon the ground in a shady place when the signal for battle was given, and there gave way to sleep, and was then roused with difficulty when the rout took place.[57] In this battle, Sulla says he lost only twenty-three men, but killed 20,000 of the enemy, and took 8,000 prisoners.[58]

Sulla captured the town of Setia. Marius, who was encamped near by, drew a little farther away. When he arrived at the so-called sacred lake [Sacriportus] he gave battle and fought bravely. When his left wing began to give way, five cohorts of foot and two of horse decided not to wait for open defeat, but lowered their standards together and went over to Sulla. This was the beginning of a terrible disaster to Marius. His shattered army fled to Praeneste with Sulla in hot pursuit. The Praenestians gave shelter to those who arrived first, but when Sulla pressed upon them the gates were closed, and Marius was hauled up by ropes. There was another great slaughter around the walls by reason of the closing of the gates. Sulla captured a large number of prisoners. All the Samnites among them he killed, because they were always ill-affected toward the Romans.[59]

Eutropius, Orosius and Diodorus preserve brief notices of the battle, which give some additional, and variant, casualty figures:

> Sulla came to battle with Marius the younger, and killed 15,000 men, with the loss of only 400.[60]
>   The greatest battle of the war was fought between Sulla and the young son of Marius at Sacriportus, where, according to Claudius, the army of Marius lost 25,000 troops.[61]
>   Marius put up a valiant struggle against Sulla, but was nevertheless defeated and sought refuge in Praeneste with 15,000 men.[62]

Plutarch has Marius catching Sulla unawares with a surprise attack, which must have been late in the day, and certainly does not have Marius sleeping during the battle. Appian chose to focus on another defection of Roman forces from the coalition to Sulla, a common theme in this war. All sources are unanimous that the battle was one of the turning points of the war. Marius appears to have had an army of over 40,000, of which only 15,000 made it into the safety of Praeneste. On this occasion, Sulla did not waste the opportunity and laid siege to the city, bottling up one of the key coalition leaders. Appian reports that Sulla had siege lines dug around the town and left the siege in the charge of a legate Q. Lucretius Ofella, a former Marian supporter, whilst he continued his campaigns northwards.[63] The *Periochae* of Livy and Velleius report that Marius' attempts to break out were repulsed.[64]

10. The Fall of Rome

With Marius defeated in western Italy and Carbo defeated in the centre, it appears that the path to Rome now lay open to Sulla. In an attempt to forestall the few remaining neutrals in the Senate from welcoming Sulla into Rome, Marius managed to send word from the besieged city of Praeneste to Rome, which was under the command of the urban praetor, L. Iunius Brutus Damasippus. Brutus then organized a massacre of the remaining neutral senators whilst the Senate was in session, some even in the Senate House itself. Amongst the victims were the *pontifex maximus* Q. Mucius Scaevola, the noted orator P. Antistius (a former ally of Sulpicius), L. Domitius (Ahenobarbus) (Cos. 94), and even a brother of the consul Carbo (see Appendix III).

In military terms, however, the massacre mattered little, as there seems to have been no major coalition forces between Sulla and Rome. That being the case, Sulla dispatched a large detachment of his army towards Rome to seize and hold the various city gates. They apparently encountered no opposition along the way, with all the towns on the route surrendering without a fight. With seemingly no ability to defend the city, certainly not in the manner of 87 BC, Brutus and the remaining coalition forces fled Rome. With a defenceless Rome before him, Sulla mustered his army in the Campus Martius and entered Rome unopposed, six years after he first seized the city. For the third time in six years, Rome had fallen to an approaching hostile army.

On this occasion, it seems that there was no bloodshed, mostly on account of there being no coalition supporters left in Rome. Sulla, however, did not savour his return for long, as the war still raged throughout central and northern Italy. He stayed long enough to seize and sell the property of the coalition leaders and summon an assembly of the people (the few that remained). We are not told what measures were passed, but the overturning of his *hostes* status and his official exile, along with that of his key supporters, must have been a key consideration.

11. The War for Central and Northern Italy

Not staying in Rome long, Sulla and his army set out north into Etruria. Appian reports his destination to be Clusium, which seems to have been the new headquarters of the coalition forces led by the consul Cn. Carbo and the former consul C. Norbanus.

Battles of River Clanis and Saturnia
On route to Clusium, Appian informs us that Sulla was twice involved in skirmishes with coalition, forces, first at the River Clanis and then at Saturnia. The location of these two battles, or skirmishes as they probably were, is interesting. The direct route from Rome to Clusium is along the Via Cassia. Yet Saturnia lies to the west of the Cassia, towards the ocean, and the River Clanis lies to the east (see Map 7). We must assume that both sides had skirmishing parties strung out on either side of the Via Cassia looking for their enemy. During the skirmish at the Clanis, Sulla defeated a small detachment of Celtiberian cavalry sent by Carbo, killing fifty, with another 270 deserting to his side. For the clash at Saturnia we have no details whatsoever.

Battle of Clusium
Sulla faced Carbo at Clusium, in what is referred to as a severe but inconclusive battle. The only details we have come from Appian, who refers to it as an all-day

battle, ended by the onset of nightfall, with no clear conclusion.[65] As is usual for this period, we are not told the size of the forces involved, yet they must have been considerable, as Carbo was later able to spare eight legions to send to Praeneste (see below). Velleius also mentions Clusium and has the two Servilius brothers playing a prominent part, though again we have no details.[66]

Sulla's march towards Clusium seems to have formed the western part of a three-pronged thrust by Sullan forces up into central Italy. In the centre we hear of Pompeius and Crassus advancing via the Via Flaminia through Umbria, and Metellus Pius advancing up the eastern coast by sea. The advance of Pompeius and Crassus was blocked by a legate of Carbo, C. Carrinas. The two forces met in battle at the city of Spoletium.

Battle of Spoletium
Appian informs us that the battle resulted in a defeat for Carrinas, who lost 3,000 men, though we are not informed of the sizes of the respective armies. Following the battle, Carrinas was besieged in Spoletium.[67]

Second Battle of Spoletium
Upon hearing of his legate's defeat, Carbo sent reinforcements to break the siege of Spoletium. However, Sulla ambushed them as they were making their way from Clusium to Spoletium, at an unknown location, and killed 2,000 of them (again, we do not know the size of the forces in total). Following this defeat, and with no hope of reinforcements, Carrinas managed to escape Spoletium under cover of a rain storm. Meanwhile, Metellus landed seemingly unopposed, in the vicinity of Ravenna on the northeast coast of Italy, and secured the region for Sulla, outflanking Carbo. With deadlock on the Via Cassia and the Via Flaminia, Appian informs us that Carbo changed tactics and dispatched a sizeable part of his army, eight legions in fact, commanded by C. Marcius Censorinus, to march south, thus bypassing Sulla, Pompeius and Crassus, and relieve the siege of Praeneste and free Marius.[68]

Unnamed Battle
Unfortunately for Marcius, these eight legions were ambushed by Pompeius. Appian preserves some details of the battle:

> Pompeius fell upon them from ambush in a defile, defeated them, killed a large number, and surrounded the remainder on a hill. Marcius made his escape, leaving his fires burning. His army blamed him for being caught in an ambush and stirred up an angry mutiny. One whole legion marched off under their standards to Ariminum without orders. The rest separated and went home in squads, so that only seven cohorts remained with their general. Marcius, having made a mess of it in this way, returned to Carbo.[69]

Thus, through battle and mutiny, Marcius managed to lose virtually the whole of the eight legions under his command, in what at best was a calculated gamble in trying to break through the Sullan forces and relieve the siege of Praeneste. The coalition forces could not sustain such losses. Following this defeat, Carbo and Norbanus retreated northwards, towards Metellus' forces.

Some relief came in the form of the Samnite army, which appeared around this time and attempted to relieve Praeneste (see below). Although the attempt was unsuccessful, the emergence of a fresh force in central Italy did force Sulla to disengage from Clusium and reinforce the siege of Praeneste by occupying the key pass that led to the city. Although the siege remained in place and Marius remained neutralized, it did provide the forces of Carbo and Norbanus with some brief respite.

Battle of Faventia

Faced with an overwhelming Sullan force to their south, and Metellus to their northeast, Carbo and Norbanus clearly needed to avoid being caught between the two forces and seemingly chose to eliminate the weaker force of Metellus and secure northern Italy. Appian again preserves the fullest account of the battle, though Orosius also adds some detail:

> About the same time, Carbo and Norbanus went by a short road to attack the camp of Metellus in Faventia just before nightfall. There was only one hour of daylight left, and there were thick vineyards thereabout. They made their plans for battle in hot temper and not with good judgment, hoping to take Metellus unawares and to stampede him. But they were beaten, both the place and the time being unfavourable for them. They became entangled in the vines, and suffered a heavy slaughter, losing some 10,000 men. About 6,000 more deserted, and the rest were dispersed, only 1,000 getting back to Ariminum in good order. Another legion of Lucanians under Albinovanus, when they heard of this defeat, went over to Metellus, to the great chagrin of their leader.[70]
>
> Metellus crushed an army commanded by Norbanus in an encounter in which 9,000 of the Marius faction were killed.[71]

Thus the coalition forces suffered another defeat in central and northern Italy and were faced with being caught in a tighter Sullan noose. The whole campaign had been marked by one disastrous defeat after another, with the coalition commanders, Carbo, Norbanus and Censorinus proving no match for their Sullan counterparts. The effect of these continuous strings of defeats was to convince the coalition armies and their allies that their cause was lost, and hence the high rate of defections.

The most notable of these defections was that of P. Albinovanus, a legate of Norbanus, who was one of the supporters of Marius and Sulpicius when they defended Rome against Sulla and Pompeius Rufus in 88 BC, and was most likely one of the twelve *hostes* declared by the consuls (see Chapter 3). Having been present at the disaster at Fidentia and lost his own legion to desertion, he determined to defect to Sulla.

Given his history, he clearly determined that he needed his defection to be of great value. To this end, he organized a feast for Norbanus and his legates, along with a number of Carbo's legates, at Norbanus' headquarters in Ariminum. All except Norbanus turned up and were promptly murdered. We are only told of two victims: C. (Coleius) Antipater and a Flavius Fimbria, brother of the coalition commander killed in Asia (see Chapter 3).[72] Such a loss not only wiped out Norbanus' command staff, but the coalition forces at his headquarters in Ariminum declared for Sulla as well. Norbanus choose this moment to flee Italy, taking ship to Rhodes, where he later committed suicide rather than be handed over to Sulla.

Norbanus' flight left only Carbo and his legates fighting in northern Italy. We are told that he again tried to send forces to relieve the siege of Praeneste, this time with two legions under L. Iunius Brutus Damasippus, but that they could not force their way past Sulla's forces, though we are not told of any actual battle. The only other military encounter we know of came at Fidentia between one of Carbo's legates, Quinctius, and a Sullan legate, M. Tarentius Varro Lucullus.

Battle of Fidentia
Plutarch and Orosius preserve accounts of the battle:

> And still further, at Fidentia, when Marcus Lucullus, one of Sulla's commanders, with sixteen cohorts confronted fifty cohorts of the enemy, although he had confidence in the readiness of his soldiers, still, as most of them were without arms, he hesitated to attack. But while he was waiting and deliberating, from the neighbouring plain, which was a meadow, a gentle breeze brought a quantity of flowers and scattered them down upon his army; they settled of their own accord and enveloped the shields and helmets of the soldiers, so that to the enemy these appeared to be crowned with garlands. This circumstance made them more eager for the fray, and they joined battle, won the victory, killed 18,000 of the enemy, and took their camp. This Lucullus was a brother of the Lucullus who afterwards subdued Mithridates and Tigranes.[73]
>
> When Lucullus was being besieged by Quinctius, he sallied forth and by a sudden attack destroyed the besieging army. More than 10,000, according to report, were slain.[74]

Once again, a coalition army was caught in a Sullan ambush, this time from a supposedly superior position of being the besieging force. Following this string of defeats, Appian tells us that the Gallic inhabitants of northern Italy defected to Metellus.[75] Appian helpfully sums up the remaining collation forces in central Italy. Carbo was headquartered at Clusium with 30,000 men. Brutus Damasippus had two legions, whilst Carrinas and Censorinus had additional forces as well. In addition, there were the 70,000 men commanded by the Samnite leaders (see below).

Thus despite all their defeats and defections, the coalition could still muster an army of more than 100,000 soldiers. Despite this, it seems that Carbo, like Norbanus before him, now lost his nerve, and he and few close confidantes took ship to Sicily, planning to seek refuge and regroup their forces in coalition-held Africa (see Chapter 7), leaving behind over 30,000 men at Clusium. Command of this coalition army now seems to have fallen to an unofficial triumvirate of Carrinas, Brutus Damasippus and Marcius Censorinus.

Second Battle of Clusium

Seemingly eager to finish off the war in Italy, it seems that Pompeius attacked the coalition forces at Clusium, hoping to take advantage of Carbo's desertion no doubt. Only Appian preserves a brief mention of this the last battle of the central Italian campaign and the penultimate battle of this war in Italy:

> ... The army around Clusium had a battle with Pompeius in which they lost 20,000. Naturally, after this greatest disaster of all, the remainder of the army dissolved in fragments and each man went to his own home. Carrinas, Marcius, and Damasippus went with all the forces they had to the pass in order to force their way through it in conjunction with the Samnites.[76]

Thus, the final remnants of Carbo and Norbanus' army were destroyed by Pompeius at Clusium. However, this did not mean the end of the war. The few forces that remained loyal were taken by the triumvirate of coalition commanders to join the 70,000-strong army of the Samnites. As shown repeatedly this year, attempts to relieve the siege of Praeneste and rescue the consul Marius (the highest ranking coalition commander still in Italy and a clear figurehead for the coalition as a whole) had proved to be impossible, due to the Sullan siege of the city. Thus the coalition forces made one last bold move: an attack on Rome itself, which was lightly defended since Sulla occupied it earlier in the year.

12. The Renewal of the Samnite Campaign

Part of the way through Appian's account of the campaign of 82 BC he suddenly introduces an army of 70,000 led by three men: M. Lamponius, Pontius Telesinus and Gutta.[77] The first two of these men were the only key surviving leaders of the Samnite alliance during the war of 91–87 BC, and were last seen (in our surviving sources at least) being defeated in their attempt to size Rhegium and take the war to Sicily (Chapter 3). The sudden appearance of this separate army in the latter stages of this war is intriguing, to say the least. From the few scattered references we have, we know that the armies of the coalition had Samnites and Lucanians amongst their number throughout the fighting of 83 and 82 BC.[78] Yet the apparent sudden emergence of this massive force led by the surviving Samnite leaders points to a new phenomenon. It appears that with Italy in chaos and Sulla gaining the upper hand, the Samnite leaders re-forged their earlier alliance and raised a fresh army to stop Sulla from gaining victory in Italy, thus uniting the two strands of the civil war.

Given the history between Sulla and the Samnite alliance and his victories against them in 89 BC, there was clearly no love lost between the two parties. Furthermore, it is clear that the alliance did not put much faith in Sulla's promises of keeping the newly established status quo. Both Florus and Velleius comment on the Samnite army:

Lamponius and Telesinus, the leaders of the Samnites, were laying waste to Campania and Etruria with even more brutality than Pyrrhus or Hannibal and were exacting vengeance on their own account under the pretence of helping their [the coalition's] cause.[79]

On the Kalends of November, Pontius Telesinus, a Samnite chief, brave in spirit and in action and hating to the core the very name of Rome, having collected about him 40,000 of the bravest and most steadfast youth who still persisted in retaining arms …[80]

Thus, for both sources, the Samnite army was fighting against Rome for their own cause, which merely overlapped with that of the coalition, in terms of ends rather than aims. This links in to the one great unknown factor about the Samnite alliance in this period: namely, what their actual status was in the period between 87 and 82 BC in Italy. The terms of the peace treaty that the surviving rebels conducted with Cinna in 87 BC are not clear beyond the issuing of citizenship to those who wanted it and the return of property and deserters (see Chapter 4). Given that they had negotiated from a position of strength and backed the winning side in 87 BC, many commentators have speculated that the Samnite alliance spent the intervening years with a far greater degree of autonomy from Rome. If that was the case, then it is clear that they believed that Sulla would not honour the Cinnan agreement and thus were forced to take the field once more as a quasi-independent alliance of states against Sulla.

In military terms, it seems at first that they were acting in concert with the remaining coalition leaders, Carbo and Norbanus, by attempting to relieve Praeneste and free Marius, taking up where the others had left off. Nevertheless, as Appian reports, this attempt was not successful, thanks to the reinforcing of the siege by Sulla himself.[81] However, with the flight of Carbo and Norbanus and the destruction of the remaining coalition forces at Clusium, this Samnite alliance army soon found itself the only opponent in the field against Sulla. Uniting with the survivors of the Clusium defeat, including the triumvirate of remaining coalition leaders, Brutus, Marcius and Carrinas, the alliance determined on a bold course of action: the seizure of Rome.

Throughout this war, control of Rome brought legitimacy, through control of the Senate and assemblies. With these organs of state, one's enemies could be declared enemies of the state and empire, and the wider world would acknowledge you as the legitimate representative of the Senate and People, providing access to far greater resources. Furthermore, although the coalition forces had been defeated in Italy, they still held the western empire and both consulships. If Rome could be retaken and held, then Marius could be freed from Praeneste and Carbo could return from Sicily. Two of the three coalition leaders with the Samnite army were serving praetors (Brutus being the urban praetor), who could legitimately direct the organs of the Republic, albeit backed up with a 70,000-strong Samnite army. Everything that Sulla had won to date could be overturned if they could seize and hold Rome.

Battle of Colline Gate

With Rome lightly defended, the united Samnite–coalition army marched swiftly towards Rome, camping in the Alban territory to the west of the River Tiber. Realizing the danger, Sulla rapidly mobilized all his forces and marched to Rome. With him was Crassus, though it seems that Pompeius, Metellus and Lucullus all remained in central and northern Italy. The Samnite–coalition forces got to Rome first, held as it was by a small Sullan garrison, but camped outside of the city waiting for Sulla, rather than take Rome itself. We can determine two reasons for this. First, the objective would have been to defeat Sulla in open battle rather than storm the city and then have to defend it. Second, attacking Rome, though militarily easy, given the uneven odds, was politically unwise, as the praetors would need all the legitimacy they could muster to control the organs of state.

Plutarch reports that a force of cavalry rode from Rome to attack the Samnite army, but was slaughtered. The only named casualty was an Ap. Claudius.[82] Having established superiority over the defenders of the city, the Samnite and coalition leaders waited for Sulla. Appian and Plutarch preserve the fullest account of the battle that followed:[83]

> [Sulla] encamped alongside the Colline Gate around the Temple of Venus about noon. The enemy were already encamped around the city. A battle was fought at once, late in the afternoon. On the right wing Sulla was victorious. His left wing was vanquished and fled to the gates. The old soldiers on the walls, when they saw the enemy rushing in with their own men, dropped the portcullis. It fell upon and killed many soldiers and many senators. But the majority, impelled by fear and necessity, turned and fought the enemy. The fighting continued

through the night and a great many were killed. The generals, Telesinus and Albinus, were killed and their camp was taken. Lamponius the Lucanian, Marcius, and Carrinas, and the other generals of the faction of Carbo, fled. It was estimated that 50,000 men on both sides lost their lives in this engagement. Prisoners, to the number of more than 8,000, were shot down with darts by Sulla because they were mostly Samnites. The next day, Marcius and Carrinas were captured and brought in. Sulla did not spare them because they were Romans, but killed them both and sent their heads to Lucretius at Praeneste to be displayed around the walls.[84]

Plutarch expands on this account, adding the detail that whilst the left flank collapsed, the right wing, commanded by Crassus won the day:

In the struggle which followed, and no other was so fierce, the right wing, where Crassus was posted, was brilliantly successful; but the left was hard pressed and in a sorry plight, when Sulla came to its assistance, mounted on a white horse that was mettlesome and very swift.[85]

... He entreated some of his men, threatened others, and laid hands on others still; but at last his left wing was completely shattered, and with the fugitives he sought refuge in his camp, after losing many friends amid acquaintances. Not a few also of those who had come out of the city to see the battle were trodden under foot and killed, so that it was thought that all was over with the city.[86]

But in the struggle near Rome, which was the last and greatest of all, while Sulla was defeated and his army repulsed and shattered, Crassus was victorious with the right wing, pursued the enemy till nightfall, and then sent to Sulla informing him of his success and asking supper for his soldiers.[87]

Plutarch reports that a number of survivors of the battle fled to the town of Antemnae, just north of ancient Rome, pursued by Crassus, who surrounded the town.[88] Sulla joined him the next day and struck a deal with a group of 3,000 of the survivors that he would grant them mercy if they turned on their fellow survivors. Only too eager to oblige the 3,000 attacked the other survivors and the town fell to Sulla easily. In total, Plutarch estimates that over 6,000, including the 3,000 traitors, mostly Samnites, were captured alive.[89]

Thus, it seems that Sulla nearly lost the battle of Colline Gate, and was forced to flee the battlefield himself, taking refuge in his own camp. Victory was only won by M. Licinius Crassus, who was the true victor. Nevertheless, the Samnite army had been destroyed and both the Samnites and the coalition had been defeated in Italy. Of the key leaders of the army, only L. Brutus Damasippus, the urban praetor, and M. Lamponius, the Lucanian commander, managed to escape. Rome and Italy fell to Sulla's control. However, the coalition forces still controlled the western half of Rome's empire and the younger Marius still held out in Praeneste.

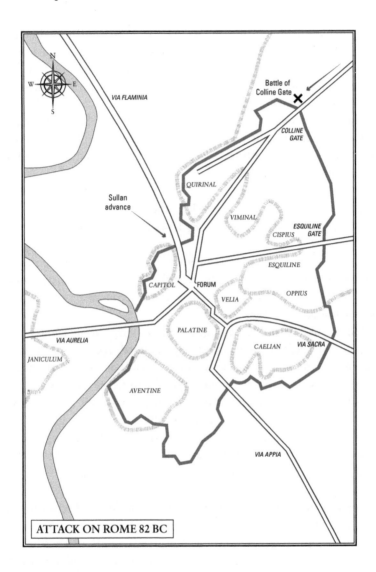

ATTACK ON ROME 82 BC

13. The Fall of Praeneste

The resolution of the siege of Praeneste was swift in coming. Upon hearing the news of the Sullan victory and seeing the grisly trophies of severed heads erected around the city, and knowing that there would be no aid from anyone in Italy, the inhabitants surrendered the city to Q. Lucretius Ofella. Unfortunately for the Praenestians, Ofella was not in a forgiving mood:

All the others who were taken in Praeneste he ordered to march out to the plain without arms, and when they had done so he chose out a very few who had been in any way serviceable to him. The remainder he ordered to be divided into three parts, consisting of Romans, Samnites, and Praenestians respectively.

1. Ruins of the Roman Forum. The turmoil in Rome was central to the events of 88 and 87 BC, with full-scale battles being fought in the streets. As the war progressed, control of Rome itself, with the Senate and Assemblies, was a key objective for all sides of the war. (*author's collection*)

2. A modern sculpture depicting
the Gracchi. Both men held the
Tribunate of the Plebs and their
reform programmes have been seen
by many (both ancient and modern)
as unleashing the violence that was
to engulf Roman politics in this
period. (*author's collection*)

3. Possible bust of C. Marius. He played
a crucial role in the wars of 88 and 87 BC,
laying siege to Rome itself and taking it by
storm. Yet he was to die a natural death,
leaving behind a legacy to be inherited by
first his son and then his nephew Caesar.
(*author's collection*)

4. Bust of L. Cornelius Sulla. A former protégé of Marius, his attacks on Rome in 88 and Italy in 83–82 were central to the first decade of the Civil War. He became overlord of Rome in 82 BC and initiated a reign of terror. He also nurtured the talents of Pompeius and Crassus, who were to dominate the New Republic. (*author's collection*)

5. Bust of King Mithridates VI of Pontus. He used Rome's internal struggles to great effect throughout the two decades of the war, even fighting under the banner of a Marius at one point. At his peak he had annexed all of Rome's eastern empire and his war with Rome extended beyond the Civil War period. (*photo courtesy of Philip Sidnell*)

6. A coin minted by the new Italian Federation. The minting of their own coinage was a tangible statement on the part of the Italian rebels, who sought to offer a viable alternative to the Roman Federation. (*author's collection*)

7. The reverse of an Italian coin minted by the new Italian Federation, and depicting a bull. The animal provided the federation with its own distinctive imagery, emphasizing a clear separation from Rome. (*author's collection*)

8. This coin issued by the Italian Federation shows four figures, each representing a different Italic people, swearing an oath of alliance. (*author's collection*)

9. Roman coin from 83 BC issued by the son of the Coalition consul Norbanus. (*author's collection*)

10. Roman coin from 83/82 BC issued by the Coalition government depicting Victory, part of a campaign of propaganda waged by both sides. (*author's collection*)

11. Sullan coin issued in 82 BC by the victorious Sullan regime, upon their seizure of Rome, depicting victory. Part of a campaign by Sulla to try to draw a line under the war. (*author's collection*)

12. Roman coin issued in 81 BC by Sulla's trusted lieutenant Q. Caecilius Metellus Pius. (*author's collection*)

13. Bust of Cn. Pompeius Magnus. The son of a Civil War commander, he dominated the latter stages of the war and came to exemplify the new generation of Civil War commanders. His alliance with Crassus brought the wars to a halt. (*author's collection*)

14. Bust of M. Licinius Crassus. Another son of a Civil War commander, he also found fame and fortune in the latter stages of the Civil War. His alliance with Pompeius brought the wars to a halt. (*author's collection*)

15. Bust of C. Iulius Caesar. Nephew to the elder Marius and cousin to the younger, Caesar took no part in the Civil War itself, and narrowly avoided being proscribed by Sulla. However, following the war he was able to inherit the Marian support and legacy. (*photo courtesy of Philip Sidnell*)

16. Bust of M. Tullius Cicero. Although he did not play an active part in the wars themselves, Cicero was in Rome during this period and provides first-hand insight into the characters and events involved. (*author's collection*)

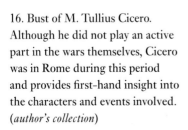

When this had been done he announced to the Romans by herald that they had merited death, but nevertheless he would pardon them. The others he massacred to the last man. He allowed their wives and children to go unharmed. He plundered the town, which was extremely rich at that time.[90]

Prior to this, Marius had sought refuge in an underground tunnel with a colleague. Fearing capture, the two men engaged in a suicide pact, but Marius struck first and with too much power leaving the other man unable to strike him through. In the end, he ordered a slave to stab him to death. Ofella cut off his head and sent it to Sulla in Rome for public display. Ofella also had executed a number of prominent coalition senators who had been with Marius in Praeneste. Others were sent to Rome for Sulla to deal with personally. With the fall of Praeneste, which was soon followed by that of Norba, Sulla had complete control of Italy and the eastern part of the empire.[91] The western part of the empire, Sicily, Spain and Africa, still remained in coalition hands.

Summary

This period of warfare raises a number of interesting points. In terms of the overall strategy, for the third time out of four, the side that took the offensive won the conflict. This happened in both 88 and 87 BC. The only exception being the Marsic and Samnite campaigns of 91–87 BC, but then they were aiming for different outcomes, namely the total defeat of Rome, rather than defeating other Romans to gain control of the city. Whilst ultimately Sulla's tactics of gaining momentum through quick victories (which put his numerically superior opponents on the back foot, whilst encouraging defections to his side) was successful, it is clear that this was not inevitable.

At times, this conflict appears to resemble previous wars, with Sulla as the new Pyrrhus or Hannibal, winning victory after victory, but constantly facing fresh Roman armies. Even after eighteen months of victories and the capture of Rome itself, he came within a whisker of total defeat at the Battle of Colline Gate, at the hands of the Samnite army. Had Crassus not been victorious on the right wing, Sulla would have been crushed and his alliance of opportunists placed under severe strain, leaving Pompeius, Lucullus and Metellus to fight the Samnites and possibly a freed Marius. What sort of Rome this would have produced is an interesting thought to contemplate?

What is clear is that Sulla was also fortunate (perhaps earning his title of Felix; see Chapter 7) in that he faced a poor calibre of opposition commanders: Carbo, Scipio, Norbanus, and even the younger Marius. The key figures that fought the wars of 88 and 87 BC, such as Marius, Cinna and Pompeius Strabo, were all dead and their successors all seemed to lack comparable military expertise. Given the strength of the coalition facing Sulla when he invaded Italy, one has to wonder whether he would have been successful if it had been led by someone with the military expertise of the elder Marius, or the leadership of Cinna. Nevertheless, Sulla was ultimately successful, in part because he attracted commanders of talent, Metellus, Lucullus, Pompeius, Crassus and the Servilii, all of whom contributed towards his victory. The clear danger lay in the fact that, whilst some of these men were supporters through genuine loyalty or shared beliefs, such as Lucullus or Metellus, others, notably Pompeius and Crassus, only supported him whilst it suited their own ends and whilst he represented the greater power. Therein lay the danger of a victory for the Sullan alliance. Sulla had won the latest round of civil warfare, which brought him control of Italy and the Senate. Yet he still faced the twin tasks of securing the rest of the Rome's empire and restoring the Republican system, so that civil warfare did not break out again after a respite.

Chapter 7

Peace in Italy; a World at War II (82–79 BC)

1. The Sullan Domination of Rome (82–79 BC)

Thus Rome once again found herself under the control of one man. However, unlike the period 86–84 BC, where first Cinna and then Carbo had dominated Rome, Sulla was in absolute control of the city in a manner in which the others had not been. Unlike 88 BC, Sulla had no consular colleague and was sole master of Rome. With military victory ensured, he set about consolidating his position. The remnants of the Senate were summoned to meet at the Temple of Bellona in the Campus Martius. To brutally emphasize the reality of the situation, Sulla had the 6,000 prisoners from Colline Gate, mostly Samnites, mustered near where the Senate were meeting and had them all slaughtered as he spoke to the Senate.

To legitimize his power, Sulla used two methods. In terms of past actions, he had an assembly called that ratified all of his acts as consul and proconsul in the period 88–82 BC. Looking forwards, he arranged for L. Valerius Flaccus, the *princeps senatus* (still protected by his kinsman's army in Gaul), to act as *interrex* in the absence of both consuls (one dead and one fled), and arranged for the assembly to elect him as dictator for an unspecified period – until the government of Rome and Italy was fully restored (based on his judgment), with full powers to pass whatever legislation he saw fit.[1] Thus Sulla elevated himself above the consulship to a level not seen in Rome since the time of the kings.

The dictatorship was an ancient office, only filled in times of military emergency, when sole rule was needed out of military necessity; and a clear check had been that it was limited to six months in duration. However, the office had not been used since the Second Punic War and had been in abeyance for 120 years. Sulla now held supreme power in Rome, far above any other magistrate and for an indeterminate time period (at his discretion). L. Valerius Flaccus became his deputy (the Master of the Horse). Consuls were still chosen (M. Tullius Decula and Cn. Cornelius Dolabella for 81 BC), but Sulla had now been placed above them. To emphasize this fact, his lictors bore twenty-four *fasces* in front of him and he maintained a bodyguard. He seems to have held the dictatorship from late 82 to 79 BC and even held the consulship of 80 BC concurrently, along with his loyal deputy, Q. Caecilius Metellus Pius.[2]

Throughout the years 82 and 81 BC, Sulla used this supreme position to enact, or in some cases re-enact, key reforms to the Roman political system, which he believed would stabilize the Republican constitution. The tribunate's powers were once again curbed, with senatorial approval needed for all legislation and any office holder disbarred from further office.[3] The number of praetors was increased to eight and quaestors to twenty. Repeated consulships were prohibited and set ages were laid down in law for the various offices of the *cursus honorum* and the order in which they must be held. The courts were reformed and the depleted Senate had 300 equestrians added to its number.[4] A fragment of Sallust even refers to marriage laws and sumptuary legislation.[5] It has been argued that his dictatorship may have had censorial powers and thus some form of census may have been conducted.[6] Thus Rome was given a Sullan constitution, in an attempt to create, or in his mind recreate, the ideal Republic.[7]

To enhance his personal image, Sulla undertook a range of measures. He celebrated a triumph, not over his civil war opponents, but over Mithridates, the Treaty of Dardanus being overlooked. He took the title of 'Felix' (lucky), ascribing his success to divine providence (rather than Crassus at Colline Gate). Gilded statues of him were raised in Rome, his monuments rebuilt and special games instituted to celebrate his achievements. In fact, Sulla summoned so many athletes from Greece to celebrate his games that Eusebius records that events at the Olympic Games had to be cancelled as a consequence.[8] Sulla also began the reconstruction of the Capitol, destroyed by fire in 83 BC, which allowed him to symbolize his rebuilding of a new Roman Republic.

Unsurprisingly, these reforms and aggrandizements had a darker side. When Sulla and Pompeius took Rome in 88 BC, twelve men were declared enemies of the state. When Marius and Cinna took Rome in 87 BC, a massacre of their opponents ensued. By 82 BC, it seems that Sulla had amassed more than just twelve enemies. The massacre of the 6,000 prisoners seems to have been merely the start of a long process of state-sanctioned murder. Rather than random acts, Sulla drew up a list of his enemies to be murdered and their lands and wealth confiscated to rebuild the state coffers. Thus were borne the infamous proscription lists. Anyone whose name was on one such list could be legally murdered, with the killer given a portion of the dead man's estate as a reward, the remainder being auctioned off and the proceeds going to the state. Furthermore, the descendants of the proscribed were barred from ever holding political office. One man who notoriously made a fortune from buying these properties, and perhaps even arranging names to be put on the lists, was M. Licinius Crassus, who soon became Rome's richest man, with an unsavoury reputation to match.

According to the sources, the original list contained just eighty names, listing prominent coalition leaders and supporters. However, this was soon followed by a second list in the hundreds and other supplementary lists covering all of Italy, thus unleashing slaughter across the city and the peninsula.[9] Sulla's murders did not restrict themselves to his enemies. Q. Lucretius Ofella, who had captured

Praeneste for Sulla (see Chapter 6), decided to stand as consul, against both Sulla's wishes and the new *cursus honorum*. Whilst campaigning in the Forum he was murdered on Sulla's orders, with Sulla himself present, again making a clear point about who ruled Rome.[10] Marius himself did not escape reprisals, despite his death some four years earlier, as Sulla had his corpse dragged from his crypt, paraded through Rome and torn apart.

One notable survivor of these proscriptions was L. Cornelius Scipio Asiaticus (Cos. 84), who famously had lost an army to Sulla without a single engagement (see Chapter 6). Appian reports that Scipio had come to some form of arrangement with Sulla, but soon violated it and was proscribed.[11] He managed to evade the assassins and lived in exile in Massilia (Marseille) for the rest of his life. A second notable survivor was a young man by the name of C. Iulius Caesar. Although he had not taken part in the coalition fighting, he had prominent Marian and Cinnan family connections. His uncle by marriage was C. Marius himself, and he was married to Cinna's daughter. When summoned before Sulla and ordered to divorce his wife, extraordinarily, he refused point blank, and later had to flee the city to evade murder. No further comment is needed on the implications for western civilization had Sulla been quicker to condemn him.

Aside from the personal slaughter, Sulla took reprisals against prominent coalition-supporting towns and cities across Italy. Walls and fortresses were destroyed, garrisons installed, land confiscated, fines levied and veteran colonies planted next to them on their confiscated lands (see below). The planting of colonies served multiple purposes. Appian reports that Sulla demobilized twenty-three legions of his veterans, creating a string of colonies across Italy, whilst the *Periochae* of Livy puts the number at forty-seven legions.[12] Not only did this demobilize his forces, but it created a string of Sullan strongholds, many planted at key strategic locations across Italy, ensuring that he had control of the peninsula and the peoples within. Not only could these veterans be used to keep any rebellious locals in check, but as they were given confiscated land, and funded from proscriptions, in theory they would have a vested interest in ensuring the Sullan legislation in Rome continued to be in force. Sulla took similar steps in Rome itself by freeing 10,000 slaves of the victims of the proscriptions and enrolling them amongst the urban plebeians, giving him a ready-made force of supporters in Rome to call on.

Sulla also seems to have taken additional precautions with respect to the foremost of the young men who followed him, by arranging a marriage alliance between himself and Cn. Pompeius. Pompeius was ordered to divorce his wife and marry Sulla's stepdaughter Amelia (the daughter of Sulla's wife's previous husband, M. Aemilius Scaurus). On paper such a marriage alliance would tie Pompeius closer to him, but the manner in which Sulla went about it only seemed to create further tensions, as Pompeius was ordered to abandon his wife and Amelia was pregnant with her husband's child at the time.[13] In any event, Amelia died in childbirth soon afterwards, negating any personal ties between the two men.

Needless to say, Sulla's period of rule seemed to create as many issues as it solved. His proscriptions caused a massive disruption to the landholding patterns of Italy, creating a large group of the dispossessed and disenfranchised, a number of whom seem to have turned to banditry. A number of those men he settled on land soon proved to be unsuited to farming, creating even more dispossessed, all of which created social discontent and therefore potential political capital (see Appendix II). With a number of the proscribed fleeing Italy, another group of exiles was created, all with friends and kinsmen back in Rome and Italy who would agitate for their pardoning and return. The emasculation of the tribunate proved to be incredibly unpopular amongst both the urban plebeians and a number of the more ambitious senators, with calls for its restoration being made almost immediately. Finally, as was seen in Italy, Africa and Asia, over the next few years, Sulla's reforms had done nothing to curb the excesses of mutinous armies or unscrupulous commanders, all of whom had seen both the horrors, but also the rewards, that naked force against one's own state could bring. In that regard, Sulla could not erase his own example, and in many respects he undermined his own authority by the method of his coming to power.

2. Renewed Civil Conflict?

Interestingly, there exists a fragment of a history by John of Antioch, a seventh century AD chronicler, which provides the following outrageous fragment of history and one which continues to baffle historians to this day.

> Upon the renewal of civil strife, the Roman Senate proposed that Sulla be granted dictatorial powers. For all the knights had banded together, wishing to rule rather than be ruled and since they repeatedly attempted to oppose the Senate the situation was intolerable to the government. Accordingly Sulla, having again attained this office, made a secret agreement with men throughout Italy, unbeknown to anyone at Rome, and ordered them to arm themselves with daggers and enter the city at the time when the Roman people would be starting to celebrate the festival of Rhea (this normally occurs about the first of January), so that with their help he might destroy the urban knights. Since the Italian rabble was hostile to the soldiers they duly appeared on the appointed day, began to riot, and by enlisting the help of the populace did away with a large number of knights. While these events were taking place in the city, reports from the subject peoples everywhere reached Rome, announcing incursions of barbarians and suggesting that the Roman consuls and praetors should occupy their territories with all speed. I give this on the authority of Plutarch. Diodorus, however, says that no such reports existed, and that Sulla concocted them as a means of distracting the people and ending the disorders. For he promptly enrolled all the armies and assigned them commanders, and thus rid the city of the whole multitude.[14]

To say that this information related in this fragment cannot be reconciled with the known history of this period would be an understatement, and a number of commentators are happy to dismiss it. Yet John quotes both Diodorus and Plutarch as his sources, though clearly Plutarch's biography of Sulla has no mention of these events. To his credit, Katz took up the challenge of trying to integrate this fragment and would date it to 88 BC, based upon John having a very distorted view of the events of that year.[15]

What we have here is an equestrian plot being foiled by Sulla, who is recalled to a second dictatorship. There is much that is unclear and some that is clearly anachronistic, such as the festival of Rhea, which did not exist in Republican times. Yet at the heart of it lies Sulla being recalled to the dictatorship to crush an equestrian plot using both men from Italy, who could easily be his veterans, and a mixture of bloodshed and deception to crush it. We know little detail of the years 81–79 BC as seen from the discussion over the length of Sulla's dictatorship. Yet it is entirely possible that he laid down his dictatorship earlier than 79 BC, only to have to take it up again when civil strife broke out in Rome. As will be discussed below (Chapter 8), such an occurrence of civil strife did soon follow his resignation of 79 BC. Furthermore, the fragments we have from Diodorus do contain a wealth of detail not found in any of our other surviving sources for the period. Thus, whilst we cannot say that this fragment can be taken at face value, we must not dismiss it or ignore its existence, as it could possibly shed light on an invaluable insight into the period 81–79, which is otherwise lost to us.

3. Civil War in Rome's Empire

As stated earlier, Sulla's victory at Colline Gate gave him control of Rome and Italy, which he could add to the Roman east, which he had already secured. Yet this victory did not automatically mean an end to the civil war as a number of coalition commanders had not only fled Italy, but had control of elements of Rome's western empire, notably Sicily, Spain and Africa. Gaul too lay under the control of the noted neutral C. Valerius Flaccus. A passage of Plutarch provides a tidy summary of the situation in the western part of Rome's empire, which faced Sulla:

> After this, word was brought to Sulla that Perperna was making himself master of Sicily and furnishing a refuge in that island for the survivors of the opposite faction, that Carbo was hovering in those waters with a fleet, that Domitius had forced an entry into Africa, and that many other exiled men of note were thronging to those parts, all, in fact, who had succeeded in escaping his proscriptions.[16]

Italy

Although Sulla had overall control of Italy after the Battle of Colline Gate, it seems that several towns rebelled against his rule, either in response to his campaign of reprisals, or for other reasons. The one clearly identified case we have was the Etruscan town of Volaterrae (Volterra), in which a garrison rebelled against its commander in c80 BC. Interestingly, the garrison was commanded by a C. Papirius Carbo, who was the brother of Carbo the consul, and chief enemy of Sulla, which shows the divisions within families the war caused.[17] We are fortunate that both Valerius Maximus and a fragment of Granius Licinianus preserve details of the rebellion:[18]

> The inhabitants of Volaterrae surrendered to the Romans, after an uprising in which the ex-praetor Carbo, whom Sulla had put in charge of them, was stoned to death (he was the brother of Cn. Carbo). The proscribed men were expelled from the city, and were cut down by cavalry sent by the consuls Claudius and Servilius.[19]
>
> Wickedly violent too was the army which took the life of C. Carbo, brother of Carbo, three times consul, who had tried somewhat abruptly and unbendingly to tighten military discipline, relaxed because of the civil wars. They thought it better to be sullied by a heinous crime than to change their depraved, vile ways.[20]

The Volaterrae incident reveals two factors. The first is that Sulla's grip on Italy was not as firm as might be thought and that he still had to campaign there as late as 80 BC. The second is that armies were still mutinying and murdering their commanders.

Sardinia

It seems that Sardinia fell to Sullan forces whilst the Italian campaign was still ongoing. All we have left in the ancient sources is a brief note in the *Periochae* of Livy, which tells us that L. Philippus (Cos. 91) captured the island from the coalition governor, the praetor Q. Antonius Balbus, who was killed. No other details are given, though Philippus' defection to Sulla's cause is an interesting point to note.[21]

Sicily

In terms of the Sicilian campaign, we know slightly more, thanks to a number of brief references to it, a result of the presence of Cn. Pompeius, who was dispatched by Sulla to retake the island. Prior to Pompeius' dispatch, Diodorus refers to Sulla negotiating with the coalition governor of the island, M. Perperna, which is interesting in itself. It would seem, therefore, that whilst campaigning in Italy he opened negotiations with at least one coalition provincial governor with an eye to reconciling them to his rule. In Perperna's case, however, it seems he was a staunch supporter of the Marii, who even threatened to invade Italy and relieve the siege of Praeneste.[22]

Following the capture of Rome, it seems that Sicily became the headquarters of the remaining coalition forces. Several sources report a gathering of the surviving coalition leaders on the island. Cn. Papirius Carbo the senior coalition leader and consul travelled from Africa to Sicily, where he was joined by M. Iunius Brutus, one of the twelve *hostes* of 88 BC.

Pompeius appears to have been dispatched by Sulla, apparently also with the command ratified by the Senate, prior to Sulla being confirmed as dictator, thus placing it almost immediately after Sulla secured Rome. All we are told is that he was dispatched with a large force, but again we are not told the size.[23] This highlights the importance and urgency that Sulla placed upon this campaign, denying the coalition leaders the chance to regroup, and on Sicily, which could be a formidable stronghold.[24] In reality, it turned out to be nothing of the sort, for when Pompeius crossed over to Sicily, Perperna fled the island without a fight.[25] Carbo and Brutus seem to have fled to the island of Cossyra, off the Sicilian coast (modern Pantelleria), but seem to have done so in haste. Orosius reports that their ultimate destination was Egypt, itself in the middle of a civil war (see below).[26]

The *Periochae* of Livy preserves a note that Carbo dispatched Brutus back to Sicily (the port of Lilybaeum), by fishing boat, to see how far Pompeius had advanced.[27] Brutus, however, was soon captured and committed suicide. Shortly afterwards, and under unknown circumstances, Carbo and a number of coalition figures were also captured by Pompeius' men. The others were executed on the spot, but Carbo was brought before Pompeius himself prior to his execution. Thus the coalition lost its most senior surviving leader and the death of the last remaining consul cleared the way for Sulla's dictatorship in Rome.

Interestingly, Perperna seems to have escaped this slaughter and laid low for several years (see Chapter 9). This is in contrast to the fate of his colleagues who seem to have gone from a position of apparent strength to one of disarray almost overnight. We do not know the details of Perperna's flight, but it does seem that he ensured his own safety, whilst leaving his colleagues behind in some difficulty. Pompeius then appears to have spent the remainder of 82 BC reordering the province and ensuring its loyalty to the new regime in Rome. However, he then received orders, from both Sulla and the Senate, to transport his army to Africa and take up command against the coalition forces there.

Africa and Numidia

Since 84 BC, the Roman province of Africa had been commanded by C. Fabius Hadrianus, who had defeated Metellus Pius and Crassus' insurrection there (see Chapter 5). However, it seems that after recovering the province, he soon became avaricious and cruel to citizen and native alike. In addition, Orosius refers to him raising a slave army in an attempt to gain personal control of Roman Africa.[28] It seems, therefore, that Fabius used the chaos of the war in Italy to attempt to break away from Roman rule and create his own quasi-independent kingdom. However, the one line of Orosius is the only source that notes this. What is clear is that at some point in 82 BC there was an uprising in the capital of Roman Africa, Utica, against Fabius, which ended in his being burnt to death in own headquarters. Cicero, who was contemporaneous with the events held him up to be a notorious example of a corrupt governor.[29]

The death of Fabius seemed to have left the province, or at least Utica, hostile to the coalition. We do not hear of any Sullan forces there, merely locals who would wish to curry favour with the new regime in Rome. However, during 82 BC, the province became one of the key destinations for coalition figures fleeing Sulla's invasion of Italy. Plutarch reports that coalition forces (of unknown size) forced an entry into the province under the command of Cn. Domitius Ahenobarbus.[30] Orosius states that Domitius was one of Cinna's sons in law (making him the brother in law of C. Iulius Caesar), but prior to the African campaign, we find no trace of him in our surviving sources.[31] Whilst we have no details of the fighting, we do know that Roman Africa quickly became a mustering point for retreating coalition forces, possibly including the consul Carbo himself for a time. Having regrouped, it seems that the key surviving coalition leaders moved back to Sicily to coordinate with M. Perperna and possibly organize a counter-attack on Italy. As detailed above, however, the swift arrival of Pompeius, combined with Perperna's swift departure, ended that plan. With the fall of Sicily, Ahenobarbus now found himself the de-facto leader of the coalition forces in the west.

In early 81 BC, Pompeius invaded Roman Africa, at the head of six legions, and with a fleet of 120 galleys and 800 transports. Upon landing at Utica, Plutarch informs us that another 7,000 coalition troops deserted to Pompeius.[32] Domitius, however, had not been idle and had forged an alliance with the Roman client state of Numidia and its king, Iarbas, and between them they had amassed an army of nearly 30,000 (now less the 7,000 that had deserted).

We are not told why the Numidians threw in their lot with the coalition at this point. Although the kings of Numidia had been clients of Marius, they had sided with Rome against him in 88 BC (see Chapter 3), yet they now actively sided against the faction that held Rome. It is possible that the Numidians themselves were undergoing another period of civil conflict, and one theory that has been advanced is that Marius helped to overthrow Hiempsal II (King of Numidia) during the 88–87 BC period and put Iarbas, a loyal puppet, on the throne (see Chapter 4).[33] Nevertheless, it does show that the coalition still had the ability to amass significant military resources and continue the civil war, despite the loss of Italy and Sicily. In any event, within days of landing at Utica, Pompeius faced Domitius and Iarbas in battle. We are fortunate that Plutarch preserves a detailed account, Orosius a briefer one:

Domitius now drew up his army against Pompeius, with a ravine in front of him which was rough and difficult to cross, but a violent storm of wind and rain began in the morning and continued to rage, so that he gave up the idea of fighting that day and ordered a retreat. But Pompeius, taking advantage of this opportunity, advanced swiftly to the attack, and crossed the ravine. The enemy met his attack in a disorderly and tumultuous fashion, not all of them, indeed, nor with any uniformity; besides, the wind veered round and drove the rain into their faces. However, the Romans also were troubled by the storm, since they could not see one another clearly, and Pompeius himself narrowly escaped death by not being recognized, when a soldier demanded the countersign from him and he gave it rather slowly. Nevertheless, they routed the enemy with great slaughter (it is said that out of 20,000 only 3,000 escaped), and hailed Pompeius as *imperator*. And when he said he would not accept the honour as long as the camp of the enemy was intact, but that if they thought him worthy of the appellation, they must first destroy that, his soldiers immediately made an assault upon the ramparts; and Pompeius fought without his helmet, for fear of a peril like the one he had just escaped. The camp was soon taken, and Domitius was slain. Then some of the cities submitted at once to Pompeius, and others were taken by storm. King Iarbus also, the confederate of Domitius, was captured, and his kingdom given to Hiempsal.[34]

After crossing to Africa, Pompeius killed 18,000 men after they had made a sortie near Utica. In this battle, the Marian leader Domitius was slain while fighting in the vanguard. This same Pompeius also pursued Iarbus, the King of Numidia, and forced Bogudes, the son of Bocchus, who was king of the Moors, to deprive Iarbus of all his troops. Pompeius put Iarbus to death as soon as he had captured the town of Bulla to which the latter had returned.[35]

Thus in one bold surprise attack, Pompeius had defeated the coalition forces in Africa and secured the province to Rome once more. He then immediately followed this with an invasion of Numidia itself, having already captured their king and swiftly subdued the province, placing a new client king on the throne (Hiempsal II). According to Plutarch, the whole campaign, from landing to subduing Numidia, took only forty days.[36]

Plutarch is swift to sing Pompeius' achievements here. Certainly, the victory was won by a bold move, and one that, as he says, could have ended in tragedy.[37] He did, however, face a scratch force of Numidians and Romans commanded by a general of whom we know nothing, other than that he allowed himself to be taken by a surprise attack. Numidia fell quickly, but then this campaign was more about the placing of a new client king on the throne, and seems to have faced little serious military opposition. Nevertheless, in less than a year Pompeius had crushed virtually all the remainder of the coalition forces in the west, and all at the age of just 24.

However, under the new Sullan system, commands such as Pompeius' were technically impossible for a young man, and he would have to wait until he was 39 (67/66 BC) for the chance to hold even a praetorship. Unsurprisingly, once he had secured Africa and Numidia, Sulla issued orders for him to send all but one legion home, await a replacement as governor of Africa, then return home and step down from a military role. It was at this juncture that the failure of the Sullan system became clear; personal ambition and command of an army were still a potent combination, and the civil war had now bred a generation of young men brought up knowing little else. Whilst officially Pompeius attempted to comply with Sulla's orders, his army apparently refused to do so, and also apparently urged him to lead them in an attack on Rome once more (such actions being commonplace now).[38] Whilst some may wish to view Pompeius' actions as wholly innocent, based on an army's loyalty to its commander, others may see a more Machiavellian motive behind all this. Pompeius, it seems, had learnt the crucial lesson of the civil war; by now the mere implied threat of an attack on Rome and the horrors that would entail, would be enough for a general to get what he wanted, even from Sulla.

With his regime barely a year old, the last thing that Sulla wanted was to have another round of civil warfare, especially against a young and talented protégé of his. It was thus arranged that Pompeius and his army returned to Rome to a hero's welcome, where Sulla saluted him as Pompeius Magnus (the Great). Further showing the power Pompeius could wield, he demanded a triumph for his African campaign, despite being just 24 and never having held a formal magistracy. Once again, Sulla refused, and once again, Pompeius showed that the implied threat of force was now just as powerful a weapon in Roman politics as force itself. Plutarch reports that Pompeius told Sulla that 'more people worship the rising sun than the setting sun;' in other words, the people and the army would follow a young charismatic general, rather than side with an aged tyrant.[39] Not wishing to plunge the Republic back into fresh warfare, Sulla caved in once again and Pompeius had his triumph, and only then disbanded his forces; remaining a quiet force in Rome for the remainder of Sulla's period of dominance.

Gaul

Securing Gaul proved to be a far easier task, as it was under the command of C. Valerius Flaccus, who throughout the preceding decade had held the Spanish and Gallic provinces, ruling them almost as a semi-autonomous fiefdom (see Chapter 5). Flaccus seems to have pursued a policy of neutrality, passively supporting whoever had control of Rome at the time. His brother had been suffect consul of 86, along with Cinna, and his kinsman was *princeps senatus* under the Cinnan regime. Yet when Sulla took Rome the Valerii Flacii effortlessly swung behind him, with L. Valerius proposing the election of Sulla as dictator and taking up the subordinate position as master of the horse. It should also be noted that he survived both the major proscriptions of 82 BC, no doubt secured by his kinsman's army stationed in Gaul. With the Valerii Flacii secure under Sulla, C. Valerius Flaccus finally returned to Rome, after more than a decade and celebrated a triumph for his campaigns in Spain and Gaul. This too was followed by the disbanding of his armies and a retirement into obscurity; a most remarkable man for his masterly inactivity during this civil war.

Spain[40]

Securing Spain, however, would prove to be another matter, as the province was commanded by Q. Sertorius, now the most senior surviving coalition commander. Sertorius had been sent to Spain in 83 BC by the coalition, possibly in disgrace for his actions during the seizure of the town of Suessa (see Chapter 6). Whilst most sources record that he won over the natives of the region by reducing the Roman burden on them, only Appian records that he clashed with the man (who is unnamed) he was sent to replace. It seems that the previous Roman governor refused to recognize his authority, probably due to a belief that Sulla was most likely to be victorious in Italy. All that Appian says is that there was trouble between the two men, but whether this led to a military clash is not stated.[41]

Nevertheless, by 82 BC, Sertorius had control of the Roman provinces in Spain and was proving to be a popular governor. With the fall of Rome, he armed both natives and Roman colonists and prepared to repel the inevitable Sullan invasion. To recover Spain, Sulla sent out a proconsul, C. Annius, who is otherwise unknown to us from our few surviving sources. Anticipating a Sullan invasion, Sertorius sent a legate, L. Iulius Salinator with 6,000 men to guard the routes across the Pyrenees. Faced with such a strong defensive position, Plutarch reports that Annius, who seems to have arrived early in 81 BC, did not attempt to force a passage but merely camped in the foothills.[42] However, once again, a military encounter was settled by a mutiny, as Salinator was murdered by a Calpurnius Lanarius, one of his legates. Upon his death, the garrison guarding the mountain passage abandoned their position, but Plutarch does not state whether they fled, or defected to Annius.[43]

All we know of the campaigns that followed is that Annius advanced into Spain, with what Plutarch describes as a large force, and routed all of Sertorius' forces in a short time.[44] Despite his acknowledged military prowess and the supposed loyalty of the natives, Sertorius' grip on Spain collapsed remarkably quickly and he found himself seeking refuge in New Carthage (Cartagene) with just 3,000 men. With no other option, he fled by sea to northern Africa and the Mauri Kingdom. However, Sertorius fared no better there than in Spain, and upon landing was attacked and driven back to sea by the Mauri.

According to Plutarch, Sertorius then returned to Spain and was again repulsed; Spann has argued that he attempted an attack on a coastal city.[45] Increasingly desperate, he then sailed to the Balearic Islands and allied with a contingent of Cilician pirates operating from there. Annius seems to have taken the initiative once more, assembling a naval force and 5,000 men and attacking

Sertorius and the pirates. As Plutarch details, the battle was abandoned due to heavy seas and strong winds, which threw Sertorius' lighter ships against the rocks. Sertorius apparently managed to escape with a few ships, but was driven out to sea by the heavy storms.[46] Abandoning Spain, he once again sought refuge in northern Africa.

Thus, by the middle of 81 BC, Spain had been recovered by the Sullan regime, which had comprehensively driven Sertorius from the province and forced him to seek refuge amongst the native kingdoms of northern Africa. One can't help but comment on the rapid collapse of Sertorius' grip on Spain. It seems that mutinies amongst his own men and the refusal of the natives to support him fatally undermined his defence of the Spanish provinces. With the fall of Spain, the Sullan regime had finally reunified Rome's empire, after a decade of division.

Egypt

Although no fighting took place in Egypt, it emerges on the periphery of the civil war. As detailed earlier (Chapter 5), Egypt had undergone its own civil war earlier in the decade, and the losing contender for the throne, Ptolemy XI Alexander, had ended up in Sulla's entourage. It is perhaps for this reason that Orosius reports that Carbo and his supporters were making for Egypt, following the fall of Sicily (see above).[47] Egypt was the Mediterranean's richest province and had a Pharaoh who would not be well disposed towards Sulla, who was harbouring his rival. In any event, the death of Carbo and his followers made the issue a moot point.[48] However, in 80 BC Sulla intervened directly and placed his man, Ptolemy XI Alexander, on the Egyptian throne. Unfortunately for him, Ptolemy promptly assassinated a rival claimant (Bernice) and was killed in a riot in Alexandria. Nevertheless, this incident shows that Sulla had designs on a closer control of Egypt and that Roman interference in that country was on the increase. Interestingly, it seems that Ptolemy XI Alexander willed his new kingdom to Rome, which brought the issue of Egyptian independence to the fore of post-civil-war Roman politics.[49] Nevertheless, Egypt retained her independence until becoming entangled in Rome's Second Civil War.

Asia Minor – The Second Mithridatic War (83–81 BC)

Although an analysis of the Mithridatic Wars falls outside the scope of this work, some mention needs to be made of the Second Mithridatic War, between 83 and 81 BC, as it highlights a number of the factors that underpinned the civil war. Upon concluding the Treaty of Dardanus with Mithridates, Sulla had left Asia under the command of a legate, L. Licinius Murena, who commanded two legions, both of which were from the army of Fimbria, who had deserted to Sulla. During 83 BC, with Sulla engaged in war in Italy, Murena launched a pre-emptive invasion of Pontus, and stirred up the former Mithridatic general Archelaus, who had defected from Mithridates when suspected of collusion with the Romans. Hampered by the treaty he had agreed with Sulla, Mithridates appealed to both the Senate and Sulla to intervene, not taking up arms to prevent Murena's plundering. During 82 BC, Murena broke off his invasion to return to allied territories with his spoils, where he was intercepted by a senatorial envoy who ordered him to desist.

However, Murena promptly ignored this order and once again invaded Pontus. This time, however, Mithridates resolved to defend himself. He intercepted Murena at an unnamed river and heavily defeated him (though as usual we have no numbers for the forces involved or the casualties). Murena was forced out of Pontus and Mithridates spent the rest of the year crushing the remaining Roman garrisons in the county. At some point early in 81 BC, Sulla directly ordered Murena to desist and restored peace with Mithridates. Murena was recalled to Rome where, extraordinarily, he was granted a triumph for his campaign.[50]

This war highlights a number of key issues that still plagued Rome. A rogue general with two rogue legions (who had betrayed both of their previous commanders) made war on a Roman ally without orders and ignored commands to withdraw. Furthermore, when Murena did finally desist, following a heavy defeat, he returned to Rome and, rather than being disciplined, was awarded a triumph. Sulla's failure to discipline Murena, combined with his reluctance to continue the war against Mithridates, showed the weakness of Sulla's position. Whilst he could command the murders of unarmed men in Italy, he now had a second general at the head of an army openly defying him and again demanding to be awarded a triumph. In terms of foreign policy, Mithridates now had a fresh victory against a Roman army and had once again suffered no adverse consequences, further enhancing his reputation. It seems that Sulla was determined to focus on political reforms and restoring unity and peace to Rome's empire, rather than foreign wars, which is itself an interesting reversal from the situation in 88 BC (see Appendix I).

On the face of it, Sullan forces had defeated the coalition forces throughout the western half of Rome's empire and killed all the leading coalition generals. However, there were two exceptions. The first was L. Cornelius Scipio 'Asiaticus' (Cos. 83). Having failed in various military campaigns in Italy and in some form of insurrection in Rome itself, he fled to Massilia, where he remained in exile for the rest of his life. He seems to have been such a peripheral figure that the Sullan regime seemed perfectly happy to allow him to live out his days. The same could not be said of the other remaining coalition leader, Q. Sertorius.

4. The Civil War in Northwest Africa (81 BC)

Of all the coalition generals, it was only Q. Sertorius who survived the warfare of the years 83/82 BC still in command of a military force. Having been driven out of Spain by the Sullan commander C. Annius (see above), Sertorius and his forces, along with a force of Cilician pirates, took refuge in northern Africa, in the Mauri Kingdom (Mauretania), where they became involved in another local civil war that was raging there. Ironically, Sertorius and his men took up arms against King Ascalis, who had apparently been overthrown, whilst his Cilician allies fought on the king's side, though we have no other details of the nature of this Maurian civil war. It soon becomes clear that, at least in Plutarch's narrative, if Sertorius was not the leader of the rebellion upon arrival, he soon became its leader, through force of arms and military success.

Unnamed Battle

Plutarch reports that Sertorius and his forces took part in a battle against King Ascalis, and that Sertorius defeated the king, though we have no other details and no independent verification of Sertorius' role.[51] Following the battle, Sertorius then laid siege to the king in the city of Tingis (modern Tangiers).

Battle of Tingis

Given Sertorius' high profile, what started as a Maurian civil war, soon transformed into a renewal of the Roman civil war, when a Roman commander named Paccianus was dispatched to defeat Sertorius. Plutarch states that he was dispatched by Sulla himself, but as Spann points out, it was more likely that he was sent by C. Annius in Spain to finish the job.[52] Again, we have few details, but once Paccianus' forces landed he moved to relieve Ascalis and gave battle to Sertorius. Once again, Roman fought Roman, this time on the very western tip of northern Africa. Sertorius was not only victorious over the forces of Paccianus, but is reported to have slain the general himself. Following the battle, Plutarch reports, the survivors of Paccianus' army joined Sertorius.[53]

Having defeated the Roman relief force, Sertorius then successfully stormed the city of Tingis, capturing King Ascalis and his brothers (though we are not informed as to their fate). Thus, by the end of 81 BC, Sertorius found himself in command of at least the city and its environs, if not the whole region of northwest Africa. Whilst on the one hand he now had a power base and additional men and resources, especially naval ones, there was the question of how long the Sullan regime would allow a coalition powerbase in northern Africa, since it would soon act as a rallying point for all the coalition survivors from the other defeats of the last two years. Again, by a process of elimination, Sertorius was now the leading figure of the coalition and the only one still fighting the Sullan regime.

5. The Renewal of Civil War in Spain (80 BC onwards)

The winter of 81/80 BC presented Sertorius with a fresh opportunity to renew the civil war in Spain. For the past decade, the ties between Spain and Rome had been loosened, not only through ongoing warfare and rebellions, but by the long period of the governorship of C. Valerius Flaccus and the only nominal acknowledgement of suzerainty to whoever happened to be in charge of Rome at the time. This would all have changed with the arrival of a fresh Sullan governor, in the form of C. Annius in 81 BC, and the expulsion of Sertorius. Roman governors would now have been eager to reassert Roman dominance over the region, which naturally would have provoked a native backlash. On this particular occasion, the Lusitanians (in modern Portugal), who had traditionally been uneasy under Roman rule, sent ambassadors to Sertorius in Tingis, offering him command of their proposed rebellion against Rome. It is not difficult to see why Sertorius eagerly accepted the offer to return to Spain. Sooner or later, Roman forces would come to dislodge him from Tingis and lay siege to the city, whereas a return to Spain offered him far larger forces than he could muster in Africa and the chance of a powerbase in the Spanish interior. Once again, a provincial rebellion and the Roman civil war became entangled.

Thus in the spring of 80 BC, Sertorius crossed from Africa to Spain and launched his insurrection. We must consider the various objectives here. For the Lusitanians and the other Spanish tribes that joined them, the clear objective was independence from Roman rule. Yet they turned to a Roman commander to achieve this, which at best would have only been an alliance of convenience. For Sertorius the aim must have been the continuation of the civil war and the conquest of Spain, to act as a powerbase for an invasion of Italy. The most interesting question centres on what would happen to Spain under a government led by Sertorius? Surely he would never have countenanced Spanish independence under his regime? All we can say is that whilst the battle to free Spain from Sullan Roman rule continued, all such thoughts must have been secondary. Both Plutarch and a fragment of Sallust record details of the crossing from northern Africa to Lusitania (see Map 12).

> For with the 2,600 men whom he called Romans, and a motley band of 700 Libyans who crossed over into Lusitania with him, to whom he added 4,000 Lusitanian slingers and 700 horsemen, he waged war with four Roman generals, under whom were 120,000 infantry, 6,000 horsemen, 2,000 bowmen and slingers, and an untold number of cities, while he himself had at first only twenty all told.[54]
>
> Therefore Sertorius, leaving behind a small force in Mauretania, took advantage of a dark night and a favourable current; he tried to move secretly and quickly, in order to make an unopposed crossing.[55]

It seems, however, that the crossing was not unopposed, and that the Sertorian fleet was intercepted off the coast of Spain, near the city of Mellaria.

Battle of Mellaria
The first battle that the Sertorian forces fought was a naval engagement, in the western straits of Gibraltar, off the city of Mellaria. The Sertorian naval forces

must have been bolstered by the capture of the port of Tingis and the seizure of Maurian, and possibly Cilician, ships.[56] Here he was faced by the pro-praetor Aurelius Cotta.[57] Again, all we know is that the Sullan forces were defeated, allowing Sertorius to land his forces and join up with the Lusitanian tribes. Furthermore, this victory allowed him to control the Straits of Gibraltar, giving him a clear line of communication between his holdings in northern Africa and western Spain and control of the Atlantic coastline of Spain.

After landing in Lusitania, it appears that Sertorius quickly spearheaded the rebellion, not only of the Lusitanians, but also a number of neighbouring Spanish tribes. The few sources that mention the early campaigns – Plutarch, Orosius and the fragments of Sallust – compress the chronology of events, so that we only have the scantest of outlines.[58] It does appear, however, that only one further engagement of note took place this year, when Sertorius faced a Roman garrison commanded by the pro-praetor Fufidius.

Battle of River Baetis

It seems that Sertorius' forces moved southwards from Lusitania into neighbouring Baetica and thus seized control of southern Spain. On the banks of the River Baetis (the modern Guadalquivir, see Map 12), the Sertorian forces confronted those of the pro-praetor Fufidius, governor of Farther Spain. A fragment of Sallust preserves some details:

> When Fufidius arrived soon afterwards with his legions, he found that the banks were steep, the ford could not easily be crossed if they had to fight, and everything was more suitable to the enemy than to his men.[59]

Thus it seems that Sertorius chose his ground well and manoeuvred Fufidius into a poor position. Plutarch records the outcome of the battle: 'he routed [Fufidius] on the banks of Baetis with the slaughter of 2,000 Roman soldiers...'[60] Thus, thanks to his two victories, Sertorius controlled the southwest of Spain.

6. The Metellan Campaign (79 BC)

Any study of the civil war in Spain is marred not only by the poor narrative for many key events we have in our surviving sources, but also by the poor chronology we are confronted with. Konrad best sums the situation up thus: 'In chronological terms, the Sertorian War is one of the most poorly documented episodes in the history of the late Republic. Whilst the general sequence of events is easily established and not seriously disputed, absolute dates are not recorded in the sources (with one exception), and hard to come by otherwise.'[61]

As noted above, the consuls of 80 BC were Sulla and his most trusted lieutenant and kinsman by marriage, Q. Caecilius Metellus Pius. For the following year, Sulla continued to hold his dictatorship and thus maintain control over Roman domestic affairs, and was awarded the province of Cisalpine Gaul, which allowed him to keep troops south of the Alps, in geographic Italy.[62] Metellus was given command of the war against Sertorius as governor of the province of Farther Spain. Nearer Spain went to a subordinate, M. Domitius Calvinus. Brunt estimates that Metellus took three to four legions with him to Spain, whilst Domitius took another two.[63] Again, our surviving sources fail us here, as we only have the scantest of evidence for the campaigns of this year; a handful of sentences only. Two battles appear to have been fought, the first of which was between the proconsul of Nearer Spain, M. Domitius Calvinus, and the forces of Sertorius, led by his quaestor, L. Hirtuleius.

Battle of the River Anas
The clash took place on the River Anas (the modern Guadiana) though exactly where on this river we do not know. Frontinus refers to Hirtuleius besieging the town of Consabura on the River Anas, though there is no explicit connection to the battle fought with Domitius and the reference is undated.[64] It is possible that Domitius was coming to the relief of Consabura or attempting to retake the town if it fell. Though a number of sources mention the battle, scant details are provided. Spann argues that Domitius would have had his full two legions with him, but we do not know the size of Hirtuleius' force.[65]

> Lucius [Marcus] Domitius, who was pro-consul of the other Spain was defeated at the hands of his [Sertorius'] quaestor [Hirtuleius].[66]

> Proconsul Lucius Manlius and Marcus Domitius [Calvinus], his deputy, were defeated in battle by quaestor Hirtuleius.[67]

> Hirtuleius, a general of Sertorius, overcame Domitius and his army.[68]

> Domitius was killed by Hirtuleius, Sertorius' general.[69]

Thus, all we know for certain is that Domitius was soundly defeated and killed in the battle. We can assume that as a result of the battle, Hirtuleius had a freer hand in reducing the other pro-Roman towns in the region and securing the Sertorian position in southern Spain.

Unnamed Battle
The second clash of the year occurred between Sertorius himself and one of Metellus' legates, L. Thorius Balbus.[70] We know even less of this clash than the previous one, other than the outcome, a Sertorian victory accompanied by the destruction of Thorius' army, with Thorius himself being killed. Even the location is disputed. Only Florus provides a location, Segovia, which was the location of a battle in 76 BC, and Florus seems to be confusing the two (see Chapter

8).[71] Due to Florus uniting both battles in his brief narrative, many have assumed that this clash also took place on or near the River Anas, but there is no evidence for the battles' location, other than Florus' placement at Segovia.[72] Konrad warns against the danger on ascribing this battle to the siege of Consabura.[73]

> The first engagements were fought by legates, Domitius and Thorius commencing operations on one side and the Hirtulei on the other. After the defeat of the latter at Segovia and the other at the River Ana ...[74]
>
> Thorius, another of the commanders sent out by Metellus with an army, he [Sertorius] slew.[75]

Given the scant details, we cannot reconstruct the circumstances behind the battle. The two pairs of armies (Sertorius and Hirtuleius, Domitius and Thorius) may have been working in concert or may have been separated by some time and merely combined in our brief sources. All we know is that, again, it resulted in a resounding victory for Sertorius, and that Thorius Balbus was killed. We can only assume that he was acting as the advance guard for Metellus, whose location at this time is unknown.

Summary

Thus the year 79 BC saw significant setbacks for the Sullan forces in Spain. Of the two proconsuls sent out to defeat Sertorius, Domitius Calvinus had been defeated and killed and a legate of Metellus, along with an unknown number of his army, had been defeated and killed also. As well as the military benefits, each victory was bound to increase the reputation of Sertorius himself and lend weight to the tribal rebellion he was spearheading. Thus in the year that Sulla abdicated his dictatorship and retired from public life, civil war was once again engulfing Rome's empire.

From Collapse to Recovery

Chapter 8

The Wars in Italy and Spain (78–77 BC)

The year 78 BC was supposed to have marked a new start for Rome. In 79 BC, following the consular elections for 78, Sulla resigned his dictatorship, as he had promised, having satisfied himself that the Republic was both restored and reformed.

Throughout his reign he had sought to portray himself as the bringer of peace and the restorer of the 'traditional' Republic, much as Augustus himself was to do half a century later. In truth, it seems that he had done neither and his reign proved as transitory as that of Cinna's a decade earlier; nothing more than a temporary respite from the civil war in Italy, accompanied by attempts to pass reforms for the longer-term stability of the Republic. However just as Cinna's regime had proved to be a temporary respite, unable to stop the civil war momentum, so it proved to be the case once again. Not only was civil war raging in Spain once more, but within a year of Sulla's resignation, the consuls went to war against each other once again, repeating the pattern set in 87 BC, which also followed Sulla stepping down from control of Rome. In 88 BC, he left Italy for Greece; in 79 BC, he left Rome to retire to his villa, where within the year he died of natural causes (an irony in itself).[1]

1. Consular Civil War in Italy

In 79 BC, Sulla had clearly hoped that by laying aside the supreme power he held, the Republic could be returned to its normal running. Yet whilst Sulla's reforms had been aimed at ending the dangers which had been at the heart of the outbreaks of the various stages of the civil war, not only were many of these issues left unresolved, but fresh flashpoints were created by Sulla's own laws and actions.

In terms of issues unresolved, the most obvious was that of the various exile groups, to which had now been added all of those who had been proscribed and fled Italy. From the Varian exiles through to the Sullan ones, there existed a diaspora of exiled Roman aristocrats scattered throughout the Mediterranean, many of whom harboured varying degrees of animosity against their own state. Significant numbers of them could be found residing under the protection of Rome's enemies, whether it be Sertorius in the west or Mithridates in the east. If this were not bad enough, the vast majority had friends and relatives still in

Rome, many of whom would be agitating for their return, and even a few who remained in close contact with them. Throughout this period it seems that each major conflict created more exiles.

When we look at issues caused by Sulla's legislation and actions, two were of paramount importance: the restrictions on the tribunate and the new 'second class' of citizens created by the proscriptions. In domestic political terms the restrictions on the tribunate, whilst seemingly sensible from a dispassionate point of view (given its recent history of being at the centre of political turbulence), were nevertheless viewed by many as a hostile act against an office of the People and a totemic reform of Sulla, which had transferred power from the People to the Senate. Furthermore, it would not only be the People who would have wanted this restriction overturned, but any ambitious politician who, either wanted the fully restored office for themselves, or wanted to manipulate it for their own ends.

In terms of the citizenry, no sooner had a second (and third) class of citizenry been wiped away by the widening of Roman citizenship to Latins and Italians and their integration into the thirty-five tribes, than a new second class were created by Sulla, albeit inadvertently. These were the *proscripiti* – the families of those men proscribed by Sulla. Though the individuals themselves may have been killed, their families had been dispossessed of their property and their descendants barred from political office. Thus, with one act, Sulla created a second class citizenry of the dispossessed and disenfranchised, not just in Rome, but throughout Italy, a class resentful at their treatment and eager for restitution.

Although Sulla may have changed some of the rules that governed the practice of politics at Rome, he could do nothing to change the mindset of the Roman politicians themselves. All he could do was to regulate their behaviour by holding onto an overriding political and military power to keep them in check. Once this power was removed, however, there was now nothing to keep them in check. This was Sulla's greatest failure in relation to his stated aim of stabilizing the Republic, but a failure that was always a possibility unless he was to assume some type of permanent monarchical power. This latter possibility, however, does not seem to have crossed his mind. This was a lesson for the next 500 years of Roman history: in the absence of a central overriding power at the heart of the Roman system, whether it be one, two, three or even four men, individual ambition would pull the system apart.

Following his withdrawal from high office, Sulla seems to have expected the Republic to be governed by the Senate, which had been moulded in his own image and filled with his supporters.[2] The problem that Sulla had was that a number of the men who followed him did not do so out of shared political or social beliefs, but from a cold and calculated political assessment that he was the most likely to win and therefore advance their own interests.[3] Amongst the victors in 82 BC stood a number of former Marian and Sulpician allies, some of whom even numbered amongst the twelve *hostes* declared by Sulla and Pompeius in 88 BC (see Chapter 6). It was to a Senate that included men such as this, that Sulla left the running of the Republic.

Many at the time would have expected that the figure to lead the breaking of the Sullan settlement would have been Sulla's own son-in-law, Pompeius Magnus, who had consistently, and publicly, shown that his own interests came first. Yet the man who took centre stage was M. Aemilius Lepidus, who campaigned for the consulship of 78 BC on a platform of anti-Sullan rhetoric and proposals to reverse a number of Sullan measures. Lepidus himself had connections to both factions; his wife was the daughter of L. Appuleius Saturninus and he had served under Cn. Pompeius Strabo. Yet when Sulla invaded Italy, we find him fighting for Sulla in Italy.[4]

However Plutarch states that one of his chief backers was Pompeius Magnus himself, who made no secret of his campaigning for Lepidus in Rome, even with Sulla present.[5] Sulla, bound by his own enforced limitations as a private citizen, could not intervene without undoing all he sought to protect. With such backing, and with such electoral proposals, Lepidus was elected as of the consul for 78 BC, ahead of his colleague, Q. Lutatius Catulus, who seems to have been a solid member of the Senate and a defender of the status quo.

Upon entering office, Lepidus apparently made a speech to the People attacking Sulla as a tyrant, and also his followers for overthrowing the state in a civil war, and denouncing the horrors of the proscriptions that followed. Sallust preserves a text of what is purported to be his speech.[6] Central to the speech are the grievances of the families of the *proscripiti*, both within Rome and the wider Italian communities. Those in Latium who had been dispossessed came in for special mention. Interestingly, the restoration of the tribunate is not mentioned by Lepidus himself. In fact, Granius Licinianus reports that when the tribunes of 78 BC asked the new consuls to restore their powers, Lepidus was the first to refuse.[7]

The first dissensions came early in 78 BC, when Sulla died, aged 60, of a wasting disease, and the proposal was made for him to be publicly commemorated (following cremation) in Rome, in the Campus Martius.[8] Naturally, Sulla's closest allies wanted to ensure a magnificent state funeral for him, and equally naturally there were a number of others who opposed it. The consuls clashed over the matter, with Lepidus opposing the lavishness of the celebrations, though he did back down over the matter.

Given the paucity of our sources, we do not have an accurate chronology for the events which followed, but it seems that Lepidus, despite all the promises, only passed (unopposed) a grain law, providing subsidized grain for the people of Rome. In addition, the sources report that promises were made for a law to recall exiles, rescind unnamed acts of Sulla and restore the original owners onto land taken for Sulla's colonies.[9] In all of these, he was opposed by the majority of the Senate and his colleague Catulus. It seems that, deprived of a fully working tribunate, Lepidus could not pass these measures into law in the face of senatorial opposition. In what seems to be a great irony, this Sullan measure worked only too well and thus meant that if Lepidus wanted to pass his measures into law, he had to do so by force, with all constitutional means blocked – an example of the law of unintended consequences, with regards to Sulla's reforms of the tribunate.

During their year in office, we have a fragment of Granius Licinianus that provides us with the sole testimony for an unusual incident, an outbreak of violence at the town of Faesulae in Etruria, to which both consuls were dispatched with an army. The fragment of Granius provides us with the following:

> The inhabitants of Faesulae broke into the strongholds of the veterans. After killing many of the veterans and reclaiming their land, they defended their actions before the Senate, on the grounds that the rural population had been forced to do this after being driven from their homes. The consuls were assigned an army and set off for Etruria, as the Senate instructed.[10]

Thus it appears that, perhaps stirred up indirectly by Lepidus, the inhabitants of an Etruscan town rebelled against Rome once more, and attacked the Sullan settlers there, leading the Senate to send both consuls, including Lepidus himself. We can see echoes of the events of 91 BC here, with Italians rising up after having the issue raised in the Senate by a leading Roman politician. The overall location is no surprise given that Etruria strongly supported the coalition against Sulla during the 83–82 BC period and suffered subsequent reprisals at his hands (see Chapter 6).

We have no details as to what actions the consuls took at Faesulae, but both soon returned to the city.[11] With both consuls now at the head of military forces in Italy once more, it seems that the Senate felt the need to make them swear that they would not resort to warfare to settle their quarrels.[12] Remarkably, they then allowed the consuls to cast lots for their consular provinces, which resulted in Lepidus being awarded Transalpine Gaul. Here we see the impotence of the system that Sulla left in his wake. The Senate seemed fearful of a return to civil war, and yet sent Lepidus to crush a rebellion in Italy at the head of an army, and then allowed him an army on the borders of Italy itself, rather than sending him out of harm's way, to the east, for example.

At what exact point Lepidus turned to open insurrection against both his colleague and the Senate we do not know, again due to the paucity of our sources. Appian refers to Lepidus being recalled to Rome, by a suspicious Senate, but whether this was from Etruria in 78 BC, when still consul, or in 77 BC as proconsul of Transalpine Gaul, is not clear.[13] Sallust preserves what purports to be a speech from the distinguished senator M. Philippus (who opposed Livius Drusus in 91 BC and survived the various purges in Rome in the period in-between).[14] The speech is an exhortation to the Senate to oppose Lepidus, who was marching towards Rome, and is set in 77 BC. It also states that Lepidus had not laid aside his consulship and thus did not return to Rome at the end of his consular year, probably indicating the time he went rogue.

By 77 BC, it seems that Lepidus had raised at least two forces: one in Cisalpine Gaul under the command of an M. Iunius Brutus (Tr Pl 83), who was the father of the slayer of Iulius Caesar, and one in Etruria under his own command.[15] Orosius interestingly refers to M. Perperna being in Liguria, and it has been suggested that he operated an additional pro-Lepidian force in this region during this insurrection.[16] Iulius Exsuperantius preserves a passage on the recruitment of Lepidus' army:

> Lepidus gathered together the dispossessed, whose land had been taken over by Sulla after his victory to make new colonies for his soldiers, and also the children of the proscribed. In this way, he collected a large army, by promising to restore their ancestral property, if they were victorious.[17]

A fragment of Sallust records that the Romans suspected that the whole of Etruria, a stronghold of coalition support, had risen in revolt.[18] In addition, Lepidus had Transalpine Gaul as his consular province, and his legate Brutus controlled Cisalpine Gaul. Thus, once again, northern and western Italy proved to be the heart of the force opposing the Senate. Interestingly, it seems that, as happened throughout this period, different conflicts overlapped, as we find a number of figures with ties to the coalition allied to Lepidus. In terms of blood ties, we find L. Cornelius Cinna, the son of the coalition leader, who joined Lepidus and then fled to Spain with Perperna, as well as an offer made to C. Iulius Caesar himself, which he wisely refused. The most prominent of the surviving coalition commanders (excluding Sertorius) was a certain M. Perperna, a fugitive coalition commander (see Chapter 8), who we find operating as a legate of Lepidus. Thus Lepidus, who backed Sulla in the war of 82–82 BC, now had a fugitive coalition element to his forces, possibly controlling Liguria (also in northern Italy). Unfortunately, how many other coalition figures or relatives sided with Lepidus is not known. The other interesting element would be if there was any contact between Lepidus and Sertorius in Spain (see below). We have no direct evidence that the two commanders were in contact, though Lepidus did now effectively control the route from Italy to Spain.

Again, we have few surviving sources for this stage of the civil war. However, it seems that Lepidus followed the precedent set by Sulla, Pompeius Rufus and Cinna, and marched his army on Rome, hoping for a knockout victory, leaving behind his legates, Brutus and Perperna, in charge of northern Italy. His colleague Catulus took command of the senatorial forces defending Rome, which was without consuls for the start of the year. Following the tumult caused by Lepidus' revolt and the dissensions between the two consuls, no elections were able to be held for 77 BC. As is common for this period, we are not given any details as to the size of the armies involved.

The Senate also took the unusual step of appointing Cn. Pompeius Magnus as a pro-praetor and gave him command of the army sent to defeat M. Iunius Brutus and recover northern Italy. This action contravened the *cursus honorum* established by Sulla, as Pompeius was yet officially too young to hold a major command of his own. It also seems strange that the Senate overlooked the fact that Pompeius was seemingly instrumental in ensuring Lepidus was elected to the consulship in the first place. Nevertheless, with a civil war breaking out in Italy once again, the Senate seems to have had no choice but to overlook both factors and chose a proven general to recover northern Italy.

The early fighting in the war seems to have been in northern Italy, with Pompeius rapidly advancing on Brutus, who was headquartered in Mutina (Modena) on the Via Amelia, controlling the route from Etruria into Cisalpine Gaul. Plutarch refers to some initial engagements between Pompeius and Brutus' forces, but we have no details, other than Pompeius was successful.[19] Brutus chose not to give battle but remained inside Mutina, to which Pompeius laid siege. At the same time, Lepidus moved through Etruria, possibly winning a victory at an unknown coastal location:

> A battle was fought on the coast of Etruria, and Lepidus started to gain the upper hand, because of the large number of soldiers who had joined his side out of hatred of Sulla's government.[20]

Lepidus then marched his army towards Rome and camped outside of the city demanding, amongst other things, that he receive a second consulship, in order to pass his reforms. Whilst this demand was not granted, it is surprising that the two consuls who were elected for the remainder of 77 BC were both kinsmen of Lepidus and Brutus: D. Iunius Brutus and Mam. Aemilius Lepidus Livianus. It is possible that they were elected as some form of compromise agreement between the Senate and Lepidus.

Whilst Lepidus was camped outside of Rome, Pompeius soon received the swift surrender of Mutina and took Brutus prisoner. Plutarch himself expresses his uncertainty over how Mutina fell, either by Brutus negotiating with Pompeius and surrendering, or via a mutiny in his army which ended in him being handed over to Pompeius. Brutus was escorted to a small town on the Po where he was murdered next day on Pompeius' orders.[21]

As well as Mutina, it seems that Lepidus also secured the route from Gaul to Spain by garrisoning the town of Alba (in modern Piedmont) under the command of his son, a Cornelius Scipio.[22] This town too was put under siege (presumably by Pompeian forces) and fell after being starved into submission. Scipio was also murdered following capture.

Battle of Rome

It seems that news of the fall of Mutina reached Rome during the ongoing negotiations, strengthening the Senate's hand. When negotiations failed both sides turned to battle, with Lepidus attacking the city. The exact location of this battle is unclear, with only Florus and Appian providing any details (see Map 11):

But Lutatius Catulus and Cnaeus Pompeius, who had been leaders and standard bearers under Sulla's domination, had already occupied the Milvian Bridge and the Janiculum Hill with another army. Having been immediately driven back by these generals at his first onslaught…[23]

A battle was fought not far from the Campus Martius. Lepidus was defeated…[24]

Florus is clearly inaccurate here in stating that Pompeius was present at the battle for Rome as he was in northern Italy at the time. This is a simple enough mistake given that there were two commanders of the overall senatorial force in this campaign and his account being a highly condensed one. Nevertheless,

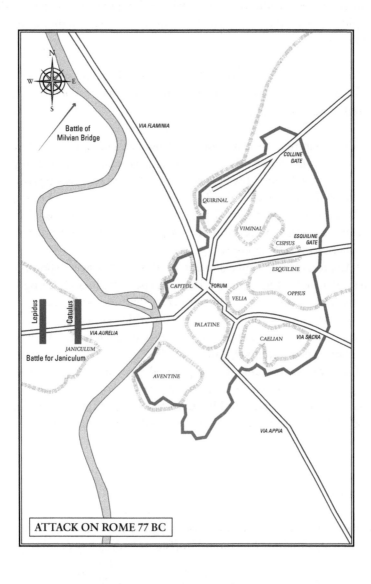

ATTACK ON ROME 77 BC

Florus does provide us with the detail that there were two thrusts to Lepidus' attack, both from the west of the city. The main attack seems to have been via the Janiculum, the same route used in the attacks of both 88 and 87 BC. Another engagement seems to have been fought further north to secure the Milvian Bridge and thus allow Lepidus' forces to cross the Tiber and approach Rome on a second front, via the Via Flaminia. We do not know where either Lepidus or Catulus were during this engagement, but as the thrust at the Janiculum was the most logical main point of attack on the city, we can speculate that they were both present.

Neither source adds any further details about the size of the forces or their dispositions. However, taking Florus' account, it seems that Lepidus was easily driven off, perhaps disheartened by the loss of Gaul. Thus the fifth attack on Rome within the last decade was defeated, as had been the previous one (the Samnite/coalition attack of 82 BC).

Unnamed Battle

With his attack on Rome repulsed, it seems that Lepidus retreated back into his heartland of Etruria. A fragment of Exsuperantius refers to Pompeius returning from Gaul and defeating and destroying Lepidus' army.

> But Pompeius returned from Gaul, in order to prevent Lepidus from harming the state by his impudent madness, and utterly defeated his army, who fled away and fell into a sudden panic. Lepidus lost the majority of his army and escaped to Sardinia …[25]

Regrettably, no other source refers to this battle between Pompeius and Lepidus, but merely notes that Lepidus was expelled from Italy.[26] This could well be the second battle to which Orosius refers. If this is the case then Pompeius can take the lion's share of the credit for defeating Lepidus, even though it was Catulus who successfully defended Rome. Again, for any meaningful details on Lepidus' activities following the defeat in Etruria we must turn to Exsuperantius. Interestingly, both Plutarch and Appian do not mention any further fighting, only that Lepidus died soon afterwards. Exsuperantius, however, paints a different picture, that of a war for control of the island.

> [Lepidus] escaped to Sardinia, from where he reduced the Roman people to neediness by hindering their trade, while he rebuilt his own forces and supplies. He fought several desperate battles in Sardinia with the pro-praetor [L. Valerius] Triarius, who defended his province so effectively that all Lepidus' plans were thwarted. Lepidus was shut out of all the towns and could not capture them because of their fortifications. So he was unable to carry out his objectives, and in the midst of his preparations he fell seriously ill and died. His partner and accomplice Perperna, in order to avoid punishment for his great crimes, crossed

over from Sardinia to Spain and joined Sertorius, who was then waging war against Rome.[27]

Thus, it seems that a drawn-out guerrilla war was averted through the death, by natural causes, of Lepidus.[28] Once again, the various conflicts of this period cross-fertilized each other, with Perperna, himself a fugitive from the war of 83–82 BC, transporting a significant portion of the Lepidian army to Spain to join the civil war being fought by Sertorius. Once again, we are not given any numbers, but Appian refers to it as the greater part of the remaining Lepidian forces, and Perperna was certainly able to fight in Spain as an independent force (see Chapter 9).[29] Despite the death of his son Scipio, Lepidus himself was survived by two other sons, L. Aemilius Lepidus Paullus (Cos. 50) and M. Aemilius Lepidus (Cos. 46 & 42), the future triumvir, both of whom became staunch supporters of Iulius Caesar.

Thus, this conflict showed both the strengths and the weakness of the Republican system in this period. Despite all the bold assertions of Sulla that he had ended the civil war, a fresh outbreak occurred within a year of his death and again another consul marched his army on Rome against his colleague. On this occasion, it seems that Lepidus was no Sulla or Cinna, given the apparent ease with which his attack on Rome was repulsed. The other notable feature is the ease with which Etruria and Gaul rose in rebellion against Rome, and the ease with which that rebellion soon collapsed.

Lepidus' death ended the immediate threat in Italy, but led to two consequences. The first was that the opponents of the Senate in Spain received reinforcements, in the form of the remnants of Lepidus' army. The second consequence was the potential threat of Cn. Pompeius Magnus. Whilst he had undoubtedly been the key to the Senate's swift victory in this war, they placed him at the head of another army, which was soon to have dangerous consequences. In 81 BC, Pompeius used his army for his own ends and faced down Sulla himself, by refusing to disband his troops. On that occasion, all he wanted was a triumph. In 77 BC, the situation was now even more balanced in his favour, as he had an army in Italy, had saved Rome from an enemy and was only facing the Senate. To no one's surprise, following his victory, Pompeius' soldiers once again refused to disband. On this occasion, the price was a command in Spain, against Sertorius. Given the situation, the Senate choose the only option they could and again acquiesced in granting him a military command, despite the strictures of the Sullan *cursus honorum*.

Thus, Pompeius, who had apparently been Lepidus' original sponsor, emerges as the one clear winner in this period of civil warfare, profiting once again from the turmoil, adding to his military reputation and showing that he had learnt a key lesson of this period; namely that the threat, or even the hint, of force could be just as powerful as the actual use of force itself, and in many cases even more powerful.

As a footnote to this phase of civil warfare in Italy, Cicero records two other mutinies in the Roman army in this period. The first seems to date from around

77 BC and occurred in the army of one of the consuls of that year, Mam. Ameilius Lepidus, although we do not know where.[30] A brief note in Cicero refers to a quaestor named C. Staienus being the instigator of a mutiny, though no other details are known.[31] The second concerns M. Atilius Bulbus, who was tried in the late 70s for treason. Cicero refers to a mutiny he attempted to instigate in a legion in Illyria under the command of C. Cosconius. Although we have no other details, Syme postulates that this was in connection with the civil war of 78–77 BC.[32] Thus we can again see that the lack of surviving sources for this period may have seriously obscured much of the detail of this phase of civil conflict. If nothing else, it again shows the instability that plagued Rome's armies during this period.

2. The Civil War in Spain (78–77 BC)

As a senior figure in the post-Sullan government, it is not a surprise that Metellus Pius remained in command of the war against Sertorius, as governor of Farther Spain. To replace the deceased Domitius Calvinus, Q. Calidius was appointed pro-praetor of Nearer Spain, but appears to have had no part in the war and returned to Rome following his year in office (where he was promptly charged with extortion). Again, we are denied a clear narrative of the year's campaigning, but our few sources do provide us with more details of some events of this year, even if the year itself is open to question.[33]

After his initial victories, the war appears to have turned into one of attrition, with both sides avoiding a set-piece battle. Sertorius appears to have avoided such a direct confrontation until he had worn his opponent down, especially as Metellus would have had a larger fighting force, and one purely of legionaries. Metellus appears to have settled on a policy of besieging towns loyal to Sertorius, thus denying him territory and support. Plutarch provides us with two good passages highlighting the different tactics, equipment and strategies the two sides used:

> For Metellus was at his wits' end. He was carrying on war with a man of daring who evaded every kind of open fighting, and who made all manner of shifts and changes, owing to the light equipment and agility of his Iberian soldiers; whereas he himself had been trained in regular contests of heavy-armed troops, and was wont to command a ponderous and immobile phalanx, which, for repelling and overpowering an enemy at close quarters, was most excellently trained, but for climbing mountains, for dealing within the incessant pursuits and flights of men as light as the winds, and for enduring hunger and a life without fire or tent, as their enemies did, it was worthless.[34]
>
> For [Sertorius] he would cut off his opponent's supply of water and prevent his foraging; if the Romans advanced, he would get out of their way, and if they settled down in camp, he would harass them; if they besieged a place, he would come up and put them under siege in their turn by depriving them of supplies.[35]

Metellus' forces were being constantly harried and worn down by Sertorius' tactics, without him needing to give battle. Metellus' army was operating in hostile territory with a long supply chain and against an enemy who seemed to melt away into the Spanish interior. Plutarch goes to great lengths to demonstrate the deteriorating morale of Metellus' men, and does provide us with an excellent example of Sertorius choosing his moment to fight openly at the siege of the town of Langobriga.[36]

Battle of Langobriga

Plutarch provides a detailed narrative of events, with Metellus attacking the town in the expectation of a short siege, due to the town's lack of water. Sertorius, however, had the town evacuate its non-essential population, leaving only the defenders, and ferried 2,000 skins of water to them, thus denying Metellus his quick siege. Regrettably for Metellus, it seems that he had only brought provisions for his men for five days, expecting a short siege, thus necessitating the need to send out foraging parties. Plutarch details the battle that followed:

> [Metellus] sent out Aquinus, at the head of 6,000 men, to forage. But Sertorius learned of this and set an ambush of 3,000 men in the road by which Aquinus was to return. These sallied forth from a shady ravine and attacked Aquinus in the rear, while Sertorius himself assailed him in front, routed him, slew some of his men, and took some of them prisoners. Aquinus, after losing both his armour and his horse, got back to Metellus, who then retired disgracefully, much abused by the Iberians.[37]

This one example perfectly illustrates the nature of the warfare during this year; with a numerically superior force being steadily worn down through attrition and ambush by a smaller native force. Whilst Sertorius was wearing down Metellus and the main Roman army, his deputy, Hirtuleius, was still operating to the north of him, in central Spain. We hear of no military activity on the part of Calidius, the governor of Nearer Spain, and we have no indication that he took any fresh legions with him. This would have left Nearer Spain with the remnants of the force defeated by Hirtuleius the previous year (one to two legions before losses).

Thus the situation for the Roman government was deteriorating further. In central Spain, Hirtuleius appeared to be operating with impunity, with few Roman forces to defend the region, whilst in southern Spain, Metellus and the main Roman army were being steadily ground down by a war of attrition. In response, the Senate ordered the proconsul of Transalpine Gaul, L. Manlius, to cross into Spain and reinforce the war effort there. Orosius provides us with details of the size of Manlius' army, which he puts at three legions and 1,500 cavalry.[38]

What he does not tell us is what Manlius was doing with such a force in the first place. Interestingly, Caesar records that an L. Manlius suffered a defeat in

Aquitania, though he does not provide the date.[39] If these legions were raised solely to reinforce Spain, then why would they not have been commanded by the new governor of Nearer Spain, Q. Calidius? Given that Pompeius had to fight a tribal war during the 77–76 BC period, it seems likely that Manlius had been sent there with fresh force to combat tribal incursion into the region. A force in Transalpine Gaul would also be able to secure and defend the route from Spain to Italy and mop up any remaining pro-Lepidian forces in the region. We are unable to tell to what degree the tribal incursions were related to the campaigns of Sertorius or Lepidus against the Senate. The clear fear here must have been that the tribes of Gaul would join in rebellion with the tribes of Spain and thus create an alliance of Gallic and Spanish tribes bearing down on Italy.

In any event, the deterioration of the war in Spain meant that Manlius and his legions were sent into Spain instead. However, before they could reach Metellus and the campaign against Sertorius they would have to pass by Sertorius' lieutenant Hirtuleius and his force, the size of which is again unknown.

Battle of Ilerda

Orosius alone provides scant details of the battle between Hirtuleius and Manlius:

> Manlius, the proconsul of Gaul, accompanied by three legions and 1,500 cavalry, crossed to Spain, where he engaged in an unequal battle with Hirtuleius. Deprived of his camp and troops by the latter, Manlius, almost alone, fled for refuge to the town of Ilerda.[40]

Thus, Hirtuleius was able to rout the three legions of Manlius and overrun his camp, though once again, we have no details as to how he actually managed to accomplish this. One of the most interesting aspects of Orosius' statement is his use of the word *iniquam* or unequal. Given the size of Manlius' army (three legions), are we to believe that Hirtuleius seriously outnumbered him? This is unlikely, given that the bulk of the rebel army fought with Sertorius and the sources frequently refer to the rebels being outnumbered. Furthermore, Hirtuleius would not have had an army solely composed of legionaries, but must have had a number of natives, and even African (Mauri), soldiers.[41] As well as unequal, *iniquam* could have the meaning of uneven, unfavourable or disadvantageous. Thus this could refer to the topography of the battlefield, with Manlius in a poor position, or even being ambushed by Hirtuleius. Given the nature of the guerrilla tactics the rebels were using, an ambush is a possibility, though it would have to be after Manlius had set up camp. Regardless, the result was the heaviest Roman defeat of the campaign to date, with three legions being routed, if not destroyed outright.

Following this battle, the sources again go silent on the campaigning for the rest of the year, but no major encounters are reported in what sources survive. We must assume therefore that the war continued as before, with Sertorius engaging in guerrilla tactics against a demoralized Metellan army in the south and Hirtuleius securing further territory in central Spain. These additional victories would have only strengthened the rebellion, and we must assume that more and more Spanish tribes defected to Sertorius with Roman rule and military might crumbling.

We only have one other reference to activities in Spain this year and it comes from a passing mention by Cicero, who states that in this year the city of Gades (modern Cadiz) on the western coast of Spain sent to Rome to formalize an alliance between the two cities.[42] Given that the region was in the process of being overrun by Sertorius, it seems that the city remained loyalty of Rome and wanted the formality of a treaty, which was granted, to ensure that even if they were overrun, they would not be thought of as colluding with an enemy of the Roman state. Regrettably, we hear no more about Gades' role in the rest of the war.

Given the events in Italy and Gaul in the year 77 BC, it is hardly surprising that our few surviving sources shift their focus to the events in Italy (see above) and our narrative for the fourth year of the civil war in Spain disappears altogether. What we can only assume is that there were no other major encounters and that the war continued in the same manner as in 78 BC, with Sertorius increasing his power and harrying Metellus' ragged army in the south and Hirtuleius securing central and possibly northern Spain. With Hirtuleius' two victories, up to five legions of senatorial forces had been defeated, and possibly destroyed, meaning that central and northern Spain had no significant Roman forces left to defend it, other than the remnants of the above armies. Certainly, we hear no more of either Calidius, the governor of Nearer Spain, except that he returned home, or of the defeated Manlius. What seems to be clear is that by beginning of 76 BC all the Spanish tribes south of the Ebro were apparently supporting Sertorius.[43]

In the absence of campaigning detail, what Plutarch does narrate is that slowly but surely Sertorius was creating a whole new infrastructure in the 'liberated' areas of Spain to support his war effort. We hear of military, political and social measures taken to Romanize the tribes that backed him and create a solid powerbase for himself in Spain. Plutarch reports that he introduced Roman arms and tactics to the tribes:

> …by introducing Roman arms and formations and signals he did away with their frenzied and furious displays of courage, and converted their forces into an army, instead of a large band of robbers.[44]

It is interesting that Sertorius created elements of a hybrid Roman–Spanish society, given that the tribes were originally rebelling against Rome. Although we are certainly seeing this from a Roman perspective, it may well be that the tribes wanted to take some of the strengths of Roman civilization without the direct control of the Senate in Rome. We are also told that Sertorius had around him a bodyguard of men, several thousand strong, who had pledged themselves to him personally and that on one occasion they rescued him from a defeat at a city they were holding (no other details are given) and carried him to the city walls and safety.[45]

In social and political terms, he bound the tribal elites to him by means of establishing a school for their children in the city of Osca (modern Huéscar), where they were educated in the Greek and Roman manner. As Plutarch states, at one stroke he was effectively holding the children of the tribal leaders as hostages, whilst educating them to grow up and support him (and his Rome), when they became adults and returned to their tribes. In terms of overall leadership, we are told that Sertorius also created a rival Senate, of 300 members, which must have contained a number of coalition exiles, such as the younger Cinna.[46] Thus Sertorius appears to have been creating a rival Roman government in exile and forging Spain from two Roman-held provinces into the heart of a new state, with which to launch his attack on Italy.

Thus by the end of 77 BC, it seems that the vast swathes of Spain south of the Ebro had been secured by Sertorius, who was busy creating a military, social and political infrastructure to unify his powerbase. Konrad provides a discussion on the extent of Sertorius' control of the Spanish provinces.[47] The only remaining Roman forces were those of Metellus in the south, who originally had six legions, but which were being constantly harried by Sertorius' guerrilla tactics and were suffering from logistical problems and declining morale. However, the year ended with the promise of reinforcements for both sides in the conflict, as the consequences from the civil war in Italy spilled over into Spain. This took the form of reinforcements for both sides, in the shape of M. Perperna and Cn. Pompeius, both of whom would ultimately transform this conflict, though for very different reasons.

Chapter 9

The War in Spain (77–74 BC)

With the extinguishing of the renewed civil war in Italy, and the reinforcements that both sides received, the Spanish theatre of war became the sole conflict zone in the civil war during the period 77 to 74 BC. Despite it being the most important phase of the civil war in Spain, this period is noted for its uncertain chronology and confused narrative in the surviving sources, to such a point that we today are unsure even of how many battles were fought in the period. In terms of chronology, some modern commentators have advocated moving events forward by a year, based on Pompeius reaching Spain early in 77 BC and starting his campaign that same year, along with an earlier date for the death of Sertorius. The analysis below is based on Pompeius reaching Spain late in 77 BC, given his activities in Gaul and not actively campaigning until 76 BC, though the death of Sertorius can be moved forward a year from the traditional view.[1]

1. The New Entrants to the War

Before analyzing the warfare of this period, it is necessary to review the two new commanders (and their forces) who entered the war and were to play such a crucial role in determining its outcome.

M. Perperna Vento

It is assumed that the Perperna who took command of the remnants of Lepidus' army in 77 BC is the same man as the former coalition governor of Sicily in 82 BC, who defied Sulla (see Chapter 6). In our surviving sources, this identification is not explicit, and he is only described as an ex-praetor who had been proscribed.[2] Given the same name, the same office and the standing of the man in 77 BC, such an identification does seem likely and it makes Perperna an important and intriguing figure in this stage of the civil war. Between the fall of Sicily to Pompeius in 82 BC and his appearance in Lepidus' army in 77 BC, we have no concrete idea of his whereabouts. Orosius does refer to Lepidus being in Liguria, but does not provide a timescale.[3] This may have been when he was operating as part of Lepidus' army in 78/77 BC, en route to Spain following Lepidus' defeat, or where he spent the years 82–77 BC. Others have speculated that he spent the years with Sertorius, thus forming a concrete link between Sertorius and Lepidus, but there is no evidence to confirm this.

What we do know for certain is that by the end of 77 BC, Perperna was in command of the remnants of Lepidus' army. Plutarch states that this force was fifty-three cohorts (500 in each), or just over 26,000 men, along with a considerable sum of money.[4] It is not clear which other Lepidian survivors went with him, but L. Cornelius Cinna, the son of the coalition leader, is recorded as fleeing to Spain following the civil war of 78–77 BC.[5] M. Marius, another relative, may well have been with him also (see Chapter 10).

Given that the senatorial forces had re-established control of Italy, whilst rebel forces were in the ascendancy in Spain, it is not surprising to see that Perperna took this force to Spain. However, as Plutarch states, it appears that Perperna did not intend to join Sertorius, but to fight his own war against the senatorial forces.[6] All surviving accounts of Perperna focus on his birth and his apparent arrogance, with Velleius stating that he was 'more distinguished for his birth than for his character'.[7] Whilst Perperna was indeed a Patrician, the sources are coloured by his later actions (see Chapter 10). By 77 BC, both Perperna and Sertorius were former praetors, and whilst Sertorius was one of the key coalition commanders in 87 BC, he had been sent to Spain in 83 BC, in partial exile, whilst Perperna seems to have been close adherent of the younger Marius and part of the new generation of the coalition (see Chapter 6). Furthermore, Perperna had followed Lepidus in his attempt to seize control of Rome, whilst Sertorius remained in Spain. Therefore, it is no surprise that Perperna was at first reluctant to place himself, and his men, under Sertorius' command.

However, once in Spain, he would have had to re-assess his position for two important reasons. Firstly, the situation in Spain had altered the balance between them, with Sertorius, as commander of a successful rebellion in the two provinces, controlling much of southern Spain. Secondly, Pompeius and his armies were approaching, and the two rebel armies would need to co-ordinate their actions to defeat him. Thus, reluctantly, Perperna led his forces to join Sertorius and placed himself under his overall command.

Cn. Pompeius 'Magnus'

For Pompeius, the civil war in Spain was an excellent opportunity. His victorious campaigns in 83–81 BC had been followed by a lull in fighting in the Roman world, except Spain, and that campaign was under the command of the Sullan veteran Q. Caecilius Metellus Pius. What faced him now would have been over a decade's wait until he could command forces again in his own right (as a praetor), and a near two-decade wait until his reached the minimum age for the consulship (42) and a leading command. The civil war in Italy in 78–77 BC gave him an excellent opportunity to take up arms again. His victories in Italy, combined with the disastrous showing of the senatorial forces in Spain, gave him the necessary circumstances to continue his military feats, whilst circumventing Sulla's *cursus honorum* once more.[8] Given the disastrous state of the war in Spain and the fact that a large fragment of Lepidus' forces were moving to Spain also, the Senate would have been well aware of the need to reinforce their Spanish armies and preferably with a fresh commander, as Metellus was proving unable to defeat Sertorius (see below).

Lepidus' attack on Rome would have made the Senate only too well aware of the potential threat from Spain and a repeat of the bloodshed of the 80s. Pompeius had a number of factors in his favour: he was a proven and battle-hardened commander, while the consuls of 76 had less battle experience and seemed to be reluctant to fight Sertorius. Furthermore, Pompeius had a large standing army in Italy and was demanding advancement, which, given his track record of refusing orders, his father's own pedigree in this area, and his closeness to his former father-in-law and mentor Sulla, made him of more immediate danger than Sertorius himself. Thus, sending Pompeius to Spain would have been a win-win situation for the Senate. They got rid of one potential threat by sending him to defeat another potential threat. If he succeeded, then the Sertorian threat was ended; if he failed, then the threat that he posed was eliminated.

There were, however, two dangers in this strategy. First, by sending him as an additional commander to Metellus and with equal standing (both had proconsular commands), there was the real danger that the two would not co-operate. This would not have been helped by the generational difference between the men; Metellus was a senior and experienced ex-consul who had been Sulla's deputy, while Pompeius was a young and arrogant commander who had been Sulla's son-in-law, and had demonstrated little appetite to conform to the Roman norms on age and respect. The second danger was farther away, and it lay in Pompeius succeeding in defeating Sertorius and returning to Italy even more powerful.

2. The Transalpine War 77–76 BC

Shortly after receiving the command, Pompeius had re-equipped his army and crossed the Alps, where it seems he fought a war against the Gallic tribes. Details of this war are limited, as the surviving narrative sources are too eager to comment on his fighting in Spain. Nevertheless, we do have some fragments that attest to the war and its scope, firstly, from a letter of Pompeius himself, preserved by Sallust:

> I admit that I entered upon this war with more zeal than discretion; for within forty days of the time when I received from you the empty title of commander I had raised and equipped an army and driven the enemy, who were already at the throat of Italy, from the Alps into Spain ... and over those mountains I had opened for you another and more convenient route than Hannibal had taken. I recovered Gaul...[9]

Cicero provides two references to the war, one a passing reference to a Transalpine War preceding the Sertorian conflict.[10] The other being: 'Gaul is my witness, through which a road into Spain was laid open to our legions by the destruction of the Gauls.'[11] We also have reference to Pompeius' action in Caesar's work on the civil wars:

Pompeius and Caesar, both patrons of our state [Massilia], one of whom has officially granted us the lands of the Volcae Arecomici and of the Helvii; the other, after conquering the Salluvii by force, has assigned them to us and increased our revenues.[12]

Thus it appears that the civil wars in Spain and Italy had stirred up the native tribes of the region into revolt, possibly attacking Rome's ally Massilia, of whom Pompeius became a patron. This would have been aided by the removal of all Roman forces from Transalpine Gaul to fight in Spain (see previous chapter). Given that Pompeius provided Massilia with lands from the Vulcae and Helvii, we can assume that they were the principal tribal opponents. Whether they were in support of Sertorius or simply rebelling against Roman domination by raiding Transalpine Gaul we will never know. All we do know is that these tribes were defeated and had to cede land to Rome's ally. Not only had Pompeius blooded his troops, but he had secured senatorial control of the strategic land corridor between Spain and Italy, thus ensuring that he could receive further reinforcements if necessary and taking the boundary of senatorial control back to the Pyrenees.[13]

3. The Early Clashes (76 BC)

With the Gallic tribes defeated, Pompeius crossed the Pyrenees into Spain in the spring of 76 BC. Orosius states that Pompeius had an army of 30,000 infantry and 1,000 cavalry, whilst Sertorius commanded 60,000 infantry and 8,000 cavalry.[14] We cannot be sure whether these figures include the armies of Metellus and Perperna. Sertorius, however, had not been idle and had been using the time to reinforce his position. Fortunately, we have a substantial surviving fragment of Livy, excerpts of which provide us with some details of this period (late 77, early 76 BC), and are worth quoting at some length:

Contrebia was reduced after forty-four days, with a large loss of soldiers. Sertorius left L. Insteius in the town with a strong garrison, and led his own force to the River Ebro. There he constructed winter quarters by the town called Camp Aelia, and remained there with his forces. By day he held conference in the town of the cities allied with him. He issued an order that throughout the province arms should be manufactured according to the capabilities of the various peoples.

He distributed the new weapons to his men through their centurions, equipped his cavalry also with new arms, distributed clothing which had been previously prepared and issued pay.

He called together embassies from all the tribes and cities and presented his thanks for the supplies they had provided for his infantry, which had been demanded. He laid before them his achievements in defending his allies and in storming the cities of his enemies, and encouraged them to continue the war after a brief explanation of the advantages of the provinces of Spain if his side had the upper hand.

As spring opened he sent M. Perperna with 20,000 infantry and 1,500 cavalry to the tribes of the Ilercaones to defend the coast of that region; he gave Perperna instructions as to the route he was to use in coming to the rescue of allied cities which Pompeius would attack, as well as those routes from which he was to attack Pompeius' own column in ambush.

At the same time, he also sent dispatches to Herennius, who was in the same region, as well as to L. Hirtuleius in the other province, instructing them how he wanted the war to be managed, especially that Hirtuleius was to protect the allied cities in such a way as not to meet Metellus in battle, since he was no match for Metellus, either in personal prestige or in military power. Sertorius said that he had no intention of meeting Pompeius head on, nor did he believe that Pompeius would offer battle.

Sertorius with his own force decided to march against the Berones and Autricones, who had, as he had learned, frequently begged aid from Pompeius during the winter.

With these thoughts in mind, Sertorius led his army up to the Ebro River through friendly territory, in a peaceful and harmless fashion. He then advanced into the territory of the Bursaones, Cascantium and Graccuris, ravaging everything and trampling the crops, and arrived at Calguris Nasica, a town of his allies.[15]

Thus Sertorius' strategy with regard to the armies of Metellus and Pompeius was clear: keep Metellus pinned down by Hirtuleius, without giving battle, and avoid battle with Pompeius, whilst protecting his allies and reducing those still loyal to Rome, who could provide aid to the invading senatorial forces. It also shows us that he took great care with the orders issued to his legates, who had explicit instructions on how to conduct the war. Furthermore, we can also see the care he took to re-equip and re-provision his army in anticipation, and made sure that all of his allies were behind him.

Regrettably, this fragment of Livy ends after recording Sertorius' advance into tribal areas still loyal to Rome, giving us a stark reminder of the details of history that have been lost to us, through the losses of works such as those of Livy. For the rest of the year's campaigning, we must fall back on briefer narrative works and compressed biographies.

It seems that Pompeius passed across the Pyrenees unopposed and pressed into Spain. Although Livy tells us that Sertorius sent Perperna to cover the coastal roads, we hear of no clashes between the two.[16] With Sertorius seeking to avoid a full-scale battle with Pompeius, it seems that Pompeius continued to advance into Spain, most likely via the eastern seaboard. Plutarch tells us that this advance caused a number of cities to either change allegiance from Sertorius to Pompeius, or at least waiver in their loyalty.[17] One such city was Lauro, the location of which is unclear, although most commentators place it on the coastal plain to the north of Valencia. It seems that Sertorius decided to take action and stop these defections by making an example of the city. In turn, Pompeius could hardly allow a defecting city to be destroyed, and so he hastened to break the siege, leading to the first clash of the war between Pompeius and Sertorius.

Battle of Lauro

Both Plutarch and Frontinus provide good accounts of the clash, which are worth quoting at length, given the paucity of our source normally:

For Sertorius was besieging that city, and Pompeius came to its assistance with all his forces. Now there was a hill which was thought to afford a good command of the city, and this hill Sertorius strove to seize in advance, while Pompeius sought to prevent him. But Sertorius got there first, whereupon Pompeius, taking position with his army, was delighted with the way things had turned out, believing that Sertorius was caught between the city and his adversary's forces; he also sent a messenger to the people of Lauro bidding them be of good cheer and take seats along their walls for the spectacle of Sertorius undergoing siege. When Sertorius heard of this, he gave a laugh, and said that to Sulla's pupil (for thus he was wont to style Pompeius in jest) he himself would give a lesson, namely, that a general must look behind him rather than in front of him. As he said this, he pointed out to his beleaguered troops, 6,000 men-at-arms, whom he had left behind at their former camp, from which he had sallied forth to seize the hill; these, in case Pompeius moved against the occupants of the hill, were to fall upon his rear. Pompeius also became aware of this all too late, and did not venture to attack Sertorius for fear of being surrounded, but he was ashamed to go away and leave the people of the city in their peril, and so was compelled to sit there quietly and see them ruined; for the barbarians gave up all hope and surrendered to Sertorius. Sertorius spared their lives and let them all go, but he burned down their city, not because he was angry or cruel, for he appears to have given way to passion less than any other general, but to put to shame and confusion the admirers of Pompeius, in order that it might be said among the Barbarians that though he was near at hand and all but warming himself at the flames of an allied city, he did not come to its relief.[18]

However, for Pompeius, the situation worsened when a foraging party fell into
an ambush:

> When Sertorius was encamped next to Pompeius near the town of Lauro in
> Spain, there were only two tracts from which forage could be gathered, one
> nearby, the other farther off. Sertorius gave orders that the one nearby should
> be continually raided by light-armed troops, but that remoter one should not
> be visited by any troops. Thus, he finally convinced his adversaries that the
> more distant tract was safer. When, on one occasion, Pompeius' troops had
> gone to this region, Sertorius ordered Octavius Graecinus, with ten cohorts
> armed after the Roman fashion, and ten cohorts of light-armed Spaniards
> along with Tarquitius Priscus and 2,000 cavalry, set forth to lay an ambush
> against the foragers. These men executed their instructions with energy; for
> after examining the ground, they hid the above-mentioned forces by night in a
> neighbouring wood, posting the light-armed Spaniards in front, as best suited
> to stealthy warfare, the shield-bearing soldiers a little further back, and the
> cavalry in the rear, in order that the plan might not be betrayed by the neighing
> of the horses. Then they ordered all to repose in silence till the third hour of
> the following day.
>   When Pompeius' men, entertaining no suspicion and loaded down with
> forage, thought of returning, and those who had been on guard, lured on by
> the situation, were slipping away to forage, suddenly the Spaniards, darting out
> with the swiftness characteristic of their race, poured forth upon the stragglers,
> inflicted many wounds upon them, and put them to rout, to their great
> amazement. Then, before resistance to this first assault could be organized, the
> shield-bearing troops, bursting forth from the forest, overthrew and routed the
> Romans who were returning to the ranks, while the cavalry, dispatched after
> those in flight, followed them all the way back to the camp, cutting them to
> pieces. Provision was also made that no one should escape. For 250 reserve
> horsemen, sent ahead for the purpose, found it a simple matter to race forward
> by short cuts, and then to turn back and meet those who had first fled, before
> they reached Pompeius' camp.
>   On learning of this, Pompeius sent out a legion under Decimus Laelius to
> reinforce his men, whereupon the cavalry of the enemy, withdrawing to the
> right flank, pretended to give way, and then, passing round the legion, assaulted
> it from the rear, while those who had followed up the foragers attacked it from
> the front also. Thus the legion with its commander was crushed between the
> two lines of the enemy. When Pompeius led out his entire army to help the
> legion, Sertorius exhibited his forces drawn up on the hillside, and thus baulked
> Pompeius' purpose. Thus, in addition to inflicting a twofold disaster, as a result
> of the same strategy, Sertorius forced Pompeius to be the helpless witness of the
> destruction of his own troops. This was the first battle between Sertorius and

Pompeius. According to Livy, 10,000 men were lost in Pompeius' army, along with the entire transport.[19]

There are brief notes in Appian, Sallust and Obsequens that also record the defeat:

> Directly Pompeius arrived in Spain, Sertorius cut to pieces a whole legion of his army, which had been sent out foraging, together with its animals and servants.[20]
>
> Laelius, the father of this Laelius, was killed by the soldiers of Hirtuleius. As Sallust says, a great number of military standards were seized along with the body of Laelius.[21]
>
> Laelius lost his life among the foragers in Spain, in the campaign against Sertorius.[22]

Thus Pompeius had been doubly defeated; first by being humiliated in his very public failure to relive the siege of Lauro, and second by losing a legion to an ambush and again being unable to save them. Not only was Pompeius visibly humbled, but the destruction of Lauro sent a message to all the other cities that had, or had considered, defecting; namely, that Pompeius could not protect them if they did. Plutarch tells us that as a consequence there were no more defections, at least this year.[23]

Whilst Pompeius was suffering reverses in northern Spain, to the south Metellus' fortunes were changing. Whilst again we have few details, it appears that Hirtuleius had disregarded Sertorius' order not to engage Metellus, and the two sides gave battle near the city of Italica Baetica (located just north of modern Seville).[24]

Battle of Italica Baetica
There is also talk of a battle of Segovia, apparently fought between these two men the next year as well. As will be discussed below, it can be argued that there was only one battle between Hirtuleius and Metellus, fought here at Italica. This battle was thus a decisive encounter for control of southern Spain. Regrettably, we have little detail on the battle itself, with only notices in Frontinus and a brief excerpt in Orosius:

> Hirtuleius engaged in battle with Metellus near the city of Italica Baetica and lost 20,000 soldiers. After his defeat he fled with a few followers to Lusitania.'[25]
>
> When Metellus Pius was waging war against Hirtuleius in Spain, and the latter had drawn up his troops immediately after daybreak and marched them against Metellus' entrenchments, Metellus held his own forces in camp till noon, as the weather at that time of year was extremely hot. Then, when the enemy were overcome by the heat, he easily defeated them, since his own men were fresh and their strength unimpaired.[26]

Metellus, in the battle in which he vanquished Hirtuleius in Spain, had discovered that the battalions of Hirtuleius which were deemed strongest were posted in the centre. Accordingly he drew back the centre of his own troops, to avoid encountering the enemy at that part of the line, until by an enveloping movement of his wings he could surround their centre from all sides.[27]

Aside from these, we only have a brief note in the *Periochae* of Livy stating that Hirtuleius was defeated.[28] This absence of detail is especially frustrating given the magnitude of the defeat and the fact that this was the first victory for the senatorial forces in the war, and an important one at that. With Hirtuleius' army destroyed, large stretches of southern Spain were now free of Sertorian forces, with the remaining ones concentrated in central Spain with Sertorius. Furthermore, the loss of 20,000 men would balance out the losses which the senatorial forces had suffered over the previous years. This major victory would also overshadow Pompeius' losses in the north and give the senatorial campaign a much needed boost.

It also seems to have turned on its head the direction of the war. In the previous years' campaigns, Metellus had seemingly been reduced to roaming southern Spain, unable to force the rebels into battle and being steadily ground down. Hirtuleius, by contrast, had won a string of victories. We must therefore assume that our surviving sources have played up the desperate situation that Metellus faced, in order to portray Pompeius in a better light. There is no mention of the battle in either of the two biographies by Plutarch (Pompeius and Sertorius), or in any of the shorter narrative accounts, Appian, Florus or Paterculus.

With the onset of winter Pompeius appears to have withdrawn back towards the Pyrenees. Appian states that Metellus also wintered by the Pyrenees, but this seems highly unlikely, given that he ended the year campaigning in southern Spain, and when the next year's campaign reopened, we again find him in the same region.[29] We are told that Sertorius and Perperna wintered in Lusitania, in the heartland of the rebel territory, where the defeated Hirtuleius had fled.[30]

As can be seen from the above, the entrance of Pompeius into the war, which must have been accompanied by much expectation on both sides, failed miserably. In fact, it was Metellus who scored the first victory of the campaign for the senatorial forces, with Pompeius being humiliated at Lauro and given a bloody nose in the battle which followed. However, the greatest victory of the year fell to Metellus when he destroyed the army of Hirtuleius, which overall meant that it was a year where the senatorial force came out ever so slightly on top.

4. Full-scale Warfare (75 BC)

If 76 BC was a year where Pompeius, Sertorius and Perperna were reluctant to commit themselves to battle, but rather followed feeling-out strategies, then 75 BC was the year that all sides appeared to commit to full-scale warfare, with three major battles culminating in the Battle of Segontia, the largest of the war. The sources present us with a number of key battles between the various armies, but each account differs from the others in terms of details, making the task of creating a coherent narrative of events notoriously difficult for this year (see below).

Non-Battle of Segovia

The key problem lies in the fact that a number of the surviving sources seem to depict elements of two battles between Hirtuleius and Metellus, traditionally assigned as the Battles of Italica Baetica in late 76 BC and Segovia in 74 BC. However, as Konrad points out, no one source states that there were actually two battles between the two men; we only assume this by combining the various scattered references across the sources.[31] Frontinus provides two separate references to the tactics used by Metellus against Hirtuleius, both different stratagems (see above), lending weight to the two-battle theory (one for Italica and one for Segovia). However, these could easily be Frontinus reporting either two different stratagems from one battle or two different accounts of the one battle from two different sources.

Another issue concerns the deaths of Hirtuleius and his brother. Orosius states that they clearly survive the first battle (Italica), while other sources depict their deaths in a subsequent encounter.[32] In Orosius, this encounter comes not only after the Battle of Lauro (76 BC) but Sucro as well (see below). Florus has only one battle, which he names as Segovia, but provides no details.[33] The disputed location of Segovia adds to the confusion, as it can be placed at a great distance from Italica.

Konrad's conclusion is that there was only one battle between Metellus and Hirtuleius, and that was Italica in late 76 BC.[34] With Hirtuleius' army crushed, he was unable to raise a fresh army and return to the field to fight the same man once again, which makes logical sense. Hirtuleius then joined up with either Sertorius or Perperna and served on their command staff, dying in battle at Segontia. To this author's mind, such an explanation seems far more logical than trying to create a two-battle scenario between the same men either side of the winter break in campaigning, especially given the complete nature of Hirtuleius' defeat at Italica. Thus, for Metellus, the year 75 BC opened with him moving from his winter quarters to link up with Pompeius to the east.

In eastern Spain, it seems that the previous year's reticence vanished also. It seems probable that Sertorius, plagued by the continuing threat of defections and weakened by the loss of Hirtuleius the previous year, had determined to defeat the senatorial forces in open battle. Whilst in 76 BC we have testimony of Sertorius deliberately avoiding battle, 75 BC saw major clashes between the two sides.

Battle of the River Turia

Pompeius advanced along Spain's eastern seaboard towards the city of Valentia (modern Valencia), where he encountered the army of Perperna and Herennius (another of Sertorius' legates), seemingly dispatched to block his attack on the city. The two armies clashed by the River Turia.[35] Again, we have few details of the battle, merely the outcome, which was a resounding victory for Pompeius, defeating both rebel commanders, killing Herennius along with 10,000 of his soldiers.[36]

> However, near Valentia he conquered Herennius and Perperna, men of military experience among the exiles with Sertorius, and generals under him, and slew more than 10,000 of their men.[37]

Following this victory, he appears to have attacked and destroyed the city of Valentia, as described by Pompeius' own words (as reported by Sallust): 'the destruction of the enemy general C. Herennius together with his army and the city of Valentia.'[38] Following the defeat, Perperna seems to have retreated southwards, towards the River Sucro.

Battle of the River Sucro

With the defeat of Perperna and Herennius, combined with the impending arrival of Metellus, it was at this point that Sertorius committed himself to battle, attempting to defeat Pompeius before the two men could combine forces. To this end, he marched to join Perperna at Sucro. In fact, Plutarch reports that Pompeius had a similar desire to give battle before Metellus could arrive; in this case out of a desire not to share any glory of the decisive victory with him. The two sides met at the River Sucro late in the day, and Plutarch provides two accounts, each with additional details, whilst Orosius has a short passage on it:

> By the River Sucro, though it was now late in the day, they joined battle, both fearing the arrival of Metellus; the one wished to fight alone, the other wished to have only one antagonist. Well, then, the struggle had a doubtful issue, for one wing on each side was victorious; but of the generals, Sertorius bore away the more honour, for he put to flight the enemy in front of his position. But Pompeius, who was on horseback, was attacked by a tall man who fought on foot; when they came to close quarters and were at grips, the strokes of their swords fell upon each other's hands, but not with like result, for Pompeius was merely wounded, whereas he lopped off the hand of his opponent. When more foes rushed upon him together, his troops being now routed, he made his escape, contrary to all expectation, by abandoning to the enemy his horse, which had golden head-gear and ornamented trappings of great value. They fought with one another over the division of these spoils, and so were left behind in the pursuit.[39]

When the fighting was at close quarters, it happened that Sertorius was not himself engaged with Pompeius at first, but with Afranius, who commanded Pompeius' left, while Sertorius himself was stationed on the right. Hearing, however, that those of his men who were engaged with Pompeius were yielding before his onset and being worsted, he put his right wing in command of other generals, and hastened himself to the help of the wing that was suffering defeat. Those of his men who were already in retreat he rallied, those who were still keeping their ranks he encouraged, then charged anew upon Pompeius, who was pursuing, and put his men to a great rout, in which Pompeius also came near being killed, was actually wounded, and had a marvellous escape. For the Libyans with Sertorius, after getting Pompeius' horse, which had golden decorations and was covered with costly trappings, were so busy distributing the booty and quarrelling with one another over it, that they neglected the pursuit. Afranius, however, as soon as Sertorius had gone off to the other wing with aid and succour, routed his opponents and drove them headlong into their camp; and dashing in with the fugitives, it being now dark, he began to plunder, knowing nothing of Pompeius' flight and having no power to keep his soldiers from their pillaging. But meanwhile, Sertorius came back from his victory on the other wing, and falling upon the straggling and confused soldiers of Afranius, slew great numbers of them.[40]

Sertorius then met Pompeius in battle and killed 10,000 of his soldiers. When Pompeius was conquering on the opposite wing, Sertorius suffered losses in almost the exact proportion to the former's gains.[41]

Thus, although both sides were victorious on a wing and suffered similar losses, it is clear that it was Pompeius who had to flee the battlefield with his men routed. The battle ended with the fall of night, which seems to have saved Pompeius' army from annihilation. The battle did not recommence the next day due to the arrival of Metellus' army, which forced Sertorius to withdraw rather than get caught between two opposing armies. Sertorius ordered his army to scatter and retreated inland to the Spanish highlands, leaving the senatorial forces with control of Spain's eastern seaboard. Whilst, on the face of it, the Battle of Sucro had been a stalemate, if not a defeat for Pompeius on the first day, ultimately, thanks to the arrival of Metellus, the senatorial forces had driven Sertorius back inland. Sertorius had once again bested Pompeius, but weight of numbers now appeared to be a factor against him. The armies of his subordinates Perperna and Herennius had been destroyed, with Herennius killed. Despite his personal standing, and undefeated status, the war appeared to be turning against him.

Pompeius thrust along the eastern seaboard, and Konrad argues that the attack on New Carthage by one of his legates (and brother-in-law), C. Memmius, dates to this period.[42]

The conflict is known only from a passing reference in Cicero. Regrettably, our narrative for the campaign then leaps forward to the next battle. We must assume that Pompeius and Metellus spent the intervening period securing control of Spain's eastern seaboard whilst tracking down Sertorius and his forces.

Battle of Segontia[43]

Again, we have few details of the circumstances building up to the battle, and the various sources give accounts that do not fit well together, and even the location is disputed. Plutarch actually places the battle near Saguntum, Appian Seguntia.[44] Modern commentators prefer to place the battle at the city of Segontia, though this in itself is problematic, as we can identify at least five of them in ancient Spain, none of which can be conclusively proven as the battle site. Konrad argues that it was fought near the River Duero and that Segontia should be identified with Langa de Duero.[45]

Whatever the location, it was the site of the greatest battle of the civil war in Spain to date, with the armies of Sertorius and Perperna clashing with those of Pompeius and Metellus for the first and last time. The circumstances that led up to the battle are unclear, but given his previous desire to avoid a set-piece battle, it seems that Sertorius had now changed tactics and was determined to end the war with one major encounter rather than continue to suffer lesser defeats, such as those suffered at Italica and Turia. There are various accounts of the battle:[46]

> Not long afterward, Sertorius fought a great battle near Seguntia, lasting from noon till night. Sertorius fought on horseback and vanquished Pompeius, killing nearly 6,000 of his men and losing about half that number himself. Metellus at the same time destroyed about 5,000 of Perperna's army. The day after this battle, Sertorius, with a large reinforcement of barbarians, attacked the camp of Metellus unexpectedly towards evening, with the intention of besieging it with a trench, but Pompeius hastened up and caused Sertorius to desist from his bold enterprise.[47]

> Quintus Metellus defeated Sertorius and Perperna with their two armies, but Pompeius, who was eager to be part of the victory, fought with dubious results.[48]

> Both sides fought splendidly. Memmius, the most capable of Pompeius' generals, fell in the thickest of the battle, and Sertorius was carrying all before him, and, with great slaughter of the enemy who still held together, was forcing his way towards Metellus himself. Then Metellus, who was holding his ground with a vigour that belied his years, and fighting gloriously, was struck by a spear. All the Romans who saw or heard of this were seized with shame at the thought of deserting their commander, and at the same time were filled with rage against the enemy. So, after they had covered Metellus with their shields and carried him out of danger, they stoutly drove the Iberians back.[49]

It has been argued that additional casualties included the Hirtuleii brothers on Sertorius' side and Memmius (Pompeius' brother-in-law), by ascribing the statement of Orosius concerning casualties to this battle (see above).[50]

Thus it seems that Sertorius was again victorious when he faced Pompeius in battle, but that the tide was again turned by Metellus, who defeated Perperna and forced Sertorius to disengage once more, or be defeated. Sertorius once again retreated back into the Spanish interior, this time with Metellus and Pompeius in pursuit. Sertorius retreated to the town of Clunia, where he successfully fought off the armies of Metellus and Pompeius, with repeated attacks on their camps and fortifications. The year ended with both senatorial commanders forced to withdraw, Metellus to Gaul, Pompeius to northern Spain, amongst loyal tribes.[51]

Thus the year ended with Sertorius suffering setbacks in battle, but still undefeated. It can be seen that this year represents a turning point in the civil war in Spain, with Sertorius out-matched by the combined armies of Pompeius and Metellus. On two occasions, at the battles of Sucro and Segontia, Sertorius was militarily successful himself (against Pompeius), but had to retire in the face of two separate Roman armies. Furthermore, his lieutenants had now all been defeated, with Hirtuleius and Herennius killed, and the remnants of Perperna's force integrated into his own.

Despite these setbacks, neither Metellus nor Pompeius were able to strike the final blow, as Sertorius' army had the ability to melt away into the Spanish interior and conduct a guerrilla campaign, to disrupt the senatorial armies, both of which retired for the winter, with Sertorius still in charge of the Spanish interior. A lack of supplies also seems to have been a serious issue for both senatorial armies for several reasons. Firstly, we must consider the devastation that Spain had suffered during these years of fighting, which was now reaching a peak, with a number of battles and sieges of key cities. Pompeius himself wrote the following (or at least that is what Sallust reports): 'That part of Nearer Spain which is not in enemy hands has been laid waste, either by us or by Sertorius, to the point of extermination, except for the coastal towns, to the stage where it is actually an expense and a burden to us.'[52]

Whilst we must allow for both possible Pompeian and Sallustian embellishments, Spain would have been devastated by this continued fighting. Furthermore, Sertorius had re-adopted his guerrilla tactics and was especially adept at the ambushing of foraging parties. All of this added up to Spain being a poor source of supplies for the armies of Pompeius and Metellus. Added to this devastation in Spain, it seemed that Gaul too was also suffering. Again, Sallust reports what purports to be Pompeius' words: 'Last year Gaul provided Metellus' army with pay and provisions; now, because of a failure of the crops, it can hardly support itself.'[53]

Thus it seems that Gaul, on the edge of famine, was unable to support the senatorial armies. This meant that supplies had to come from the rest of Rome's empire. However, it seems that the key sea routes were blocked or at least severely compromised by the activities of the Cilician pirates. We have little direct reference to their activities in the west, but Plutarch does refer to Sertorius cutting off the supplies of Pompeius and Metellus, including 'their maritime supplies by besetting the coast with piratical craft'.[54]

As we shall see below, the Senate took steps to clear the supply routes to the west. However, in the short term, this meant that whilst the two senatorial armies were victorious on the battlefield, it seems that they were losing the logistical war. A measure of the senatorial commanders' frustration can be seen by the reports that Metellus offered up a huge reward, of money and land, along with a free pardon to any exile, who assassinated Sertorius. At this point of the war, we have no reports of anyone attempting to claim the reward.

Metellus appears to have wintered in Gaul, adding to the burden of an overstretched province, whilst Pompeius seems to have wintered in Celtiberia, apparently continuing to reduce the local towns and cities. It was during the winter of 75/74 BC that he sent his infamous letter to the Senate, preserved by Sallust, demanding fresh troops, monies and supplies. In addition to summing up the desperate situation of his own army and the regions of Spain and Gaul (as seen above), his letter included the following statements:

> Thus the situation of my army and that of the enemy is the same; for neither is being paid and either, if victorious, can march into Italy. I draw your attention to this state of affairs and ask you to take notice of it and not to force me to solve my difficulties by abandoning the interest of the state for my own.[55]
>
> I myself have exhausted not only my means, but even my credit. You are our last resort; unless you come to our aid, my army, against my wishes, but as I have already warned you, will cross into Italy and bring with it the whole Spanish War.[56]

Whilst the debate will forever rage over the accuracy of the wording in Sallust, we must assume that the content and tone were the ones of Pompeius' letter to the Senate. If that is the case then it is an extraordinary document, in which a senatorial commander threatens to abandon the war and let Sertorius invade Italy, or be 'forced', by his own army to invade Italy and bring the civil war with it. Once again, we see the Pompeian tactic of claiming that his army was making demands rather than him. This tactic was used in both 80 and 77 BC when his army refused orders to disband, leaving him apparently powerless to defy them. As Sallust reports, the threats worked, and the consuls dispatched fresh monies, supplies and legions to Pompeius to continue the war in Spain.[57]

5. A Year of Sieges (74 BC)

Following the flurry of military activity in 75 BC, with a number of important battles, the war in 74 BC, by contrast, appears to have been one of siege and counter-siege. Sertorius returned to his strategy of avoiding set-piece battles and grinding the two senatorial armies down with his guerrilla tactics, whilst Metellus and Pompeius, perhaps slowed down by the lack of men and supplies, at least in the beginning of the year, seemed unable to fully campaign. As we would expect, the few surviving sources retain no sense of chronology for the year's campaigns. Both Metellus and Pompeius set about attacking the towns and cities which were loyal to Sertorius, whilst being harried by Sertorius in return. Sertorius and Perperna again appear to have wintered in Lusitania in the heartland of the rebellion.[58]

Metellus is recorded as making further progress against Sertorius in this year, aided by an increasing tide of defections from Sertorius. The losses of the previous year, whilst not actual defeats in battle, must have dented his aura of invincibility and indicated that he was unlikely to be victorious in the war, to the point of being able to drive Pompeius and Metellus out of Spain and invade Italy. Furthermore, Pompeius' letter to the Senate (see above) points out that the Sertorian forces were suffering from a lack of supplies also, due to the devastation caused by the continued fighting in Spain. Appian records the following:

> At this time, many of the soldiers of Sertorius deserted to Metellus, at which Sertorius was so angered that he visited savage and barbarous punishments upon many of his men and became unpopular as a consequence.[59]

Whilst Metellus was making apparent headway against Sertorius, both by desertions and sieges, Pompeius by contrast appeared to be continuing in his difficulties. We do not know at what point his reinforcements from Italy arrived; all we do know is that he suffered reversers at the sieges of Palentia and Calagurris, as reported in Appian:

> While Pompeius was laying siege to Palentia and undermining the walls with wooden supports, Sertorius suddenly appeared on the scene and raised the siege. Pompeius hastily set fire to the timbers and retreated to Metellus. Sertorius rebuilt the part of the wall which had fallen and then attacked his enemies, who were encamped around the castle of Calagurris and killed 3,000 of them. And so this year went by in Spain.[60]

The *Periochae* of Livy has the following: 'in every aspect of war and the art of soldiery, he [Sertorius] was their equal... and having made them to break off the siege of Calagurris, he forced them to retreat in different regions, Metellus to Hispania Ulterior, Pompeius to Gaul.[61]

Perperna, however, appears to have been active in the field also, attacking towns loyal to Metellus and Pompeius, yet seems to have avoided the main areas of conflict in Spain. A fragment of Sallust, which is commonly dated to this year, records him capturing the town of Cales in northwest Spain, though again this is impossible to date with any certainty.[62]

Thus it seems that again Sertorius was victorious against Pompeius' forces, but lost ground to Metellus. The senatorial forces again appeared to be slowly gaining the upper hand by reducing the towns and cities loyal to Sertorius, securing fresh supplies and reinforcements, whilst encouraging defections amongst Sertorius' men. Yet as the year drew to a close, Sertorius remained at large, Spain remained largely out of senatorial control, and Pompeius and Metellus appeared to be no nearer to clinching a decisive victory in the war.

Whilst the year 74 BC saw stalemate in Spain, two new wars beset Rome this year, both of which had an impact on the civil war being fought in Spain, namely, the Third Mithridatic War and another major campaign against the Cilician pirates. Whilst the full details of these wars falls beyond the scope of this present work (see Appendix I), both contained elements that affected the fighting in Spain.

6. The Piracy Campaign (74 BC onwards)

The removal of the great naval powers of the region, notably Rhodes, combined with Roman indifference to naval issues, had allowed piracy in the Mediterranean to flourish, and one particular hotbed was centred on the lawless regions of Cilicia, in southeast Asia Minor. On occasions the Senate tuned its attentions to the piracy problem, most notably in 102 BC, with the appointment of M. Antonius (grandfather of the triumvir) to a command to combat the piracy problem in the eastern Mediterranean. Whilst he seems to have made some inroads into the problem, for a generation at least, the chaos of this period had led to a resurgence of piratical activity, disrupting trade across the whole Mediterranean. In the western Mediterranean, Sertorius allied with Cilician pirates as early as 81–80 BC, whilst by 74 BC the pirates seem to have totally disrupted the naval routes between Italy and Spain, though whether this was through alliance with Sertorius or not is unknown.

Thus in 74 BC, tiring of the problem in both the west and the east, the Senate appointed another M. Antonius (the son of the commander of the 102 BC expedition and father of the triumvir) to another extraordinary naval command, tasked with clearing the Mediterranean of the pirate threat. Whilst the spur for this command is usually ascribed as the outbreak of the Third Mithradatic War (see below), Antonius spent the first year of his campaign clearing pirates from the western Mediterranean, around the coasts of Liguria, Spain and Sicily, and thus aided the Senate in securing the supply routes to its commanders in Spain, especially Pompeius, again easing the conditions of warfare for the senatorial commanders.[63] A fragment of Sallust preserves a narrative of an engagement Antonius fought with Ligurian tribes allied to the pirates, who then considered finding shelter with Sertorius:

When, on the summons of the Terentuni, the Ligurian detachments had withdrawn into the Alps, the question was raised about sailing on to join Sertorius. Since it seemed a good idea to Antonius and the others to hasten their voyage towards Spain, they reached the territory of the Aresinarii after four days with their whole force of warships.[64]

7. The Civil War Spreads East

Whilst the additional naval support provided by Antonius in his war against the pirates of the Mediterranean looked like a further tightening of the noose around Sertorius in Spain, events in the east allowed for a massive (albeit temporary) escalation of the civil war. At some point in 75/74 BC period, King Nicomedes IV of Bithynia (see Map 9) died and bequeathed his kingdom to the Roman people.[65] As his kingdom lay between the Roman province of Asia and the Pontic Kingdom of Mithridates VI, the Senate, not wanting Mithridates to seize the leaderless kingdom, eagerly accepted the bequest and declared Bithynia a Roman province. Unsurprisingly, Mithridates VI did not take kindly to the Romans annexing a prize he had long sought and bringing their empire to his own borders, and thus declared war on Rome, sparking the Third Mithridatic War. Whilst the full details of this war fall outside of the scope of this work, there was one crucial element that tied this war to the civil war raging in Spain. At some point in either 75 or 74 BC, Mithridates sent envoys to Spain to conduct a treaty of alliance with Sertorius and his government in exile.[66] As Appian reports, the driving force behind this alliance seems to have come from two former coalition commanders, who had served under Flaccus and then Fimbria in Asia Minor (see Chapter 5), and had taken shelter with the court of Mithridates:

> Two members of his [Sertorius'] faction, Lucius Magius and Lucius Fannius, proposed to Mithridates to ally himself with Sertorius, holding out the hope that he would acquire a large part of the province of Asia and of the neighbouring nations. Mithridates fell in with this suggestion and sent ambassadors to Sertorius. The latter introduced them to his Senate and felicitated himself that his fame had extended to Pontus, and that he could now besiege the Roman power in both the Orient and the Occident. So he made a treaty with Mithridates to give him Asia, Bithynia, Paphlagonia, Cappodocia, and Galatia, and sent Marcus Marius[67] to him as a general and the two Luciuses, Magius and Fannius, as counsellors.[68]

Plutarch reports a variation on the terms of the treaty:

> So Mithridates sent envoys to Iberia carrying letters and oral propositions to Sertorius, the purport of which was that Mithridates for his part promised to furnish money and ships for the war, but demanded that Sertorius confirm him in the possession of the whole of Asia, which he had yielded to the Romans by virtue of the treaties made with Sulla. Sertorius assembled a council, which he called a Senate, and here the rest urged him to accept the king's proposals and be well content with them; for they were asked to grant a name and an empty title to what was not in their possession, and would receive therefore that of which they stood most in need. Sertorius, however, would not consent to this. He said

he had no objection to Mithridates taking Bithynia and Cappodocia, countries used to kings and of no concern whatever to the Romans; but a province which Mithridates had taken away and held when it belonged in the justest manner to the Romans, from which he had been driven by Fimbria in war, and which he had renounced by treaty with Sulla, this province Sertorius said he would not suffer to become the king's again; for the Roman state must be increased by his exercise of power, and he must not exercise power at the expense of the state.[69]

Orosius also records the alliance: 'Fannius and Magius fled from the army of Fimbria and joined Mithridates. On their advice the latter made a treaty with Sertorius through the offices of ambassadors whom he had sent to Spain.[70]

Thus in Plutarch's version, Sertorius agreed to cede to Mithridates Bithynia and Cappodocia, but not Asia. Given that its revenue was crucial to the Roman state, this is hardly surprising. Despite this, it seems that a treaty was concluded and Sertorius and his Senate agreed that Cappodocia and Bithynia were to be ceded to Mithridates.[71] Plutarch details the practical terms of the treaty: 'Sertorius sending him [Mithridates] a general and soldiers, while Sertorius was to receive from Mithridates 3,000 talents and forty ships.'

For Plutarch and Orosius, it is the two coalition commanders L. Fannius and L. Magius, who were the driving forces behind this alliance, linking Mithridates' struggle to their own and fanning the flames of the civil war in Asia once more, leaving Rome to fight on two fronts. Appian has a variation on their role, placing them both as firm followers of Sertorius, seemingly making him the driving force for this alliance, and seems to believe that they were in Spain with him prior to being sent to serve under Mithridates. Given that they fled to Mithridates whilst in the east, it seems that both men stayed there in the intervening period, as part of the wider Roman exile community in the Pontic court (see Chapter 11). How much prior contact the two had with Sertorius is unknown.[72] Thus, by 74 BC, a second front of the civil war had been opened, in Asia Minor. As part of the alliance, Sertorius sent a general to fight alongside Mithridates, and the other Roman exiles in Pontus: his name was M. Marius.

Chapter 10

War on Two Fronts: Spain and Asia (74–71 BC)

Marius and the Roman exiles in Asia

Marius is an intriguing figure, first appearing in Spain serving under Sertorius, as a quaestor in 76 BC. All we have as background for that man is that he was a senator who had fled to Sertorius, but crucially we do not know when.[1] The obvious question is what was his relationship to C. Marius? Ultimately, we have no evidence; we know he was a senator who had to flee Rome and that Sertorius thought him totemic enough to be the figurehead for the coalition armies in Asia. Given that he was a Roman senator who was proscribed, the most logical assumption is that he was indeed a close relation of the elder Marius, but we do not know if he fled Rome in 82 or 78/77 BC. He could have fled Rome in 82 BC directly to Spain or been on Sicily along with M. Perperna.

We know little of the wider family of the elder C. Marius, but we do know of an M. Marius who served as praetor and pro-praetor in Spain in 102–101 BC, leading Evans to speculate that he was a younger brother of C. Marius.[2] Given that they had the same name, it is not beyond the realms of possibility that this M. Marius was the son of this possible younger brother and thus nephew of the seven-time consul himself.[3] In any event, having a Roman army led by a Marius was of significant propaganda value, and so the civil war, for so long now confined to the west, spread once again, this time to Asia Minor. Plutarch describes Marius as being Sertorius' choice to spearhead the eastern rebel forces, whilst Orosius reports a slight variation on this story:

> Sertorius sent M. Marius to him [Mithridates] for the purpose of ratifying the treaty. Mithridates kept him by his side and in a short time appointed him general in place of Archelaus.[4]

Aside from Marius, we have reports of a number of prominent Roman exiles at the court of Mithridates, who had gathered there over the years. The earliest of these reported figures is C. Appuleius Decianus (Tr Pl 98) who was prosecuted and exiled following his year of office for being a supporter of the murdered tribune L. Appuleius Saturninus (see Chapter 1). Whether he fled east to Mithridates directly, or made his way slowly there over the years is not known.[5]

The most notable of the exiles were the aforementioned coalition commanders L. Fannius and L. Magius, who had served under Fimbria in the east in the campaigns against Mithridates of 86–85 BC. They seem to have been at Mithridates' court for at least a portion of the intervening decade, becoming trusted advisors on Roman matters. The final named individual is a Roman senator named Attidius, though his identity and reasons for seeking refuge at the Pontic court are unknown.[6]

Aside from these five named individuals, Memnon refers to a number of Roman exiles, all proscribed men, being killed in the decisive battle of the eastern phase of the civil war (see below).[7] Thus, all the indications are that by this point there was a sizable gathering of exiled and proscribed Roman senators, mostly lesser coalition figures, in the court of Mithridates VI, who were now able to utilize the forces of Mithridates in the continuation of their war against the Senate in Rome. Fannius and Magius were not the only reminders of the previous civil war campaigns in Asia, as a large part of the senatorial army fighting Mithridates and the coalition commanders came from the army of Fimbria himself, which had been left as a permanent force in Asia by Sulla, when he left the east to invade Italy:

> The Fimbrians, as they were called, had become unmanageable, through long lack of discipline. These were the men who, in collusion with Fimbria, had slain Flaccus, their consul and general, and had delivered Fimbria himself over to Sulla. They were self-willed and lawless, but good fighters, hardy, and experienced in war. However, in a short time Lucullus pruned off their insolent boldness, and reformed the rest.[8]

Thus a large contingent of the senatorial forces were from a former coalition army, that had connived at the murder of their consular commander Flaccus in 85, and then promptly betrayed their new commander Fimbria; following which they had been left in Asia as a permanent presence for the intervening decade. Furthermore, they now faced some of their own former commanders, in the form of Fannius and Magius, and the opposing general, a relation of elder Marius.

2. Civil War in Asia

In the opening period of the war, not only were the coalition forces led by M. Marius, but it seems that the Pontic forces were as well (at least nominally):

> He [Marius] was assisted by Mithridates in the capture of certain cities of Asia, and when he entered them with fasces and axes, Mithridates would follow him in person, voluntarily assuming second rank and the position of a vassal. Marius gave some of the cities their freedom, and wrote to others announcing their exemption from taxation by grace of Sertorius, so that Asia, which was

once more harassed by the revenue-farmers and oppressed by the rapacity and arrogance of the soldiers quartered there, was all of a flutter with new hopes and yearned for the expected change of supremacy.[9]

Thus, rather than appear as a foreign invader, Mithridates wisely appeared to be subordinate to the Roman general and was appointed representative of one of Rome's two Senates. Marius appears to have played this role with considerable skill, appearing as a Roman general freeing them from the hated tax collection process imposed on them by the Senate of Rome. The Roman senatorial forces in Asia were commanded by both consuls of 74 BC, M. Aurelius Cotta and L. Licinius Lucullus.[10] Though Cotta arrived in the east first, it was Lucullus who soon assumed overall command of the Third Mithridatic War and led the bulk of the fighting against Marius in these eastern civil war campaigns.

A clash between Lucullus and Marius was awash with overtones of the previous phases of the civil war and the history behind it. Lucullus was not only a protégé of Sulla, but is suspected of being the only one of Sulla's officers who did not desert Sulla when he marched his army on Rome in 88 BC (see Chapter 3).[11] As we have seen (Chapter 5), he served as Sulla's legate in the First Mithridatic War and had always been seen as a close adherent to Sulla, with whom he was related through marriage; both had married into the Caecilii Metelli. In point of fact, his maternal uncle was Q. Caecilius Metellus Numidicus himself, Marius the elder's former mentor and then long-time enemy. Though the full details of the Third Mithridatic War fall outside the scope of this work, we do have a number of references to the activities of Marius and his coalition forces and his subsequent battles with Lucullus.

Battle of Chalcedon
The first key battle of the Third Mithridatic War was a Mithridatic victory over the consul Cotta in late 74 BC at Chalcedon. Marius and his forces played a part in that victory:

> Marius and Eumachus, who were dispatched by Mithridates as generals against Lucullus, assembled a great army in short time and engaged in battle with P. Rutilius [Nudus] near Chalcedon; he and the greater part of his army were slain there.[12]

The Non-Battle of Otryae
Following this defeat, Cotta and his forces were held up in the city of Chalcedon, awaiting reinforcements and rescue by Lucullus. As Lucullus' army approached, Marius was sent to stop him. The two forces met at Otryae:

[Lucullus] led his army against Mithridates, having 30,000 foot-soldiers, and 2,500 horsemen. But when he had come within sight of the enemy and seen with amazement their multitude, he desired to refrain from battle and draw out the time. But Marius, whom Sertorius had sent to Mithridates from Spain with an army, came out to meet him, and challenged him to combat, and so he put his forces in array to fight the issue out. But presently, as they were on the point of joining battle, with no apparent change of weather, but all on a sudden, the sky burst asunder, and a huge, flame-like body was seen to fall between the two armies. In shape, it was most like a wine-jar, and in colour, like molten silver. Both sides were astonished at the sight, and separated. This marvel, as they say, occurred in Phrygia, at a place called Otryae.[13]

Thus the first clash between Lucullus and Marius was aborted due to a natural phenomenon. Lucullus' force went on to Chalcedon and lifted the siege, though we have no details of Marius' involvement in the fighting. The forces next met a few months later, during early 73 BC, following the Mithridatic siege of the city of Cyzicus, which also saw another notable incident involving the former Fimbrian element of Lucullus' army:

The Fimbrian soldiers were concerned that their leaders would regard them as disloyal because of their crime against Flaccus, and they secretly sent to Mithridates, promising to desert to him. Mithridates thought this message was a stroke of luck, and when night came he sent Archelaus to confirm the agreement and to bring the deserters over to him. But when Archelaus arrived, the Fimbrian soldiers seized him and killed his companions.[14]

Appian adds the detail that this was orchestrated by none other than L. Magius himself, who once again decided to change sides and this time betrayed Mithridates to Lucullus, after securing amnesty.[15] Appian adds the crucial detail that Magius did so following the death of Sertorius in Spain. As the Cyzicus campaign dates from 73 BC, this is a crucial piece of evidence for the argument that Sertorius was assassinated in 73 BC, and not 72 BC (see below).[16] Thus both Magius and the Fimbrian legions completed a full circle of betrayals and placed themselves firmly in the camp of the Roman Senate. The various clashes of the Cyzicus campaign turned the tide of the war against Mithridates and Marius. Again, the chronology for this period is open to dispute, but the year 73 BC is considered to be the most likely.[17]

Battle of the River Aesepus
The first clash between Lucullus and Marius came at the River Aesepus, and is recorded in brief detail by Memnon, Appian and Orosius:

He [Mithridates] appointed Hermaeus and Marius to lead the foot-soldiers, with an army of over 30,000 men, while he made his way back by sea. Various disasters occurred as he boarded the triremes, because the men who were still waiting to board them grasped the ships and hung onto them, both the ships which were already full and the ones which remained. So many men did this that some of the ships were sunk and others were capsized. When the citizens of Cyzicus saw this, they attacked the Pontic camp, slaughtered the exhausted troops who were left there and pillaged everything that had been left in the camp. Lucullus pursued the army as far as the River Aesepus, where he surprised it and killed a great number of the enemy.[18]

Nevertheless Mithridates continued his efforts, hoping still to capture Cyzicus by means of the mounds extending from Mount Dindymus. But when the Cyziceans undermined them and burned the machines on them, and made frequent sallies upon his forces, knowing that they were weakened by want of food, Mithridates began to think of flight. He fled by night, going himself with his fleet to Parius, and his army by land to Lampsacus. Many lost their lives in crossing the River Aesepus, which was then greatly swollen, and where Lucullus attacked them.[19]

Soon afterwards he attacked and defeated Marius and put him to flight in a battle in which more than 11,000 of Marius' troops, according to report, were killed.[20]

Thus, the first battle between Lucullus and Marius ended with a Marian defeat, and the loss of 11,000 men. The Marian forces had been in retreat following the failure at Cyzicus and were ambushed by Lucullus when attempting to cross a swollen river. The aborted siege of Cyzicus proved to be a turning point in the war; Mithridates' forces had suffered an earlier defeat at the River Rhyndacus, with heavy losses, and now came this rout at Aesepus.[21] The sources report that, whilst Mithridates himself had escaped by ship, the land army was in headlong retreat with Lucullus at its heels. The remnants of the army seem to have made for the coastal city of Lampsacus to await naval rescue. Lucullus followed them and laid the city under siege. A Mithridatic fleet arrived and spirited the survivors away, except for a rearguard commanded by M. Marius:

Mithridates sent ships for those who had taken refuge in Lampsacus, where they were besieged by Lucullus, and carried them away, together with the Lampsaceans themselves. Leaving 10,000 picked men and fifty ships under Marius (the general sent to him by Sertorius), and Alexander the Paphlagonian, and Dionysius the eunuch, he sailed with the bulk of his force for Nicomedia. A storm came up in which many of both divisions perished.[22]

Battle of Tenedos

With the main fleet escaping, Marius appears to have escaped Lampsacus himself with his army on board the ships that had been left for him. Lucullus, whose fleet had not been able to prevent the evacuation of Mithridates' army, now gave chase to the Marian fleet and engaged them near the island of Tenedos, near Lemnos. Appian, Plutarch and Orosius preserve accounts of the battle:[23]

He overtook Marius and Alexander and Dionysius on a barren island near Lemnos (where the altar of Philoctetes is shown with the brazen serpent, the bows, and the breastplate bound with fillets, to remind us of the sufferings of that hero), and dashed at them in a contemptuous manner. They stoutly held their ground. He checked his oarsmen and sent his ships toward them by twos in order to entice them out to sea. As they declined the challenge, but continued to defend themselves on land, he sent a part of his fleet around to another side of the island, disembarked a force of infantry, and drove the enemy to their ships. Still they did not venture out to sea, but hugged the shore, because they were afraid of the army of Lucullus. Thus they were exposed to missiles on both sides, landward and seaward, and received a great many wounds, and after heavy slaughter took to flight. Marius, Alexander, and Dionysius the eunuch were captured in a cave where they had concealed themselves. Dionysius drank poison which he had with him and immediately expired. Lucullus gave orders that Marius be put to death, since he did not want to have his triumph graced by a Roman senator, but he kept Alexander for that purpose.[24]

Accordingly, Lucullus put to sea at once, captured these, slew their commander, Isodorus, and then sailed in pursuit of the other captains, whom these were seeking to join. They chanced to be lying at anchor close to shore, and drawing their vessels all up on land, they fought from their decks, and sorely galled the crews of Lucullus. These had no chance to sail round their enemies, nor to make onset upon them, since their own ships were afloat, while those of their enemies were planted upon the land and securely fixed. However, Lucullus at last succeeded in disembarking the best of his soldiers where the island afforded some sort of access. These fell upon the enemy from the rear, slew some of them, and forced the rest to cut their stern cables and fly from the shore, their vessels thus falling foul of one another, and receiving the impact of the ships of Lucullus. Many of the enemy perished, of course, and among the captives there was brought in Marius, the general sent from Sertorius. He had but one eye, and the soldiers had received strict orders from Lucullus, as soon as they set sail, to kill no one-eyed man. Lucullus wished Marius to die under the most shameful insults.[25]

Lucullus later met this same Marius in a naval encounter and sank or captured thirty-two of the royal ships and also a great many transports. Many of those whom Sulla had proscribed were killed in that battle. On the next day Marius was dragged out from a cave in which he was hiding and paid the penalty that his hostile intentions merited.[26]

Cicero refers to the battle on three occasions in his various speeches, and is the only source to name its location, Tenedos:

> I say that he also, when general, defeated and destroyed that great and well-appointed fleet, which the chiefs of Sertorius' party were leading against Italy with furious zeal.[27]
>
> Do you think that that naval battle at Tenedos, when the enemy's fleet were hastening on with rapid course and under most eager admirals towards Italy, full of hope and courage, was a trifling engagement, an insignificant contest?[28]
>
> Ours is the glory which will be for ever celebrated, which is derived from the fleet of the enemy which was sunk after its admirals had been slain, and from the marvellous naval battle off Tenedos.[29]

Thus this naval battle ended the Asian campaigns of the civil war. The Ciceronian references are interesting, as he refers to them as an invasion fleet heading to Italy rather than a rearguard action to escape Lampsacus and retreat to safer territory. It is conceivable that, feeling abandoned by Mithridates, the Roman contingent had decided to abandon the Asian campaign and return to Spain and rejoin Sertorius. In any event, Marius and a significant proportion of the Roman exile community were killed. Despite Cicero, it is difficult to see this incident as being anything other than a sacrifice by Mithridates, placing Marius and a number of his fellow exiles in the rearguard to buy his own forces time to retreat. This assessment would be enhanced if Sertorius himself was now dead and the alliance broken (see below).

Of the other Roman exiles at the Mithridatic court, L. Magius presumably continued the war in Lucullus' entourage, whist L. Fannius escaped and continued to fight with Mithridates, but seems to have also defected back to the Roman side and Lucullus, possibly facilitated by his old colleague Magius, and we find him fighting Tigranes in 68 BC.[30] The son of Decianus, who accompanied his father into exile, returned to Rome following the general amnesty in 70 BC (see Chapter 11) and is mentioned in relation to his business dealings in Asia by Cicero. The only other exile still recorded at the court of Mithridates was Attidius, who became a close confidante of Mithridates himself, but was executed by the king in 67 BC after being implicated in a plot to assassinate him.

Thus by his swift actions and military acumen, Lucullus ended the eastern campaigns of the civil war, which had so briefly threatened to plunge Rome into a two-pronged war, in little more than a year. Marius and his fellow exiles seemed to have suited Mithridates' purposes when he was on the offensive, especially by legitimizing his invasion of Roman territory, but they soon found themselves sacrificed when the tide of the war turned. With the death of Marius, and his colleagues' defection back to Rome, combined with Mithridates retreating across Asia Minor, the alliance between him and the exiled government in Spain, which had promised so much, fell into abeyance. Once again, Spain became the sole focus of the civil war.

4. The War in Spain (73–71 BC)

The key issue facing any analysis of this phase of the civil war in Spain concerns the death of Sertorius. Under the traditional dating, the year 73 BC apparently continued in the same vein as 74 BC, with no major clashes, but with Pompeius and Metellus reducing the remaining Sertorian allied towns and cities by siege. Appian only makes a vague statement about there being no great battles and a campaign of sieges, whilst both he and Plutarch start stressing that the morale of the Spanish tribes was undermined by the military superiority of the senatorial forces and that in response Sertorius became more tyrannical, even going so far as to attack the children of the tribal leaders who were being educated at his Roman school in Osca (see Chapter 9), apparently killing a number and selling the survivors into slavery.[31] However, as Plutarch also reports, dissatisfaction amongst Sertorius' followers extended beyond the Spanish tribes and into the rebel Senate itself.[32]

Traditionally, by 72 BC Sertorius' descent into tyranny leads to conspiracy, as detailed in both Appian and Plutarch.[33] Given the deaths of Hirtuleius, Herennius and M. Marius, the key surviving coalition general was M. Perperna, and the conspiracy centres upon him. According to Appian's account, the initial conspiracy was discovered but not Perperna's role as mastermind. A second attempt was planned for a banquet at which Sertorius and his bodyguards were plied with wine and then murdered.

From Plutarch's account and a fragment of Sallust, we are given the names of a number of the other conspirators: M. Antonius, Aufidius, L. Fabius Hispaniensis, Manlius, Octavius Graecinus and C. Tarquitius Priscus.[34]

Unfortunately, there are a number of indications that this assassination actually occurred in 73 BC, not 72 BC, as traditionally believed. Both Bennett and Konrad provide the best arguments.[35] There are several indicators to this shift in chronology. Firstly, we have the evidence that Appian provides for the betrayal of L. Magius from the coalition forces in Asia to Lucullus, as news of Sertorius' death had reached them. Again, the Cyzicus campaign itself is difficult to date, but it has been argued that it dates from autumn 73 BC. As Bennett argues, the consuls elected in late 73 for 72 BC were Pompeian allies, and when in office they carried laws to validate grants of citizenship Pompeius had made in Spain, the argument being that they were elected with the expectation of quick victory on the news of Sertorius' death.[36] There is also an intriguing sentence in the *Periochae* of Livy that states that for 73 BC, 'It [the book] also contains an account of Cn. Pompeius' victorious war against Sertorius in Hispania.' The key question is why was it victorious if no major engagements were fought?[37] Again, unfortunately, the *Periochae* of Livy itself is uncertain on its exact year-on-year chronology.

Ultimately, we have no exact chronology for this period, and the year of Sertorius' assassination cannot be dated with absolute certainty. Nevertheless, the evidence does indicate that the assassination took place early in 73 and not 72 BC. This re-assessment removes the additional year of Sertorius' campaign in the narrative of our sources, and has him being murdered whilst still scoring victories in his guerrilla tactics. This does not mean that his rule had not become harsher or that his allies were deserting him through 74 BC as the tide of the war turned.[38]

The murder of Sertorius had a major impact on both sides of the Mediterranean. Naturally enough, as senior surviving commander of the coalition forces, Perperna took charge of the war in Spain. Whilst competent enough, he was no match for Sertorius in either his military prowess or his leadership skills. Sertorius' death robbed the coalition forces of a charismatic figurehead, a general who fought with Marius himself and who had gone through the war avoiding outright defeat, always seeming to bounce back stronger. Perperna, on the other hand, whilst competent, had a string of military defeats to his name and, if the sources are to be believed, the personality of a true Roman patrician.

Both Appian and Plutarch report that, although Sertorius' unpopularity had been growing, neither the solders nor the tribal leaders took kindly to seeing such a great leader murdered in such a fashion. Ironically, it seems that Perperna himself was made a bequest in Sertorius' will.[39] Appian reports the measures that Perperna was forced to take in order to quell rebellions amongst the soldiers and other Roman commanders:

And they would not have abstained from violence had not Perperna bestirred himself, making gifts to some and promises to others. Some he terrified with threats and some he killed in order to strike terror into the rest. He came forward and made a speech to the multitude, and released from confinement some whom Sertorius had imprisoned, and dismissed some of the Spanish hostages. Reduced to submission in this way, they obeyed him as praetor (for he held the next rank to Sertorius), yet they were not without bitterness toward him even then. As he grew bolder, he became very cruel in punishments, and put to death three of the nobility who had fled together from Rome to him, and also his own nephew.[40]

Whilst Perperna may have been able to control the Roman contingent, as Plutarch reports, the tribal elements of the armies were another matter:

Well, then, most of the Iberians immediately went away, sent ambassadors to Pompeius and Metellus, and delivered themselves up to them; but those who remained Perperna took under his command and attempted to do something.[41]

With the rebellion faltering and his own authority in question, Perperna seems to have continued his campaign through the rest of 73 BC, but by early the following year he seems to have decided to gamble everything on one decisive battle with Pompeius, which, given his previous record against him, was a bold move indeed.

Unnamed Battle

Both Appian and Plutarch preserve short narratives of the battle between Pompeius and Perperna, though the location of the clash is unknown:

> As Metellus had gone to other parts of Spain, for he considered it no longer a difficult task for Pompeius alone to vanquish Perperna, these two skirmished and made tests of each other for several days, but did not bring their whole strength into the field. On the tenth day, however, a great battle was fought between them. They resolved to decide the contest by one engagement, Pompeius because he despised the generalship of Perperna; Perperna because he did not believe that his army would long remain faithful to him, and he could now engage with nearly his whole strength. Pompeius, as might have been expected, soon got the better of this inferior general and disaffected army. Perperna was defeated all along the line and concealed himself in a thicket, more fearful of his own troops than of the enemy's. He was seized by some horsemen and dragged toward Pompeius' headquarters, loaded with the execrations of his own men, as the murderer of Sertorius, and crying out that he could give Pompeius a great deal of information about the factions in Rome. This he said either because it was true, or in order to be brought safe to Pompeius' presence, but the latter sent orders to kill him before bringing him into his presence, fearing lest the news that Perperna wanted to communicate should be the source of new troubles at Rome. Pompeius seems to have behaved very prudently in this matter, and his action added to his high reputation. So ended the war in Spain with the life of Sertorius. I think that if he had lived longer the war would not have ended so soon or so successfully.[42]

Accordingly, Pompeius took the field against him at once, and perceiving that he had no fixed plan of campaign, sent out ten cohorts as a decoy for him, giving them orders to scatter at random over the plain. Perperna attacked these cohorts, and was engaged in their pursuit, when Pompeius appeared in force, joined battle, and won a complete victory. Most of Perperna's officers perished in the battle, but Perperna himself was brought before Pompeius, who ordered him to be put to death. In this he did not show ingratitude, nor that he was unmindful of what had happened in Sicily, as some allege against him, but exercised great forethought and salutary judgement for the commonwealth. For Perperna, who had come into possession of the papers of Sertorius, offered to produce letters from the chief men at Rome, who had desired to subvert the existing order and change the form of government, and had therefore invited Sertorius into Italy. Pompeius, therefore, fearing that this might stir up greater wars than those now ended, put Perperna to death and burned the letters without even reading them.[43]

Thus, it seems that Perperna fell into a Pompeian trap and his army was wiped out. Once again, Perperna proved that in battle he was no Sertorius. Both sources chose to focus on Pompeius' summary execution of Perperna, akin to that of Carbo in 82 BC. As with Lucullus' execution of M. Marius the year before, both senatorial commanders chose the easier option of ending further resistance with a swift execution (both men were already declared enemies of the state), rather than bring them back to Rome to re-open old wounds. Certainly, no Roman could parade another in a triumph, and the embarrassing fact that Roman was fighting Roman needed to be downplayed.

Both sources also focus on the letters of support that first Sertorius, and then Perperna, had in their possession from figures within the Senate in Rome. Pompeius seemingly made a public show of telling everyone that he had burnt these treasonable letters without reading them, but one has to wonder whether he really did decline to read them first, or whether he perhaps made copies. Such leverage would be invaluable in his forthcoming political career, and it is hard to believe that such a consummate politician as Pompeius would pass up such an opportunity. Certainly, Pompeius' prudence in this matter was not so subtle as to prevent such stories circulating in Rome at the time and in the histories which followed.[44]

Appian's comments about the war in Spain being over with Sertorius' death, whilst reflecting a commonly held view, are not to be accepted at face value. Certainly, we have to say that Perperna was no Sertorius, and that the alliance of rebellious tribes and coalition forces from the civil war that had been forged by Sertorius were not guaranteed to survive his death. Yet a victory for Perperna would have injected fresh energy into the campaign and may have held this alliance together, which probably explains Perperna's rash move to fight a man who had already defeated him. With Perperna dead, it seems that the Sertorian Senate soon fell apart. As a postscript to his life of Sertorius, Plutarch records the fate of the other assassins (see Appendix III):

> Of Perperna's fellow conspirators, some were brought to Pompeius and put to death; others fled to Africa and fell victims to the spears of the Mauri. Not one escaped, except Aufidius, the rival of Manlius; he, either because men did not notice him or because they did not heed him, came to old age in a barbarian village, a poor and hated man.[45]

The reference to some of the remaining commanders fleeing to Africa is interesting, as the city of Tangis (Tangiers) was Sertorius' initial springboard for his invasion of Spain and presumably remained under his control throughout this period. From Plutarch's reference, it seems that the native Mauri, following the death of Sertorius, soon determined to show their loyalty to Rome by murdering its enemies. Interestingly, the civil war campaigns in Spain and Asia both featured a mixture of native rebellions acting in concert with, or being spearheaded by, exiled Roman elements. In 85 BC, Sulla made a treaty with Mithridates, whilst a decade later it was Sertorius and a Marius. Such a mixture of conflicts can be seen with the war in 87 BC, whereby the Samnites, still fighting the Italian war, found themselves on the winning side of Rome's civil war (albeit temporarily). This seems to have been a two-way process. For the factions not in control of Rome, these rebellions provided fresh forces for their fight against their enemies, whilst for the natives these civil war factions provided unparalleled opportunity to take advantage of a divided Rome and bolster their own campaigns. Ultimately, however, these alliances between natives and Roman factions were only ever going to be 'marriages of convenience', for whichever faction gained control of Rome, none would countenance the break-up of Rome's empire, nor a diminution in its might (however paradoxical that may have seemed).

In Spain, the death of Perperna did not signal the outright ending of hostilities, and it seems that a handful of Spanish cities did continue their rebellion against Rome. Both Florus and Orosius preserve some details of the aftermath of the defeat:

> After Sertorius had been brought low by treachery in his own camp and Perperna had been defeated and given up, the cities of Osca, Termes, Ulia, Valentia, Auxum and Calagurris (the last after suffering all the atrocities of starvation) themselves entered in alliance with Rome.[46]
>
> Later, however, a greater part of the army of Sertorius followed Perperna. Pompeius, however, defeated him and slaughtered his whole army. He at once received the voluntary surrender of all the cities with the exception of Uxama and Calagurris, which continued their resistance. Of these cities Pompeius captured Uxama, whilst Afranius destroyed Calagurris with a final slaughter and burning after the city had been worn down by a continuous siege and compelled by its pitiable hunger to cannibalism.[47]

Thus the war in Spain dragged on for a little time longer, possibly even into 71 BC (again the sources are unclear), and Pompeius spent the rest of his time restoring order to the province and reorganizing it. In 71 BC, both he and Metellus finally withdrew and set off for Italy. However, this does not automatically mean that the First Civil War had come to an end. Similar lulls in the fighting were experienced between 86–84 and again in 81–80 BC. Whilst all bar one of the original coalition commanders had been killed (the exception being L. Cornelius Scipio Asiaticus), the civil war had already entered its second generation and one of its leading figures, the now victorious Cn. Pompeius Magnus, had already threatened to return with his army to Italy in an aggressive manner, and had a track record for not being able to obey senatorial commands to disband his armies. Furthermore,

Pompeius had been presented with another golden opportunity to postpone disbanding his armies and returning to Italy at the head of his legions. During 73 BC, a small and seemingly insignificant slave revolt took place at a gladiatorial *ludus* in Capua. On any other occasion, this event would barely rate a footnote in history. This occasion, however, proved to be quite different. The leader of the revolt was a slave named Spartacus.

5. Crassus, Pompeius and the Servile War in Italy

As the decades pass, the myth of Spartacus in popular culture seems to continue to grow, and this is matched by the exponential growth in the number of volumes devoted to his exploits. Although a detailed analysis of this conflict falls outside of the scope of this work, the conflict does contain some interesting factors surrounding causes and effects that need to be explored in terms of the First Civil War.

The first factor to be noted is the fact that greatest slave revolt in the ancient world occurred in the period of Rome's First Civil War, which leads to questions surrounding whether the civil war facilitated the development of this slave revolt into what it later became. This is not to say that every civil war was accompanied by a slave revolt, but then this civil war did have some rather unique circumstances, in terms of the devastation that the previous decade of fighting had had on Italy and the massive disruption to the established social order accompanied by the proscriptions. Furthermore, there were several occasions when one faction of the war called for slaves to revolt, as seen in Rome in both 88 and 87 BC.

In terms of the devastation factor, there had been peninsula-wide fighting throughout the Italian War, the war of the duumvirate and again following the Sullan invasion. Such devastation would not be recovered from easily and we still do not have a clear understanding on the economic effects that Italy was suffering under, especially from the point of view of the peasant classes. Furthermore, the Sullan proscriptions had overturned long-established land-holding patterns, which would have had a knock on effect on both the local economies and the established social order. It is notable that the servile armies contained more than just slaves, but a number of free peasants as well, as Plutarch notes:

> They were also joined by many of the herdsmen and shepherds of the region, sturdy men and swift of foot, some of whom they fully armed, and employed others as scouts and light infantry.[48]

Thus the slave rebellion seems to have been a focus for wider social dissatisfaction. In terms of the slaves themselves, many would have found themselves with new masters as a result of the Sullan proscriptions and the exiling of a number of Rome's prominent men, all of whom had landed estates. Furthermore, we must consider the wider implications of a period that had seen the established social order and the certainties it produced overturned in a matter of years. Men that had been allies for centuries now found themselves at war with each other: Roman vs. Italian, Italian vs. Italian, and finally, Roman vs. Roman, undermining the whole social fabric of ancient Italy.

As if this were not enough, we must also consider whether the fear of Roman power had been diminished. As we have seen throughout this work, one of the effects of the implosion of the Roman system was that the sense of the might of Rome was greatly diminished. By 73 BC, Rome was assailed by an alliance of native and Roman rebels in the west and a similar alliance of Roman rebels and native powers in the east, and the loss of control of the seas and coastline to the pirate threat. With one of the key foundations of slavery being the mightier subduing the weak, what effect would the mightier being humbled have on the weak?

Finally, we have the issue of the poor quality of military response from Rome. Had the initial Roman force under C. Claudius Glaber crushed the revolt in its initial stages, as was expected, the world would not have heard of Spartacus. This was followed by further Roman defeats, until M. Licinius Crassus, a former civil war commander (see Chapter 6), brought Roman might to bear and accomplish a sound Roman victory.[49] From the descriptions in the ancient sources, Spartacus hardly emerges as a new Hannibal, but more of a man who exploited poor-quality Roman leadership and military force. With so many of Rome's experienced military men dead, exiled or fighting on either side of the civil war, we have to ask ourselves whether this had an effect on the quality of the men left in Italy, at all levels. On several occasions, the sources note the reluctance of magistrates in the 70s to fight in Spain. Thus we must ask ourselves whether the effects of the First Civil War were key factors in the success of the Spartacan Servile War and whether without these, a small slave revolt in Capua would have produced such as result.

Whilst the death of Spartacus and the destruction of his army at the Battle of Silarus ended the immediate threat for Rome, the victorious campaign led to two potentially disastrous consequences, in the forms of Pompeius and Crassus. For Pompeius, the war had given him the prefect excuse to retain command of his army and march it through Italy in the name of protecting the Republic from destruction at the hands of the slave army, with the agreement of the Senate. Furthermore, as he was travelling through Italy, he encountered a force of 5,000 slaves feeling from the fighting in the south, which presented him an opportunity too good to miss, as Plutarch observes:

Even in this success, however, fortune somehow or other included Pompeius, since 5,000 fugitives from the battle fell in his way, all of whom he slew, and then stole a march on Crassus by writing to the Senate that Crassus had conquered the gladiators in a pitched battle, but that he himself had ended the war entirely.[50]

Thus, despite the fact that it was Crassus who had defeated Spartacus and saved the Republic, Pompeius still managed to attempt to cash in on the glory and advance his own successes, none of which would have endeared him to Crassus. As we have already seen (Chapter 6), Crassus and Pompeius had been rivals since their time serving under Sulla during his invasion of Italy. Both men had followed similar beginnings, being the sons of commanders who had contested the Battle for Rome in 87 BC, and both of whom, as young men without official command, had raised armies and joined Sulla. Crassus joined the Sullan campaign in Africa and then joined Sulla himself in Greece, while Pompeius later joined Sulla in Italy. However, despite these similar beginnings, the intervening years had seen them taking divergent paths, Pompeius with a string of military commands, all of which contravened the *cursus honorum*, Crassus immersing himself in Roman political life, amassing a fortune and a network of patronage and contacts.

Whilst Pompeius' victory in Spain had elevated his position further, Crassus' more immediate victory over Spartacus, which was won on the battlefield, rather than via assassination, put him on a par with Pompeius once more. Velleius records a glowing tribute for Crassus, which must have captured the mood of at least some of the people at the time: 'The glory of ending this war belongs to Marcus Crassus, who was soon by unanimous consent to be regarded as the first citizen in the state.'[51]

Furthermore, Crassus had earned his position by observing the *cursus honorum* and was of the correct age for advancement to consulship, and had never defied a senatorial order to disband his army or threatened them in an open letter. Thus by late 71 BC, Rome was faced with two commanders with a long-standing rivalry, both of whom expected to be rewarded for their efforts in recent wars, and more importantly, both of whom had battle-hardened armies within a few days' march from Rome.[52] Furthermore, both were key supporters of Sulla in his attack on Rome, and the slaughter that followed. It is hardly surprising then that the sources report that there were fears within both the Senate and the people that a fresh phase in Rome's twenty-year civil war was imminent.[53]

Chapter 11

The Rise of the New Republic (71–70 BC)

The Rise of the New Duumvirate

It seems however that both Pompeius and Crassus had learnt from their mentor's mistakes: why use blatant force when the threat of force was enough? This was a tactic that Pompeius had already used on both Sulla and the Senate on two previous occasions (see Chapter 7). It seems that on this occasion Crassus too used this tactic. Furthermore, the two men, who clearly had no personal liking for each other, both seemed to come to a fundamental realization, namely, that whilst separately they were strong, in alliance they would be unstoppable. And so was born a new duumvirate, one which was to dominate Roman politics for the next twenty years. In many ways, the alliance of Pompeius and Crassus harks back to that of Marius and Cinna, another temporary alliance to gain control of Rome. Both men determined that they wanted the same thing: in this case, the consulship and the chance to enact political reform. To those ends, not only did they temporarily unify their efforts, but in public they seemed to play off each other. Pompeius declared that he would disband his army, but only after he had been awarded a triumph, whilst Crassus stated that he too would disband his army, but only after Pompeius had done so.

Thus, with two armies camped outside of Rome, Pompeius and Crassus both stood for the consulship. Of the two, Crassus was of the correct age and had held the correct pre-requisite offices, whilst Pompeius was only thirty-four (eight years too young) and had held no prior elected political office. Nevertheless, faced with such an overwhelming alliance of patronage, money and popularity, not to mention outright military force, the Senate gave way, and Pompeius was granted dispensation (most likely by *plebiscitum*). With the last barrier removed, both men stood for the office of consul and were easily elected. If the resources of this alliance were not enough, Pompeius had campaigned on the restoration of the power of the tribunate, a popular move amongst the people, and one which would have smoothed his dispensation no doubt.

Upon taking office, neither man immediately disbanded his army. Appian reports that both men publicly reconciled before the people in what seems to have been a stage-managed piece of theatre. At an assembly of the people, a number of soothsayers prophesied consequences for Rome if the consuls did not reconcile, though given the previous twenty years, one did not need divine inspiration to come to that conclusion. Next came the pleas and lamentations of the people. Finally, Crassus theoretically got off his curule chair and offered his hand in friendship to Pompeius, who accepted. Then, to wild celebrations amongst the people, both men issued orders for their armies to disband.

To Appian, this reconciliation marked the end of his first book on the history of Rome's civil wars, signalling a turning point: when Roman politicians chose to renounce the violence of the previous years. In many respects, this seems to have been exactly what Pompeius and Crassus wanted: to be seen as the joint restorers of peace to Rome, much as their mentor had claimed over a decade earlier, and presumably Cinna before him. On this occasion, however, it proved to be the case, though not because of the theatrics.

As consuls, the pair passed or sponsored a number of key pieces of legislation. The full powers of the tribunate of the plebs were restored, returning the office to its pre-civil war position. Not only did this give the pair popular support, but it once again removed control of legislation from the Senate and gave it back to men who could be sponsored to provide a supportive piece of legislation. Pompeius himself would make good use of the tribunate to further his military career. The consuls also restored the office of censor, which had elapsed since it was last held in 86 BC. The men chosen were the consuls of 72 BC, who had stood aside to allow Crassus his command against Spartacus. However, aside from this short-term repayment of a political debt, the censors undertook a severe purge of the Senate, eliminating sixty-four senators, and we must assume that few allies of the consuls were amongst them.

More importantly, it meant that a full census of the new citizens could be held (for the first time since full enfranchisement had been offered). The census of 70 BC reveals that there were now just over 900,000 Roman citizens, as opposed to the 463,000 in 86 BC. Thus we can see the Roman citizenship doubling in this period. Despite this, a number of commentators have pointed out that this figure is far short of the total male population of Italy; by 28 BC, under Augustus, the figure was over 4,000,000 citizens. However, it must be remembered that as a result of the various conflicts of the 80s BC, Roman citizenship had merely been offered to those who wanted it, and this did not mean all male citizens in Italy initially took up this offer. Nevertheless, by holding this census, the issue of Roman citizenship could be finally clarified officially and thus concluded as a political issue.

Aside from the consular measures, there were three other key pieces of legislation passed this year that contributed to the consular programme of ending the civil war. Firstly, came two laws from a tribune named Plotius: firstly, a possible law authorizing land distribution for the discharged soldiers of Pompeius and Metellus (the Spanish veterans); and secondly, what was effectively an amnesty law, restoring citizenship to those followers of Lepidus and Sertorius. Thus we can see the consuls making immediate use of a tribune to pass major legislation. The discharge of troops would mean that, as well as there being no more armies in

Italy, Pompeius (like Marius and Sulla before him) had a large group of veterans beholden to him. The law restoring citizenship to the exiles was also a major step forward. For the last two decades, each regime had exiled its opponents, stripping them of their citizenship. This law, effectively an amnesty, drew a line under the divisions that the previous decades of civil warfare had caused and ended what must have been a continual source of rancour within the oligarchy. Again, there would have been considerable patronage for the consuls who had arranged these men's returns.

The final law came from a praetor, L. Aurelius Cotta, and reformed the composition of the juries once more. This time, juries were to be drawn in three equal parts from the Senate, the equestrians and a third grouping, the *tribuni aerarii*, whose exact nature is much debated. Drawing the composition of juries in equal numbers from the main two groups of equestrians and senators, along with a third balancing force, ensured that no one group dominated the juries and swung decisions in their favour, and again removed what had been a major point of political dissension for the last fifty years.

The consuls took one other major step to ensuring the end of the civil war, by stepping down from office and becoming private citizens once more, as Sulla himself had done. However, there was one key difference. When Sulla had stepped down from his dictatorship in 79 BC, he had retired from active political life, and even when he did intervene, he seemed to be ignored, being so hated by the people (Chapter 8). Pompeius and Crassus, however, remained in Rome, refusing pro-consular commands, and they remained there until 67 BC (in Pompeius' case). This apparent inactivity has caused much modern debate. However, one obvious solution is that they had learnt from Sulla's mistakes. When he had stepped down and quit Rome, tensions arose almost immediately amongst the oligarchy, leading to renewed civil war. As with Sulla, a number of measures passed by Pompeius and Crassus were contentious, notably the restoration of the tribunate, and possibly the amnesty. Given all of these factors, it can be argued that Pompeius and Crassus remained in Rome to ensure that their settlement of 70 BC was not undone by those who opposed it, or those who followed them, and that the peace that they had restored actually held.

Thus this duumvirate seem to have become the temporary guardians of the restored Republic, ensuring that there was not the vacuum in power that had happened when Sulla retired, and acting as guarantors of peace. Neither man needed political office to achieve this. Both had the money and prestige to create large factions of supporters within the oligarchy, in both the Senate and the equestrian order. Pompeius had the military glory, with his label of Magnus, and had immense popularity amongst the populace. Although neither had a mobilized army, both had access to large numbers of veterans, and both were battle-hardened commanders with a string of victories to their names. In short, there was no one amongst the oligarchy to effectively oppose them. However, this guardianship was only ever meant to be temporary, and the two men would have been eager to pursue their own careers once more, Pompeius in the field, Crassus in Rome. Here was highlighted the fatal flaw of the post-civil-war Republic: the need for a permanent arbiter of peace.

The End of the First Civil War

Thus, to this author's mind, the year 70 BC marked the end of the First Civil War. As has been shown, an end to a period of fighting did not automatically mean an end to the civil war. Fighting had stopped in 88, 87 and 82 BC, and soon flared up again. Sulla's victory in 82 merely mirrored that of Marius and Cinna in 87 BC and seemed to mark little more than the end of a particular phase of the war. For the Sullan regime, the high point came in the middle of 81 BC, when all provinces of Rome's empire were reunited under the control of Rome. However, this control proved to be illusory and a fresh phase of the civil war soon re-opened in Spain, ultimately spreading to Asia Minor, not to mention the fighting that continued in Italy throughout the period of Sulla's dominance. By 71 BC, the Spanish and Asian phases of the civil war had ended, with the deaths of M. Marius in the east and Sertorius and Perperna in the west.

However, what we have seen here is that civil wars do not end when there is a lull in the fighting; they end when a workable political solution is put into place and adhered to. It was only with Pompeius and Crassus refusing to take up arms and follow the cycle of conflict that had been created that this seemingly endless cycle of civil war came to a conclusion. They cemented their decision not to take up arms with reforms that removed a number of points of tension. Exiles were recalled, healing some of the rifts that had appeared within the senatorial elite. The tribunate was restored, removing that as a source of tension between the People and the Senate, and within the senatorial elite itself, though this obviously restored the office as a source of future problems. The courts were reformed, with neither the senators, nor the equestrians holding the balance of power. A census was held to embed the new citizens within the Roman system. Finally, armies were demobilised and the two most powerful individuals or 'warlords' of this period of the civil war laid down their arms and determined to work within the system, returning once more to the Roman aristocratic notion of placing a high premium on their own interests, without overtly harming the interests of the state.

In many ways, this sums up the whole period of the civil war: when key Roman leaders placed their own interests at such a premium, that the interests of the state were positively harmed by their actions. Throughout the Republic, there had always been individuals who stretched the boundaries of what actions they could get away with within the system, from Sp. Cassius in the fifth century through to Scipio Africanus. Yet the Roman system had always been flexible enough to accommodate these individuals without breaking. It was not until this period, and the double shock of the Italian War, and the coups of 88 BC and 87 BC, that this flexibility finally snapped. What Pompeius and Crassus did in 70 BC was not take Rome by overt force, as Sulpicius and Marius, Sulla and Pompeius Rufus, and Cinna and Marius all had, but merely use their collective *auctoritas*, backed up by the implied threat of force, to achieve a temporary dominance. Thus, not only had peace been restored, but the standard workings of the Republican system had been restored, albeit in a modified form.

The New Post-Civil War Republic

If we are to argue that it was Pompeius and Crassus who restored the Republic rather than Sulla, we have to acknowledge that the Republic they restored was not the one which had disintegrated in 91 BC, but was a newer version. Recently, Flower has published a masterful argument setting out the theory that there were a number of new versions, or phases, of the Republic within its near 500 year period of existence, which would make it more akin to the modern French Republic. Flower has provided a wonderful framework for historians to utilize, and the arguments provided here coincide with her overall theory, albeit differing on when a particular Republic started. Nevertheless, some key features of this new Republic need to be identified.

Firstly, it must be acknowledged that although the duumvirate of Pompeius and Crassus provided solutions to many of the key issues that were factors in the collapse of the Republic into civil war and issues that arose during the period, they did not answer all of them, and several were left unresolved altogether. Perhaps the most notable factor in this new Republic was that of citizenship, which was now no longer a running sore between the peoples and communities of Italy, with all free citizens south of Cisalpine Gaul, being able to take up Roman citizenship if they so desired it. This does not mean that by 70 BC every free-born inhabitant held Roman citizenship, but it does mean that as the century progressed more and more would take it up, all of which greatly accelerated the Romanization of Italy and the move toward a more unified Italy, which we see by the time of the Empire.

In political terms, although control of the courts seems to have been removed as a major political issue, the office of the tribunate of the plebs was another matter. In the space of the two decades, it had been thoroughly reformed by Sulla (either once or twice) and then fully restored by Pompeius and Crassus. Thus, the office had come full circle and was still as dangerous a weapon in the wrong hands as it had been in 91 BC with Livius Drusus, or 88 BC with Sulpicius. Certainly, Pompeius was to make good use of it in the years to come, and no permanent solution was found until Augustus took tribunician power himself, which formed the basis of an Emperor's domestic power for the next 200 years.

Although a political amnesty had been issued with the recall of exiles, which would have gone a long way to healing rifts within the senatorial aristocracy and robbed any of Rome's external enemies of the chance to use a Roman figurehead (as Mithridates had done with M. Marius), there still remained the issue of the Sullan *proscripiti*, in terms of the future disenfranchisement of their descendants and the dispossession of their lands. All this did was create a vast body of the dispossessed and disenfranchised, who would have been hoping or even working to overturn the Sullan proscriptions, many of whom were of senatorial stock. This would not only create tensions within the new system, but would be a vast pool of support for any politician tempted to take up the cause. As detailed below (Appendix II), several did so, including, ultimately, a certain nephew of Marius and former son in law of Cinna, by the name of C. Iulius Caesar.

Furthermore, there is the matter of all the veterans being given land. The concept had originated with Ti. Sempronius Gracchus, who legislated for providing farmers who had lost their land through military service with fresh land to farm. However, the mass mobilizations of the 80s and 70s, combined with Marius' (temporary) abolition of the land qualification as a precursor to military service meant that there would have been a number of veterans given land that had not been farmers in the first place and would have been unsuited to the role. Added to this is the matter of the devastation caused by the various wars raging across Italy, including the Servile War and issues with taking land off individuals or communities who had been dispossessed, and the disruption that this caused. All of this meant that there would have been a number of veterans giving up or losing their land and drifting back to Rome.

The key issue which the new Republic faced, however, was the spectre of violence. Essentially this was a Republic born out of civil war, and although the fighting had ceased and Pompeius and Crassus temporarily acted as its guarantors, there was nothing in the new system that enshrined this stewardship. Control of the armies remained with the same class of men who had caused the war, and in many cases the same men who had so willingly participated in it. The loyalty of armies still seemed to be to their commander, not so much as clients to a patron, but as citizens to a legally appointed representative of the Republic. If that representative should determine that a fellow Roman was an enemy of the state, then would future Roman armies behave any differently to those of this period?

Furthermore, there was the issue of precedent. In a system based on *mos maiorum* (or established practice), a range of unsavoury, but undoubtedly successful practices had been introduced, ranging from consuls using their armies to seize control of Rome, to tribunes using mobs to seize control of Rome, and the exiling and murder of one's political opponents, through to Pompeius and Crassus' own brand of leverage, invoking the horror of the civil war without actually indulging in the deeds. Pompeius and Crassus, whether acting together or independently, may have been happy to rule out a return to civil war and use their vast resources to act as unofficial guarantors of the peace, but others would surely not take the same view, nor would those two men be around forever. It is interesting to consider that within just three years of Crassus being killed in the aftermath of the Battle of Carrhae and the failed invasion of Parthia, Rome fell into fresh civil war, between two men, one of whom was the nephew of Marius and son-in-law of Cinna, while the other was the son of Pompeius Strabo and the son-in-law of Sulla (Caesar and Pompeius).

However, this does not mean that this new Republic was doomed to failure or that the end of the Republican system was inevitable. In fact, as this work has hopefully shown, the Republican system was strong enough at its core to survive the full-scale collapse it suffered during this period and actually reform itself. In many ways, it can be argued that the Republican system did not actually end dramatically, but that it merely evolved itself into something new. Whilst this new Republic, did indeed face its own collapse into civil war (the second one, traditionally dating from 49 BC to 31 BC), a new Republic arose out of those ashes, one fashioned by C. Iulius Caesar 'Octavianus' (or Augustus, as he became known), a great nephew of Marius, and one in which the principal of a permanent stewardship of the Republic as a guarantor of peace became enshrined.

It can be said that all political systems are created with the seeds of their own destruction within them, and this new Republic created in 70 BC was no different. In this respect, it was just the same as the one that had collapsed in 91 BC, albeit with different seeds. Whilst the seeds may have been there, they needed an individual, or a collection of individuals, to cultivate them, which in the end always returns us to the individuals involved and the choices they made.

Conclusion

What can we say about this collapse of the Roman Republican system? Ultimately, all civil wars come about due to the inflexibility of a particular system in accommodating the needs and desires of individuals, or groups of individuals, within that system. Rome's First Civil War contained both factors (groups and individuals) and had two crucial origins. First came the inability to reform the citizenship issue and the desires of the Italians. This was allied to the inability to accommodate the competing desires of the leading men of state, usually the consuls and tribunes, in the period 91–87 BC, be they Livius Drusus and Marcus Philippus, Sulpicius and Pompeius Rufus, Marius and Sulla, or Cinna and Octavius. The interaction of these two factors led to the collapse of the Republican system and the deaths of several hundred thousand Romans and Italians (including civilians). Yet despite these horrendous losses, as in most cases, conflict breeds resolution, and a new Republic was able to emerge from the slaughter, with many of the issues that caused the collapse resolved (see above).

However, just as important as why a system collapsed, is why it survived. Not only did a new Republic emerge in 70 BC, but transitional arrangements during

91–70 BC ensured that despite the seemingly continuous battles, warfare and slaughter, the core of the system continued to function. Among of the most remarkable elements of any civil war are the people who do not get involved and the work they do to ensure the day-to-day work of administrating a system gets done despite the chaos. For Rome, this even included the military, with a number of foreign wars being fought and territory defended by generals not involved in the civil war, from C. Valerius Flaccus in the 80s through to the generals of the 70s (see Appendix I). The historical narrative, especially a fragmentary one, is always going to focus more on the participants than these others, the 'neutrals' as it were. The only ones we hear of occupy the top levels of Roman society, from the generals in the field to the non-affiliated senators, yet there would have been so many more, from the ordinary citizens through to the local officials. It was all of these people that kept Roman society together and ensured that when the fighting died down and a political solution was found, there was something still left to govern.

Externally, though Rome at times looked weak, many allies and potential enemies were not certain that Rome would fall, and were fearful of reprisals if they sided against her. Both in the long term and the short (whether it be Hannibal or the Cimbri and Teutones), Rome had undergone periods of crisis and near collapse and survived. This was reinforced by the Roman ability to wage civil warfare at the same time as external warfare, sometimes even within the same area of campaign, as seen in Greece and Asia in the 80s. Thus an internal collapse of Rome did not become a full-scale collapse, and again allowed the Romans time to get their house in order.

Thus, when all is said and done, despite the temporary collapse of the Republican system, there seemed to be enough people who believed in the concept of Rome, both internally and externally, to ensure that those participants were given enough time to reconstruct the working of the system.

Appendix I

On the Offensive – Roman Expansion
in the 70s BC

As noted earlier, one of the most notable features of Rome's First Civil War was her ability to conduct both civil warfare and external warfare simultaneously. Whilst the earlier chapters have covered the external wars of the 80s, the 70s BC saw a greater military effort on Rome's part, and an actual expansion of Rome's empire. Although the full details of these wars fall outside the scope of this study, some detail is important if we are to understand the full impact on Rome of fighting both civil wars and external wars at the same time and the tremendous strain that this placed on her resources. As Orosius himself states, at one point in 78–77 BC, the Romans were engaged in four wars at the same time: the civil war in Spain, and wars in Illyria, Cilicia and Macedonia, all of which put a huge strain of Rome's manpower resources and ensured that the civil war would not receive the Senate's full attention.[1]

Cilicia

Asia Minor saw a considerable amount of Roman military activity in this period and was the source of an expansion of Rome's empire. The earliest military activity of the 70s BC came in 78 BC, the year of Sulla's death, and saw P. Servilius Vatia, the consul of 79 BC, launch major offensives in southern Asia Minor centred on Cilicia. Unlike previous campaigns in this region, this does not seem to have been another campaign against the pirates of the region but a major assault on the peoples of Cilicia and surrounding areas. The timing is interesting, coming after Sulla had left office, and it seems that's Sulla's resignation and death saw a major expansion of Roman military effort. Both Eutropius and Orosius preserve accounts of Vatia's campaign (in fact, they are almost word-for-word), and both show the extent of his campaign:

> Publius Servilius, an energetic man, was sent, after his consulate, into Cilicia and Pamphilia. He reduced Cilicia, besieged and took the most eminent cities of Lycia, amongst them Phaselis, Olympus, and Corycus. The Isauri he also attacked, and compelled to surrender, and, within three years, put an end to the war. He was the first of the Romans that marched over Mount Taurus. On his return, he was granted a triumph, and acquired the surname of Isauricus.[2]

Thus the regions of Cilicia, Pamphilia, Lycia and Isauria were subdued in a three-year-long campaign, which saw Roman forces cross the Taurus Mountains for the first time in their history. This campaign is often described as one against the pirates of the region, but Servilius' actions seem to have been aimed at something far greater, namely securing the region to Rome. Cilicia, or a portion of it, seems to have been made a Roman province around the time of Antonius' campaign against the pirates there (102–100 BC), but this is far from clear.

Even if it had been technically declared Roman territory, Rome never had the chance to subdue the whole region in the intervening period, and it was only now that they choose to do so, again highlighting their post-Sullan expansionist policies, even though civil war raged in Spain. Again, we are not clear whether the region was formally made into a province under Servilius, but it formed part of Pompeius' eastern settlement in 64 BC.

Ironically, Appian informs us that Servilius' campaign did little to stamp out the piracy problem, but then he seems to have been rather busier subduing the interior of these regions. Certainly, the pirate attacks continued in both frequency and boldness, reaching the coastline of Sicily and Italy itself. This in turn led to the campaign by M. Antonius in 74 BC (see below).

Bithynia

As well as increasing their territory in southern Asia Minor, the Romans annexed the kingdom of Bithynia in the north. In 74 BC, Rome's old ally King Nicomedes IV of Bithynia died, bequeathing his kingdom to the Roman people. Given that Mithridates VI was his neighbour and had annexed the kingdom on several occasions, this bequest provided him with the opportunity not only safeguard his kingdom but to thwart Mithridates' plans and possibly provoke him by bringing Roman territory right up to his border. If this was his plan, then it failed in the short term but succeeded in the longer term. Given the danger which Mithridates posed, the Senate acted quickly and voted to annex Bithynia as a Roman province. Mithridates, however, acted equally as quickly and invaded and annexed Bithynia, sparking off the Third Mithridatic War (see below), the ultimate conclusion of which saw the creation of a new Roman province of Pontus and Bithynia on the north coast of Asia Minor, giving Rome a presence on the Black Sea for the first time.

Pontus and Armenia

Although the details of the Third Mithridatic War fall outside of the scope of this work (see Chapter 10), this new generation of Roman commanders was unwilling to follow Sulla, who on two occasions had come to a negotiated settlement with Mithridates. The war drew in Mithridates' ally Tigranes, and the Armenian Empire, and saw Roman armies penetrating the regions of the east to a far greater extent than ever before, reaching as far east as the shores of the Caspian, into the

Parthian Empire and ultimately into Syria and Jerusalem. By the settlement of Pompeius in the 60s BC, Rome had acquired Pontus and annexed Syria, creating a permanent presence in the Middle East.

Crete

In 74 BC, the pirate problem of the eastern Mediterranean had reached such a stage that the Senate created an extraordinary command, with *imperium infinitum* being awarded to M. Antonius, whose father had commanded a similar campaign against the pirates in 102–100 BC. His initial campaign focussed on the west, in Liguria, Spain and Sicily, perhaps to break their alliance with Sertorius (see Chapter 10). By 72 BC, his focus had shifted to the island of Crete. Appian states that the Cretans favoured Mithridates and gave the pirates a safe haven. When his embassy to the Cretans was rebuffed, Antonius seems to have gone to war with the Cretans as well as the pirates infesting the island. Appian also states that he did not achieve much of note, but was awarded the title Creticus anyway.[3] However, other sources, such as Florus, state that Antonius was actually defeated by the Cretans, in either late 72 or early 71 BC, and forced to conduct a peace treaty with them.[4] Soon afterward, Antonius died and the campaign petered out, leaving the pirates to be dealt with by Pompeius, and the Cretans by Q. Caecilius Metellus Creticus in the 60s.[5]

Cyrene

The Ptolemaic kingdom of Cyrene had been bequeathed to Rome in 96 BC, but beyond securing some royal estates, Rome had left the kingdom to its own devices.[6] However, in 75 BC, this seemed to change, and one of the Quaestors, P. Cornelius Lentulus Marcellinus, was sent to the kingdom to organize it as a new Roman province.[7] This extended Rome's holdings on the northern African coast and took Rome's empire to the borders of Ptolemaic Egypt, whose own independence came under close Roman scrutiny during the 60s.[8]

Macedonia and Thrace

By the early 70s BC, once again, Macedon appears to have been invaded by Thracian tribes, in particular the Scordisci, who had fought a bitter war against Rome at the time of the Northern Wars.[9] C. (Cn). Cornelius Dolabella (Cos. 81) was dispatched and fought there between 80 and 77 BC. He returned to Rome to celebrate a triumph, but we have no other details of his campaigns. In 78 BC, the Roman proconsul Ap. Claudius Pulcher was dispatched to Macedonia, and by 77 we are told that he scored a number of victories over the tribes, especially around Mount Rhodopa, though no details are given.[10] However, Claudius seems to have caught a disease whilst in Macedonia and died in 76 BC. His successor, C. Scribonius Curio, crossed into Thrace. Eutropius has the following excerpt:

> Cnaeus Scribonius Curio, on the termination of his consulship, was sent to succeed him. He conquered the Dardanians, penetrated as far as the Danube, and obtained the honour of a triumph, putting an end to the war within three years.[11]

Thus Roman forces took the offensive and drove deep into the Balkans, defeating the Dardani, who were the regional power, and reaching the Danube for the first time. The Dardani had been humbled, and Roman power extended into the Balkans, though without any formal annexation of territory. Syme himself states that 'the march to the Danube was a spectacular achievement, not to be repeated for fifty years,' and that the conquest of the Dardani has been 'undeservedly neglected in the historical record'.[12]

Curio returned to Rome in 72 BC to celebrate another triumph for this theatre of war. His replacement was M. Terentius Varro Lucullus, who continued to extend Roman power throughout the sub-Danubian region. He defeated the tribe of the Bessi, captured the town that would become Adrianople (Uscudama), and advanced towards the shores of the Black Sea, reducing the Greek cities of the region. Thus, despite the ongoing civil and Mithridatic Wars, Rome took great strides towards subduing the Balkans between Macedonia and the Danube, without annexing any territory, but taking Roman influence to the western shores of the Black Sea.

Illyria

Illyria also seems to have been the site of a major war fought by the Romans. In 78 BC, C (Cn). Cosconius began a two-year campaign on the Dalmatian coast.[13] We posses no other details as to why the war was fought, nor details of the campaign, except for an excerpt of Eutropius:

> Cnaeus Cosconius was sent into Illyricum as proconsul. He reduced a great part of Dalmatia, took Salonae, and, having made an end of the war, returned to Rome after an absence of two years.[14]

Summary

Thus, we can see that the 70s saw a massive expansion of Roman military activity across the Mediterranean, greatly extending both Rome's physical empire and its regions of influence. It was in this period that Roman armies reached the Danube and crossed the Taurus Mountains for the first time, and the two additional provinces of Bithynia and Cyrene were annexed, from bequests. It is noticeable that almost immediately upon Sulla's resignation as dictator, the Senate launched three major campaigns, in Illyria, Macedonia and Cilicia, all confirming and extending Roman influence in these regions. Although the timing may have been a coincidence, it is tempting to see Sulla as having adopted a passive foreign policy during his tenure, with the focus being on internal (re)integration of Rome's existing territories. Furthermore, all this military activity put large armies under the command of others and allowed them personal glory in the form of triumphs, both of which seem to foreshadow aspects of the Augustan Principate. It may well be that with the experience of Pompeius fresh in his mind, Sulla did not want to encourage unnecessary military activity. With Sulla out of the picture, however, it seems that the rest of the Senate were eager to gain military glory and pursue an aggressive foreign policy.

One other interesting aspect is the effect of the lack of a surviving detailed narrative source for this period. As can be seen, there were a number of other important wars taking place, yet our narrative is skewed towards Spain, with Pompeius and Sertorius, and the east, with Mithridates. Having examined the other fragmentary sources, it is clear that our whole view of Roman military activity in this period is unbalanced by the random vagaries of which ancient sources survived.

The final aspect to note is that whilst all of these wars were continuous with the civil war still raging in Spain and also in Italy, it largely explains why the Spanish campaigns seem to have been under resourced. It also helps to explain the reluctance of some members of the oligarchy to serve in these wars, when there were far more glorious foreign adventures to be had, which perhaps sums up the general Roman elite's attitude to the civil wars. If nothing else, it seems that this expansionist policy channelled the efforts and ambitions of a number of the Roman oligarchy into what was a far more beneficial outlet than that found in the 80s.

Appendix II

The Second Civil War (63–62 BC)[1]

A Divided Republic

Whilst the Consulships of Pompeius and Crassus had brought an end to the conflicts that formed the First Civil War and resolved a number of the underlying issues which had both caused and perpetuated it, the new Republic which emerged in 70 BC still faced a number of issues and underlying tensions. As with all conflicts of this nature there were winners and losers at all levels of Roman society. Within the Roman oligarchy there had been a huge number of casualties, both in the fighting and in the Sullan proscriptions that followed. Whilst a number of prominent families survived, there were many who hadn't, and their place had been taken by the rise of a new 'Sullan' aristocracy.

As we have seen Sulla had created a new Republic, one which reduced the popular element (which, as he saw it, had been responsible for the collapse of the Republic between 133–91 BC) and one which centred power on the Senatorial oligarchy. The problem was that even after the Proscriptions, this oligarchy was as fractured as ever. There were the old families who had survived only by pledging token allegiance to whichever faction was ruling Rome at the time, those who followed Sulla, but only out of a desire to back the winning side and those who enthusiastically followed Sulla. Of all the factions it was only the hardcore Marian and Cinnan supporters who had been purged.

Outside of the oligarchy, the situation in Rome and Italy was just as fractured. In Rome itself the urban populace held no great loyalty for any faction and would have supported whoever offered them the most. However they were kept in check with the virtual abolition of the Tribunate of the Plebs, the most convenient tool for harnessing popular support. In Italy itself, there were winners, such as the Sullan veterans in their new colonies, losers such as the peoples who had supported Marius and Cinna and had their lands removed and simply those who had suffered from the years of armies marching up and down Italy devasting the local economies.

The Anti-Sullan Backlash (70–63 BC)

Thus, for the New Republic to survive a figurehead was required to oversee these various factors, a role which Sulla himself had probably hoped to enjoy, albeit without any formal Dictatorial powers, a prototype Princeps. His early death removed this role from the equation and, as we saw, the civil war conflicts continued. As we have also seen, the election of Pompeius and Crassus destroyed the Sullan Republic and replaced it with a new Pompeian-Crassan one. Again, both men would have realised that simply passing laws would not ensure the survival of their new Republic and so both men chose to remain in Rome throughout 69 and 68 BC to ensure that their successors did not overturn their reforms.

Yet the Consulships of Pompeius and Crassus saw something else; the start of a backlash against the new Sullan elite. Though both men were the perhaps the two most notorious of Sulla's supporters in the middle years of the civil war, neither fell into the camp of hardcore Sullan supporters. Both were opportunistic young men, both of whom had lost their fathers in the early years of the war, both of whom had raised 'illegal' armies and joined Sulla, more out of opportunism than conviction. With the Pompeian-Crassan settlement dismantled the Sullan Republic, the new Sullan elements of the oligarchy found their newly elevated position under threat.

The most immediate consequence was the Censorship of 70–69 BC, of Cn. Cornelius Lentulus Clodianus and L. Gellius Publicola, which saw sixty-four Senators purged from the Senate and we can be sure that none of Pompeius or Crassus' supporters were amongst them. The bulk of the exclusions therefore would have fallen upon the new Sullan element of the oligarchy. Worse was to follow when several ambitious young Roman noblemen took up the cause of righting the wrongs committed during the Sullan purges. The first sign of this anti-Sullan backlash (at least in our surviving sources) seems to have been in 66 BC when the Tribune Memmius prosecuted M. Terentius Varro Lucullus for his actions as Sulla's Questor.[2]

We do not know whether this was a genuine attempt to attack Sulla's junior officers or part of an ongoing feud between Memmius and Marcus' brother L. Licinius Lucullus (Cos. 74 BC). In any event Lucullus was acquitted; but then Sulla had been granted formal pardon for all acts committed during the civil war, which presumably extended to those of his officers, following his orders. Nevertheless, the charge is an interesting one and does perhaps indicate the general mood of the people was favourable to opening these recent wounds, even if the Senate was not.

By 64 BC however we see further prosecutions of the lesser members of the new Sullan aristocracy by two other young Roman aristocrats. The first was none other than M. Porcius Cato, scion to a famous Roman family, albeit one who's star had faded. Cato in particular made a very public (and popular ploy) to recover monies that had been awarded to those who had committed murder in Sulla's proscriptions.

Thus, Cato launched a high-profile attack on the Sullan profiteers (despite their acts being legal at the time) and recovered monies they had been paid out and then handed them over to be tried for murder. This will have undoubtedly made him a number of enemies from within the ranks of Sullan veterans, not to mention those in the Senate who had also profited. Yet such moves allowed him to gain a reputation as a staunch defender of the state finances and a man of the utmost probity; not to mention someone who was not afraid to tackle an obvious (though legal) injustice.

Another young man who took a similar route and started prosecutions of those who had taken part in Sulla's proscriptions was another young man from a distinguished but faded Roman family; a certain C. Iulius Caesar. Caesar had first come to notice under the Sullan Dictatorship when as a young man he defied Sulla's order to divorce his wife (Cinna's daughter). To make matters worse, he was related (by marriage) to the elder Marius; his aunt being Marius' wife. Having done nothing in person to offend the Sullan regime, and not having any great wealth, Caesar had survived the proscriptions and emerged as the closest living relative to the great Marius; a fact he proudly traded on early in his political career in the 60s BC.

Thus as the 60s BC progressed, the Sullan faction within the oligarchy found itself increasingly under attack in this new Pompeian-Crassan Republic. The most senior men of the Sullan faction were Q. Caecilius Metellus Pius, who had returned from Spain and was an old man (dying in c. 63 B) and L. Licinius Lucullus, who returned to Rome from the Eastern Wars in 66 BC, but was met with prosecution and attempts to block his Triumph. This in turn limited his involvement in domestic politics (retaining his imperium, he had to remain outside of the Pomerium) until 63 BC. Thus attention would have turned to the next generation of the Sullan faction, the obvious candidate being Sulla's only son Faustus. Yet by the mid-60s he was too young to fully take part in Roman politics (being born in the early 80s BC). Thus attention would have fallen on Sulla's nephew (of the same name); P. Cornelius Sulla, who was eligible to stand for election in 66 BC, presumably carrying the hopes of an increasingly concerned Sullan faction.

The Rise and Fall of Cornelius Sulla (65 BC)

As it initially turned out, Cornelius Sulla did not disappoint, being elected as Consul for 65 BC, along with his running mate P. Autronius Paetus. Yet in an extraordinary twist, both men were disbarred from office having been successfully prosecuted for electoral bribery, a common enough practice in Roman elections. Yet what was uncommon was that both men were convicted and disqualified from holding public office, and stripped of their Senatorial membership, an almost unheard-of occurrence in the Republic and one which must strike us as suspicious. We must ask ourselves whether it was mere random chance that the only Consul Designates to be stripped of their office in this period included the leading member of the Sullan family or was there a move amongst their opponents to ensure that another Sulla was not elected, one who would surely have defended the Sullan legacy. If so, then it ties in with the moves to prosecute lower level Sullan supporters.

Having been stripped of the Consulships, their electoral rivals and accusers (Cotta and Torquatus) were elected in their place (adding insult to injury). Thus, for the second time, a Cornelius Sulla had been robbed of his crowning achievement. This happened to his uncle in 88 BC, when as Consul he was stripped of the command against Mithridates. The elder Sulla responded by marching his army on Rome and ignited another major conflict in the First Civil War. His nephew however had no such military resources, though there were rumours of his involvement in a plot or coup. Here we must be incredibly careful as for many of our sources the events that occurred in 63 BC confirmed that rumours of the alleged plot in 65 BC. Dio presents a succinct summary:

> Publius Paetus and Cornelius Sulla, a nephew of the great Sulla, who had been elected Consuls and then convicted of bribery, had plotted to kill their accusers, Lucius Cotta and Lucius Torquatus, especially after the latter had also been convicted. Among others who had been suborned were Cnaeus Piso and also Lucius Catilina, a man of great audacity, who had sought the office himself and was angry on this account.
>
> They were unable, however, to accomplish anything because the plot was revealed beforehand, and a bodyguard given to Cotta and Torquatus by the Senate. Indeed, a decree would have been passed against them, had not one of the Tribunes opposed it. And when Piso even then continued to display his audacity, the Senate, fearing he would cause some riot, sent him at once to Spain, ostensibly to hold some command or other; there he met his death at the hands of the natives whom he had wronged.[3]

The problem we have is that all accounts of this were written after the events of 63 BC, when a genuine coup attempt occurred. Furthermore, it is clear that Cicero, in the elections in 64 BC, not only voiced this rumour, but embellished it greatly to tar his electoral opponent, Catilina. Certainly, there are unusual elements to this case; the fact that the Senate granted the Consuls a bodyguard (as far as we are aware) and that Cn. Calpurnius Piso was given an unusual command in Spain, by decree of the Senate; questor pro-praetore.

The Coup of 63 BC and the Outbreak of the Second Civil War

Thus we can see that by the late 60s BC, the Sullan faction found itself on the backfoot and under attack, which must have stung them greatly given that they assumed they were the victors of the First Civil War. Events came to a head in 63 BC with the elections for the offices of 62 BC. The candidate who attached himself most to the Sullan faction was a certain. L. Sergius Catilina, a minor

Roman aristocrat who had been rejected the previous year for the Consulship (beaten by none other than M. Tullius Cicero). Clearly thinking over his previous rejections, Catilina latched on to the various political reforms which had been frustrated by Cicero during 63 BC, again showing the dangers of the Senate not taking a lead in dealing with these issues. Dio mentions both land distribution and the cancellation of debts.[4]

The bulk of the supporters of these measures seemed to be veterans from Sulla's new colonies, many of which had become impoverished in the intervening years and resentful; given their role in putting Sulla and his supporters in power. Thus a disgruntled Sullan faction member united with a disgruntled Sullan veterans, all of whom felt that they had been robbed of the spoils of their victories.

Determining what happened next is a perfect example of the frustration of having a contemporary source written by one of the key men involved, but one which presents us with a completely biased picture of what actually happened and why. Even the very name of this event is a red herring; the so called 'Conspiracy of Catiline'; placing everything at the foot of a man who has become one of the late Republic's pantomime villains. Yet Catilina was a convenient scapegoat for events which showed just how flawed this new Republic really was and his swift elimination could re-assure the Senatorial oligarchy that the problem had been dealt with. However, as it is clear, Catalina was not the cause of the issues which faced the new Republic, but merely a symptom.

What is clear is that a group of the Senatorial nobility, all with affiliations to the Sullan faction, organised a coup in Rome and an uprising in Italy. Frustratingly what is unclear is who organised it and why? Cicero would like us to believe that Catalina was its mastermind, whilst others saw the shadowy hand of Crassus in the background. What is clear is that there were a few key ringleaders of this attempted coup; P. Cornelius Lentulus Sura, C. Manlius and Catalina himself.

Cornelius Lentulus is an interesting character and one who had fallen behind the shadow of Catalina in this matter yet was of senior rank to him. Lentulus hailed from one of Rome's oldest and most noble families; the Cornelli and his branch of the family had been one of the most successful, with the family first achieving the Consulship in 324 BC and holding it virtually every generation since. In his youth Lentulus himself had followed Sulla and held the Questorship in 81 B.C when Sulla himself was Consul.

Thus Lentulus was part of the Sullan oligarchy which ruled the Republic in the aftermath of Sulla's victory, a point confirmed when he was elected to the Consulship of 71 BC. Yet he had clearly fallen foul of either Pompeius or Crassus (or both) as he was immediately purged from the Senate during the Censorship of 70 BC, as had one of the current Consuls (C. Antonius). It is unsurprising that man of his character did take this humiliation lying down and he stood for, and won, one of the Praetorships for 63 BC and thus was a serving Praetor this year (for a second time). Furthermore, it is reported, though with what accuracy we will never know, that Lentulus firmly believed in a purported Sibylline Oracle:

These recited forged oracles in verse purporting to come from the Sibylline books, which set forth that three Cornelii were fated to be monarchs in Rome, two of whom had already fulfilled their destiny, namely, Cinna and Sulla, and that now to him, the third and remaining Cornelius, the heavenly powers were come with a proffer of the monarchy, which he must by all means accept, and not ruin his opportunities by delay, like Catilina.[5]

C. Manlius by contrast was a different character altogether. We are told that he was a Sullan veteran, who became leader of the Sullan veterans in Etruria. The main surviving sources portray him as nothing more than an agent of Catilina, yet he seems to have been a power in his own right. Thus, we can see Manlius, rather than an agent of Catilina, as the leader of a group of Sullan veterans looking for allies amongst the Roman oligarchy. The key question still remains as to what this disparate group of men were hoping to achieve? Clearly as late as mid 63 BC Catilina and Manlius were hoping to achieve the election of Catilina to the Consulship, no doubt followed by legislation to alleviate the plight of the Sullan veterans, with either fresh measures on land distribution and debt relief.

When this electoral route failed then they began to think of extra-constitutional means. Here we must remember that all of the key men involved had been part of the winning side of the First Civil War yet (for different reasons) noel had been able to reap the rewards they felt they were due (though in most cases they had and then had squandered them). As was common throughout the period that preceded the First Civil War, when Roman oligarchs found the constitutional route blocked, they turned to violence, and here all the men had seen first-hand the rewards that violence could bring, which was perhaps Sulla's greatest and most lasting legacy.

To those ends this new faction planned to seize power in the Republic both via a coup in Rome, supported by levied armies of veterans in Italy and even uprisings in Gaul (which would most likely have been suppressed by the new regime anyway). The new Consuls (for 62 BC) were to be murdered, as was Cicero, whilst Antonius (the other Consul) was believed (at least by them) to be sympathetic to their cause.

Thus, with Pompeius absent, this faction would seize power in Rome and enact a coup along the lines of those of 88 and 87 BC. With both Consuls elect dead; no doubt Lentulus and Catilina would be appointed as new Consuls, who would then use their forces to intimidate a freshly purged Senate to legitimise their seizure of power, as it had done in 88, 87, 82 and 70 BC. We get the sense that once in power this faction would then attempt to turn the clock back to the Sullan Republic, as it had been in 82–70 BC with the hardcore Sullan faction (as they saw themselves) in power and benefiting from power. The Sullan veterans would no doubt be handsomely rewarded again, which would merely re-start the cycle of reward and impoverishment.

We can also argue that this was a Sullan backlash against the manner in which this new Pompeian-Crassan Republic was developing, which had seen the hardcore Sullan faction lose their monopoly on power and gradually finding themselves losing the victory they had fought so hard to earn. Yet the great irony is that Sulla, for all his faults, did not fight the First Civil War to simply ensure that his followers would be rich and powerful. Furthermore, this coup went against everything that Sulla had wanted for the new Republic, namely an end to the political violence and bloodshed and unified Senatorial oligarchy.

The Bloody Failure of the Coup of 63 BC

Unfortunately for the coup plotters however, their planning was shambolic. Whilst Manlius fulfilled his part and raised an army of Sullan veterans and the disaffected, the plot in Rome ended in dismal failure. In a closely interconnected oligarchy, word of the plot soon leaked, brought about by a failure to act swiftly and a desire to include an ever growing range of figures, many of whom were only lukewarm in their support for the coup; they may have supported its aims but did not want to risk active involvement.

Once Catalina had failed in his attempt to gain power via election to the Consulship, they should have acted. What seems to have happened is that they made two crucial mistakes. The plot called for co-ordinated action between the insurrections in Italy and the coup in Rome. What happened in fact is that news of Manlius raising his army reached the Senate, along with reports of revolts breaking out in other parts of Italy. Thus, the Senate was fully warned and was allowed time to act, raising forces and dispatching commanders to deal with the Italian elements of the plot (see below). The SCU was passed and the Consuls (both of them) were ordered to defend the Republic. Antonius was assigned the task of defeating the rebel army whilst Cicero (with his total lack of military experience) stayed in Rome to deal with the coup threat.

In response, the coup plotters only made a feeble attempt to assassinate Cicero, who was tipped off, and the plot came to nought. Thus, Cicero and the Senate had ample time to prepare a response to the outbreak of a Second Civil War in Italy and the moment was lost. Furthermore, many in the Senate were now aware that the rebels in Italy had allies amongst the Senatorial oligarchy who were planning a coup and Catilina soon came under suspicion. Cicero naturally wasted no time in making a series of speeches to the Senate (the Catilinarians) condemning his old rival; but as yet had no hard evidence.

This evidence was soon provided by none other than Lentulus himself, who in seemingly a last throw of the dice attempted to involve the Gallic tribe of the Allobroges in the plot. The Allobroges were a Gallic tribe who lived to the very north of Rome's province of Transalpine Gaul and how had been defeated by Rome during a war in the 120s BC. Lentulus gambled that they would want to rebel from Roman rule and thus aid the coup in Rome and the rebellion in

Italy. That they were considering rebelling can hardly be in doubt, but that they would throw in their lot with a group of Roman aristocrats, whose plot was looking decidedly shaky and who, even if they took power, were hardly likely to grant them their independence was highly unlikely. Thus to throw suspicion off themselves they betrayed the plot and the Senate had the evidence they needed.

Catilina had by this point had wisely left Rome to join with Manlius and his army, whilst the others were rounded up in Rome; and thus, the coup failed miserably. Cicero and the Senate were now left with the thorny issue of what to do with the plotters. Though the coup had failed miserably, Italy was now in the throes of another civil war (its second) with the Senate understandably concerned about the dangers of Manlius' rebel army and a number of other uprisings in Italy, and its own lack of military resources. Furthermore Catalina, one of the key plotters was now the de-facto leader of the rebellion or at least its figurehead, though Manlius seems to have been the more militarily qualified. Under Roman law, the plotters would have to be tried for treason, though it was known that they had many sympathisers within the oligarchy, who had not been implicated; the Tribune elect L. Calpurnius Bestia for one. Thus, a conviction could not be guaranteed.

What followed was one of the most notorious debates in Senatorial history, who's details can be found in both Cicero and Sallust, about the fate of the plotters.[6] In the end, and with the civil war in Italy looming, the majority of the Senate agreed with Cato, and Cicero was instructed to arrange the execution (murder) of the prisoners. Thus, on the 5th December, Lentulus, a serving Praetor (though he was compelled to abdicate his office first) was murdered on the orders of the Senate along with four of his noble colleagues[7] (with a number of others condemned in absentia (including Catilina).

The Sullan Legacy and the Second Civil War in Italy (63–62 BC)

Whilst the attempted coup in Rome receives the bulk of the coverage in our surviving sources (especially Cicero), the real threat to the Republic came from the uprisings which these Roman noblemen had encouraged. Rebellions sprung up throughout Italy and we must ask ourselves what motivated these men to rise up and take arms against Rome, in what must surely be considered to be the Second Civil War. One thing we can be certain of, is that these rebels did not do so to support a failed Roman politician, or his colleague spurred on by oracles from the gods. The majority of these men took up arms against their own state as they saw it as the only way to resolve their grievances and thus we can clearly see that the faults of the Republic, which had brought about the First Civil War, were still present in this new Republic.

We can see impoverished and embittered Sullan veterans from the new colonies, those dispossessed by either the Sullan proscriptions or the creation of the Sullan colonies, and those who had taken to banditry and could see the spoils that could be accumulated as the victorious side in a civil war. Harrison presents the best modern analysis of the factors that seem to have been present in this period.[8]

We must not forget that Italy had been badly affected by the Sullan invasion of 83 BC and subsequent peninsula wide war (83–82 BC). Both the social and economic patterns of Italy were further disputed by the Sullan colonies being created and the changes to landholding brought about by the proscriptions. This was then followed by the demands of the continuing Civil Wars in Spain and the East, followed by the disruption and devastation caused by the Spartacan Slave Rebellion. The scale of the rebellions can be seen from the sources:

> Thereupon by decree of the Senate Quintus Marcius Rex was sent to Faesulae and Quintus Metellus Creticus to Apulia and its neighbourhood. Both these generals were at the gates in command of their armies, being prevented from celebrating a Triumph by the intrigues of a few men, whose habit it was to make everything, honourable and dishonourable, a matter of barter. Of the Praetors, Quintus Pompeius Rufus was sent to Capua and Quintus Metellus Celer to the district of Pisa, with permission to raise an army suited to the emergency and the danger.[9]
>
> At about this time there were disturbances in both Transalpine and Cisalpine Gaul, as well as in the Picene and Bruttian districts and in Apulia; for those whom Catilina had sent on ahead were doing everything at once, acting imprudently and almost insanely. By their meetings at night, by their transportation of arms and weapons, and by their bustle and general activity they caused more apprehension than actual danger.[10]

By far the biggest threat came from C. Manlius, who was able to raise an army of at least ten thousand men from Etruria. Despite these various uprisings, the Senate found itself in a better position than it should have been. Outside of Rome were several returning armies, with their commanders awaiting Triumphs. This gave the Senate sufficient forces to immediately counter the largest threat; C. Manlius (and soon Catilina himself), in Etruria, whilst still being able to send another four commanders to various parts of Italy; Faesulae, Apulia, Capua and Pisa.

The second advantage the Senate had was the disorganised nature of their opposition. Whilst Manlius was able to put an army into the field to possibly march on Rome in support of the coup, the other regions seemed uncoordinated and unfocussed; more intent on local rebellion than a knockout attack on Rome itself. This allowed the Senate to focus on the clearest danger; the army of Manlius and Catilina.

This disorganised nature of the rebellion played another crucial role in the Senate's eventual victory. As discussed earlier, the rebellions in Italy should have coordinated with the coup in Rome, but whilst Manlius fulfilled his part superbly,

Catilina and Lentulus squandered their opportunity. Further damage was done to their cause as it seems that they had informed their army that they were to support a coup in Rome. When that failed, and the plotters were executed, their force realised that the prospect of a quick win had disappeared and that they would have to face the full force of the Roman state. We are told that this resulted in mass desertions.

Nevertheless, Catilina and Manlius preserved the nucleus of an army. yet whilst they still had numbers, their quality was poor. Thus, this seems to have been an army in name only, more a rag-tag collection of poorly armed veterans and poor citizens. Facing them were the armies of Q. Metellus Celer and the Consul C. Antonius, both with large armies of veteran soldiers. We are told that Celer had three legions of his own and Antonius an equally large army. Thus, the army of Catilina and Manlius was seriously outnumbered, both in terms of numbers and quality of soldiers.

Realising the forlorn state of this situation, Catalina and Manlius gave up on the idea of a march on Rome and apparently tried to march their army into Transalpine Gaul, and possibly over the Alps, no doubt hoping to stir up further rebellion as they went. Unfortunately, they were trapped when Metellus marched ahead of their route and blocked their path, with Antonius trailing them. Faced with being caught between two opposing armies, Catilina and Manlius chose to attack Antonius' army presumably to force an escape route. The result was the Battle of Pistoria in January 62 BC. Given the disparity between the two sides, both in terms of numbers and quality, the result was a forgone conclusion and the rebel army was annihilated, with both Catilina and Manlius killed in the fighting (Antonius sent Catalina's head to Rome as proof).

Yet whilst the largest threat had been crushed, the war did not end there and military operations in Italy continued throughout 62 BC. We see that a number of the newly elected Praetors were fighting across Italy; M. Calpurnius Bibulus in central Italy against the Paeligni sand Q. Tullius Cicero (the younger brother of the Consul) in Southern Italy in Bruttium. Though we have insufficient information, it would be worth speculating on connections between those regions that rebelled during this war and those that had during the First Civil War, to see if again it was unfinished business for them. Yet these rebellions were isolated ones and by the end of 62 BC had all been extinguished in Italy, though the Allobroges did indeed start a rebellion of their own, which continued until 61 BC.

Summary

Thus, we can see that these events allow us to argue both for the inherent weakness of this new Republic and its underlying strength. Within just seven years of the end of the First Civil war, Roman citizens were taking up arms against the Republic encouraged by elements of the ruling oligarchy. Though the military conflicts did not continue for years, as they had in the first war, this still constituted a civil war, with Roman citizen fighting Roman citizen across Italy.

We can see that though Pompeius and Crassus dealt with many of the underlying issues that caused the First war, a number of fresh issues had arisen which had not been addressed notably those who had lost out either politically or economically from the first war or since.

This second war can be seen as a backlash from the Sullan supporters and veterans whose victory had seemingly turned sour and who felt robbed and embittered by subsequent events.

Furthermore the Senatorial oligcrahy, in whom, Sulla had seemingly placed so much faith was as factional and fractious as ever without someone (or some two) to keep them in check and it is no surprise that these events exploded when Pompeius was absent. Crassus role as ever was obscure at the time as has bene ever since. Yet despite Pompeius' absence, this new Republic actually held together remarkably well when faced with renewed civil war and did not collapse as its predecessors had, though they were helped by the ineptitude of the coup plotters and the rebel leaders. Had they faced a more organised opponent then the outcome may well have bene different, as was shown just over a decade later (in 49 BC).

Two Decades of Bloodshed – Roman Senatorial Causalities in the First Civil War

As can be seen, the death toll from this series of wars was on a massive scale, both in terms of quantity and quality. Although there was no one battle to compare to a Cannae or an Arausio, as detailed above, there were a huge number of smaller-scale battles throughout the twenty years of conflict, across the whole Mediterranean world. Furthermore, its very nature as a civil war meant that Roman and Italian casualties were far higher than in a normal Roman-versus-non-Roman conflict.

The sources are divided on the death toll of the civil war in the 80s BC. Appian and Diodorus provide figures of around 100,000 killed in combat alone.[1] Orosius, supported by Eutropius, puts the death toll of the conflicts up until 82 BC at 150,000 dead, in combat alone. As Orosius points out, this figure 'does not include innumerable peoples over all Italy who were slaughtered without any consideration'.[2] Velleius, meanwhile, states the death toll at 300,000 for both sides.[3] If we add in the civilian deaths and the combat from the 70s BC, then it is clear that the First Roman Civil War would have had a death toll running into the hundreds of thousands.

For the Roman oligarchy, at no time since the Second Punic War had such high casualty figures been suffered. According to Orosius, 'the census also shows that twenty-four men of consular rank, six of praetorian rank, sixty with the rank of aediles, and almost 200 senators were destroyed.' As well as the usual losses in combat, however, this period saw a number of prominent Romans being either murdered in mutinies or murdered by their fellow nobles, whether after capture or in a more formal proscription, and even a handful of suicides.

The following lists are of the known members of the Roman oligarchy who died during this period, collected by type of death to show the true scale of the losses sustained.

Assassinated

91 BC   M. Livius Drusus   (Tr. 91)
             Assassinated during the night on the streets of Rome

Killed in Battle

90 BC   P. Rutilius Lupus   (Cos. 90)
             Killed at the Battle of the River Tolenus by a Marsic army
90 BC   Q. Servilius Caepio
             Killed in an unnamed battle by the Marsi
89 BC   T. Didius   (Cos. 98)
             Killed in an unknown battle against the Samnite allianace
89 BC   A. Gabinius
             Killed during a siege against the Lucanians
87 BC   C. Milonius
             Killed during the Battle of the Janiculum
82 BC   Ap. Claudius
             Killed when leading a cavalry charge against the Samnite
             army, whilst defending Rome
82 BC   C. Marcius (Censorinus)   (Pr. 82)
             Killed in the Battle of Colline Gate, fighting Sulla
81 BC   Cn. Domitius Ahenobarbus
             Killed in battle in northern Africa, fighting Pompeius
81 BC   Paccianus
             Killed in battle with Sertorius at Tingis (Tangiers)
79 BC   M. Domitius Calvinus   (Pr. 80)
             Killed in the Battle of the River Anas whilst fighting Hirtuleius
79 BC   L. Thorius Balbus
             Killed whilst fighting Sertorius in a battle in Spain
76 BC   Laelius, D.
             Killed in the Battle of Lauro, whilst fighting Sertorius
75 BC   C. Herennius
             Killed in the Battle of Valentia, whilst fighting Pompeius
75 BC   L. Hirtuleius and Hirtuleius
             Killed in the Battle of Segontia, whilst fighting Pompeius and
             Metellus
75 BC   C. Memmius
             Killed in the Battle of Segontia whilst fighting Sertorius and
             Perperna
74 BC   P. Rutilius (Nudus)
             Killed in battle near Chalcedon whilst fighting Pompeius
             M. Marius

62 BC	L. Sergius Catilina	(Pr. 68)

Killed in the Battle of Pistoria by forces commanded by
the consul C. Antonius

62 BC   C. Manlius
Also killed in the Battle of Pistoria by forces commanded
by the consul C. Antonius

Murdered during Riots in Rome

89 BC	A. Sempronius Asellio	(Pr. 89)

Murdered when attacked by a mob of creditors during
daylight on the streets of Rome

88 BC   Pompeius Rufus
Son of the consul of 88 BC, he was murdered by supporters
of Sulpicius during the tumult

Murdered/Executed following Capture

90 BC	L. Postumius	(Pr. 90)

Murdered by the Samnites following his capture at Nola

88 BC   M. Aquillius   (Cos. 101)
Murdered by having gold poured down his throat following
his capture by Mithridates

82 BC   C. Carrinas   (Pr. 82)
Murdered at Sulla's command following the Battle of
Colline Gate

82 BC   L. Iunius Brutus Damasippus   (Pr. 82)
Murdered at Sulla's command following the Battle of
Colline Gate

82 BC   Cn. Papirius Carbo   (Cos. 85, 84
                                                       and 82)
Murdered on the command of Pompeius following his capture on
the island of Cossyra

82 BC   Q. Antonius Balbus   (Pr. 82)
Murdered by the Sullan commander L. Philippus after
the capture of Sardinia

77 BC   M. Iunius Brutus
Murdered on the orders of Pompeius following his capture at
Mutina

77 BC   Cornelius Scipio
Murdered on the orders of Pompeius following his capture
at Alba

73 BC	M. Marius	
	Murdered on the orders of Lucullus following his capture at the Battle of Tenedeos	
72 BC	M. Perperna	(Pr. 82)
	Murdered on the orders of Pompeius following his capture at an unnamed battle in Spain	
72/71 BC	M. Antonius; L. Fabius Hispaniensis; Manlius; Octavius Graecinus; C. Tarquitius Priscus	
	All of the conspirators who murdered Sertorius (excepting Aufidius) were themselves murdered, either by Pompeius or by the Mauri	
63 BC	P. Cornelius Lentulus Sura	(Pr. 63)
	Executed without trial on the orders of Cicero for his part in the attempted coup	
63 BC	C. Cornelius Cethegus; L. Statilius; A. Gabinius Capito; M. Ceaparius	
	All were executed without trial on the orders of Cicero for their part in the attempted coup of 63 BC	

Murdered During a Mutiny

91 BC	Q. Servilius	(Pr. 91)
	Murdered in Asculum by the inhabitants	
89 BC	L. Porcius Cato	(Cos. 90)
	Murdered during the Battle of Lake Fucinus, possibly by the younger C. Marius	
89 BC	A. Postumius Albinus	(Cos.99)
	Murdered during the siege of Pomepii	
88 BC	M. Gratidius	
	The legate of Marius sent to take command of Sulla's army; he was murdered when they mutinied against the change of command	
88 BC	Q. Pompeius Rufus	(Cos. 88)
	Murdered when attempting to assume command of the army of Pompeius Strabo	
86 BC	L. Valerius Flaccus	(Cos. 86)
	Murdered during a mutiny instigated by his deputy, C. Flavius Fimbria	
84 BC	L. Cornelius Cinna	(Cos. 87–84)
	Murdered by elements of his army in Italy as they were waiting to cross to Illyria	
82 BC	C. Fabius Hadrianus	(Pr. 85/84)
	Murdered during an uprising in Utica	

82 BC	C. (Coelius) Antipater	
	Murdered during a mutiny organized by P. Albinovanus	
82 BC	Flavius Fimbria	
	Murdered during a mutiny organized by P. Albinovanus	
81 BC	L. Iulius Salinator	
	Murdered by one of his commanders in a mutiny whilst guarding the Pyrenees crossing into Spain	
80 BC	C. Papirius Carbo	(Pr. 81)
	Murdered during a mutiny by the garrison of Volaterrae	
73 BC	Q. Sertorius	
	Murdered in Spain, in a conspiracy instigated by his deputy M. Perperna	

Murdered during a Proscription[4]

88 BC	P. Sulpicius	(Tr. Pl. 88)
	Murdered after being declared an enemy of the state, following the capture of Rome by Pompeius and Sulla	
87 BC	Cn. Octavius	(Cos. 87)
	Murdered by Censorinus following the capture of Rome by Marius and Cinna	
87 BC	P. Licinius Crassus	(Cos. 97)
	Murdered by Fimbria following the capture of Rome by Marius and Cinna	
87 BC	M. Antonius	(Cos. 99)
	Murdered at his villa following the capture of Rome by Marius and Cinna	
87 BC	L. Iulius Caesar	(Cos. 90)
	Murdered in Rome following its capture by Marius and Cinna	
87 BC	C. Iulius Caesar Strabo	(Aed. 90)
	Murdered in Rome following its capture by Marius and Cinna	
87 BC	Q. Ancharius	(Pr. 88)
	Murdered by Marius' bodyguard following the capture of Rome	
87 BC	P. Licinius Crassus (junior)	
	Murdered by Fimbria following the capture of Rome by Marius and Cinna	
87 BC	Atilius Serranus; P. Lentulus; C. Nemetorius; M. Baebius	
	All murdered during the slaughter that followed the capture of Rome by Marius and Cinna.	

86 BC	Sex. Lucilius	(Tr.Pl. 87)
	Thrown from the Tarpeian Rock following his year of office on the orders of Marius	
82 BC	Q. Mucius Scaevola	(Cos. 95)
	Murdered by Iunius Brutus, on the orders of the younger Marius	
82 BC	L. Domitius Ahneobarbus	(Cos. 94)
	Murdered by Iunius Brutus, on the orders of the younger Marius	
82 BC	P. Antistius	(Tr. 88)
	Murdered by Iunius Brutus, on the orders of the younger Marius	
82 BC	Papirius Carbo	
	Murdered by Iunius Brutus, on the orders of the younger Marius	
82 BC	M. Marius Gratidianus	(Pr. 85)
	Murdered by Catilina following the Sullan capture of Rome	
82 BC	P. Laetorius	
	Murdered during the Sullan Proscriptions	
82 BC	Venuleius	
	Murdered during the Sullan Proscriptions	
81 BC	Q. Lucretius Ofella	
	Murdered on Sulla's orders for standing for the consulship against his wishes	

Natural Causes

Ironically, four of the main protagonists of the civil war died of natural causes, though none apart from Marius could claim to have died peacefully.

90 BC	Sex. Iulius Caesar	(Cos.91)
	Died of disease whilst besieging Asculum	
87 BC	Cn. Pompeius Strabo	(Cos. 89)
	Died as disease struck his camp, followed by a lightning strike	
86 BC	C. Marius	(Cos. 107, 104–100 and 86)
	Died in his bed of old age and the exertions of the previous year	
78 BC	L. Cornelius Sulla	(Cos. 88 and 80, Dict. 82–79)
	Died in 78 BC of a wasting disease	
77 BC	M. Aemilius Lepidus	(Cos. 78)
	Died in Sardinia of disease	

Suicide

87 BC	L. Cornelius Merula	(Cos. 87)
	Committed suicide when prosecuted following the duumvirate's capture of Rome	
87 BC	Q. Lutatius Catulus	(Cos. 102)
	Committed suicide when prosecuted following the duumvirate's capture of Rome	
87 BC	P. Coelius	
	Committed suicide following the fall of Placentia	
87 BC	L. Petronius	
	Committed suicide following the fall of Placentia	
85 BC	C. Flavius Fimbria	
	Committed suicide in Pergammum following the defection of his army to Sulla	
82 BC	C. Marius	(Cos. 82)
	Committed suicide in Praeneste, as the city fell to Sullan forces	
82 BC	M. Iunius Brutus	(Pr. 88)
	Committed suicide at Lilybaeum in Sicily following his capture by Pompeius' forces	
82/81 BC	C. Norbanus	(Cos. 83)
	Committed suicide in Rhodes when faced with being handed over to Sulla	

Notable Survivors of the Civil War who were later Killed

53 BC	M. Licinius Crassus	(Cos. 70 and 55)
	Murdered whilst negotiating with the Parthians following his defeat at the Battle of Carrhae	
48 BC	Cn. Pompeius Magnus	(Cos. 70, 55 and 52)
	Murdered by a Roman centurion in Egypt, following his defeat at the Battle of Pharsalus	
44 BC	C. Iulius Caesar	(Cos. 59, 48, 46, 45, 44)
	Famously murdered in the Senate House by a conspiracy of senators	
43 BC	M. Tullius Cicero	(Cos. 63)
	Murdered during a proscription ordered by M. Antonius	

Notes and References

All translations are taken from the Loeb unless otherwise specified (*), and amended by the author where necessary. Below is a list of the full titles of the ancient works referenced and their modern short codes.

Amm. Marc.   Ammianus Marcellinus – *History of Rome*

App. *BC*   Appian – *Civil Wars*
App. *Mith.*   Appian – *Mithridatic Wars*
App. *Ib.*   Appian – *Spanish Wars*
App. *Ill.*   Appian – *Illyrian Wars*
App. *Sic.*   Appian – *Sicilian Wars* (Fragments)

de vir. ill. *   Unknown – *Lives of Famous Men*
Dio.   Dio Cassius – *History of Rome*
Diod.   Diodorus – *Library of History*

Eutrop. *   Eutropius – *Epitome of Roman History*
Exsuper. *   Iulius Exsuperantius – *Epitome of Roman History* (Fragments)

Fest. *   Festus – *Lexicon* (Fragments)
Flor.   Florus – *Epitome of Roman History*
Frontin. *Str.*   Frontinus – *Stratagems*

Gell.   Gellius – *The Attic Nights*
Gran. Lic. *   Granius Licinianus – *Epitome of Roman History* (Fragments)

Iustin *   Justin – *Epitome of Pompeius Trogus' History of the World*

Jerome *Chr.* *   Jerome – *Chronicon* (Timeline of History)
John of Antioch * John of Antioch – *Chronicle of History* (Fragments)
Joesph. *AJ* *   Josephus – *Antiquities of the Jews*

Liv.   Livy – *History of Rome*
Liv. *Per.*   The *Periochae of Livy*

Macr. *Sat.* *   Macrobius – *The Saturnalia*
Mem. *   Memnon – *History of Heracleia* (Fragments)

Obseq.	Iulius Obsequens – *Summary of Livy*
Oros.	Orosius – *Seven Books against the Pagans*
Ovid. *Fasti.*	Ovid – *Calendar of Festivals*
Plin. *NH*	Pliny – *Natural History*
Plut. *Cat. Min.*	Plutarch – *Life of Cato the Younger*
Plut. *Crass.*	Plutarch – *Life of Crassus*
Plut. *Luc.*	Plutarch – *Life of Lucullus*
Plut. *Mar.*	Plutarch – *Life of Marius*
Plut. *Pomp.*	Plutarch – *Life of Pompeius Magnus*
Plut. *Sert.*	Plutarch – *Life of Sertorius*
Plut. *Sull.*	Plutarch – *Life of Sulla*
Quinct. *Inst.*	Quintilian – *Institutes of Oratory*
Sall. *Cat.*	Sallust – *The Conspiracy of Catiline*
Sall. *Hist.* *	Sallust – *Histories* (Fragments)
Sis. *	Sisenna – *History of Rome* (Fragments)
Strabo	Strabo – *Geography*
Suet. *Iul.*	Suetonius – *Biography of Iulius Caesar*
Tac. *Ann.*	Tacitus – *Annals of Roman History*
Val. Max.	Valerius Maximus – *Memorable Doings and Sayings*
Vell.	Velleius Paterculus – *History of Rome*

Cicero – Works

Cic. *Brut.*	*Brutus*
Cic. *De. Or.*	*On the Ideal Orator (de Oratore)*
Cic. *Div.*	*On Divination (de Divintaione)*
Cic. *Lael.*	*Laelius on friendship*
Cic. *ND.*	*On the Nature of the Gods (de Natura Deorum)*

Cicero – Speeches

Cic. *Arch.*	*In Defence of Archias*
Cic. *Balb.*	*In Defence of Cornelius Balbus*
Cic. *Cael.*	*In Defence of Caelius*
Cic. *Cat.*	*Against Catiline*
Cic. *Clu.*	*In Defence of Cluentius*
Cic. *Div. in Caec.*	*Against Caecilius*
Cic. *Dom.*	*On his House*
Cic. *Flacc.*	*In Defence of Flaccus*
Cic. *Font.*	*In Defence of Fonteius*

Cic. *Leg. Agr.*	On the Agrarian Law of Rullus
Cic. *Man.*	In Favour of Pompeius' Command
Cic. *Mil.*	In Defence of Milo
Cic. *Mur.*	In Defence of Murena
Cic. *Pis.*	Against Piso
Cic. *Verr.*	Against Verres

| Ascon. * | Asconius – *Commentaries on Cicero's Speeches* |
| Schol. Bob. * | Scholia Bobiensia – *Commentary on Cicero's Speeches* |

Cicero – Letters

| Fam. | Cicero – *Letters to his Friends* |

Latin Inscriptions

| CIL | *Corpus Inscriptionum Latinarum* |

Chapter One

1. Sall. *Cat.* 10. See R Syme, *Sallust* (London, 1964), pp. 240–273.
2. App. *BC.* 1.1–2. Plutarch (*Sull.* 7.2), based on the memoirs of Sulla, naturally blamed Marius. Florus (1.9.3) blamed both men.
3. See TP Wiseman, 'The Two-Headed State: How Romans Explained Civil Wars' in B Breed, C Damon and A Rossi (eds.), *Citizens of Discord* (Oxford and New York, 2010), pp. 25–44.
4. In 485, 439 and 394 BC respectively. See P Panitschek, 'Sp. Cassius, Sp. Maelius, M. Manlius als exempla maiorum', *Philologus* 133, 1989, pp. 231–245; C. Smith, 'Adfectatio regni in the Roman Republic' in S Lewis (ed.), *Ancient Tyranny* (Edinburgh, 2006), pp. 49–64; M Lowrie, 'Spurius Maelius: Dictatorship and the *Homo Sacer*' in B Breed, C Damon and A Rossi (eds.), *Citizens of Discord* (Oxford and New York, 2010), pp.171–186.
5. Val. Max. 4.7.1, Cic. *Lael.* 37.
6. App. *BC.* 1.20.
7. See L Taylor, 'Forerunners of the Gracchi', *Journal of Roman Studies* 52, 1962, pp. 19–27 and E Badian, 'Tribuni Plebis and Res Publica' in J Linderski (ed.), *Imperium Sine Fine* (Stuttgart, 1996), pp.187–214.
8. KJ Hölkeskamp, *Reconstructing the Roman Republic* (Oxford, 2010), pp.107–124.
9. In 209 BC, twelve Roman colonies, with Latin rights, refused to supply troops to Rome's war effort, claiming they were not able (Liv. 27.9). They too were made an example of (Liv. 29.15).
10. A McDonald, 'Rome and the Italian Confederation (200–186 BC)', *Journal of Roman Studies* 34, 1944, p. 33.
11. The first expulsion of non-citizens from Rome, whether they be Latins or Italians, occurred in 187 BC. Others followed in 177, 168 and 126 BC. See R Husband, 'On the Expulsion of Foreigners from Rome', *Classical Philology*, July, 1916, pp.315–333.
12. See Mouritsen, *Italian unification: A study in ancient and modern historiography* (London, 1998), p.111.
13. See McDonald (1944), pp.11–33.

14. See V Shochat, 'The Lex Agraria of 133 BC and the Italian Allies', *Athenaeum* 48, 1970, pp. 25–45; E Badian, 'Roman Politics and the Italians (133–91 BC)', *Dialoghi di Archeologia* 4–5, 1970–71, pp.373–409; J Richardson, 'The Ownership of Roman Land: Tiberius Gracchus and the Italians', *Journal of Roman Studies* 70, 1980, pp. 1–11; R Howarth, 'Rome, the Italians, and the Land', *Historia* 48, 1999, pp. 282–300; and H Mouritsen, 'The Gracchi, the Latins, and the Italian Allies', in L de Ligt and S Northwood (eds.) *People, Land and Politics, Demographic Developments and the Transformation of Roman Italy 300 BC–AD 14* (Leiden, 2008), pp. 471–483.

15. App. *BC*. 1.19.

16. See P Conole, 'Allied Disaffection and the Revolt of Fregellae', *Antichton* 15, 1981, pp. 129–130.

17. App. *BC*. 1.21, Val. Max. 9.5.1. See A Hands, 'Land and Citizenship, 125–122 BC', *Mnemosyne* 29, 1976, 176–180.

18. Mouritsen (1998), pp. 118–121.

19. Cicero refers to the revolt as the *bellum Fregellanum* (*Leg Agr*. 2.90). Mouritsen (1998), pp.118–119, and Conole (1981), pp. 129–140, both argue that Fregellae was part of a larger planned Latin revolt, but that Fregellae jumped the gun and their destruction stopped the others.

20. See Conole (1981), pp.132–133.

21. See G Sampson, *The Crisis of Rome. The Jugurthine and Northern Wars and the Rise of Marius* (Barnsley, 2010), pp.192–200.

22. Sampson (2010), pp. 212–214.

23. E Badian, 'Caepio and Norbanus. Notes on the Decade 100–90 BC', *Historia* 6, 1957, pp. 318–346, and E Gruen, 'Political Prosecutions in the 90's BC', *Historia* 15, 1966b, pp. 32–64.

24. See T Carney, 'Was Rutilius' Exile Voluntary or Compulsory', *Acta Juridica*, 1958b, pp. 242–244, and R Kallet-Marx, 'The Trial of Rutilius Rufus', *Phoenix* 44, 1990, pp.122–139

25. See note 11.

26. Ascon. 68C.

27. Ap. *Ib*. 99–100, Liv. *Per*. 70, Plut. *Sert*. 3.3, Sall. *Hist*. 1.88M, Gell. 2.27.2, Frontin. *Str*. 1.8.5 and 2.10.1, Obseq. 48, Cic. *Pis*. 58, Ascon. 14C, Plut. *Crass*. 1.1, 4.1–2 respectively.

28. Ap. *Ib*. 100.

29. Diod. 37.5a.

30. Liv. *Per*. 70, Obseq. 48 and 53.

31. Liv. *Per*. 70, App. *Mith*. 121, Iust. 39.5.2, Cic. *Leg. Agr*. 2.51, Sall. *Hist*. 2.41, Obseq. 49, Eutrop. 6.11.3, Jerome. *Chr*. 1922 and 1952, Amm. Marc. 22.16.24.

32. G Sampson, *The Defeat of Rome, Crassus, Carrhae and the Invasion of the East* (Barnsley, 2008), pp. 32–55.

33. App. *Mith*. 10–15, see D Glew, 'Mithridates Eupator and Rome: A Study of the Background of the First Mithridatic War', *Athenaeum* 55, 1977, pp. 380–405, B McGing, *The Foreign Policy of Mithridates VI Eupator, King of Pontus* (Leiden, 1986), S Dmitriev, 'Cappodocian Dynastic Rearrangements on the Eve of the First Mithridatic War', *Historia* 55, 2006, pp. 285–297.

34. Plut. *Mar*. 31.3.

35. See T Luce, 'Marius and the Mithridatic Command', *Historia* 19, 1970, pp.161–194, and L Ballesteros Pastor, 'Marius' Words to Mithridates Eupator (Plut. *Mar.* 31.3)', *Historia* 48, 1999, pp. 506–508.

36. See G Sumner, 'Sulla's Career in the Nineties', *Athenaeum* 56, 1978, pp. 395–396, P Cagniart, 'L. Cornelius Sulla in the Nineties: a Reassessment', *Latomus* 50, 1991, pp. 285–303, and T Brennan, 'Sulla's Career in the Nineties', *Chiron* 22, 1992, pp.103–158.

37. Plut. *Sull.* 5.3–6, Liv. *Per.* 70, Vell. 2.24.3. See A Keaveney, 'Roman Treaties with Parthia circa 95–circa 64 BC', *American Journal of Philology* 102, 1981, pp.195–212, and Sampson (2008), pp. 86–87.

38. M Olbrycht, 'Mithridates VI Eupator and Iran', in J Hojte (ed.) *Mithridates VI and the Pontic Kingdom* (Aarhus, 2009), pp. 163–190, argues that Mithridates II of Parthia was sponsoring Mithridates VI in his activities in Asia Minor to reduce Roman influence.

39. Cic. *De.Or.* 1.24–25.

40. See E Hardy, 'Three Questions as to Livius Drusus', *Classical Review* 27, 1913, pp. 261–263, P Seymour, 'The Policy of Livius Drusus the Younger', *English Historical Review* 29, 1914, pp. 417–425, A Hands, 'Livius Drusus and the Courts', *Phoenix* 26, 1967, pp. 268–274, E, Weinrib, 'The Judiciary Law of M. Livius Drusus (Tr. Pl. 91 BC)', *Historia* 19, 1970, pp. 414–443, E Gabba, *Republican Rome: The Army and the Allies* (trans. P Cuff) (Oxford, 1976), pp.131–141, A Marshall, 'Livius Drusus and the Italian Question', *Historical Papers* 11, 1976, pp. 93–103, R Evans, 'The characters of Drusus and Sulpicius', *Questioning Reputations* (Pretoria, 2004), pp. 133–159.

41. Again, there is a debate over whether this proposal was aimed at all Latins and Italians or just Latins. Mouritsen (1998), pp. 120–122, again argues that it was intended for the Latins only, but then this does not explain the Italian reaction.

42. App. *BC.* 1.35–36

43. Val. Max. 3.1.2, Plut. *Cat. Min.* 2, Vict. *de vir. ill.*. 80.1. See C Dart, 'Qvintus Poppeadivs Silo Dvx et Avctor of the Social War', *Athenaeum* 98, 2010, pp. 111–126.

44. Diod. 37.11. See H Rose, 'The Oath of Philippus and the Di Indigetes', *Harvard Theological Review* 30, 1937, pp. 165–181, who argues that the wording Diodorus presents was his own creation, and L Taylor, *Party Politics in the Age of Caesar* (Berkeley, 1949), p.45–46, who argues that it could well be the genuine wording.

45. Val. Max. 9.5.2, *de vir. ill.*. 66.8.

46. *de vir. ill.*. 66.8.

47. Plut. *Cat.Min.* 2.3, Val. Max. 3.1.

48. Liv. *Per.* 71.

49. Flor. 2.6.8.

50. Dio (28. *fr.*96) and the *Periochae* of Livy (*Per.*71) refer to the conspiracy, but not the part Drusus played.

51. Diod. 37.11.

52. Given his apparent role in unveiling the conspiracy, it could have been by either Romans or Italians. Cicero (*ND* 3.81) accuses Q. Severus Varius Hybrida (Tr. Pl. 90) as being the assassin.

53. Ascon. 69.

54. App. *BC.* 1.38.

55. App. *BC.* 1.38, Diod. 37.13.2, Liv. *Per.* 72, Vell. 2.15.1, Flor. 2.6.9, Obseq.

Chapter Two

1. L. Lucceius, a friend of Cicero, wrote a history of the Social and Civil Wars in c56 BC. See Cic. *Fam.* 5.12.2.

2. The *Periochae* of Livy (*Per.* 72), Orosius (5.18.8), Eutropius (5.3.1) and Florus (2.6.5), all of whom are based on Livy, have elements of the same list. For this period we do not have the books of Livy himself, but must rely on the *Periochae* (or summary) of Livy for information.

3. Diod. 37.2.5.

4. App. *BC.* 1.39.1.

5. E Salmon, 'Notes on the Social War', *Transactions and Proceedings of the American Philological Association* 89, 1958, pp. 159–184.

6. Diod. 37.2.7.

7. Diod. 37.2.4–7. Also see Strabo. 5.4.2.

8. Dart argues that such descriptions are indeed a Romanized version of the Italian command, rather than representing the actuality, which he argues was each of the two federations having a *dux* in supreme command, with a commander for each of the major races, and no annual elections to Italian magistracies. See C Dart, 'The "Italian" Constitution in the Social War: A Reassessment (91 to 88 BC)', *Historia* 58, 2009, pp. 215–224.

9. See E Salmon, 'The Cause of the Social War', *Phoenix* 16, 1962, pp. 107–119, and P Brunt, 'Italian Aims at the Time of the Social War', *Journal of Roman Studies* 55, 1965, pp. 90–109.

10. App. *BC.* 1.39.1.

11. See Conole (1981), pp. 129–140.

12. Flor. 2.6.6–8.

13. Plut. *Sert.* 4.1–5, Sall *Hist.* 1.77.

14. Mem. 20.

15. App. *BC.* 1.39.

16. P Brunt, *Italian Manpower 225 BC–AD 14* (Oxford, 1971), pp. 435–440.

17. CIL I². 867–874.

18. The other named legates were Q. Servilius Caepio, C. Perperna, M. Valerius Messala (see App. *BC.* 1.40).

19. Oros. 5.18.10.

20. See A Keaveney, *Rome and the Unification of Italy* (London, 1987), pp. 215–219, for the possible identifications of the commanders and the Italian peoples.

21. App. *BC.* 1.47, Oros. 5.18.17.

22. Keaveney (1987), pp. 131–132.

23. Again, see Keaveney (1987), pp. 216–217.

24. App. *BC.* 1.41.

25. Oros. 5.18.11–14.

26. App. *BC.* 1.43.

27. Oros. 5.18.11–13. Also see Dio. *fr.* 98.1–2.

28. Brunt (1971), p.435.

29. Obsequens (55), however, ascribed the loss to a failed sacrifice.

30. Liv. *Per.* 73.

31. T Broughton, *The Magistrates of the Roman Republic, Volume II, 99 BC–31 BC* (New York, 1952), pp. 30–32.

32. Liv. *Per.* 73.
33. Oros. 5.18.14.
34. App. *BC.* 1.44.
35. App. *BC.* 1.46.
36. Liv *Per.* 73, Oros. 5.18.16.
37. Diod. 37.15.1–3.
38. See Plutarch (*Mar.* 33.2) for a reported clash between the two men.
39. Cic. *Phil.* 12.27.
40. Mattingly and Keaveney argue that this Sulpicius was P. Sulpicius, the tribune of 88 BC. See H Mattingly, 'The Consilium of Cn. Pompeius Strabo in 89 BC', *Athenaeum* 53, 1975, pp. 264–265, and Keaveney (1987), p.209.
41. App. *BC.* 1.47.
42. Oros. 5.18.17.
43. He came from a different branch of the Iulii than Lucius, and the men may have been cousins.
44. App. *BC.* 1.48.
45. See Broughton (1952), pp. 27–31.
46. Diod. 37.19.3–20.1.
47. Diod. 37.16.1. Orosius (5.18.17) also names him as an Italian leader.
48. Liv. *Per.* 72.
49. The *Periochae of Livy* (*Per.* 73) and Orosius (5.18.11) state that Caesar fought Samnites. Appian (*BC.* 1.41) states that the enemy commander was Vettius Scato without naming the peoples he commanded.
50. Ibid.
51. App. *BC.* 1.41.
52. App. *BC.* 1.42.
53. Ibid.
54. Having been captured along with his father and held as a hostage for the last 15 years.
55. App. *BC.* 1.42. Appian continually refers to L. Caesar as Sex (his brother), who was not the consul this year.
56. Oros. 5.18.11.
57. App. *BC.* 1.45.
58. Frontin. *Str.* 1.5.17.
59. Oros. 5.18.16
60. Liv. *Per.* 73. Diodorus preserves details of the famine in the city during the siege (Diod. 37.19.1–2.). Strabo 5.238) states that in his day the city was still deserted.
61. Keaveney (1987), p.140.
62. App. *BC.* 1.41.
63. Frontin. *Str.* 2.4.16.
64. Diod. 37.23.
65. App. *BC.* 1.42.
66. Oros. 5.18.17.
67. Liv. *Per.* 74.
68. App. *BC.* 1.49.
69. Oros. 5.18.17.
70. Liv. *Per.* 73.
71. App. *BC.* 1.49.

72. Sis. *fr*.119 contains references to the issuing of citizenship.
73. CIL. 1.709.
74. Cic. *Balb*. 21.
75. Gell. *NA*. 4.4.3.
76. *Ad Herenn*. 3.2.2.
77. E Bispham, *From Asculum to Actium: The Municipalization of Italy from the Social War to Augustus* (Oxford, 2007), pp. 161–204.
78. Ibid, pp. 172–173.
79. Cic. *Arch*. 7.
80. *Schol Bob*. 175.
81. See U Ewins, 'The Enfranchisement of Cisalpine Gaul', *Papers of the British School at Rome* 23, 1955, pp. 73–98.
82. App. *BC*. 1.49. See R Lewis, 'Appian *BC* I, 49, 214. Rome's New Tribes 90–87 *BC*', *Athenaeum* 46, 1968, pp. 273–291.
83. Bispham (2007), pp. 162–171.
84. App. *BC*. 1.49.
85. Ibid.
86. Freedmen had been used in the military during the Second Punic War. During the Jugurthine and Northern Wars Marius had recruited citizens without land. See Sampson (2010), pp.180–191.
87. The 'Hybrida' refered to his mixed parentage, his mother being Spanish and Varius himself possibly being born in Surco. Cicero (*ND*. 3.81) accuses him of murdering Livius Drusus and Q. Caecilius Metellus Numidicus (the latter by poison).
88. See E Gruen, 'The Lex Varia', *Journal of Roman Studies* 55, 1965, pp. 59–73, E Badian, 'Quaestiones Variae', *Historia* 18, 1969, pp. 447–491, F. Porra, 'La legge Varia del 90 e quella Sulpicia dell' 88 a.C: il problema degli esuli', *Annali della Facoltà di Lettere* 35, 1973, pp. 13–28.
89. Cic. *Brut*. 305, *ND*. 3.81, Val. Max. 8.6.4.
90. Plut. *Mar*. 33.6.
91. App. *BC*. 1.50.
92. Ibid.
93. Dio. *fr*.100.
94. Liv. *Per*. 75, Oros. 5.18.24.
95. Although Orosius names the battle as Lake Facinus, the word *facinus* in Latin can refer to an evil deed.
96. Liv. *Per*. 75.
97. Oros. 5.18.24.
98. Private armies who followed their patron as an individual rather than as the duly appointed representative of the state. See R Morstein–Marx, 'Consular Appeals to the Army in 88 and 87: the locus of legitimacy in late–Republcian Rome', in H Beck, A Dupla, M Jehne and F Pollo (eds.), *Consuls and Res Publica* (Cambridge, 2011), pp. 259–278.
99. App. *BC*. 1.50, Vell. 2.16.4, Liv. *Per*. 75, Eutrop. 5.3.2.
100. We have no further names for him other than Sulpicius. Broughton (1952), p. 37, argues that it was Ser. Sulpicius Galba.
101. Oros. 5.18.25, Liv. *Per*. 76.
102. Liv. *Per*. 76. The latter campaign took place in 88 *BC*, see Chapter 3.

103. App. *BC*. 1.48. Orosius (5.18.21) also has the suicide of Vidacilius.
104. Oros. 5.18.21.
105. Vell. 2.21.1.
106. Oros. 5.18.26.
107. This is not explicitly attested by any ancient source, but a number of them refer to him having legates of his own, and it follows the pattern set with Marius and Rutilius the year previously. See Broughton (1952), p. 38.
108. Plin. *NH*. 3.70.
109. Oros. 5.18.22.
110. Vell. 3.16.2.
111. App. *BC*. 1.50.
112. See A Keaveney, 'Sulla, the Marsi, and the Hirpini', *Classical Philology* 76, 1981, pp. 292–296.
113. App. *BC*. 1.51.
114. Ibid.
115. Ibid.
116. Ovid. *Fasti*. 6.567.
117. App. *BC*. 1.52.
118. Ibid.
119. Liv. *Per*. 75, Diod. 37.2.8.
120. App. *BC*. 1.52.
121. Broughton (1952), p.39, postulates that he may have been the same man who was a proconsul c.78 BC, but does not explain the massive gap in his career nor this absence during the intervening years of the civil war.
122. Liv. *Per*. 76.
123. Flor. 2.6.13.
124. Vell. 2.15.3.
125. Brunt (1971), pp. 439 and 696–697.
126. The Northern Wars against the Cimbri and Teutones, which saw one of Rome's greatest ever defeats, at Arausio, and an invasion of Italy itself. See Sampson (2010), pp. 133–141.
127. Oros. 5.18.30.
128. Brunt (1971), pp. 438–439.
129. Oros. 5.18.27–29.
130. See C Barlow, 'The Roman Government and the Roman Economy, 92–80 BC', *American Journal of Philology* 101, 1980, pp. 202–219.
131. App. *BC*. 1.54.
132. Barlow (1980), pp. 202–219.
133. App. *BC*. 1.54, Liv. *Per*.74, Val. Max. 9.7.4.
134. Ibid.
135. Fest. 516L.
136. This is explicitly attested in Cicero (*Arch*. 11).
137. Plutarch (*Mar*. 36.5) tells the story of a prophecy that was made during Marius' youth concerning seven Eagle chicks in a nest that he caught in his cloak, which was interpreted as signalling seven Consulships. At this point he remained on six. We have no way of telling whether this prophecy was a later invention or how much credence Marius made of it during his lifetime.

Chapter Three

1. App. *BC*. 1.53.
2. Diod. 37.2.9–10.
3. Obseq. 56.
4. See Broughton (1952), p. 43 and p. 45.
5. Obseq. 56.
6. Diod. 37.2.10.
7. Ibid.
8. Liv. *Per.* 76, *de vir. ill.* 63. Confusingly, Orosius had a Poppaedius killed at the battle of Teanus River in 89 by Sulpicius (Oros. 5.18.25).
9. Liv. *Per.* 76.
10. *de vir. ill.* 63.1.
11. Many commentators have made Mamercus a legate of Metellus, but this is never attested anywhere in the ancient sources.
12. Diod. 37.2.11.
13. Sampson (2010), pp. 46–49, 53–55 and 98–99.
14. Oros. 5.18.30.
15. Liv. *Per.* 74.
16. Dio. *fr.* 101.
17. M Olbrycht, 'Mithridates VI Eupator and Iran', in J Hojte (ed.) *Mithridates VI and the Pontic Kingdom* (Aarhus, 2009), pp. 163–190. For good background on Mithridates, see B McGing (1986) or P Matyszak, *Mithridates the Great* (Barnsley, 2008).
18. E Badian, 'Sulla's Cilician Command', *Athenaeum* 37, 1959, pp. 279–303, P Cagniart, 'L. Cornelius Sulla in the Nineties: a Reassessment', *Latomus* 50, 1991, pp. 285–303, and T Brennan, 'Sulla's Career in the Nineties', *Chiron* 22, 1992, pp. 103–158.
19. Plutarch (*Sull.* 24) gives the figures as 150,000, whilst Memnon (22.9) and Valerius Maximus (9.2e3) state 80,000. See also App. *Mith.* 22–23, 58 and 62, Oros. 6.2.2–3, Liv. *Per.* 78, Dio. *fr.* 101, Vell. 2.18.1.–2, Flor. 1.40.7–8, Cic. *Man.* 7, Tac. *Ann.* 4.14.
20. Plut. *Sull.* 6
21. The tribune is only identified as a Pompeius, but modern commentators have argued that it was the same man. See Broughton (1952), pp. 2–3.
22. Cic. *Lael.* 2.
23. Val. Max. 3.5.2.
24. Technically, lots were used to distribute the command between the two consuls, but with a partnership such as this and a clear military favourite, this seems to have been arranged (Vell. 2.18.2).
25. See Lewis (1968), pp. 273–291.
26. Vell. 2.20.2, App. *BC.* 1.49, Sis. *fr.* 17.
27. See A Lintott, 'The Tribunate of P. Sulpicius Rufus', *Classical Quarterly* 21, 1971, pp. 442–453, T Mitchell, 'The Volte-Face of P. Sulpicius Rufus in 88 BC', *Classical Philology* 70, 1975, pp. 197–204, C Chapman, 'Cicero and Sulpicius Rufus (Tr. Pl. 88 BC)', *Acta Classica* 22, 1979, pp. 61–72, J Powell, 'The Tribune Sulpicius', *Historia* 39, 1990, pp. 446–460, R Lewis, 'P. Sulpicius' Law to Recall Exiles, 88 BC', *Classical Quarterly* 48, 1998, pp. 195–199, R Evans, 'The Characters of Drusus and Sulpicius', *Questioning Reputations* (Pretoria, 2004), pp. 133–159.
28. *Ad Herenn.* 2.45, Liv. *Per.* 77. See Lewis (1998), pp.195–199.

29. See B Katz, 'Caesar Strabo's Struggle for the Consulship – and more', *Rheinisches Museum für Philologie* 120, 1977, pp. 45–62, A Keaveney, 'Sulla, Sulpicius and Caesar Strabo', *Latomus* 38, 1979, pp. 451–460, and J Beness, 'Sulpicius (Tr. Pl. 88 BC) and the Pompeii', *Electronic Antiquity* 1.3, 1993.

30. Ascon. 25C. See also Quinct. *Inst.* 6.3.75 and Macr. *Sat.* 1.11.32.

31. As voting had to be conducted in person in Rome, the vast majority of the new citizens would not be able to afford to leave their jobs to travel to Rome (and back) to vote regularly.

32. Plut. *Sull.* 7.2.

33. Plut. *Sull.* 8.3.

34. See Plut. *Mar.* 36.5 for the prophesy of Marius' catching a nest with seven eagle chicks in it.

35. When Ti. Sempronius Gracchus deposed M. Octavius.

36. See G Sampson, *A Re-examination of the Office of the Tribunate of the Plebs in the Roman Republic (494–23 BC)* (Manchester, Unpublished Thesis, 2005).

37. Plut. *Sull.* 9, App. *BC.* 1.57.

38. Morstein-Marx (2011), pp. 259–278.

39. See A Keaveney, *Lucullus: A Life* (London, 1992), p. 7 and pp.17–18.

40. Val. Max. 9.7 *ext.* 1, Oros. 5.19.4.

41. See Morstein-Marx (2011), pp. 273–274.

42. Plut. *Sull.* 9.2.

43. Plut. *Mar.* 35.5 and *Sull.* 9.1.

44. App. *BC.* 1.57.

45. Plut. *Sull.* 9.5.

46. App. *BC.* 1.58.

47. Plut. *Sull.* 9.5–6.

48. Florus (2.21.7) has Sulpicius and Albinovanus as the leaders of the defenders, both of whom he labels as consuls, which is an interesting slip. Possibly, Albinovanus was a fellow tribune. Another remoter possibility is that Albinovanus was the suffect consul who replaced Pompeius and who, due to questionable legitimacy and his short tenure of office, was never officially recognized as consul.

49. App. *BC.* 1.58.

50. App. *BC.* 1.59.

51. Flor. 2.21.7.

52. The phrase '*civitatatis statum ordinavit*' is used (Liv. *Per.* 77).

53. Flor. 2.9.8, Plut. *Sull.* 10.1, Val. Max. 3.8.5, Velleius (2.19.1) labels it a law.

54. B Katz, 'The First Fruits of Sulla's March', *L'antiquité classique* 44, 1975, pp. 102–104, disagrees and thinks it was agreed in the Senate and then put to a popular vote.

55. Val. Max. 3.8.5.

56. Appian (*BC.* 1.60) states that there were around twelve *hostes* in total. Ten of these can be identified with some degree of certainty: Marius and Sulpicius, C. Marius (jnr.), M. Iunius Brutus, P. Cornelius Cethegus, Cn. and Q. Granius, P. Albinovanus, M. Laetorius, Q. Rubrius Varro. See R Bauman, 'The Hostis Declarations of 88 and 87 BC', *Athenaeum* 51, 1973, pp. 270–293 and Katz (1975), pp. 105–115.

57. They were joined by Cethegus, the Granii, Albinovanus, Laetorius and others (App. *BC.* 1.62).

58. Velleius (2.19.1) has Sulpicius being hunted down by horsemen and killed in the Laurentine marshes, whilst the others sources have him being betrayed by a slave whilst hiding in his villa. According to the sources, Sulla then rewarded the slave with his freedom, and then had him hurled from the Tarpeian Rock for the act of treachery (Plut. *Sull.* 10.1).

59. Ti. and C. Sempronius Gracchus, L. Appuleius Saturninus and M. Livius Drusus.

60. Fest. 516L.

61. App. *BC.* 1.59. Katz (1975), pp. 117–120, again argues that this was actually accomplished in 88 BC.

62. See E Badian, 'Lucius Sulla: The Deadly Reformer', in A Dunston (ed.) *Essays on Roman Culture* (Sydney, 1970), pp. 35–74, E Gabba, *Republican Rome, The Army and the Allies* (Oxford, 1976), pp. 131–141. A Keaveney, *Sulla, The Last Republican* (London, 1982).

63. We have no details concerning where or whom he fought.

64. Plut. *Sull.* 10.3, although the manuscript names him as a Servaeus. See Broughton (1952), p. 4.

65. Having been a Metellan client, Marius usurped the command against Jugurtha from Metellus and then supported the tribune Saturninus in exiling Metellus. See Sampson (2010), pp. 192–200.

66. Plut. *Mar.* 40.3–4

67. E Badian, 'Notes on Provincial Governors from the Social War down to Sulla's Victory', *Proceedings of the African Classical Association* 1, 1958, pp. 1–18.

68. Plut. *Sull.* 10.3.

69. Plut. *Sull.* 10.4, Dio. *fr.* 102.3.

70. Dio. *fr.* 102.5.

71. See Vell. 2.24.2. We are not told how many, but as six fled to Cinna and one was executed, it can only be a maximum of three.

72. Plut. *Sull.* 10.4.

73. App. *BC.* 1.63. Translation amended by the author.

74. Vell. 2.20.1. This overlooks the murders during the Marsic and Samnite campaigns (see Chapter 2).

75. Sampson (2010), pp. 180–191.

76. App. *BC.* 1.64.

77. KJ, Hölkeskamp (2010), pp. 107–124.

Chapter Four

1. See J Ramsey, 'Mithridates, the Banner of Ch'ih-Yu, and the Comet Coin', *Harvard Studies in Classical Philology* 99, 1999, pp. 197–253.

2. Plut. *Sull.* 7.4 , Liv. *fr.* 15. See J Heurgon, 'The Date of Vegoia's Prophesy', *Journal of Roman Studies* 49, 1959, 41–45.

3. Cic. *Div.* 1.4. See TP Wiseman, 'Lucretius, Catiline and the Survival of Prophesy', in *History and Imagination Eight Essays on Roman Culture*, (Exeter, 1994) pp. 58–59.

4. Dio. *fr.* 102.7.

5. Broughton (1952), p. 48.

6. 135–132 and 104–100 BC. See Sampson (2010), pp. 201–203.

7. Diod. 37.2.13–14.

8. App. *Mith.* 29.
9. Plut. *Sull.* 11.4–5.
10. Appian (*BC.* 1.64) names Capua, whilst Velleius (2.20.4.) names Nola. The *Periochae* of Livy (*Per.* 79) does not give a location, but is the only one to name Ap. Claudius.
11. App. *BC.* 1.64.
12. Cic. *Font.* 4.3 and Liv. *Per.* 76.
13. Flor. 2.21.9–10.
14. This is interesting in itself as six of the ten tribunes later fled with Cinna. The use of the majority in vetoing a proposal is also an interesting and little explored feature of the tribunate. See G Sampson, 'A Re–examination of the Office of the tribunate of the plebs in the Roman Republic (494 – 23 BC)' (Manchester, Unpublished Thesis, 2005), pp. 211–213.
15. App. *BC.* 1.64.
16. Exsup. 25–26.
17. Plut. *Sert.* 4.5.
18. App. *BC.* 1.65, *de vir. ill..* 69.
19. See Brunt (1971), pp. 440–441.
20. E Fentress, 'Tribe and Faction: The Case of the Gaetuli', *Mélanges de l'Ecole francaise de Rome Antiquité* 94, 1982, pp. 327–329.
21. Plut. *Mar.* 41.2. Fentress (Ibid) argues that they were Gaetulians not Mauri.
22. Gran. Lic. 16–17.
23. Flor. 2.8.21.
24. App. *BC.* 1.67, Plut. *Mar.* 41.2.
25. See B Katz, 'The Selection of L. Cornelius Merula', *Rheinisches Museum für Philologie* 122, 1979, pp. 162–166.
26. Dio. *fr.* 102.7.
27. Gran. Lic. 20–21.
28. Vell. 2.21.2.
29. Brunt (1971), p. 440.
30. We have few clear details surrounding the wider family of Marius; at least one brother and one step-brother are known. Certainly, the late Republic saw a number of Marii holding junior magistracies.
31. Gran Lic.17.
32. For the fleet, see Plut. *Mar.* 42.1.
33. Gran. Lic. 18. The Valerius is not clearly identified. Broughton postulated that it may have been. L. Valerius Flaccus, the consul of 86. Broughton (1952), p. 53.
34. Most notably in the Gothic Wars of the sixth century AD.
35. App. *BC.* 1.67, Val. Max. 4.7.5.
36. Gran. Lic. 20.
37. Broughton (1952), p. 51 and p.53.
38. Livy (1.33.6–7) states that the Janiculum was added to the city's fortifications to stop attacking armies using it as a strong point.
39. App. *BC.* 1.68.
40. Gran. Lic. 18–20.
41. Vell. 2.213.
42. Oros. 5.19.

43. Tac. *Hist.* 3.51.
44. Plut. *Mar.* 42.2.
45. Liv. *Per.* 80.
46. Lovano (2002), pp. 41–42.
47. Gran. Lic. 18.
48. Tac. *Hist.* 3.51.
49. The *Periochae* of Livy is condensing a huge amount of original Livian narrative into short sentences and could easily have integrated different battles.
50. In fact, we have a number of references to Ap. Claudii throughout the period, with no clear idea of how many there were, but they appear on all sides of the conflict.
51. Appian (*BC.* 1.69) names Marius, but it may have been one of the younger Marii. Orosius (5.19) adds the details of the slaughter.
52. Gran. Lic. 22.
53. Gran. Lic. 22. See O Watkins, 'The Death of Cn. Pompeius Strabo', *Rheinisches Museum für Philologie* 131, 1988, pp. 143–150, T Hillard, 'Death by Lightening, Pompeius Strabo and the People', *Rheinisches Museum für Philologie* 139, 1996, pp. 136–145, and T Hillman, 'Cinna, Strabo's Army, and Strabo's Death in 87 BC', *L'antiquité classique* 65, 1996, pp. 81–89.
54. App. *BC.* 1.69. See Lovano (2002), pp. 42–43.
55. Gran. Lic. 23–24.
56. Diod. 38.2.
57. App. *BC.*1.70, Plut. *Mar.*43.1.
58. App. *BC.* 1.70.
59. Diod. 38.2.
60. Plut. *Mar.* 42.4.
61. App. *BC.* 1.71.
62. Gran. Lic. 24.
63. App. *BC.* 1.72.
64. Sampson (2010), pp. 167–179.
65. App. *BC.* 1.73.
66. Ibid.
67. Plut. *Mar.* 44.6, *Sert.*5.5, Oros. 5.19.24.
68. App. *BC.* 1.74.
69. Ibid.
70. Liv. *Per.* 80.
71. Broughton (1952), p. 51 and p. 53.
72. E. Salmon, *Samnium and the Samnites* (Cambridge, 1967), pp. 376–379.
73. Liv. *Per.* 80.

Chapter Five

1. Dio. 31. *fr.*104. If we combine the two sources it would seem that Marius' son was tribune this year; a point not usually noted.
2. Liv. *Per.* 80.
3. See Lovanao (2002), pp. 53–77.
4. See C Barlow, 'The Roman Government and the Roman Economy, 92–80 BC', *American Journal of Philology* 101, 1980, pp. 202–219.

5. Plin. *NH*. 33.132 and 34.27.
6. See E Badian, 'Waiting for Sulla', *Journal of Roman Studies* 52, 1962b, pp. 47–61.
7. See Brunt (1971), pp. 91–99 and Lovano (2002). pp. 61–63.
8. The figure comes from Jerome. *Chr*. 173.4
9. It may fall into the Census of 86/85, given the notoriously inaccurate dating of The *Periochae* of Livy.
10. Liv. *Per* 84.
11. Lovano (2002), pp. 61–63.
12. Cic. *Dom*. 84.
13. App. *BC*. 1.53.
14. Cic. *Brut*. 303.
15. See Badian (1958), pp. 1–18 and Lovano (2002) pp. 79–103.
16. See Badian (1958), pp. 7–8.
17. Ibid.
18. App. *Ib*. 100.
19. Son of the consul of 86 BC, he fled to his uncle following the murder of his father in Asia by Fimbria. Cic. *Flacc*. 63.
20. Some manuscripts give the name as Caelius, which some modern commentators have amended to Caecilius. See Broughton (1952), p.25, and Badian (1958), p.12, who identify him as the consul of 94 BC.
21. Liv. *Per*. 73.
22. Badian (1958), p. 12.
23. Val. Max. 4.7.5.
24. Badian (1958), pp. 12–13.
25. Badian (1958), p. 1.
26. Plut. *Mar*. 40.3–4.
27. By reason of a superior *imperium* to Sextilius, see Badian (1958), p. 1.
28. This version of events would explain the odd two to three year gap between Metellus gaining control of Africa and the Cinnan regime attempting to dislodge him.
29. Plut. *Crass*. 6.2.
30. Liv. *Per*. 84.
31. Sampson (2010).
32. Plut. *Mar*. 40.5.
33. Plut. *Luc*. 2.3–4, Joseph. *AJ*. 14.114.
34. Vell. 2.24.3. This is often combined with Sulla's meeting with a Parthian ambassador in the 90s, but Velleius is quite clear on the timing.
35. Liv. *Per*. 70, Obseq. 53.
36. Cic. *Pis*. 84.
37. Dio. 30–35. *fr*.101. Jerome (*Chr*. 174.1) dates the sacking of the Temple to 83 BC, to synchronize it with the destruction of the Capitol in Rome.
38. App. *Ill*. 5, though the dating is contentious. See Broughton (1952), p. 59.
39. Liv. *Per*. 74 and 76.
40. Oros. 5.18.30.
41. App. *Mith*. 35.
42. Mem. 22.12.
43. App. *Ill*. 5.

44. Eutrop. 5.7.1.
45. Gran. Lic. 27–28. The campaigns are also mentioned by the *Periochae* of Livy (*Per.* 83) and the *de viris illustribus* (75).
46. See E Badian, 'Rome, Athens and Mithridates', *American Journal of Ancient History* 1, 1976, pp. 105–128, C Habicht, 'Zur Geschichte Athens in der Zeit Mithridates VI', *Chiron* 6, 1976, pp. 127–142, M Hoff, 'Laceratae Athenae: Sulla's Siege of Athens in 87/6 BC and its Aftermath' in M Hoff and S Rotroff (eds.), *The Romanization of Athens* (Oxford, 1997), pp. 33–51.
47. Mem. 22.
48. App. *Mith.* 45, Oros. 6.2.4–7.
49. App. *Mith.* 51.
50. Plut. *Sull.* 20.1.
51. App. *Mith.* 51.
52. Mem. 24.
53. App. *Mith.* 52.
54. The site widely believed to be Troy is certainly that of Ilium. Whether it is the site of Troy has recently been disputed by the research of Dr I McGregor-Morris and Dr J Moore.
55. Liv. *Per.* 83.
56. App. *BC.* 1.77.
57. App. *BC.* 1.78.

Chapter Six

1. There is significant confusion around the son of Marius. The *Periochae* of Livy (Per.86) has him as being younger than 20 when elected consul in 83 BC. Yet Orosius has him serving in Porcius Cato's army in 89 BC, and he was old enough to declared *hostis* in 88 BC, and serve possibly as tribune in 86 BC (based on Dio.). In truth, we know little about Marius' children, and it could possibly be that there was more than one son, though this remains speculation.
2. App. *BC.* 1.82; 200 cohorts of 500 men. Brunt argues that this could well have been an accurate figure. See Brunt (1971), pp. 442–443.
3. App. *BC.* 1.82.
4. App. *BC.* 1.79. Again, see Brunt for confirmation of these figures. Brunt (1971), pp. 442–443.
5. Plutarch has him landing at Brundisium (*Sull.* 27.1) but later has him landing at Tarentum (*Sull.* 27.4) as well.
6. Vell. 2.25.1.
7. Exsup. 43–44.
8. Vell. 2.25.3 and Plut. *Sull.*5 respectively.
9. Appian (*BC.* 1.84) states that the battle took place at Canusium, possibly mistaking it for Casilinum in Campania.
10. Vell. 2.25.4, Plut. *Sull.* 27.4 .
11. Plut. *Sull.* 27.5.
12. Flor. 2.9.19.
13. Oros. 5.20.
14. Eutrop. 5.7.4.

15. App. *BC*. 1.85.
16. Plut. *Sull*. 28.1–3. Also see Eutrop. 5.7.4.
17. Plut. *Sert*. 6.2.
18. Exsup. 49.
19. Plut. *Sull*. 28.2–3.
20. Vell. 2.25.3.
21. P Spann, *Quintus Sertorius and the Legacy of Sulla* (Fayetteville, 1987), p. 36.
22. Plut. *Sert*. 4.3.
23. Vell. 2.25.3.
24. Plut. *Sert*. 6.2.
25. Exsup. 50.
26. Diod. 38.16.
27. App. *BC*. 1.86.
28. Ibid.
29. Liv. *Per*. 85.
30. App. *BC*. 1.86.
31. The date of the fire comes from Plutarch (*Sull*. 27.6–7). See H Flower, 'Remembering and Forgetting Temple Destruction. The Destruction of the Temple of Jupiter Optimus Maximus in 83 BC', in G Gardner and K Osterloch (eds.). *Antiquity in Antiquity* (Tübingen, 2008), pp. 74–92.
32. App. *BC*. 1.86.
33. Plut. *Pomp*. 6.4, App. *BC*. 1.80.
34. See Broughton (1952), p. 65 for possible identification of this man.
35. Plut. *Pomp*. 7.1–2.
36. Plut. *Pomp*.7.3.
37. Diod. 38.16.
38. Plut. *Crass*.6.2.
39. Crassus' date of birth is not clear, but must have been around 112 BC. See Sampson (2008), pp. 57 and 64–65.
40. Plut. *Crass*. 6.2–3.
41. Plut. *Crass*. 6.1, App. *BC*.1.86.
42. See note 399 for a discussion on the various ages assigned to C. Marius. Velleius (2.26.1) has him as twenty–six. Sallust (*Hist*. 1.35) records that Marius' widow objected to her son becoming consul this year, as did the *de viris illustribus* (68).
43. Liv. *Per*. 86.
44. Exsup. 50.
45. App. *BC*. 1.86.
46. Exsup. 47.
47. Brunt (1971), pp. 442–443.
48. Val. Max. 7.6.4, Plin. *NH*. 3.16.
49. From the large increase in the number of coins for this period. See Barlow (1980), pp. 204–205.
50. App. *BC*. 1.87.
51. The latter detail comes from Orosius (5.20.5).
52. Plut. *Crass*. 6.5.
53. App. *BC*. 1.87.

54. Oros. 5.20.5.
55. App. *BC.* 1.88.
56. Only Appian (*BC.* 1.88) records the battle.
57. This allegation is repeated in the *de viris illustribus* (68).
58. Plut. *Sull.* 28.4–8.
59. App. *BC.* 1.87.
60. Eutrop. 5.8.1.
61. Oros. 5.20.6.
62. Diod. 38.15.
63. App. *BC.* 1.88.
64. Liv. *Per.* 87, Vell. 2.27.6.
65. App. *BC.* 1.89. The battle is also referred to in the *Periochae* of Livy (*Per.* 86).
66. Vell. 2.28.1.
67. App. *BC.* 1.90.
68. Ibid.
69. App. *BC.* 1.90.
70. App. *BC.* 1.91.
71. Oros. 5.20.7.
72. App. *BC.* 1.91.
73. Plut. *Sull.* 27.7.
74. Oros. 5.20.3.
75. App. *BC.* 1.92.
76. Ibid.
77. App. *BC.* 1.90.
78. Such as at the Battle of Sacriportus, see Appian (*BC.* 1.87).
79. Flor. 2.8.22.
80. Vell. 2.27.1.
81. App. *BC.* 1.90. See R Lewis, 'A Problem in the Siege of Praeneste, 82 BC', *Papers of the British School at Rome* 39, 1971, pp. 32–39.
82. Plut. *Sull.* 29.3.
83. The battle is also mentioned in Oros. 5.20.9, Vell. 2.27.1–3, Flor. 2.9.22–23, Liv. *Per.* 88, Sall. *Hist.* 1.34L, Strabo. 5.249, Eutrop 5.8.1.
84. App. *BC.* 1.93.
85. Plut. *Sull.* 29.5.
86. Plut. *Sull.* 29.7.
87. Plut. *Crass.* 6.6.
88. Plut. *Sull.* 30.1–3.
89. Ibid.
90. App. *BC.* 1.94.
91. For the fall of Norba see Appian (*BC.* 1.94).

Chapter Seven

1. See F Vervaet, 'The Lex Valeria and Sulla's Empowerment as Dictator (82–79 BC)', *Cahiers Glotz* 15, 2004, pp. 37–84.
2. Even though Appian states that he held the dictatorship until 79 BC (*BC.*1.103), a number of modern scholars have tried to argue against this, preferring a date in either 80 or 81 BC.

Recently, Vervaet has argued that there is nothing wrong with Appian's chronology and that Sulla did indeed hold the dictatorship until the beginning of 79 BC, coming full circle. See E Badian, 'Forschungsbericht: From the Gracchi to Sulla', *Historia* 11, 1962, p. 230, B Tywman, 'The Date of Sulla's Abdication and the Chronology of the First Book of Appian's Civil War', *Athenaeum* 54, 1976, pp. 271–295, F Hurlet, *La dictature de Sylla: monarchie ou magistrature republicaine?* (Rome, 1993), pp. 67–69, A Jenkins, 'Sulla's Retirement', *Studies in Roman History and Latin Literature* VII, 1994, pp. 132–142, F Hinard, 'Dion. Cassius et l'Abdication de Sylla', *Revue des Études Anciennes* 101, 1999, pp. 427–432, Vervaet (2004), pp. 58–69, A Keaveney, 'The Terminal Date of Sulla's Dictatorship', *Athenaeum* 93, 2005, pp. 423–439.

3. See Sampson (2005), pp. 357–366.
4. For the similarities between these reforms and those proposed by Drusus, see E Gabba (1976), pp. 131–141.
5. Sall. *Hist.* 1.53.
6. Vervaet (2004), p. 47.
7. See Badian (1970).
8. Euseb. *Chron.* 211.
9. Orosius (5.21) states 80 and then 500. Appian (*BC*. 1.95) has 40 senators and 1,600 equestrians initially.
10. App. *BC*. 1.101, Liv. *Per.* 89, Plut. *Sull*.33.5–6, 40.7; Ascon. 91L, Dio. 37.10.2.
11. App. *BC*. 1.95.
12. App. *BC*. 1.100, Liv. *Per.* 89.
13. Plut. *Pomp.* 9.
14. John of Antioch, *fr*.68, translated by F Walton, 'A Neglected Historical Text', *Historia* 14, 1965, p. 245.
15. Katz (1975), pp. 122–125.
16. Plut. *Pomp.* 10.1.
17. Another Carbo had been murdered in the Marian-ordered proscription of 82 BC.
18. Liv. *Per.* 89 also mentions the revolt, but with no details.
19. Gran. Lic. 39.
20. Val. Max. 9.7.3.
21. Liv. *Per.* 86.
22. Diod. 38.14.
23. Plut. *Pomp.* 10.1.
24. Liv. *Per.* 89.
25. We are not told where he fled to. Spain is usually mentioned by modern commentaries, but not the ancient ones.
26. Oros. 5.21.11.
27. Liv. *Per.* 89.
28. Oros. 5.20.3.
29. Cic. *Verr.* 2.1.70.
30. Plut. *Pomp.* 10.1.
31. Oros. 5.24.16.
32. Plut. *Pomp.* 11.2.
33. See Fentress (1982).
34. Plut. *Pomp.* 12.1–4.
35. Oros. 5.21.13–14.

36. Plut. *Pomp.* 12.5.
37. Plut. *Pomp.* 12.1.
38. See T Hillman, 'Pompeius in Africa and Sulla's Orders to demobilize (Plutarch, Pompeius 13, 1–4)', *Latomus* 56, 1997, pp. 94–106.
39. Plut. *Pomp.* 14.3.
40. The best modern sources for Sertorius' campaigns in Spain are Spann (1987) and C Konrad, *Plutarch's Sertorius. A Historical Commentary* (Chapel Hill, 1994).
41. App. *BC*. 1.86.
42. Plut. *Sert.* 7.1. See Konrad (1994), pp. 99–100.
43. Plut. *Sert.* 7.2.
44. Ibid.
45. Plut. *Sert.* 7.3. Spann (1987), p.48.
46. Plut. *Sert.* 7.3–4.
47. Oros. 5.21.11.
48. It is interesting to note that Egypt was the destination for Pompeius following his defeat at the Battle of Pharsalus in 48 BC.
49. See I Shatzman, 'The Egyptian Question in Roman Politics (59–54 B.C)', *Latomus* 30, 1971, pp. 363– 369, and M Siani–Davies, 'Ptolemy XII Auletes and the Romans', *Historia* 46, 1997, pp. 306–340.
50. Appian provides the only detailed narrative for this war. (App. *Mith.* 64–66). Also see Mem. 26. Cic. *Mur.* 15, Liv. *Per.* 86.
51. Plut. *Sert.* 9.1–2.
52. Plut. *Sert.* 9.3, Spann (1987), pp. 51–52.
53. Ibid.
54. Plut. *Sert.* 12.2.
55. Sall. *Hist.* 1.93.
56. As noted earlier (Plut. *Sert.* 9.2), his former Cilician allies had chosen to fight on the side of King Ascalis and may therefore have been captured when Tingis fell.
57. It could have been either of the brothers, Caius or Marcus; both became consuls (75 and 74 BC respectively). See P Spann, 'C., L. or M. Cotta and the "Unspeakable" Fufidius: A Note on Sulla's Res Publica Restituta', *Classical Journal* 82, 1987, pp. 306–309, and C Konrad, 'Cotta off Mellaria and the Identities of Fufidius', *Classical Philology* 84, 1989, pp. 119–129.
58. See Konrad (1994).
59. Sall. *Hist.* 1.95.
60. Plut. *Sert.* 12.3.
61. C Konrad, 'A New Chronology of the Sertorian War', *Athenaeum* 83, 1995, p.157.
62. Gran. Lic. 32. This was not considered to be part of Italy proper, which only reached unto the River Rubicon.
63. Brunt (1971), pp. 470–471.
64. Frontin. *Str.* 4.5.19.
65. Spann (1987), p. 66.
66. Plut. *Sert.* 12.3–4. See Konrad (1994), pp.129–133.
67. Liv. *Per.* 90.
68. Oros. 5.23.3.
69. Eutrop. 6.1.2. The battle is also mentioned in Sall. *Hist.* 1.111M and Flor. 2.10.6–7.
70. Florus (2.10.6) has the other of the Hirtulei brothers commanding against Throuis.

71. C Konrad, 'Segovia and Segontia', *Historia* 43, 1994b, pp. 444–445.
72. See Spann (1987), pp. 65–66.
73. See Konrad (1994), p. 133.
74. Flor. 2.7.6.
75. Plut. *Sert.* 12.3. Cic. *Fin.* 2.63 also mentions that he died in battle.

Chapter Eight

1. For his abdication, see endnote 491. For his death, see T Carney, 'The Death of Sulla', *Acta Classica* 4, 1961, pp. 64–79.
2. See E Hardy, 'The Number of the Sullan Senate', *Journal of Roman Studies* 6, 1916, pp. 59–62, J Hawthorn, 'The Senate After Sulla', *Greece & Rome* 9, 1962, pp. 53–60, R Evans, 'The "Consulares" and "Praetorii" in the Roman Senate at the beginning of Sulla's Dictatorship', *Athenaeum* 61, 1983, pp. 521–528, F Santangelo, 'Sulla and the Senate: A Reconsideration', *Cahiers Glotz* 17, 2006, pp. 7–22.
3. See A Keaveney, 'Who were the Sullani?', *Klio* 66, 1984, pp. 114–150.
4. L Hayne, 'M. Lepidus (Cos. 78): A Re–Appraisal', *Historia* 21, 1972, pp. 661–688, V Arena, 'The Consulship of 78 BC. Catulus versus Lepidus: an optimates versus populares affair', in H Beck, A Dupla, M Jehne and F Pollo (eds.), *Consuls and Res Publica* (Cambridge, 2011), pp. 299–318.
5. Plut. *Pomp.* 15.1.
6. Sall. *Hist.* 1.48. The speech, as we have it, is worded as though Sulla is still alive.
7. Gran. Lic. 34. Sallust preserves a purported speech from one of Lepidus' opponents, Philippus, in the Senate, in which he claims that Lepidus was planning on restoring the powers of the tribunate (Sall. *Hist.* 1.67) but there is no other source to directly connect him to this at this time. See B Marshall and J Beness, 'Tribunician Agitation and Aristocratic Reaction 80–71 BC', *Athenaeum* 75, 1987, pp. 361–378.
8. See Plut. *Sull.* 36–38 and App. *BC.* 1.105.
9. App. *BC.* 1.107, Flor. 2.11.1–5, Exsuper. 35–37, Gran. Lic. 34, Liv. *Per.* 90.
10. Gran. Lic. 34–35.
11. See F Santangelo, *Sulla, the Elites and the Empire* (Leiden, 2007) pp. 181–183. Cicero (*Cat.* 3.6.14 and *Mur.* 24.49) refers to Sullan settlers from Faesulae in Catiline's army in 63 BC (see Appendix II).
12. Cicero (*Cael.* 70) refers to law passed by a Q. Catulus in a time of civil dissension on the use of violence.
13. App. *BC.* 1.107.
14. Sall. *Hist.* 1.67.
15. This Brutus was a different person to the M. Iunius Brutus who was declared *hostis* by Sulla in 88 BC, who was a praetor in that year.
16. Oros. 5.24.16. See Konrad (1994), pp. 147–148.
17. Exsuper. 34.
18. Sall. *Hist.* 1.64.
19. Plut. *Pomp.* 16.3.
20. Exsuper. 38.
21. Plut. *Pomp.* 16.4–5. Frontinus (*Str.* 1.9.3) also refers to Pompeius' men slaughtering the 'Senate of Milan'; though the reference is undated this conflict would seem the most logical.
22. Believed to be his eldest son, who had been adopted into the Cornelii Scipiones to renew an alliance between the two families. See L Hayne, 'M. Lepidus (Cos. 78): A

Re–Appraisal', *Historia* 21, 1972, pp. 661–688. The Alba in question is never explicitly attested as that in modern Piedmont.

23. Flor. 2.11.6–8.
24. App. *BC*. 1.107.
25. Exsuper. 39.
26. App. *BC*. 1.107, *de vir. ill.*. 77.3.
27. Exsuper. 39–42. Asconius (19C) also refers to Valerius Triarius' fighting Lepidus.
28. Appian (*BC*. 1.107), Plutarch (*Pomp.* 16.9), Florus (2.11.7) and Pliny (*NH.* 7.122 and 186) all agree that he died of natural causes, with the additional stress of a divorce. The *Periochae* of Livy (*Per.* 90) and Cicero (*Cat.* 3.24) merely state that he died.
29. App. *BC*. 1.107.
30. See Broughton (1952), p.89 for the dating.
31. Cic. *Clu.* 99.
32. R Syme, *Rome and the Balkans 80 BC–AD 14* (Exeter, 1999), p.168.
33. Again, see Konrad (1995), pp.157–187 for the issues of dating the years of the war securely to an actual calendar year.
34. Plut. *Sert.* 12.5.
35. Plut. *Sert.* 13.3.
36. Plut. *Sert.* 12.5.
37. Plut. *Sert.* 13.5.
38. Oros. 5.23.4.
39. Caes. *BG*. 3.20.1.
40. Oros. 5.23.4.
41. We find Mauri soldiers operating under Sertorius in Spain at the siege of Langobriga (Plut. *Sert.* 13.5).
42. Cic. *Balb.* 34.
43. Plut. *Sert.* 16.1.
44. Plut. *Sert.* 14.1.
45. Plut. *Sert.* 14.4–5.
46. App. *BC*. 1.108.
47. Konrad (1994), pp.150–151.

Chapter Nine
1. See Konrad (1995), pp. 157–187 for a summary of the key arguments.
2. Both Velleius and Valerius Maximus refer to him as being an ex–praetor. Velleius alone remarks that he had been proscribed (Vell. 2.30.2, Val. Max. 6.2.8). Plutarch (*Sert.*15.1) also states that he was 'of the same faction as Sertorius; in other words a Marian supporter. See Konrad (1994), p.146 for further details.
3. Oros. 5.24.16
4. Plut. *Sert.* 15.3.
5. Suet. *Iul.* 5.
6. Plut. *Sert.* 15.1.
7. Vell. 2.30.1.
8. See R Smith, 'Pompey's Conduct in 80 and 77 BC', *Phoenix* 14, 1960, pp. 1–13, T Hillman, 'Pompeius and the Senate: 77–71', *Hermes* 118, 1990, pp. 444–454 and F Vervaet, 'Pompeius' Career from 79 to 70 BC: Constitutional, Political and Historical Considerations', *Klio* 91, 2009, pp. 406–434.
9. Sall. *Hist.* 2.98. Appian (*BC*. 109) also records his crossing of the Alps.

10. Cic. *Mil.* 28.
11. Cic. *Mil.* 30.
12. Caes. *BC.* 1.35.
13. See C Ebel, 'Pompey's Organization of Transalpina', *Historia* 29, 1975, pp. 358–373.
14. Oros. 5.23.6, quoting Galba.
15. Liv. *fr.*18.
16. Ibid.
17. Plut. *Sert.* 18.2.
18. Plut. *Sert.* 18.2–6.
19. Frontin. *Str.* 2.5.31.
20. App. *BC.* 1.109.
21. Sall. *Hist.* 2.30. The obvious oddity here is the Sallustian report of Hirtuleius' troops being involved, given that he was to the south of the country fighting Metellus. This can be cleared up by the fact that it is reported that there were several Hirtuleii (brothers) serving under Sertorius, and it may have been one of those who was legate in Sertorius' army.
22. Obseq. 58.
23. Plut. *Sert.* 18.6.
24. It was also the birthplace of the Emperor Hadrian.
25. Oros. 5.23.10.
26. Frontin. *Str.* 2.1.2.
27. Frontin. *Str.* 2.3.5.
28. Liv. *Per.* 91.
29. App. *BC.* 1.109.
30. Sall. *Hist.* 2.82 refers to Metellus being provisioned from Gaul, but the year is unclear and may refer to an earlier one.
31. Konrad (1995), p. 442.
32. Oros. 5.23.12, Liv. *Per.* 91.
33. Flor. 2.10.7.
34. Konrad (1994b), p. 445, though he adopts a revised chronology for the war and dates it to 76 BC.
35. Sall. Hist. 2.46.
36. Plutarch (*Pomp.* 18.3) is the only source to provide details of the clash.
37. Plut. *Pomp.* 18.3.
38. Sall. *Hist.* 2.82.6.
39. Plut. *Pomp.* 19.1–3.
40. Plut. *Sert.* 19.2–5.
41. Oros. 5.23.12.
42. See Konrad (1995), p.186. Broughton (1952), p.93 and Spann (1987), p.104 assign it a year earlier.
43. The location of the battle is unclear. See P Spann, 'Saguntum vs. Segontia: A Note on the Topography of the Sertorian War', *Historia* 33, 1984, p. 116–119 and Konrad (1994b), pp.440–453.
44. Plut. *Sert.* 21.1, though the manuscript may be corrupted for the location. See Spann (1984), p.117.
45. Spann (1984), pp. 118–119, (1987), p.115, and Konrad (1994), pp. 447–451. Both Cicero (*Balb.*5) and Sallust (*Hist.* 2.98) make reference to a clash near the river Duero, which

makes the Segontia at Langa de Duero the most likely on a range of topographical and geographical factors.

46. Sallust's Histories (2.55–59), refer to military encounters in this period, but cannot be ascribed to any particular encounter with any certainty.
47. App. *BC.* 1.110.
48. Liv. *Per.* 92.
49. Plut. *Sert.* 21.1–2.
50. Oros. 5.23.12 .
51. Plut. *Sert.* 21.3–4, Liv. *Per.* 92.
52. Sall. *Hist.* 2.82.9.
53. Ibid.
54. Plut. *Sert.* 21.5.
55. Sall. *Hist.* 2.82.7.
56. Sall. *Hist.* 2.82.9–10.
57. Sall. *Hist.* 2.82.10.
58. App. *BC.* 1.111.
59. App. *BC.* 1.112.
60. Ibid.
61. Liv. *Per.* 93.
62. Sall. *Hist.* 3.30.
63. Drawn together from brief notes by Cicero: *Div in Caec.* 55, *Verr.* 2.2.8, 3.213–218, Sall. *Hist.* 3.4–7, Tac. *Ann.* 12.62.
64. Sall. *Hist.* 3.6.
65. The sources are again unclear as to the exact timing. See D Glew, 'Between the Wars: Mithridates Eupator and Rome, 85–73 BC', *Chiron* 11, 1981, pp. 109–130 and B McGing, 'The Date of the Outbreak of the Third Mithridatic War', *Phoenix* 38, 1984, pp. 12–18.
66. As is common in this period, an exact chronology is impossible to determine, but the *Periochae* of Livy (*Per.* 93) and Plutarch (*Sert.* 23–24) place it in this period.
67. Appian actually names him as Marcus Varius, whilst Plutarch, Orosius and Memnon name him as Marius. To what extent this is a consequence of poor manuscript tradition is unclear.
68. App. *Mith.* 62.
69. Plut. *Sert.* 23.3.
70. Oros. 6.2.
71. For more details on the coalition Senate, see Spann (1987), pp. 169–174.
72. See Konrad (1994), pp. 191–192.

Chapter Ten

1. Plut. *Sert.* 24.3.
2. R Evans, 'Gaius and Marcus Marius in Iberia and Gaul: Family Affairs and Provincial Clients', *Acta Classica* 50, 2008, pp. 77–90.
3. M. Marius Gratidianus was a son of Marius' sister.
4. Oros. 6.2.
5. See G Kelly, *A History of Exile in the Roman Republic* (Cambridge, 2006), pp. 180–181 for a fuller discussion.
6. Ibid, pp. 187–188.

7. Mem. 28.
8. Plut. *Luc.* 7.1–2.
9. Plut. *Sert.* 24.3–4.
10. Lucullus held command in Cilicia, Cotta in Bithynia.
11. A. Keaveney, *Lucullus. A Life* (London, 1992), pp. 17–18.
12. Oros. 6.2.13. Also see App. *Mith.* 71.
13. Plut. *Luc.* 8.5–7.
14. Mem. 28.
15. App. *Mith.* 72.
16. See Konrad (1995), pp. 175–176 for a fuller discussion.
17. See Broughton (1952), pp. 106–108 and W Bennett, 'The Death of Sertorius and the Coin', *Historia* 10, 1961, pp. 459–472.
18. Mem. 28.
19. App. *Mith.* 76.
20. Oros. 6.2.
21. App. *Mith.* 75.
22. App. *Mith.* 76.
23. Eutropius (6.6.3 and 6.8.2) also refers to it on two occasions.
24. App. *Mith.* 77.
25. Plut. *Luc.* 12.2–5.
26. Oros. 6.2.21–22.
27. Cic. *Man.* 21.
28. Cic. *Mur.* 33.
29. Cic. *Arch.* 21.
30. Dio. 36.8.2.
31. App. *BC.* 1.113, Plut. *Sert.* 25.4.
32. Plut. *Sert.* 25.1.
33. App. *BC.* 1.113.
34. Plut. *Sert.* 26–27, Sall. *Hist.* 3.83. See C Konrad, 'Some Friends of Sertorius', *American Journal of Philology* 108, 1987, pp. 519–527.
35. Bennett (1961), pp. 459–472, Konrad (1995), pp. 157–187.
36. Bennett (1961), pp.466–467.
37. Liv. *Per.* 94.
38. Konrad (1995), based on earlier commentators, has argued that this re–assessment means re-dating the whole chronology of the civil war in Spain. This in part rests on the sources' accounts being a coherent narrative, which must be moved as a whole a year further back. Whilst there is enough evidence to support moving the murder of Sertorius back a year and disposing of the vague narrative for the campaigns of 73 found in Appian and Plutarch, this author believes that there is not yet enough evidence to warrant a wholesale alteration to the chronology of the war, given the belief that Pompeius did not start campaigning in Spain until 76 BC. Nevertheless, Konrad's arguments are fundamental to any analysis of the civil war in Spain and may yet be proven correct.
39. App. *BC.* 1.114.
40. Ibid.
41. Plut. *Sert.* 27.1.
42. App. *BC.* 1.115.
43. Plut. *Pomp.* 20.2–3.

44. See B Katz, 'Sertorius' Overlooked Correspondent?', *Rheinisches Museum für Philologie* 126, 1983c, pp. 359–362.
45. Plut. *Sert.* 27.4.
46. Flor. 2.30.9.
47. Oros. 5.23.14.
48. Plut. *Crass.* 9.3. See P Piccinin, 'Les Iialiens dans le "Bellum Sparticium"', *Historia* 53, 2004, pp. 173–199.
49. Sampson (2008), pp.62–68.
50. Plut. *Pomp.* 21.2.
51. Vell. 2.30.6.
52. Metellus Pius, the third triumphant commander, followed the correct procedure and disbanded his army after he had crossed the Alps. (Sall. *Hist.* 4.43).
53. App. *BC.* 1.121.

Appendix I

1. Oros. 5.23.
2. Eutrop. 6.3, Oros. 5.23, Liv. *Per.* 90.
3. App. *Sic.* 6.1.
4. Flor. 1.42.7, Diod. 40.1.
5. Liv. *Per.* 97.
6. See D Braund, 'Royal Wills and Rome', *Papers of the British School at Rome* 51, 1983, pp. 16–57.
7. Sall. *Hist.* 2.40–41, App. *BC.* 1.111, Eutrop. 6.11.3.
8. I. Shatzman, 'The Egyptian Question in Roman Politics (59–54 B.C)', *Latomus* 30, 1971, pp. 363–369. M. Siani–Davies, 'Ptolemy XII Auletes and the Romans', *Historia* 46, 1997, pp. 306–340.
9. See Sampson (2010), pp. 46–49 and 98–99.
10. Liv. *Per.* 91.
11. Eutrop. 6.2.1.
12. See R Syme (1999), p. 13. For the other campaigns, see pp. 133–137.
13. This Cosconius is most often identified with the Cosconius who fought against the Italians in 89 BC. See Broughton (1952), p.88. However, I would argue that the elapsed time is too great, and that given Cosconius' military success and expertise, had he survived, we should have heard of him in the intervening wars. To my mind, the elder Cosconius died sometime shortly after 90 BC, and the Cosconius here is his son.
14. Eutrop. 6.4. Also see Oros. 5.23.23, Cic. *Clu.* 97.

Appendix II

1. This appendix is a slimmed down version of Chapter Three in G. Sampson (2019). *Rome, Blood & Power. Reform, Murder and Popular Politics in the Late Republic 70–27 BC*, pp. 58–86 and finally answers a question posed in response to my paper 'Still Waiting for Sulla' at the 2002 Classical Association Conference.
2. Plut. *Luc.* 37.1.
3. Dio. 36.44.3.
4. Dio. 37.30.1.
5. Plut. *Cic.* 17.5.
6. Cic. *Cat.* 4.1–24, Sall. *Cat.* 50.1–55.6.

7. P. Cornelius Lentulus Sura, M. Caeparius, C. Cornelius Cethegus, P. Gabinius Capito, L. Statilius.

8. I. Harrison. (2008). 'Catiline, Clodius, and Popular Politics at Rome during the 60s and 50s BC', *Bulletin of the Institute of Classical Studies* 51, pp. 95–118.

9. Sall. *Cat*. 30.3.

10. Sall. *Cat*. 42.

Appendix III

1. App. BC. 1.103, Diod. 37.29.5.

2. Oros. 5.22, Eutrop. 5.9.2.

3. Vell. 2.15.3.

4. For a more detailed analysis, see F Hinard, *Les Proscriptions de la Rome républicaine* (Rome, 1985).

Bibliography

Abbott, F. (1915). 'The Colonising Policy of the Romans from 123 to 31 BC', *Classical Philology* 10, 365–380.

Alexander, M. (1990). *Trials in the Late Roman Republic 149 BC to 50 BC* (Toronto).

Arena, V. (2011). 'The consulship of 78 BC. Catulus versus Lepidus: an optimates versus populares affair', in H. Beck, A, Dupla, M. Jehne & F. Pollo (eds). *Consuls and Res Publica* (Cambridge), 299–318.

Ashby, T. (1909). 'An Important Inscription Relating to the Social War', *Classical Review* 23, 158–159.

Badian, E. (1955). 'The Date of Pompey's First Triumph', *Hermes* 83, 107–118.

——. (1956). 'Q. Mucius Scaevola and the Province of Asia', *Athenaeum* 34, 104–123.

——. (1957). 'Caepio and Norbanus. Notes on the Decade 100–90 BC', *Historia* 6, 318–346.

——. (1958) 'Notes on Provincial Governors from the Social War down to Sulla's Victory', *Proceedings of the African Classical Association* 1, 1–18.

——. (1958b). *Foreign Clientelae (264–70 BC)* (Oxford).

——. (1959). 'Sulla's Cilician Command', *Athenaeum* 37, 279–303.

——. (1961). 'Servilius and Pompey's First Triumph', *Hermes* 89, 254–256.

——. (1962). 'Forschungsbericht: From the Gracchi to Sulla', *Historia* 11, 197–245.

——. (1962b). 'Waiting for Sulla', *Journal of Roman Studies* 52, 47–61.

——. (1963/64). 'Marius and the Nobles', *Durham University Journal* 25, 141–154.

——. (1964). 'Where was Sisenna? *Athenaeum* 42, 422–431.

——. (1967). 'The Testament of Ptolemy Alexander', *Rheinisches Museum für Philologie* 110, 178–192.

——. (1969). 'Quaestiones Variae', *Historia* 18, 447–491.

——. (1970). 'Lucius Sulla: The Deadly Reformer', in A. Dunston (ed.) *Essays on Roman Culture* (Sydney), 35–74.

——. (1970–71). 'Roman Politics and the Italians (133–91 BC)', *Dialoghi di Archeologia* 4–5, 373–409.

——. (1972). 'Tiberius Gracchus and the Beginnings of the Roman Revolution', *Aufsteig und Niedergang der Römischen Welt* 1.1, 668–731.

——. (1973). 'Marius' Villas: The Testimony of the Slave and the Knave', *Journal of Roman Studies* 63, 121–132.

——. (1976). 'Rome, Athens and Mithridates', *American Journal of Ancient History* 1, 105–128.

——. (1983). 'The Silence of Norbanus', *American Journal of Philology* 104, 156–171.

——. (1990). 'The Consuls 179 – 49 BC', *Chiron* 20, 371–413.

——. (1996). 'Tribuni Plebis and Res Publica', in J. Linderski (ed.) *Imperium Sine Fine* (Stuttgart), 187–214.

Baker, G. (1927). *Sulla the Fortunate: Roman General and Dictator* (New York).

Ballesteros Pastor, L. (1999). 'L'an 88 av. J.-C.: presages apocalyptiques et propaganda déologique', *Dialogues d'histoire anciennes* 25, 83–90.

——. (1999b). 'Marius' Words to Mithridates Eupator (Plut. Mar. 31.3)', *Historia* 48, 506–508.

Balsdon, J. (1938). 'The History of the Extortion Court at Rome 123–70 BC', *Papers of the British School at Rome* 14, 98–114.

——. (1951). 'Sulla Felix', *Journal of Roman Studies* 41, 1–10.

Barlow, C. (1980). 'The Roman Government and the Roman Economy, 92–80 BC', *American Journal of Philology* 101, 202–219.

Batsone, W. (2010). 'Word at War: The Prequel', in B. Breed, C. Damon & A. Rossi (eds.) *Citizens of Discord: Rome and Its Civil Wars* (Oxford). 45–71.

Bauman, R. (1973). 'The Hostis Declarations of 88 and 87 BC', *Athenaeum* 51, 270–293.

Bellen, H. (1975). 'Sullas Brief an den Interrex L. Valerius Flaccus. Zur Geneese der sullanischen Diktatur', *Historia* 24 (1975) 554–569.

Beness, J. (2000). 'The Punishment of the Gracchani and the Execution of C. Villius in 133–132', *Antichton* 34, 1-17.

——. (2005). 'Scipio Aemilianus and the Crisis of 129 BC', *Historia* 54, 37–48.

Beness, J & Hillard, T. (2008). 'From Marius to Sulla. Part 1', *Ancient History* 38, 56–83.

Bennett, H. (1923). *Cinna and his Times* (Chicago).

Bennett, W. (1961). 'The Death of Sertorius and the Coin', *Historia* 10, 459–472.

Béranger, J. (1966) 'La date de la Lex Antonia de Termessibus et le tribunat Syllanien', *Melanges D'Archéologie et D'Histoire offerts à Andre Piganiol* 2, 723–737.

Bispham, E. (2007). *From Asculum to Actium: The Municipalization of Italy from the Social War to Augustus* (Oxford).

Botsford, G. (1913). 'On the Legality of the Trial and Condemnation of the Catilinarian Conspirators', *Classical Weekly* 6, 130–132.

Braund, D. (1983). 'Royal Wills and Rome', *Papers of the British School at Rome* 51, 16–57.

Breed, B, Damon, C & Rossi, A. (2010). *Citizens of Discord. Rome and its Civil Wars* (Oxford).

Brennan, T. (1992). 'Sulla's Career in the Nineties', *Chiron* 22, 103–158.

——. (2000). *The Praetorship in the Roman Republic Volumes 1 & 2* (Oxford).

Broughton, T. (1952). *The Magistrates of the Roman Republic Volume II 99 BC–31 BC* (New York).

——. (1960). *The Magistrates of the Roman Republic; Supplement* (New York).

——. (1986). *The Magistrates of the Roman Republic Volume 3, Supplement* (Atlanta).

Brown, R. (2003). 'The Terms *Bellum Sociale* and *Bellum Civile* in the Late Republic', *Studies in Latin Literature and Roman History* 11, 94–120.

Brunt, P. (1956). 'Sulla and the Asian Publicans', *Latomus* 15, 17–25.

——. (1962). 'The Army and the Land in the Roman Revolution', *Journal of Roman Studies* 52, 69–86.

——. (1965). 'Italian Aims at the Time of the Social War', *Journal of Roman Studies* 55, 90–109.

——. (1971). *Italian Manpower 225 BC–AD 14* (Oxford).

——. (1988). *The Fall of the Roman Republic and Related Essays* (Oxford).

Bulst, C. (1964). 'Cinnanum Tempus: a reassessment of the 'Dominatio Cinnae'', *Historia* 13, 307–337.

Burton, P. (2014). 'The Revolt of Lepidus (Cos. 78 BC) Revisited', *Historia* 63, 404–421.

Cagniart, P. (1991). 'L. Cornelius Sulla in the Nineties: a Reassessment', *Latomus* 50, 285–303.

Carney, T. (1955). 'Notes on Plutarch's Life of Marius', *Classical Quarterly* 5, 201–205.

——. (1958). 'The Death of Marius', *Acta Classica* 1, 117–122.

——. (1958b). 'Was Rutilius' Exile Voluntary or Compulsory', *Acta Juridica* 242–244.

——. (1960). 'The Death of Ancharius', *Hermes* 88, 382–384.

——. (1960b). 'Plutarch's Style in the Marius', *Journal of Hellenic Studies* 80, 24–31.

——. (1960c). 'Cicero's Picture of Marius', *Wiener Studien* 73, 83–122.

——. (1961). 'The Death of Sulla', *Acta Classica* 4, 64–79.

——. (1961b). 'The Flight and Exile of Marius', *Greece & Rome* 8, 98–121.

——. (1962). 'The Picture of Marius in Valerius Maximus', *Rheinisches Museum für Philologie* 105, 308–337.

——. (1970). *A Biography of C. Marius* (Chicago).

Chapman, C. (1979). 'Cicero and Sulpicius Rufus (tr. pl. 88 BC)', *Acta Classica* 22, 61–72.

Coello, J. (1995–96). 'C. Flavivs Fimbria, Consular y Legado en la Provincia de Asia (86/84 a. de C.)', *Studia historica historia Antigua* 13–14, 257–275.

Conole, P. (1981). 'Allied Disaffection and the Revolt of Fregellae', *Antichton* 15, 129–140.

Crawford, M. (1998). 'How to Create a Muncipium: Rome and Italy after the Social War', in M. Austin, J. Harries & C. Smith (eds.) *Modus Operandi. Essays in Honour of Geoffrey Rickman* (London), 31–46.

D'Arms, J. (1968). 'The Campanian Villa of C. Marius and the Sullan Confiscations', *Classical Quarterly* 18, 185–188.

Dart, C. (2009). 'The 'Italian' Constitution' in the Social War: A Reassessment (91 to 88 BC)', *Historia* 58, 215–224.

——. (2010). 'Qvintus Poppeadivs Silo Dvx et Avctor of the Social War', *Athenaeum* 98, 111–126

——. (2010b). 'Deceit and the Struggle for Roman Franchise in Italy' in A. Turner, K. O. Chong-Gossard and F. Vervaet (eds.) *Public and Private Lies: The Discourse of Despotism and Deceit.* (Leiden), 91–105.

——. (2014). *The Social War, 91 to 88 BC: A History of the Italian Insurgency against the Roman Republic* (London).

David, J-M. (1996). *The Roman Conquest of Italy* (Oxford).

de Blois, L. (1987). *The Roman Army and Politics in the First Century BC* (Amsterdam).

de Ligt, L. & Northwood, S. (eds.) (2008). *People, Land, and Politics: Demographic Developments and the Transformation of Roman Italy 300 BC–AD 14* (Leiden).

de Sanctis, G. (1976). *La Guerra Sociale* (Firenze).

di Bella Farina, M. (1997). *Sulla: The Rise of a Revolutionary Republican* (New Orleans).

Dowling, M. (2000). 'The Clemency of Sulla', *Historia* 49, 303–340.

Dyson, S. (1985). *The Creation of the Roman Frontier* (Princeton).

Dzino, D. (2002). 'Annus Mirabilis: 70 BC Re-examined', *Ancient History* 32, 99–117.

Eckert, A. & Thein, A. (eds.). (2019). *Sulla: Politics and Reception* (Berlin).

Evans, R. (1983). 'The 'Consulares' and 'Praetorii' in the Roman Senate at the beginning of Sulla's Dictatorship', *Athenaeum* 61, 521–528.

——. (1994). *Gaius Marius: A Political Biography* (Pretoria).

——. (1997). 'The Augustan 'Purge' of the Senate and the Census of 86 BC', *Acta Classica* 40, 77–86.

—— (2004). 'The military reputation of Gaius Marius', *Questioning Reputations* (Pretoria), 11–35.

——. (2004b). 'Pompey in the 70s', *Questioning Reputations* (Pretoria), 37–64.

——. (2004c). 'The characters of Drusus and Sulpicius', *Questioning Reputations* (Pretoria), 133–159.

——. (2008). 'Gaius and Marcus Marius in Iberia and Gaul: Family Affairs and Provincial Clients', *Acta Classica* 50, 77–90.

Flower, H. (2008). 'Remembering and Forgetting Temple Destruction. The Destruction of the Temple of Jupiter Optimus Maximus in 83 BC', in G. Gardner & K. Osterloch (eds.). *Antiquity in Antiquity* (Tübingen), 74–92.

——. (2010). *Roman Republics* (Princeton).

——. (2010b). 'Rome's First Civil War and the Fragility of Republican Political Culture', in B. Breed, C. Damon & A. Rossi (eds.) *Citizens of Discord: Rome and Its Civil Wars* (Oxford). 73–86.

Frank, T. (1933). 'On Some Financial Legislation of the Sullan Period', *American Journal of Philology* 54, 54–58.

Frassinetti, P. (1972). 'Sisenna e la guerra sociale', *Athenaeum* 50, 78–113.

Frier, B. (1971). 'Sulla's Propaganda: The Collapse of the Cinnan Republic', *American Journal of Philology* 92, 585–604.

Gabba, E. (1950). 'Lex Plotia Agraria', *Parola del Passato* 5, 66–68.

——. (1954). 'Le origini della Guerra Sociale e la vita politica romana dopo l'89 a.C.' *Athenaeum* 32, 41–114.

——. (1955). 'Note Appianee', *Athenaeum* 33, 218–230.

——. (1956). *Appiano e la storia delle guerre civili* (Florence).

——. (1956b). 'Il ceto equestre e il Senato di Silla', *Athenaeum* 34, 124–138.

——. (1964). 'M. Livio Druso e le riforme di Sulla', *Annali della Scuola Normale Superiore di Pisa* 33 (Pisa), 1–15.

——. (1967). (ed.) *Appiano Bellorum Civilium Liber Primus* (Amsterdam).

——. (1972). 'Mario e Silla', *Aufstieg und Niedergang der Römischen Welt* 1.1, 764–805.

——. (1976). *Republican Rome, The Army and the Allies* (Oxford).

Galassi, F. (2014). *Catiline, The Monster of Rome: An Ancient Case of Political Assassination* (Pennsylvania).

Glew, D. (1977). 'Mithridates Eupator and Rome: A Study of the Background of the First Mithridatic War' *Athenaeum* 55, 380–405.

——. (1977b). 'The Selling of the King: A Note on Mithridates Eupator's Propaganda in 88 BC', *Hermes* 105, 253–256.

——. (1981). 'Between the Wars: Mithridates Eupator and Rome, 85–73 BC', *Chiron* 11, 109–130.

Gordon, T. (1744). 'Of the Resignation of Sylla', *Political Discourses in the Works of Sallust* (London), Discourse III.

Greenhalgh, P. (1980). *Pompey. The Roman Alexander* (London).

Gruen, E. (1965). 'The Lex Varia', *Journal of Roman Studies* 55, 59–73.

——. (1966). 'The Dolabellae and Sulla', *American Journal of Philology* 87, 385–99.

——. (1966b). 'Political Prosecutions in the 90's BC', *Historia* 15, 32–64.

——. (1969). 'Notes on the 'First Catilinarian Conspiracy'', *Classical Philology* 64, 20–24.

——. (1971).'Pompey, Metellus Pius and the Trials of 70–69 BC', *American Journal of Philology* 92, 1–16.

——. (1974). *The Last Generation of the Roman Republic* (Berkeley).

——. (1996). 'Roman Oligarchy: Image and Perception' in J. Linderski, (ed). *Imperium Sine Fine* (Stuttgart), 215–225.

Habicht, C. (1976). 'Zur Geschichte Athens in der Zeit Mithridates VI', *Chiron* 6, 127–142.

Hall, U. (1977). 'Notes on M. Fulvius Flaccus', *Athenaeum* 55, 280–288.

Hands, A. (1967). 'Livius Drusus and the Courts', *Phoenix* 26, 268–274.

Hantos, T. (1988). *Res Publica Constituta. Die Verfassung des Diktators Sulla* (Stuttgart).

Hardy, E. (1913). 'Three Questions as to Livius Drusus', *Classical Review* 27, 261–263.

——. (1916). 'The Number of the Sullan Senate', *Journal of Roman Studies* 6, 59–62.

——. (1917). 'The Catilinarian Conspiracy in Its Context: A Re-Study of the Evidence', *Journal of Roman Studies* 7, 153–228.

Harris, W. (1972). 'Was Roman Law imposed on the Italian Allies?', *Historia* 21, 639–645.

——. (1979). *War and Imperialism in Republican Rome 327–70 BC* (Oxford).

——. (1982). 'The Italians and the Empire', in W. Harris (ed.) *The Imperialism of Mid-Republican Rome* (Rome), 89–107.

Harrison, I. (2008). 'Catiline, Clodius, and Popular Politics at Rome during the 60s and 50s BC', *Bulletin of the Institute of Classical Studies* 51, 95–118.

Hawthorn, J. (1962). 'The Senate After Sulla', *Greece & Rome* 9, 53–60.

Hayne, L. (1972). 'M. Lepidus (Cos. 78): A Re-Appraisal', *Historia* 21, 661–688.

Heftner, H. (2006). 'Der Beginn von Sullas Proskriptionen', *Tyche* 21, 33–52.

Henderson, J. (2003). 'Sulla's List: The First Proscription', *Parallax* 9, 39–47.

Heurgon, J. (1959). 'The Date of Vegoia's Prophesy', *Journal of Roman Studies* 49, 41–45.

Hill, H. (1932). 'Sulla's New Senators in 81 BC', *Classical Quarterly* 26, 170–177.

Hillard, T. (1996). 'Death by Lightening, Pompeius Strabo and the People', *Rheinisches Museum für Philologie* 139, 136–145.

Hillman, T. (1990). 'Pompeius and the Senate: 77–71', *Hermes* 118, 444–454.

——. (1992). 'Plutarch and the First Consulship of Pompeius and Crassus', *Phoenix* 46, 124–137.

——. (1996). 'Cinna, Strabo's Army, and Strabo's Death in 87 BC', *L'Antiquité Classique* 65, 81–89.

——. (1997). 'Pompeius in Africa and Sulla's Orders to demobilize (Plutarch, Pompeius 13, 1–4), *Latomus* 56, 94–106.

——. (1997b). 'The Serpent and the Flower: Pompeius Strabo and Q. Sertorius, 89–87 BC', *Studies in Roman History and Latin Literature* VIII, 85–115.

Hinard, F. (1985). *Les Proscriptions de la Rome Républicaine* (Rome).

——. (1985b). *Sylla* (Paris).

——. (1985c). 'La déposition du consul de 88, Q. Pompeius Rufus, et la première prise de Rome par les armes', *Kéntron* 1, 3–5.

——. (1999). 'Dion. Cassius et l'Abdication de Sylla', *Revue des Études Anciennes* 101, 427–432.

——. (2008). *Sullana Varia. Aux sources de la première guerre civile romaine* (Paris).

Hölkeskamp, KJ. (2010). *Reconstructing the Roman Republic* (Princeton).

Hoff, M. (1997). 'Laceratae Athenae: Sulla's Siege of Athens in 87/6 BC and its Aftermath', in M. Hoff & S. Rotroff (eds.) *The Romanization of Athens* (Oxford), 33–51.

Howarth, R. (1999). 'Rome, the Italians, and the Land', *Historia* 48, 282–300.

Hurlet, F. (1993). *La dictature de Sylla: monarchie ou magistrature republicaine?* (Rome).

Husband, R. (1916). 'On the Expulsion of Foreigners from Rome', *Classical Philology*, 315–333.

Hyden, M. (2017). *Gaius Marius: The Rise and Fall of Rome's Saviour* (Barnsley).

Jal, P. (1963). *La Guerre Civile a Rome* (Paris).

Jehne, M. (2009). Diplomacy in Italy in the Second Century BC', in C. Eilers (ed) *Diplomats and Diplomacy in the Roman World* (Leiden), 143–170.

Jehne, M & Pina Polo, F. (eds.) (2015). *Foreign Clientelae in the Roman Empire: A Reconsideration* (Stuttgart).

Jenkins, A. (1994). 'Sulla's Retirement', *Studies in Roman History and Latin Literature* VII, 132–142.

Kallet-Marx, R. (1989). 'Asconius 14–5 Clark and the Date of Q. Mucius Scaevola's Command in Asia', *Classical Philology* 84, 305–312.

——. (1990). 'The Trial of Rutilius Rufus', *Phoenix* 44, 122–139

Katz, B. (1975). 'The First Fruits of Sulla's March', *L'antiquité classique* 44, 100–125.

——. (1976). 'Studies on the Period of Cinna and Sulla', *L'antiquité classique* 45, 497–549.

——. (1976b). 'The Siege of Rome in 87 BC', *Classical Philology* 71, 328–336.

——. (1977). 'Caesar Strabo's Struggle for the Consulship –and more', *Rheinisches Museum für Philologie* 120, 45–62.

——. (1979). 'The Selection of L. Cornelius Merula', *Rheinisches Museum* für *Philologie* 122, 162–166.

——. (1981). 'Sertorius, Caesar and Sallust', *Acta Antiqua Academiae Scientiarum Hungaricae* 29, 285–313.

——. (1982). 'Notes on Sulla's Ancestors', *Liverpool Classical Monthly* 7, 148–149.

——. (1983). 'Notes on Sertorius', *Rheinisches Museum für Philologie* 126, 44–68.

——. (1983b). 'Sertorius' Overlooked Correspondent?', *Rheinisches Museum für Philologie* 126, 359–362.

Keaveney, A. (1978). 'Pompeius Strabo's Second Consulship', *Classical Quarterly* 28, 240–241.

——. (1979). 'Sulla, Sulpicius and Caesar Strabo', *Latomus* 38, 451–460.

——. (1981). 'Sulla, the Marsi, and the Hirpini', *Classical Philology* 76, 292–296.

——. (1982). *Sulla, The Last Republican* (London).

——. (1982b). 'Sulla and Italy', *Critica Storia* 19, 499–544.

——. (1982c). 'Young Pompey: 106–79 BC', *L'antiquité classique* 51, 111–139.

——. (1983). 'Studies in the Dominatio Sullae', *Klio* 65, 185–203.

——. (1983b). 'Caesars in the Social War', *Rheinisches Museum für Philologie* 126, 273–281.

——. (1983c). 'What Happened in 88?', *Eirene* 20, 53–86.

——. (1984). 'Who were the Sullani?', *Klio* 66, 114–150.

——. (1987). *Rome and the Unification of Italy* (London).

——. (1992). *Lucullus. A Life* (London).

——. (1995). 'Sulla's Cilician Command: The Evidence of Apollinaris Sidonius', *Historia* 44, 29–36.

——. (2005). *Sulla, The Last Republican, Second Edition* (London).

——. (2005b). 'The Terminal Date of Sulla's Dictatorship', *Athenaeum* 93, 423–439.

——. (2006). 'The Exile of L. Cornelius Scipio Asiagenus' *Rheinisches Museum für Philologie* 149, 112–114.

——. (2007). *The Army in the Roman Revolution* (London).

——. (2010). 'Cicero Pro Sulla 60–62 and the Sullan Settlement of Italy', *Athenaeum* 98, 127–138.

Keller, J. (2007). 'Rome and Her Italian Allies: Conflicting Interests and Disintegration', in R. Roth & J. Keller (eds.) *Roman by Integration: Dimensions of Group Identity in Material Culture and Text* (Portsmouth), 43–58.

Kelly, D. (1970). 'Evidence for Legislation by Tribunes 81–70 BC', in. B. Harris (ed.) *Auckland Classical Essays* (Auckland), 133–142.

Kendall, S. (2012). 'Appian, Allied Ambassadors and the rejection of 91: why Romans Chose to Fight the Bellum Sociale', in S. Roselaar (ed.) *Processes of Integration and Identity Formation in the Roman Republic* (Leiden), 105–121.

——. (2013). *The Struggle for Roman Citizenship: Romans, Allies, and the Wars of 91–77 BC* (Piscataway).

Kindahl. P. (1968). *Caius Marius* (New York).

Konrad, C. (1987). 'Some Friends of Sertorius', *American Journal of Philology* 108, 519–527.

——. (1988). 'Metellus and the Head of Sertorius', *Gerión* 6, 253–261.

——. (1989). 'Cotta off Mellaria and the Identities of Fufidius', *Classical Philology* 84, 119–129.

——. (1994). *Plutarch's Sertorius. A Historical Commentary* (Chapel Hill).

——. (1994b). 'Segovia and Segontia', *Historia* 43, 440–453.

——. (1995). 'A New Chronology of the Sertorian War', *Athenaeum* 83, 157–187.

Lange, C. (2013). 'Triumph and Civil War in the Late Republic', *Papers of the British School at Rome* 81, 67 – 90.

Lange, C. & Vervaet, F. (2019). 'Sulla and the Origins of the Concept of Bellum Civile' in C. Lange, & F. Vervaet (eds.), *The Historiography of Late Republican Civil War* (Leiden), 17–28.

Letzner, W. (2000), *Lucius Cornelius Sulla: Versuch einer Biographie* (Munster).

Levick, B. (1982b). 'Sulla's March on Rome in 88 BC', *Historia* 31, 503–508.

Lewis, R. (1968). 'Appian BC I, 49, 214: Rome's New Tribes 90–87 BC', *Athenaeum* 46, 273–291.

——. (1971). 'A Problem in the Siege of Praeneste, 82 BC', *Papers of the British School at Rome* 39, 32–39.

——. (1998). 'P. Sulpicius' Law to Recall Exiles, 88 BC', *Classical Quarterly* 48, 195–199.

Linderski, J. (1966). 'Were Pompey and Crassus Elected in Absence to their First Consulship?', in *Mélanges offerts à Kazimierz Michałowsk* (Warsaw), 523–526.

Lintott, A. (1968). *Violence in Republican Rome* (Oxford).

——. (1971). 'The Tribunate of P. Sulpicius Rufus', *Classical Quarterly* 21, 442–453.

——. (1971b). 'The Offices of C. Flavius Fimbria', *Historia* 20, 696–701.

Long, G (1866). *Decline of the Roman Republic Volume 2* (London).

——. (1869). *Decline of the Roman Republic Volume 3* (London).

Lovano, M. (2002). *The Age of Cinna: Crucible of Late Republican Rome* (Stuttgart).

Luce, T. (1970). 'Marius and the Mithridatic Command', *Historia* 19, 161–194.

Mackay, C. (2000). 'Sulla and the Monuments: Studies in Public Persona', *Historia* 49, 161–210.

Magie, D. (1950). *Roman Rule in Asia Minor* (Princeton).

March, D. (1989). 'Cicero and the Gang of Five', *Classical World* 82, 225–234.

Malden, H. (1886). 'The Battle at the Colline Gate, BC 82', *Journal of Philology* 15, 103–110.

Marshall, A. (1976). 'Livius Drusus and the Italian Question', *Historical Papers* 11, 93–103.

Marshall, B. (1972). 'The Lex Plotia Agraria', *Antichton* 6, 43–52.

——. (1985). 'Catilina and the Execution of M. Marius Gratidianus', *Classical Quarterly* 35, 124–133.

Marshall, B. & Beness, J. (1987). 'Tribunician Agitation and Aristocratic Reaction 80–71 BC', *Athenaeum* 75, 361–378.

Mattingly, H. (1975). 'The Consilium of Cn. Pompeius Strabo in 89 BC', *Athenaeum* 53, 262–266.

Matyszak, P. (2008). *Mithridates the Great: Rome's Indomitable Enemy* (Barnsley).

——. (2013). *Sertorius and the Struggle for Spain* (Barnsley).

——. (2014). *Cataclysm 90 BC: The Forgotten War that Almost Destroyed Rome* (Barnsley).

McDonald, A. (1944). Rome and the Italian Confederation (200–186 BC), *Journal of Roman Studies* 34, 11–33.

McGing, B. (1984). 'The Date of the Outbreak of the Third Mithridatic War', *Phoenix* 38, 12–18.

——. (1986). *The Foreign Policy of Mithridates VI Eupator, King of Pontus* (Leiden).

Messer, W. (1920). 'Mutiny in the Roman Army. The Republic', *Classical Philology* 15, 158–175.

Millar, F. (1986). 'Politics, Persuasion and the People before the Social War (150–90 BC)', *Journal of Roman Studies* 76, 1–11.

Mitchell, T. (1971). 'Cicero and the Senatus 'consultum ultimum'', *Historia* 20, 47–61.

——. (1975). 'The Volte-Face of P. Sulpicius Rufus in 88 BC', *Classical Philology* 70, 197–204.

Morley, N. (2001). 'The Transformation of Italy, 225–28 BC', *Journal of Roman Studies* 91, 50–62.

Morstein-Marx, R. (2011). 'Consular Appeals to the Army in 88 and 87: the locus of legitimacy in late-Republican Rome', in H. Beck, A, Dupla, M. Jehne & F. Pollo (eds). *Consuls and Res Publica* (Cambridge), 259–278.

Mouritsen, H. (1998). *Italian unification: a study in ancient and modern historiography* (London).

——. (2008). 'The Gracchi, the Latins, and the Italian Allies', in L. de Ligt & S. Northwood (eds.) *People, Land and Politics, Demographic Developments and the Transformation of Roman Italy 300 BC–AD 14* (Leiden), 471–483.

Naco del Hoyo, T, Antela-Bernáardez, B, Arrayás-Morales, I & Busquets-Artigas, S. (2009).

'The Impact of the Roman Intervention in Greece and Asia Minor upon Civilians (88–63 BC).', in B. Antela-Bernáardez & T. Naco del Hoyo (eds.) *Transforming Historical Landscapes in the Ancient Empires* (Oxford), 33–51.

Nagle, D. (1973). 'An Allied View of the Social War', *American Journal of Archaeology* 77, 367–378.

Panitschek, P. (1989). 'Sp. Cassius, Sp. Maelius, M. Manlius als exempla maiorum', *Philologus* 133, 231–245.

Patterson, J. (2012). 'Contact, Co-operation and Conflict in Pre-Social War Italy', in S. Roselaar (ed.) *Processes of Integration and Identity Formation in the Roman Republic* (Leiden), 215–226.

Pfeilschifter, R. (2007). 'The Allies in the Republican Army and the Romanisation of Italy', in R. Roth & J. Keller (eds.) *Roman by Integration: Dimensions of Group Identity in Material Culture and Text* (Portsmouth), 27–42.

Piccinin, P. (2004). 'Les Itialiens dans le 'Bellum Sparticium'', *Historia* 53, 173–199.

Porra, F. (1973). 'La legge Varia del 90 e quella Sulpicia dell' 88 a.C: il problema degli esuli', *Annali della Facoltà di Lettere* 35, 13–28.

Powell, J. (1990). 'The Tribune Sulpicius', *Historia* 39, 446–460.

Raaflaub, K. (1996). 'Born to Be Wolves? Origins of Roman Imperialism', in R. Wallace & E. Harris (eds). *Transitions to Empire*, 273–314.

Ramage, E. (1991). 'Sulla's Propaganda', *Klio* 73, 93–121.

Ramsey, J. (1982). 'Cicero, pro Sulla 68 and the Catiline's Candidacy in 66 BC', *Harvard Studies in Classical Philology* 86, 121–131.

——. (1999). 'Mithridates, the Banner of Ch'ih-Yu, and the Comet Coin', *Harvard Studies in Classical Philology* 99, 197–253.

Rawson, E. (1979). 'L. Cornelius Sisenna and the Early First Century BC', *Classical Quarterly* 29, 327–346.

——. (1987). 'Sallust on the Eighties?', *Classical Quarterly* 37, 163–180.

Reams, L. (1993). 'Censorinus, Sulla and Marius', *Rheinisches Museum für Philologie* 136, 281–288.

Reid, J. (1915). 'Problems of the Second Punic War: III. Rome and Her Italian Allies', *Journal of Roman Studies* 5, 87–124.

Reiter, W. (1978). 'M. Fulvius Flaccus and the Gracchan Coalition', *Athenaeum* 56, 125–144.

Ridley, R. (2000). 'The Dictator's Mistake: Caesar's Escape from Sulla', *Historia* 49, 211–229.

——. (2003). 'The Contradictory Revolution: The Italian War (91–89)', *Ancient History* 33, 31–57.

Rosenblitt, A. (2019). *Rome after Sulla* (London).

Roselaar, S. (2010). *Public Land in the Roman Republic: A Social and Economic History of Ager Publicus in Italy, 396–89 BC* (Oxford).

——. (ed.) (2012). *Processes of Integration and Identity Formation in the Roman Republic* (Leiden).

——. (ed.) (2015). *Processes of Cultural Change and Integration in the Roman World* (Leiden).

——. (2015). 'Italian allies and access to ager Romanus in the Roman Republic', *Mélanges de l'École française de Rome Antiquité* 127.

——. (2019). *Italy's Economic Revolution: Integration and Economy in Republican Italy* (Oxford).

Rowland, R. (1966). 'Numismatic Propaganda under Cinna', *Transactions and Proceedings of the American Philological Association* 97, 407–419.

Ryan, F. (1996). 'The Lectio Senatus after Sulla', *Rheinisches Museum für Philologie* 139, 189–191.

Salmon, E. (1935). 'Catiline, Crassus, and Caesar', *American Journal of Philology* 56, 302–316.

——. (1936). 'Roman Colonisation from the Second Punic War to the Gracchi', *Journal of Roman Studies* 26, 47–67.

——. (1953). 'Rome and the Latins: I', *Phoenix* 7, 93–104.

——. (1953b). 'Rome and the Latins: II', *Phoenix* 7, 123–135.

——. (1955). 'Roman Expansion and Roman Colonization in Italy', *Phoenix* 9, 63–75.

——. (1958). 'Notes on the Social War', *Transactions and Proceedings of the American Philological Association* 89, 159–184.

——. (1962). 'The Cause of the Social War', *Phoenix* 16, 107–119.

——. (1964). 'Sulla Redux', *Athenaeum* 42, 60–79.

——. (1967). *Samnium and the Samnites* (Cambridge).

——. (1970–71). 'Discussion on the Period 130–80 BC', *Dialoghi di Archeologia* 4–5, 371–372.

——. (1982). *The Making of Roman Italy* (London).

Sampson, G. (2001). *Crisis and Renewal; The Two Decades of the First Civil War 91–70 BC* (Manchester, Unpublished Thesis).

——. (2005). *A re-examination of the office of the Tribunate of the Plebs in the Roman Republic (494 – 23 BC)* (Manchester, Unpublished Thesis).

——. (2008). *The Defeat of Rome. Crassus, Carrhae and the Invasion of the East* (Barnsley).

——. (2010). *The Crisis of Rome. The Jugurthine and Northern Wars and the Rise of Marius* (Barnsley).

——. (2017). *Rome, Blood and Politics: Reform, Murder and Popular Politics in the Late Republic 133–70 BC* (Barnsley).

——. (2019). *Rome, Blood and Power: Reform, Murder and Popular Politics in the Late Republic 70–27 BC* (Barnsley).

Santangelo, F. (2006). 'Sulla and the Senate: A Reconsideration', *Cahiers Glotz* 17, 7–22.

——. (2007). *Sulla, the Elites and the Empire* (Leiden).

——. (2008) 'Cicero and Marius'. *Athenaeum* 2008, 597–607.

——. (2014). 'The Politics of the 70s BC: a Story of Realignments?', *Journal of Roman Studies* 2014, 104, 1–27.

——. (2015). *Marius* (London).

Scardigli, B. (1971). 'Sertorio: problemi cronologici', *Athenaeum* 49, 229–270.

Shochat, V. (1970). 'The Lex Agraria of 133 BC and the Italian Allies', *Athenaeum* 48, 25–45

Seager, R. (1964). 'The First Catilinarian Conspiracy', *Historia* 13, 338–347.

——. (ed.) (1969). *The Crisis of the Roman Republic* (Cambridge).

Seleckij, B. (1982). 'Sulla's financial resources at the time of the war with Mithridates', *Vestnik Drevnej Istorii* 160, 63–75.

Shatzman, I. (1974). 'Scaurus, Marius and the Metelli: A Prosopographical-Factional Case', *Ancient Society* 5, 197–222.

Sherwin-White, A. (1954). 'Violence in Roman Politics', *Journal of Roman Studies* 46, 1–10.

——. (1973). *The Roman Citizenship* (Oxford).

——. (1977). 'Ariobarzanes, Mithridates, and Sulla', *Classical Quarterly* 27, 173–183.

——. (1984). *Roman Foreign Policy in the East 168 BC to AD 1* (Oklahoma).

Siani-Davies, M. (1997). 'Ptolemy XII Auletes and the Romans', *Historia* 46, 306–340.

Smith, C. (2006). 'Adfectatio regni in the Roman Republic', in S. Lewis (ed.) *Ancient Tyranny* (Edinburgh), 49–64.

——. (2009). 'Sulla's Memoirs', in C. Smith & A. Powell (eds.). *The Lost Memoirs of Augustus and the Development of Roman Autobiography* (Swansea), 65–86.

Smith, R. (1955). 'Violence in Roman Politics', *Journal of Roman Studies* 46, 1–10.

——. (1957). 'The Lex Plotia Agraria and Pompey's Spanish Veterans', *Classical Quarterly* 7, 82–85.

——. (1957b). 'The Conspiracy and the Conspirators', *Greece & Rome* 4, 58–70.

——. (1958). *Service in the Post Marian Army* (Manchester).

——. (1960). 'Pompey's Conduct in 80 and 77 BC', *Phoenix* 14, 1–13.

——. (1977). 'The Use of Force in Passing Legislation in the Late Republic', *Athenaeum* 55, 150–174.

Sordi, M. (1973). 'La legatio in Cappadocia di C. Mario nel 99–98 a.C.', *Rendiconti dell' Instituto Lombardo* 107, 370–379.

Spann, P. (1984). 'Saguntum vs. Segontia: A Note on the Topography of the Sertorian War', *Historia* 33, 116–119.

——. (1987). *Quintus Sertorius and the Legacy of Sulla* (Fayetteville).

——. (1987b). 'C., L. or M. Cotta and the 'Unspeakable' Fufidius: A Note on Sulla's Res Publica Restituta', *Classical Journal* 82, 306–309.

Steel, C. (2013). *The End of the Roman Republic 146 to 44 BC: Conquest and Crisis* (Edinburgh).

——. (2014). 'Rethinking Sulla: the Case of the Roman Senate', *Classical Quarterly* 64, 657–668.

——. (2014b). 'The Roman Senate and the post-Sullan res publica', *Historia* 63, 323–339.

Stevenson, G. (1919). 'Cn. Pompeius Strabo and the Franchise Question', *Journal of Roman Studies* 9, 95–101.

Stockton, D. (1973). 'The First Consulship of Pompey', *Historia* 22, 205–218.

Sumi, G (2002) 'Spectacles and Sulla's public image', *Historia* 51: 414–32.

Sumner, G. (1978). 'Sulla's Career in the Nineties', *Athenaeum* 56, 395–396.

Syme. R. (1999). *Rome and the Balkans 80 BC–AD 14* (Exeter).

——. (2016). 'The Abdication of Sulla', in R. Syme and F. Santangelo (eds.). *Approaching the Roman Revolution: Papers on Republican History* (Oxford), 56–78.

——. (2016b). 'M. Aemilius Lepidus (Cos. 78 BC)', in R. Syme and F. Santangelo (eds.). *Approaching the Roman Revolution: Papers on Republican History* (Oxford), 93–110.

——. (2016c). 'P. Sulla (Cos. cand 66 BC)', in R. Syme and F. Santangelo (eds.). *Approaching the Roman Revolution: Papers on Republican History* (Oxford), 169–172.

Tatum, J. (2011). 'The Late Republic. Autobiography and Memoirs in the Age of the Civil Wars', in G. Marasco (ed.). *Political Autobiographies and Memoirs in Antiquity* (Leiden), 161–87.

Taylor, L. (1949) *Party Politics in the Age of Caesar* (Berkeley).

——. (1962). 'Forerunners of the Gracchi', *Journal of Roman Studies* 52, 19–27.

Telford, L. (2014). *Sulla: A Dictator Reconsidered* (Barnsley).

Thein, A. (2006). 'Sulla the weak tyrant', in S. Lewis (ed.) *Ancient Tyranny* (Edinburgh), 238–249.

——. (2010). 'Sulla's Veteran Settlement Policy', in F. Daubner (ed). *Militärsiedlungen und Territorialherrschaft in der Antike* (Berlin), 79–99.

——. (2013). 'Rewards to Slaves in the Proscriptions of 82 BC', *Tyche* 28, 163–175.

——. (2014). 'Reflecting on Sulla's Clemency', *Historia* 63, 166–186.

——. (2015). 'Sulla and the Tarpeian Rock in 88 and 82 BC', *Ancient Society* 45 171–186.

——. (2016). 'Booty in the Sullan Civil War of 83–82 BC', *Historia* 65, 450–472.

——. (2017). 'Percussores: a study in Sullan violence', *Tyche* 32, 235–50.

Torelli, M. (1995). *Studies in the Romanization of Italy* (Edmonton).

Tweedie, F. (2012). 'The Lex Licinia Mucia and the Bellum Italicum', in S. Roselaar (ed.) *Processes of Integration and Identity Formation in the Roman Republic* (Leiden), 123–140.

Twyman, B. (1972). 'The Metelli, Pompeius and Prosopography', *Aufsteig und Niedergang der Römischen Welt* 1.1, 816–874.

——. (1976). 'The Date of Sulla's Abdication and the Chronology of the First Book of Appian's Civil War', *Athenaeum* 54, 271–295.

——. (1979). 'The Date of Pompeius Magnus' First Triumph', *Studies in Latin Literature and Roman History* I, 175–208.

Urso, G. (2016). 'Cassius Dio's Sulla: Exemplum of Cruelty and Republican Dictator', in C. Lange & J. Madsen (eds.). *Cassius Dio. Greek Intellectual and Roman Politician* (Leiden) 13–32.

Valgiglio, E. (1956). *Silla e la crisi repubblicana* (Florence).

Vanderbroeck, P. (1988). *Popular Leadership and Collective Behaviour in the Late Roman Republic (ca. 80–50 BC)* Amsterdam.

van Ooteghem, J. (1954). *Pompée le grand, bâtisseur d'Empire* (Brussels).

——. (1959). *L. Licinius Lucullus* (Brussels).

——. (1959). *L. Marcius Philippus et sa famillie* (Brussels).

——. (1964). *Caius Marius* (Brussels).

——. (1967). *Les Caecilii Metelli de la République* (Brussels).

Verboven, K. (1994). 'The Monetary Enactments of M. Marius Gratidianus', *Studies in Latin Literature and Roman History* VII, 117–131.

Vervaet, F. (2004). 'The Lex Valeria and Sulla's Empowerment as Dictator (82–79 BC)', *Cahiers Glotz* 15, 37–84.

——. (2009). 'Pompeius' Career from 79 to 70 BC: Constitutional, Political and Historical Considerations', *Klio* 91, 406–434.

——. (2010). 'Metellus and Pompeius in Spain, 77–71 BC: Reinventing the Past in the Face of War', in B. Antela-Bernáardez & T. Naco del Hoyo (eds.) *Transforming Historical Landscapes in the Ancient Empires* (Oxford), 53–61.

——. (2018). 'The Date, Modalities and Legacy of Sulla's Abdication of his Dictatorship: a Study in Sullan Statecraft', *Historia Antigua*, 31–82.

Volkmann, H. (1958). *Sullas Marsch auf Rom Der Verfall der römischen Republik* (Munich).

Walton, F. (1965). 'A Neglected Historical Text', *Historia* 14, 236–251.

Watkins, O. (1988). 'The Death of Cn. Pompeius Strabo', *Rheinisches Museum für Philologie* 131, 143–150.

Weinrib, E. (1970). 'The Judiciary Law of M. Livius Drusus (tr. pl 91 BC)', *Historia* 19, 414–443.

Wiseman, T. (1994) 'Lucretius, Catiline and the Survival of Prophesy', in *History and Imagination. Eight Essays on Roman Culture*, 49–67.

——. (2010). 'The Two-Headed State: How Romans Explained Civil Wars', in B. Breed, C. Damon & A. Rossi (eds.) *Citizens of Discord: Rome and Its Civil Wars (Oxford)*. 25–44.

Woolliscroft, D. (1988). 'Sulla's Motives', *Liverpool Classical Monthly* 13, 35–39.

Worthington, I. (1992). 'Coinage and Sulla's Retirement', *Rheinisches Museum für Philologie* 135, 188–191.

Wulff-Alonso, F. (2002). *Roma e Italia de la Guerra Social a la retirada de Sila (90–79 a.C.)* (Brussels).

Wylie, G. (1992). 'The Genius and the Sergeant: Sertorius versus Pompey', *Studies in Latin Literature and Roman History* VI, 145–162.

Yavetz, Z. (1963). 'The Failure of Catiline's Conspiracy', *Historia* 12, 485–499.

Index